VALERY CHKALOV:

Vancouver USA's Russian Hero

English translation and Introduction
by Jess V. Frost

Book and cover design:
Anita Jones, Another Jones Graphics

ISBN 13: 978-1-4196-6230-0
ISBN 10: 1-4196-6230-9

Printed in the United States

About the Translator

Jess V. Frost met Valeria Chkalova on a trip to Moscow soon after the dedication of the monument to her father in Vancouver in 1975. He has been a close friend of the family since that time, traveling many times to Russia as a member of the original Chkalov Transpolar Flight Committee, and as founder and President of the Valery P. Chkalov Cultural Exchange Committee.

Frost received a Masters Degree in International Relations Education from Central Washington State University in 1961.

He received two National Defense Education Act Grants to study Russian at Indiana University in 1964-65, and was awarded a second Masters Degree in Russian. In 1967, he won a post-graduate IREX Award to study at Moscow State University.

Frost and Valeria Chkalova have agreed to donate all proceeds from the sale of this book to the Valery P. Chkalov Cultural Exchange Committee in honor of her father's wish that "the peoples of Russia and the United States live on this same globe peacefully and with cooperative effort decorate this ocean of human life."

CONTENTS

Note:
    There are two types of footnotes:
    The author's are in the Reference List as end notes.
    The translator's are at the bottom of the page in which the text appears and are in bold type.

INTRODUCTION

Valery Chkalov has often been called the Russian Charles Lindbergh. The analogy is grossly inadequate — and unfortunate. Chkalov was truly a man of epic proportions: a daredevil test pilot, who also dared to defy Stalinist convention, and even Stalin himself.

He was a patriot; a man of the people, who loved his Russia and what he thought it stood for. The problem for Valery Chkalov was that he believed in the Communist ideal — not the practice, the ideal. He was an individualist in a communist society. He broke the rules of flight when they held him back professionally. He broke the rules of sycophancy in the Communist state when they contradicted his and the stated Communist ideals of a just, classless, society.

These values made him immensely popular in Russia, an idol really, but at the same time led to his death, according to his daughter, Valeria Chkalova. Such popularity was often a death sentence from a jealous Stalin, who insisted on being the "One True Communist God."

THE VANCOUVER CONNECTION

"Hey, guys! Get a move on! General Marshall is waiting for us!" shouted Valery Chkalov, pilot of the just completed world-record transpolar flight from Moscow to Vancouver, USA.

Alexander Belyakov and Georgy Baidukov, navigator and copilot, looked at one another. "I didn't expect anything like this," Belyakov said, smiling.

"I didn't understand Valery," responded Baidukov. "Is it a general or a marshal that's meeting us""

"I don't think there are any marshals in the United States," Belyakov answered.

Copilot Baidukov's confusion was understandable. They had just flown 63 hours and 16 minutes in the cold, cramped cockpit of the long-winged (112 feet) ANT-25; and after expecting to reach San Francisco, these first transpolar fliers were forced to land on a small, rain-soaked field in Vancouver, WA.

It was June 20, 1937. Ice, head winds, cyclones, and a forced change of course, had depleted their fuel supply and forced them to land 600 miles short of their San Francisco goal, with only 10 gallons of fuel left.

Little did they know they would be met and hosted in this tiny town by the soon to be famous general and future U.S. Secretary of State, George C. Marshall. Perhaps more surprising to these Russian heroes was the stream of cars headed across the Oregon-Washington Interstate Bridge to greet them.

The three adventurers had intended to land at Portland's Swan Island, but "the thousands of people waving their hands and hats frightened them off," Baidukov was later to write. Chkalov had read that the French had torn Lindbergh's plane apart for souvenirs and he was afraid it would happen here.

Much had been endured: The high altitude caused nosebleeds, magnetic storms made the compass spin, clouds hid the sun for positioning, cyclones, head winds, and near fatal icing forced a change in course, the engine overheated, drinking water froze, radio contact was lost for 12 hours. After all that, they weren't going to risk having their plane torn apart by eager souvenir hunters.

World attention had been focused on the flight for several days. Georgy Baidukov describes the following scene in his book _Chkalov_:

"_As soon as the chief pilot appeared on the balcony (of General Marshall"s home), the huge crowd came alive: Hats flew into the air; applause broke out; one could hear the powerful outbursts:_

"'_Hurray Russian fliers! Hurray..._'

"_America's largest broadcaster, the National Broadcasting Corporation, had prepared everything for a program, which would have an audience of more than 12 million Americans._"

The three Russian fliers went on a triumphal tour of America, which culminated in a New York ticker-tape parade and a meeting with President Franklin D. Roosevelt in the White House. They turned out to be as skilled at diplomacy as they were at flying.

WHAT MONUMENT?

Unfortunately, as Ms. Chkalova points out, the flight was soon forgotten amid the crises of approaching World War II. It took détente (a period of relaxed U.S.-Soviet relations), an embarrassing question and two enterprising Americans to revive Vancouver's memory 37 years later. Détente brought the Soviet fishing trawler *Posyet* into Portland for supplies in the spring of 1974. Dick Bowne, a Clark County Public Utility District engineer, and Peter Belov, consultant to Columbia Machine, Inc. of Vancouver, invited two of the ship's officers to Bowne's home in Vancouver for the evening.

While crossing the Interstate Bridge, the officers asked to see "the monument" at Pearson Airfield, where Chkalov landed. There was no monument. The embarrassed Bowne and Belov had to explain that Vancouver had forgotten its role in the history of the world's first transpolar flight and the three famous Russian heroes.

Though strangers before they met on the *Posyet*, Bowne and Belov resolved then and there to do something to commemorate the event. Perhaps "a small marker" would be both possible and appropriate.

THE CHKALOV TRANSPOLAR FLIGHT COMMITTEE

Belov took the idea to his employers at Columbia Machine, which had been working on a Russian marketing attempt. Owner Fred Neth had relatives still living in Russia, and Norm Small, international sales representative for the company, had been a World War II fighter pilot. They volunteered company support.

From there the plan took off. The Chkalov Transpolar Flight Committee consisted of: President Norman Small, Vice President Alan Cole, and members Dick Bowne, Peter Belov, Fred Neth, Ken Puttkamer, Mayor Lloyd Stromgren, Steve Small, Steve Smut, Dick Osborne, Danny Greco, Thomas Taylor, and Jess Frost.

Alan Cole (owner of Portland's Premier Gear Co.) became committee president in 1977 and contributed immensely to its considerable diplomatic and cultural accomplishments in succeeding years. As the Cold War and U.S-Soviet relations worsened, Alan and the committee were able to keep the focus on the three brave pilots and their fantastic flight and out of the ideological struggle.

It was a human, person-to-person effort, appreciated on both sides of the Iron Curtain and contributed significantly to melting the icy atmosphere of the Cold War. Soviet citizens, thanks to the prominent nationwide Soviet press coverage of the committee's efforts, knew Vancouver, USA, better than Vancouver, Canada.

On October 17, 1995, Alan Cole was awarded the Russian Federation Order of Friendship "For meritorious service in developing cooperation between American and Russian civic service organizations...." President Boris Yeltsin signed the accompanying certificate.

In a follow up telegram, Prime Minister Viktor Chernomyrdin congratulated "Our dear friends—the founders of the Chkalov Transpolar Flight Committee...for your many years of civic activity ...directed at strengthening the friendship...between the Russian and American peoples." He went on to note that, "This served as a beginning of the melding of the American and Russian peoples."

Ninety-seven local companies donated money, labor and materials to complete the Chkalov monument by June 20, 1975, in time to play a role in Vancouver's 150th birthday party that summer.

The "small marker" had turned into a $75,000 ($200,000 in today's money) monument of considerable proportions when measured by Vancouver and, indeed, U.S. standards. The state of Washington donated land along the edge of Pearson field and beside highway 14 for the development of a park to complement the monument. Birch trees, flowers and shrubbery were added to give it a "Russian touch" in an attractive setting.

Chkalov Monument

As a result of Highway 14 improvements, the monument was moved in 1996 to its present location closer to the spot where the ANT-25 came to rest in 1937 and next to the Pearson Air Museum. It lost its beautiful park, but its location is perhaps more historically relevant. The museum itself contains an outstanding exhibit of the 1937 fight history and memorabilia.

Videotape with historic shots of the plane's Moscow departure and the story of the flight is constantly on display. A large scale-model of the ANT-25 can also be seen there.

Many gifts were brought from Russia and placed in the Marshall House for Vancouver and its tourists to enjoy. A huge bust of Valery Chkalov and an English translation of Georgy Baidukov's book *Chkalov*, signed by both President Jimmy Carter and General Secretary Leonid Brezhnev, attract much attention.

THE 1975 DEDICATION

Citizen contribution to the monument was exceptional, and the Russian response to this contribution exceeded all expectations. Among the many gifts to come were three bronze plaques of the ANT-25 and the Soviet Press's 1937 account of the flight, which were presented to the committee and compose the centerpiece of the monument.

In addition, the Russians sent their finest airliner, an IL-62M, to follow Chkalov's route over the pole and to carry Belyakov and Baidukov once more to Vancouver. Valery Chkalov's children, Igor, Valeria and Olga, were also present, as were the families of Baidukov and Belyakov.

Ambassador and Mrs. Anatoly Dobrynin from Washington, D.C., Consul General and Mrs. Alexander Zinchuk from San Francisco, plus 11 other diplomatic dignitaries, represented the Soviet Union.

The Governor, later U.S. Senator, Dan Evans, headed the Washington State delegation, which was made up of state senators and representatives. Sol Polansky, deputy director of the Office of Soviet Affairs, represented Washington, D.C. and Mayor and Mrs. James Gallagher represented the city of Vancouver.

A new street, Chkalov Drive, was also dedicated on June 20th. It was located on a barren rural field in 1975. Promises to the Russians that it would grow into one of the busiest of Vancouver's urban centers were received at the time by Russians, and some Chkalov Committee members, with a considerable degree of skepticism.

Such high-level attention to its efforts was beyond the wildest dreams of our Chkalov Committee. Finally, the committee and its contributors were flown to San Francisco in the IL-62M for an elaborate reception at the Soviet Consulate.

The Chkalov delegation then repeated the 1937 itinerary by flying to Washington, D.C. to be greeted at the White House by President Gerald Ford.

THE YEARS SINCE

Delegations from Vancouver have been invited to Moscow and delegations have been invited from Moscow to Vancouver many times since to commemorate the 1937 flight and the construction of the monument.

In addition, ambassadors, diplomats, cosmonauts and good-will groups have stopped by to pay tribute to the monument and what it represents in U.S.-Russian relations. One of the most memorable early visits was that of Russian Cosmonauts Alexei Leonov and Valery Kubasov, who, in 1975, traded capsules with American astronauts in the Apollo-Soyuz mission.

Georgy Baidukov greeting Jess Frost at the 1987 50th Anniversary Celebration. Vancouver Mayor Bruce Seidel looks on from the left.

Large delegations were exchanged on the flight's 50th and 60th anniversaries. In 1997, an Aeroflot Ilyushin-96 was chartered to take almost 100 Vancouverites to Russia for a marvelous commemorative program in St. Petersburg and Moscow.

On November 18, 1999, The Valery P. Chkalov Cultural Exchange Committee was incorporated and received 501(3) status to continue the work of the Transpolar Flight Committee.

Its first exchange included the 2000 visit by Gherman Titov, the second man to orbit the earth (the first to do it 24 times). He gave an eloquent presentation to the city council describing the beauty of the earth from space, and a heartfelt plea for Russian-American cooperation to protect this "vulnerable, tiny, cosmic spec we call home."

In 2002, General Nikolai Moskvitelev, Russian Air Force Commander from 1977-1987, led the Russian delegation. As Kelly Adams of The Columbian reported, "With his shock of white hair and perfect posture, Moskvitelev moved with the regal bearing of a visiting head of state."

Kelly continues, "He placed his hand on his heart and bent forward in a reverential bow to the crowd" and told them, "'I present myself to you with special humility.'" He then surprised and impressed those in attendance further by getting down on his knees, leaning over and kissing the ground under the monument's arch in honor of his country's famous hero. The moment was captured by Columbian photographer Troy Wayrynen in a unique photo of this former Russian Air Force Chief honoring Valery Chkalov's achievement in bringing our two countries closer together in peace.

In 2004, a Vancouver delegation was invited to Moscow, Nizhni Novgorod, and Chkalovsk to celebrate their hero's 100th birthday, February 2nd. Our delegation was treated royally and shown on Russian national television in a huge celebration in the Rossia Hotel by Red Square, and as we placed flowers by Valery Chkalov's grave by the Kremlin wall.

We then traveled to Nizhni Novgorod, the capital of the "Province" where he was born and raised. There we were received by Governor Khodyrev and toured their Kremlin on the banks of the Volga River. We placed flowers again on a huge statue of Valery Chkalov overlooking the Volga. The next day we were sent in a chartered bus with police escort along snow-covered roads on a 1 1/2-hour trip to the village of Chkalovsk,

Russian cosmonaut remembered as man of dignity

Gherman Titov, who circled globe at age 25, made an impression on his Vancouver hosts

> "I would want people here to know the Russian people have lost a great man in their culture."
>
> MARCIA ROSS
> *Titov's host
> in Vancouver*

BY MARGARET ELLIS
Columbian staff writer

A Russian hero, Gherman Titov cemented Soviet success in space flight when he became the second Russian to see space. The 65-year-old explorer died Wednesday in the carbon monoxide poisoning in the sauna of his Moscow apartment.

He was the first to stay in space for 25 hours, and at age 25 was the youngest person ever to orbit Earth. But Titov was a pioneer in another respect.

He visited Vancouver this spring as part of an effort to foster under-

standing between the United States and Russia, and to celebrate the 63rd anniversary of Valery P. Chkalov's flight from Moscow to Vancouver.

"He told the city council that we all needed to learn from the international space station," said Jess Frost, president of the Valery P. Chkalov cultural exchange committee, the group that organized the visit.

Marcia Ross invited Titov and two other Russian dignitaries to

Fallen hero:
Gherman Titov, right, the second Russian to orbit the Earth, touched the lives of Vancouver residents last spring. He's seen here with Jess Frost. Titov died Wednesday.

FILES/The Columbian

Titov

Friends in Vancouver recall Russian hero's spirit

From page C1

stay in her Vancouver home. She said his heroic spirit came through across language and cultural barriers.

"There are people who carry themselves with such great dignity, and he was one of them," she said.

wanted to know more about other places."

It was easy to see why Titov, who held the Soviet Union's highest awards, became a hero to his people.

"He was clearly a man that justified great respect," said Ross.

But another side of his nature came out during the weeklong stay.

Every morning he walked Ross' Labrador puppy around her neighborhood.

"My picture of him is standing in his business suit in his bare

Jess Frost introducing Cosmonaut Titov Gherman at the Chkalov Monument, June 20, 2000.

Vancouver and CCEC members were saddened to learn of the death of Gherman Titov. He impressed us all with an eloquent address in June, 2000, before the City Council, noting the vulnerability of our small planet and the necessity of Russian-American cooperation and friendship.

8

Valery's birthplace. Here we saw the actual plane he, Georgy Baidukov and Alexander Belyakov flew to Vancouver.

Our respect for these adventurers grew immensely on seeing the narrow, sparse cabin and primitive equipment they had to rely on to cover the unknown expanses of snow and ice separating our two continents and peoples.

On returning to Vancouver, we hosted our new Russian friends with a Mayor's reception at the Marshall House, a rededication of the Chkalov Monument, and an evening dinner at the Pearson Air Museum. Also included in their stay was a trip to Olympia to be received by Governor Gary Lock and Supreme Court Chief Justice Gerry Alexander.

THE MEANING OF THE MONUMENT

The original intent of the monument was to honor three brave pioneers who were first to fly across the North Pole in a dangerous 63 hour 16 minute flight. It's now tied to larger considerations of American-Russian relations.

The Chkalov monument will be here for a long time, forever reminding us that human qualities of courage, cooperation and friendship transcend those of narrow nationalism. No one has said it better than Valery Chkalov, son of a half-deaf boilermaker from a tiny village on the Volga River. From the balcony of the Marshall House on June 20, 1937, 18 months before he was to die in a fatal plane crash, he said:

"There are two rivers, the Columbia and the Volga, which are found on two different continents, have different dispositions and characters …. They flow, however, on one and the same planet, not troubling one another and, in the final analysis, turn out to be elements of one and the same ocean. And so must the peoples of the Soviet Union and the United States live on this same globe peacefully and with cooperative effort decorate this ocean of human life."

Chkalov closed by saying, *"We bring the great American people wishes of happiness and well being from our great people on the red wings of the ANT-25, having overcome all obstacles of which nature is capable."*

The obstacle of understanding Russia, however, still must be overcome. From Will Roger's declaration that, "Whatever you say about Russia, it's true," to Gen. Nathan F. Twining, Chief of Staff of the USAF, on returning from Russia on July 4, 1956, that, "Nobody is an expert on

Russia. There are just varying degrees of ignorance," to Winston Churchill's exasperated, "Russia is a riddle, wrapped in a mystery inside an enigma," it's clear that Russia presents us with a challenge to understanding.

It's also clear that Valery Chkalov, Georgy Baikukov and Alexander Belyakov were first to present America with a bridge to that understanding by bringing "… the great American people wishes of happiness and well being … on the red wings of the ANT-25 …" and connecting our two peoples.

Vancouver's Valery P. Chkalov Cultural Exchange Committee has taken Chkalov's two rivers metaphor for its mission statement. It hopes to continue the great tradition of friendly people-to-people exchanges initiated by "our" courageous Russian pilots. We are certain the people of Vancouver and this metropolitan area will continue to show first class hospitality to Russians who travel to this side of the world to pay their respects to us and to their heroes, who have over the years become symbolic citizens of our community.

Finally, I hope this translation of Valeria Chkalova's biography of her father, in this 70th anniversary year of the flight, will add to our knowledge, appreciation, and understanding of Valery Chkalov, his crew, their flight, and, in some small way, to improved American-Russian relations.

Jess V. Frost, translator
President
The Valery P. Chkalov Cultural Exchange Committee
January 29, 2007

A Note to the Reader

Many books about my father, Valery Pavlovich Chkalov, have been published in the 20th Century. Mother, Olga Erazmovna, has written about him, as have his friends, Georgy F. Baidukov, Alexander V. Belyakov, M. V. Vodopyanov; writers N. N. Bobrov and I. S. Rakhillo; myself; and many others.

February 2, 2004, however, is his 100th birthday, and thoughts return to this man's life.

Father died when he was only 34 years old, but in this short life he was able to accomplish more than most do in a full lifespan. How was he able to do this? They say I resemble my father. Perhaps that is why I so wanted to understand my father better as a person—I was not yet four years old when he died. I wanted to know the whole truth of his life, without exaggeration or distortion, exactly as it was. This forced me to begin a serious search of archival documents in order to form a more complete picture of his professional, social and political life.

I found much new material about his famous flights, about the profession of test pilot, and about his tragic death. It was necessary, of course, to declassify most documents. They had been stamped "Secret" or "Top Secret," and were inaccessible for reading or study; therefore, the readers of this book will be the first to make their aquaintance.

This new material gave me the opportunity to write a documented work about the life of a courageous, unusually driven man, a pilot "from God," a marvelous family man, husband and father. He and mother made an ideal pair, fulfilling each other's lives. My mother was forced to raise and educate us alone. It is in memory of these wonderful people that I would like to dedicate this book.

My wish is that this book will present the reader with a more complete impression and understanding of Valery Chkalov, one of the best pilots in our country in the 1930s, a person whose name has inspired thousands of young people to take to the sky and whose name was given to a generation of boys in our country.

And I believe that today he could be a favorite hero to Russia's young generation: a hero to use as an example, a hero to emulate. His name to this day remains an example of courage, love for homeland, and respect for our people.

I wish to express my gratitude to Anatoly Anatolievich Demin, a specialist on the history of the development of aviation in our nation, for his helpful advice and valuable comments.

Valeria V. Chkalova
Ph.D., Engineering Sciences
Laureate Government Prize Winner

APPEAL TO RUSSIAN YOUTH
FROM THE ASSOCIATION OF HEROES OF
THE SOVIET UNION
AND THE HEROES OF RUSSIA

To the Youth of Russia:

A new century has arrived, in which **YOU**, our young men and women, will have the responsibility to write a new chapter in the history of our country!

Every generation gives birth to its heroes, whose names are remembered by humanity, and are recorded in the book of the life of our planet with golden letters.

Among **YOU**, and of this we have no doubt, there will also be heroes—heroes of your time, heroes of Russia!

People are like events: the further they recede into history, the more significance they acquire in the lives of the people, the nation and epoch.

VALERY CHKALOV fits this category perfectly. No matter the time that has passed, and the highly developed level of our aviation, we will always, with increasing pride, remember the name of this person, who represents the powerful sources of this development.

CHKALOV lived only 34 years. Contemporary aviation has surpassed the most daring **CHKALOV** speculations, but his life and example to this day continue to attract wide attention and admiration.

We are certain that the example of **CHKALOV**—the example of a courageous, talented individual with a serious approach to his profession, a respect for the common man, a fervent and sincere love for his homeland, and a wish to bring fame to our Russia—will live on in the memory of our young generation.

A. N. Kvochur
Hero of the Russian Federation; Honored Test Pilot of the USSR

V. G. Korzun
Hero of the Russian Federation; Colonel; Cosmonaut-Pilot

M. P. Odintsov

Twice Hero of the Soviet Union; General-Colonel; Honored Military
Pilot

V. V. Sivko

Hero of the Russian Federation; Vice President,
Russian Association
of Heroes.

A. A. Chilingarov

Hero of the Soviet Union; Laureate Government Prize Winner USSR;
President, Association of Polar Explorers.

THEY WERE FIRST AND REMAIN FIRST, FOREVER

On December 16, 1903, on sandy hills in North Carolina in a little village called Kitty Hawk, there was something strange being built on the shoreline next to a large barn. Two young men stood close by. A stranger walked by. He watched from all sides and finally asked, "What's this strange contraption"? "It's a flying car, an airplane," answered one of the young men. The stranger looked doubtful. "Are you saying this thing is going to fly in the air and you're really going to fly on it"? "Yes, that's exactly what we're hoping to do," the other answered, laughing, "if there'll be a strong enough wind tomorrow." "I don't think that's going to fly in any kind of a wind," said the stranger. After observing a while longer and shaking his head, the stranger went on his way. The young men laughed. These were the Wright brothers, Wilbur and Orville, the sons of Milton Wright, who lived in Dayton.

Wilbur Wright
(1867-1912)

Orville Wright
(1871-1948)

On the morning of December 17, a strong wind was blowing. The brothers sat by a small stove warming themselves. It was 10:00.

"We can't wait any longer."

The chosen spot was about 150 feet from the hangar. A pre-arranged signal was given to the rescue station on the seashore and four men and a boy came running. These five people would be the only witnesses to the plane's flight.

The wind froze fingers and penetrated coats. But no matter — the plane was placed on the rails facing directly into the wind.

Each brother wanted to be the first to fly. Wilbur took out a coin.

"Heads or tails"?

"Heads," answered Orville.

The coin flew into the air and fell into Wilbur's palm — "Heads!"

Orville jumped to his feet like a boy and ran to the plane. He settled himself into the pilot's "cradle." He grabbed the lever designed to lift the plane into the air with one hand and, with the other, the steering mechanism. Wilbur started the engine. They allowed it to warm up for several minutes, then Orville shouted to his brother, "Is everything ready"? Wilbur shook his head. Orville unfastened the rope holding the plane in place. The contraption slowly moved forward. Wilbur ran along side, supporting the edge of the right wing.

The wind was so strong, the plane moved very slowly at first. For 50 feet, it tottered on the rails, with Wilbur supporting the right wing.

The first picture of an airplane was taken at this point, rising in the air on the power of a motor. Wilbur was still running alongside at the edge of the wing, with the plane about three feet off the ground.

The plane gathered speed and rose a bit more. Wilbur stopped. The flight was not even: the plane rose to perhaps 12 feet, then descended to mere inches above the ground. But it was flying! On the fourth dip, it landed on the sand. The plane had been in the air for 12 seconds and had traveled 120 feet from its departure point.

The was the first time a plane had left the earth with the help of a motor, rose to a higher level, and without the loss of speed successfully landed at a spot on the same level as the point of departure. Man had flown!

At noon Wilbur made the fourth and final flight. The plane flew 750 feet in 59 seconds. The brothers immediately sent their father a telegram describing their success.

And so from December 17, 1903, mankind was no longer tied to Earth. He could now fly.

This first flight lasted only 12 seconds. "True, not a long time, if we compare it with the flight of birds. But this was the first event in history when a machine carrying a person rose into the air with its own power and in free flight covered a horizontal distance not lessening its speed and finally landing on earth without damage or injury," wrote the brothers.[1]

Newspapers little trusted the rumors about the successful flight by the Wright brothers at Kitty Hawk. They found, however, one reporter, a Mr. Moore from Norfolk, Virginia, who believed that something important had happened on the sandy mounds of North Carolina.

On the evening of December 17, he sent detailed notes about the flights of the Wright brothers to a Mr. Glenon, the publisher of the Virginia Pilot. Glenon knew that Moore was credible and on the next morning his paper, the only one in the United States, gave a detailed description of the events in Kitty Hawk. Glenon also sent a short announcement to other newspapers. On the morning of December 18, short descriptions of the flights appeared in Washington, New York, Philadelphia, Chicago and other cities.

Only 34 years later, on June 18, 1937, a single engine plane, the ANT-25, with a three-man crew commanded by Valery Pavlovich Chkalov, and with copilot Georgy Fillipovich Baidokov and navigator Alexander Vasilievich Belyakov, took off from Moscow's Shchelkovo Airfield. It flew across the North Pole in 63 hours and 16 minutes, covering 5,288 miles and landed at Pearson Field in the City of Vancouver, Washington, USA.

This nonstop transpolar flight from Moscow to America, the first in history, united two continents and announced the beginning of transcontinental aviation.

On December 17, 1938, the Soviet Union's most important newspaper, *Pravda*, published an article by Valery P. Chkalov, *"Pioneers of Contemporary Aviation,"* honoring the 35th anniversary of the Wright brothers' first flight:

"Contemporary aviation, unquestionably, owes its beginning to the brothers Wright. They were the first to correctly solve the problems of flight in a heavier than air apparatus. Of course it was primitive, perhaps even naïve, but they were the first to fulfill the dream, which had possessed the minds of men for centuries.

"On December 17th it will be 35 years since that first Wright brothers' flight. Their biography is full of fascinating interest, but deals little with the struggle these young inventors had to deal with in order to achieve their goal.

"Many brave inventors died during their attempted flights. After some small success, there would come a long period of disillusionment. During one such period, the Wright brothers entered the arena. These were two modest workers, masters of the bicycle. From childhood, they were taken by technology. Learning about the tragic flights of the glider inventor, Otto Lilienthal, the young brothers became extremely interested in his experiments. They began to eagerly study all of the special literature on gliding at that time. During long, sleepless nights, the Wright brothers spent hours doing all kinds of calculations, comparisons, and experiments. They finally reached the conclusion that in order to solve the problem of aviation, one must go through the stage of motorless flight. Several years passed before the Wrights had built their first glider. The experience they gained was priceless. The young Americans then gradually moved from the glider to the first motored airplane with maneuvering mechanisms and a propeller. The first flight was on December 17, 1903. The flight shocked the entire world. The Soviet Union with respect remembers these two American inventors—the pioneers of aviation ...."

CHAPTER ONE

Difficult Beginnings

CHILDHOOD

On February 2, 1904, in the city of Vasileva, a son was born to peasants, Pavel Grigorievich Chkalov and his wife, Irina Ivanovna. Both were Russian Orthodox Christians. There has remained very little in history about the village of Vasileva and Chkalov family roots. Vasileva was one of the most ancient small villages on the Volga River. It was founded some time in the 12th century and its name was tied with the Russian prince Vasily Yurievich, the son of Yury Dolgoruky. Vasileva was built with the goal of defending the border of a larger city, Radilov, which was surrounded by high earth embankments with strengthened oak walls, military towers, and gun slots, which commanded the Volga and the left bank of the plain.

Vasileva where Chkalov was born and raised. It was renamed Chkalovsk after his successful flight to Vancouver.

The first documentation of Vasileva was in 1405. From the 14th to the 18th centuries, Vasileva was located in the territory ruled by the Shuisky princes. It then was transferred to the property of the Moscow Voznesyensky Convent and from 1764 came under the national economy. The main occupation of the population of Vasileva was making pottery, earthenware, and baking and selling bread. Since a large trade route passed through the village, every spring barge haulers gathered from the various villages along the river to work.

In 1883, they began to build structures for the repair of the dredging fleet. This provided the opportunity to provide a convenient boatyard for winter moorage of boats and the repair of the dredging machines and earth carriers.

These events changed the face of Vasileva. Construction of new roads and homes began where skilled workers lived. By 1924, Vasileva's boatyard had become a factory for shipbuilding and repair.

In 1937, Vasileva and the Vasileva region were renamed Chkalovsk and the Chkalovsk Region. This was done by a declaration of the Central Committee of the Communist Party on July 27, 1937, after the heroic flight of Valery Chkalov, Georgy Baidukov, and Alexander Belyakov across the North Pole to America. Chkalovsk in the years of the Second World War gave the country four more heroes of the Soviet Union. In 1955, Chkalovsk received the status of a city.

From regional documents of the time and research into the Chkalov family history, it is apparent that the Chkalovs were barge haulers. "The Chkalov family, according to oral history, came from the Upper Volga and they turned up in our region somewhere in the 19th century, specifically in the village of Poteryakhino. Vasileva was one of the centers for the hiring of barge haulers. In Vasileva there was a harbor where boats were wintered." Poteryakhino was located seven kilometers from Vasileva.

Anna Pavlovna Chkalova, Valery Chkalov's older sister, remembers: "Our great grandparents were not peasants of landowners, but belonged to the Monastery of the Trinity of St. Sergey. Our roots belong to the Volga. Valery's grandfather came, as they had for centuries, to this port of longshoremen on the Volga and his grandfather was a barge hauler, who pulled the barges up the Volga with long straps. It is said that great grandfather was born on the Volga during a flood on a drifting ice floe. This drifting ice floe is called a "Chka". From this comes the family name of Chkalov.

In history we find a name of Yevdokim Chkalov. His second son, Mikhail Yevdokimovich, had a son, Grigori Mikhailovich Chkalov — the grandfather of Valery Pavlovich Chkalov, who is considered the founder of the family. During the summer, the Chkalovs were barge haulers. In the winter, they transported passengers. Grigory Mikhailovich had six children, two daughters and four sons. Among them was Pavel Grigorivich, the future father of Valery Pavlovich Chkalov. Pavel Grigorivich started his working life as a longshoreman for nine years. During the winter, he pounded nails with his father. He was illiterate; therefore, wanted all of his children to go to school. He bought himself a primer to teach himself to read and began to study grammar while raising his family. He next went to work in Yaroslavl with friends and became a caulker. Later in Vasileva, he became a master riviter in the large boilers of steamships. Pavel Grigorivich, like his father, was unusually strong. As his family remembered, he cracked pistachios and walnuts with his teeth as if they were sunflower seeds. He defeated seven opponents at one time in a fight, and once, on a bet, lifted his friend on a stool with his teeth.

He loved his work and always produced beautifully finished goods. He was considered the most skillful master in the shipyard and was called the artist of the boiler room. Richard Mazing, the shipyard boss, said he had golden hands. About himself, Pavel said that he could never be a lathe operator, but from iron he could make anything. He had a marvelous memory and did all his calculations in his head. Pavel chose someone from his native village, Arina Ivanovna Kozhirnova, for his wife. She was broad-shouldered and strong, with blue eyes. Her character was firm, but she was unusually kind and helped all of her friends. She was generous to the poor. Arina was a happy person, loved to joke, and had a beautiful singing voice. Pavel loved his wife and they were happy together. Arina was a fine housekeeper and very hospitable. She baked very tasty pirogy, and on Sundays all of the shipyard friends would gather in Pavel's and Arina's home.

In his work repairing steamships, barges, and skows, Pavel earned enough money to build a home, which he built by himself on a hill by his father's home and with his permission. This house now stands in Chkalovsk and is a memorial museum to Valery P. Chkalov. Pavel and three of his friends then bought a steamship, the Ruslov, from a Nizhni Novgorod merchant. He was to pay for it in installments over a 10-year period. Pavel was chosen out of the four owners to be in charge. They rebuilt the steamship, but Pavel had a lot of trouble with it. The merchant had deceived the four men. Claiming not to have received all of the required payments, the merchant sued them.

As a result, the steamship was repossessed. When the revolution came in 1917, the ship was nationalized and it carried Red Army soldiers and, in one battle, it was sunk. When the Ruslov was repossessed, it stood idle for four years. Pavel and his friends bought another ship named the Pretok, which had burned and only the hull and part of its engine remained. The boilers were useless. Pavel repaired them himself. He repaired the whole ship and began to pay back his friends for their investments. But in 1913 he had to sell this second ship because he could not afford it. At this time, it would have been possible perhaps to barter the ship, but Pavel's work ethic persuaded him again to go to work as a boilerman.

In 1904, Pavel and Arina's 10th child was born. The baby was strong, but the birth was difficult and long. Anna Pavlovna remembers that as a result both Arina and the infant suffered. The baby was born unconscious. They slapped and shook him, but nothing helped. To give birth to a dead child was considered a grievous sin. Someone suggested burning a black rag to create a lot of pungent smoke and force the baby to breathe it in. The burning rag was placed under the baby's nose. He sneezed. "Thank God," everyone shouted in one voice, "He'll live!"

Having issued his first cry, the baby was not about to stop. He was quiet for a few seconds, however, when the local priest baptized him with icy water from the Volga. A thick steam emanated from the baby's body. Later, Pavel stood by the bedside proud and silent. On the congratulations of his friends, he answered laconically, "My son will be sturdy," and he asked, "What will we name him, Mother"? She answered, "Valerian, after your friend, Gikhun." After the boy had grown a bit, his father named him Volka.

The small Valerian had withstood the icy bath calmly, without a cry. But after this watery procedure, they say his voice strengthened and he began to cry louder. Valerian cried this way for the first six weeks, announcing his birth to everything around him. When he started to walk, he tried to climb on everything he could—and then fall, from the stairs, from a chair, from the table, and he would fall, without fail, on his forehead. He fell so often that there seemed to be a permanent, painful, lump on his forehead. That earned him the name of "Valerian with a Star."

And like all children, he put everything in his mouth. When he swallowed a thimble, Arina stuck her hand in his mouth, grabbed the thimble on her finger and pulled it out. Arina Ivanovna died when Valerian was six years old. All the difficulty of raising the small boy now was on the shoulders of his sister, Anna. She taught him well: not to cry from injury or offense, to be independent, and to always work up to his ability.

Valerian helped her care for the garden. Pavel forged a small shovel for him, with which he dug in the earth where it was necessary and where it wasn't. He loved his older sister, and after many years, he gave Anna a book describing his transpolar flight to America. In it he wrote, "Sister! How strange it is that not long ago you raised this disobedient mischief maker, in general a hooligan, and now all the world knows this man, but remember, Nura, this has not spoiled me, nor will it. I'm the same Volka I was earlier, only a bit more serious and now a grown person. Dear sister, I give you this book to read knowing that it was very difficult, but we overcame the difficulties and in this you played a most important role — I'm your brother. You will always be in my thoughts."

The family was large and within six months Pavel brought a stepmother into the home, Natalya Grigorievna, but Valerian, being accustomed to his older sister, paid more attention to her than to this new stepmother.

In the winter, Valerian went outside with an Astrakhan hat and a short sheepskin coat — a hand-me-down from his older brother, Alexei — with a red sash. For this he received the nickname Shortcoat. As soon as he got outside, however, he would untie the sash, throw his hat on the back of his head, and unbutton his coat, in spite of the below freezing temperature. By the time he was six, he could swim like a fish and dive. Anna had to watch over him carefully. He was reckless and foolhardy.

All of his childhood he spent on the Volga. In the winter, he rode sleighs and skied, and in the summer he swam. "My childhood was stormy and mischievous," he said much later.

"He was recklessly brave," remembered his stepmother, Natalya. During the spring breakup of ice in the Volga, huge chunks would grind against one another, raising mounds of ice. Volka and his friends would play king of the mountain on these mounds. "It was impossible to look at what he was doing, where ever these ice blocks were colliding, there would we would find our Volka."

"Your Volka is a Cossack chieftain," the old men shook their heads, "but he's going to lose his head. He's going to cause you a lot of trouble, Pavel." Valery's strict father answered quietly, "Yes, he's my little rogue." Pleased, he turned and left. He was like his father in build and in his unusual physical strength. Valery matured early and became very strong for his age, and so was chosen by his friends as their gang leader. He took part in fistfights, which at that time were often part of the holiday celebrations in Vasileva. With great enthusiasm and energy he threw himself into these rough games. In them, he could show his remarkable strength, agility, and quick thinking, which earned the admiration of his friends. This competitive effort to be first turned up in him early. It is apparent that this was genetically Chkalov. His father remembered that no one could swim across the Volga as fast as Valery or dive under the rafts or attach himself to the rudder of a moving barge. "I was a very healthy kid," he later told us. "I could dive under a raft and was able to count up to 40 logs."

He started school at age seven and was a good student, but never received higher than a C for his behavior. Studies came easy to him and didn't demand much effort. Arithmetic was especially easy for him and was his favorite subject.

What character traits distinguished Valery during his childhood? "He was very kind," remembered Natalya. "We had a large orchard at home and he was always giving apples to his friends."

He was always helping everyone and defending the weak. He was goal oriented and persistent, clever, brave and strong. These characteristics helped Pavel, it is told, when a wager was made with the merchant Kolchin, from whom he bought the steam barge Ruslov. The barge at that time was repossessed due to the false testimony of Kolchin and was standing idle in the harbor. This was a time of Maslenitsa when in Vasileva troika races were organized. Pavel and his shipyard friends approached the shore of the frozen Volga. Kolchin was there with his coachman, Yashka, who bragged that no one could overtake him on his sleigh. "And if we come from that mountain," asked Pavel, "could you be passed?" "From the mountain, all the better!" interrupted his enemy. At that moment, Valery turned up on his skies.

Grigory Baidukov describes the following episode: "Pavel turned to Kolchin and suggested a wager of whatever he would like, betting that

Yashka on his troika could not reach the Volga from the mountain beforeValery on his skies. Kolchin with great passion shouted, "I'll bet the steam barge!" The boilermaker invited everyone who heard to be witnesses. They gave the signal and the race began. Valery set out in a rush, but fell on the turns and Yashka in his troika was getting farther and farther ahead. It was clear to the observers that the skier was losing. There only remained two more turns, and in the distance the road was straight to the Volga. Valery also understood that to follow the troika was a losing proposition. He remembered the face of his father having been insulted by Kolchin. Suddenly, he made what seemed a crazy decision. Leaving the road, turning neither right nor left, heading straight to the precipice, flying over it like a bird and landing from the air on the snowy cover of the Volga. With great speed, his skis slid on the river's surface. Valery, not able to stay on his feet, fell head over heels, breaking one of his skis. Kolchin's troika rushed onto the ice 30 second later."

A gripping story! Whether true or not, it's difficult to say. We only know that Pavel never paid his 4,000 rubles for the boat, and after the death of Kolchin his son never asked Pavel for anything.

In 1916, Valery finished the fourth grade in the village school. Pavel very much wanted his children to have an education. The oldest brother, Nikolai, was studying in a Nizhni Novgorod school, but was drafted in the First World War and killed at the front. Anna was the oldest and received a domestic education, which allowed her to pass exams to become a village teacher without attending lectures. Brother Alexei studied in a technological institute in St. Petersburg. His sister Sonia studied in a school in Gorodets.

Natalya convinced Valery to apply to the Cherepavedsky Mechanics Institute, which prepared skilled technicians for all Russia. He agreed. The competition was fierce, but he passed the entrance exams. According to the archives, Chkalov passed the first year successfully and entered the second. He only studied in the second class a half year. Since this was 1918, and the civil war in the country had produced famine, destruction, and chaos, the school had no heat, so classes were suspended and he returned home.

On returning home, Valery began to work as a blacksmith striker with his father. Every day between 10 and 12 hours, he was lifting and pounding with a huge mallet. This work, however, strengthened him.

Probably it was at this time, in spite of the fact that Valery was only 14 years old, that his childhood ended.

YOUTH

In 1918, Valery began to work as a stoker or fireman in a dredging machine, where he worked a bit longer than one year, and in the spring of 1919, having returned to Vasileva, began to work as a stoker on the passenger ship, Baiyan.

This was a difficult time, but he never forgot about his family. He caught typhus and had no money, but in the spring of 1919 he returned to Vasileva, bringing a sack of flour and two sacks of potatoes to his sisters, Anna and Sonia.

It was in 1919 in Nizhni Novgorod that Valery for the first time saw a seaplane: "My childhood dreams to accomplish something unusual took a new direction: I began to dream about learning to fly."

He was only 15 when he lied about his age by one year and in August 1919 volunteered for the Red Army. They took him into the Fourth Kanavinsky Aviation Park in the Nizhni Novgorod aircraft engine repair shop. In this endeavor, his sister Sonia's husband, Vladimir Frolishchev, helped him.

In this aviation park, Valery became acquainted with all types of planes that were used by the Red Army. The foreign models, Morany, Vuazeny, Farmany, seemed to him miracles of technology.

For a whole year, Chkalov worked in the park as an assembler of airplanes, and day and night he dreamed about flying. But he could get no one to teach him. This was a time of war. "I recall the great envy I experienced during the dozens of times I spent in the air on repaired airplanes. I recall the passion I felt when I studied these planes and so worshipped and idolized the pilots who would sometimes take me up. After every such flight, I would go to the head of our park and ask: 'Comrade leader, I want to be a pilot.'"

But he was such a good worker, and skilled workers were rare, that no one would let him go.

At this time, there was only one theoretical aviation school in the entire country and for a boy of only four years' village education and an incomplete course of study at the Cherepovetsky Mechanical Institute, admittance to this school was impossible. But with his work on the repair and assembly of planes he was given the opportunity to study aviation technology. Having placed before himself this goal, he worked hard for its realization. He began to read voraciously. He conversed with the pilots and aviation mechanics, so gradually he prepared himself for this aviation school. At last, in August 1921, for his good work, the administration of the air park fulfilled his wish and sent him to the theoretical aviation school in Yegorevsk. My father's dream had come true. This was the first Soviet school for pilots. Soldiers came to this school from the front in gray, torn overcoats and ragged shoes to quickly learn to fly and again return to the front.

He still had a long way to go before could perform solo flights. The order to enter this theortical school of the Red Army is dated August 18, 1921. It says in part, "Valerian Chkalov shall be included in the list of students who will pursue their studies in the Yegorevsky Theoretical Aviation School … ." Apparently, this was the last document that mentions his name as Valerian. Later documents all have him listed as Valery, which was more understandable and easier to pronounce.

This school had its origin in the Gatchinsky Military Aviation School, which in 1914 was transformed into the Aviation Department of the Officers Flying School.

In the Aviation Section, before its transformation, the famous Russian pilot, Lieutenant Peter Nikolaevich Nesterov, studied. He received worldwide renown in 1913 for performing the first acrobatic figure called the Death Loop.

Many of the first heroes of the Soviet Union graduated from the Yegorevsky Theoretical Aviation School: A. V. Lyapidevsky, N. P. Kamanin, G. F. Baidukov, I. P. Mazuruk, and V. K. Kokkinaki.

In 2002, this school for pilots, now the Yegorevsky Aviation Technical College of Civil Aviation, was given the name V. P. Chkalov.

Chkalov immediately attracted attention on entering the school with his intense efforts and skillful flying ability. He studied hard.

He mastered theory surprisingly quickly, as well as the construction of engines, and very often helped the slower students. One of his classmates said it all seemed so easy for him. Listening to lectures, he could memorize them so he did not even have to write summaries. If he did come across a difficult problem, he wouldn't leave his desk until it was solved.

The following words became the motto of his life: "Whatever you decide to be, be the best." Specifically, not the "first," but the "best." It was with this motto that he began his journey in aviation.

He loved sports and particularly loved to play soccer. He favored the attack, but physically he was much more suited to the defense.

He belonged to a drama circle and took part in plays. They said he was a good actor. He was more suited to the comic roles, though, and played them selflessly, giving himself completely to his natural sense of humor.

"I remember an event in the Yegorevsky School," writes one of his classmates, Makarsky. "Before the evening roll call we were usually in our rooms. Someone thought up the following contest: After the command 'prepare for the evening roll call!' we undressed down to our underwear and crawled under the covers. Before the command 'on your feet' there remained a certain number of minutes, so each of us holding back tried as best we could to remain for as long as possible under the covers. Suddenly, one person would jump up, another, a third, a fourth and quickly dress and a minute later the command would ring out. The logic of each contest presupposed an accurate calculation and the establishment of a record.

"Once when we had all jumped off our cots and began to dress, Chkalov continued to lie there. He was making complicated calculations. We didn't bother him. Suddenly came the command, 'On your feet!' Chkalov remained calm. Three or four second later and Chkalov was already in his boots, his coat and hat, and ran to take his place in line. The roll call ended and the command 'Dismissed' should have been given, but the sergeant for some reason hesitated. Then he called Chkalov forward. The command 'About face' was issued. Chkalov spun quickly, fulfilling this simple command and loud laughter shook the walls of this old monastery — the traitorous coat, when he turned, opened widely enough so that he demonstrated to the whole brigade the white color of his undershorts."

D. P. Ananev, the head of the flying school, who taught him his first flights, remembers, "When I arrived at the airfield, I was presented with a new student. A stocky, solidly built Chkalov reminded me of a Volga bargehauler … .

"Chkalov and I got into our 'Farman.' I flew the plane, and he sat behind me. We took off. I tentatively observed my passenger. I remember how happily, with wide-open eyes, he looked all around, but I was a bit surprised—he sat in the plane as if he had flown dozens of times. After the flight I remember my conclusion. Student Chkalov would be a good pilot."[3]

Chkalov gave the impression of someone brave, and of inquiring mind. He mastered the landing of his plane at the school airport in a very short time. The landing demanded highly accurate calculations and considerable skill, since the airport was only 100 meters wide and on one side flowed the river Gusyanka and on the other was a ditch and a swamp. Young student Chkalov always made exact calculations and made his landings perfectly.

There was still another event in his life that took place during this period at Yegorevsk. He got married to a Lida Krylovaya. He was only 17 and there were no children. Nothing is known about her. Pavel, and especially his older sister Anna, tried to dissuade him. But eventually there were disagreements, as Anna remembers. They divorced when he went to Borisoglebsk Military School alone.

Chkalov had finished the Yegorevsky Theoretical School with the grade of Good in the spring of 1923. The whole graduating class was assigned the name Red Commanders and they were sent in 1923 to the city of Borisoglebsk to attend school for practical training. The school had just opened.

"Our first practice turned out to be not flying but construction," remembered Makarsky. On the airfield there was an old building which had been a riding school and we had to change it into a hangar. At that time the whole country was building and we had the right to expect some help. We worked with enthusiasm, happily—because before us stood our long awaited flights.

"Finally three new planes arrived, the Avro, in which we were to receive our practice flights. We had to wash these planes, clean them, and change their motors.

"From the general graduating class 10 people had been chosen for flight training. In the selection they took note of the evaluations of the Yegorevsk Theoretical School. Chkalov was chosen to be one of the honored 10.

"We didn't begin to fly immediately. We learned only how to taxi on the ground and for that there was a special plane with cut wings.

"We would taxi almost until flight. I remember once how Chkalov unwillingly jumped out of his plane and hurried to take his place in line again for a second 'flight.' Everybody took this training very seriously, but there were several extraordinary occurrences, which for many years formed part of the oral history of the school.

"On the airfield very often cows were pastured, and I don't know whether it came from the initiative of the cows themselves or from their owners, but at times during our taxiing it was necessary to make very complicated maneuvers to avoid unpleasant collisions. Once student Tsurenko, not understanding a cow's intentions, cut into the poor animal with his propeller and killed it on the spot.

"Soon we were confronted by a crying woman. It was necessary for the school to buy her dead cow. For several days we had marvelous meat borsch and in our hearts we were thanking Tsurenko, but of course the meat ran out and we were placed back on our earlier rations.

"During the next taxiing practice when Tsurenko approached his plane Chkalov's voice unexpectedly rang out, 'Tsurenko, do your best and get us another cow or else we will be put back on the same nasty grub.'

"Tsurenko started off amid general laughter ... ."

The flight instructor of the Borisoglebsk Military Pilot School, Hero of the Soviet Union, N. F. Popov, remembered that among the present young replacement students, "... there stood out a young lad with strong broad shoulders. He had an eagle's nose, heavy brows, blond hair, and his eyes showed attention and concentration. His speech was slow, calm, and thoughtful.... He was distinguished by his strong character ... ."

The flight instructor valued his courage, and cool head. In flying with the instructor he was unusually careful not to interrupt him. Having made a landing, he would hurry to debrief with the instructor, who had evaluated his flight. "Sitting just one time in the training plane in the instructor's seat, one felt that this youth, not having flown 10 hours yet, would force this plane to submit to his will, would rule over her ... ."

Chkalov's creative talents already began to show themselves in this school. When he received the assignment of performing solo aerobatics, and was given a plane designed only for simple aerobatics, he performed complex ones.

On responding to his instructor's comments, he said, "I wanted to show you that I can do not only simple aerobatics, but complex ones too

... I wanted to squeeze from the plane everything, and to show what it's capable of." And as it turned out, planes of this type in the future performed all of the figures of aerobatics, including the death loop.

In this school, Chkalov mastered landing his plane on a chosen spot. He always tried to do more than he was asked. If they told him to do a loop, he would do three. According to his fellow students, already in this period he had mastered the classical flying skills.

In one of the evaluations of this period, it's said, "Chkalov is a premier example of a thoughtful and attentive pilot who, during the course of his flight lessons, proved to be circumspect and disciplined ... "From the very first, Chkalov showed great skill in the flight program. He was always confident and calm during flight. He had a quick mind and acted with energy and decisiveness, uncovering the reasons for his mistakes and successfully correcting them ... I suggested that he is perfectly fitted to be a military pilot."

Chkalov finished the Borisoglebsk School with the grade of "Outstanding." He was recommended as a future fighter pilot. On leaving the school, he left the following note, "I am happy that I graduated from this school with the first graduating class, but I'm still sad to leave. Here we built everything with our own hands. Take care of this school, dear friends." Of the 45 people who finished the Borisoglebsk School, Chkalov was in the top 10 and was sent for further study to the Moscow Aviation School.

He entered the school on November 1, 1923. Here he learned to fly faster, more modern aircraft.

His first instructor in this Moscow School of Advanced Aviation was Alexander Ivanovich Zhukov, who had by this time taught about 300 student pilots.

Zhukov was a surprising and unusually modest person, a marvelous pilot, a master of advanced aerobatics. He was one of the first fighter pilots to have tested Soviet fighters designed by N. N. Polikarpov at the dawn of Soviet aviation. In 1940, he participated in test flying our first jet planes, the high altitude fighters MIG-1 and MIG-3 of the design bureau Mikoyan and Gurevich. A. I. Zhukov remembers, "I met Chkalov in November 1923. It was a fresh, frosty morning. They were rolling out planes from the hangar, engines were being tested, and the engines hummed across the Khodynsky Airfield. The mechanics and I were looking over my plane. Suddenly I heard someone shout, 'Are you Comrade Zhukov?' 'Yes.' I turned around and saw several young pilots in identical new overcoats and helmets. A red cheeked sturdily built fellow with a tightly pulled belt, and his hand thrown to his helmet in salute, announced in a Volga accent, 'Are you the chief instructor of the first group? Student Chkalov reporting. I've been assigned to your group for further studies.' We exchanged greetings. In his firm handshake, I felt his strength, and so it turned out that I was to be the first instructor of Valery Chkalov in the Moscow School of Advanced Flight for Red Army Pilots. After me, he studied flight with instructors Lopping and Trofimov. Valery came to us right after finishing the Borisoglebsky School having accumulated only a few hours of flight. In Moscow, he was to perfect advanced aerobatics and to master new types of aircraft. We had new foreign planes at that time …

"On looking over an unfamiliar plane, Chkalov never asked unnecessary questions, but if he didn't understand something completely, he was not afraid to ask two or three times if necessary. Then, having understood the heart of the matter, he would become quiet and again listen attentively, looking as if perhaps he didn't quite believe it. His calm, slow movements inspired in oneself trust even before his flight began."

In his instructor's book, Zhukov wrote, "Chkalov was uncomplicated, sociable, and strong with an incessant thirst for flight and especially for advanced piloting and aerobatics." Being a master himself, Zhukov wrote, "I loved aerobatics myself. You can imagine what a pleasure it was to teach Valery Chkalov and to observe his daring, beautiful air figures … Valery Chkalov was a born pilot. He became a genuine artist of the most complex aerobatics only thanks to his constant practice and untiring effort."

On November 14, 1923, Zhukov writes about one of Chkalov's flights on the Fokker C3 biplane, "In front of me in the open forward cockpit I could see the broad shoulders of Chkalov and his head in the leather helmet with his goggles strapped on the back. We communicated by means of a special system: a receptacle that was tied to our partner with a rubber hose and fastened to a metal 'ear' in our helmets. 'Can you hear? Are you ready for the flight?' I asked. 'I hear fine,' rumbled Chkalov's mellow bass voice. 'I'm ready for the flight.' We taxied to the start, avoiding the snowy mounds. The runway was clear … My left hand was on the gas, my right was on the steering. My feet were on the pedals. I remembered how smoothly Valery completed all his preparations. I was ready to help at any minute. I pushed the gas forward. The motor roared. The whole plane shook as if impatient to fly, and rushed forward, faster and faster.

"The foot pedals were being manipulated too sharply, controlling the direction of flight. I could feel the steering lever was being handled with too much strength. The plane was jumping up and down over the snowy mounds. I tried to soften the movement of the pedals with my feet and to hold back the steering lever. No use! The strength of this young fellow! I wanted to correct him, to overpower his steering actions. I'm no weakling. I had never experienced anything like this and the Fokker was gathering speed. It was useless to struggle with this student.

"'Stop pushing the steering lever,' I shouted to him. 'You're strong as a bear.' He didn't have time to answer, but I could feel he began to steer more softly. 'That's it, lighter, lighter, hold it there. Let the plane move freely. It will even itself out.'

"I could see that Valery understood. We were moving well and left the earth. Gathering altitude, Chkalov worked efficiently. His actions were persistent, solid. What he did didn't need to be redone. But his first turn was too sharp. I told him about this. 'Yes, sir, I understand,' I hear him answer.

"He turned his head toward me and nodded. I could see his smile flash under the glass of his goggles. I understood that he was happy. He was flying himself and enjoying it. We finished the flight with a circle and came in to land. His calculations were good, but Chkalov was moving in too fast and pushed the plane too hard on the descent. I wanted to tell him about this, but he suddenly turned to me and I saw that the end of the rubber tube going from my speaker to his ear had fallen out of Valery's helmet. I could say nothing to him. I tried to pull back on the gas lever, but it worked poorly. I again felt the strength of his hand. He had a death grip on it, and so we landed at much too high a speed.

"We taxied to the start for a second flight. Chkalov put the end of the rubber tube back in his helmet and asked, 'What's your evaluation, Comrade instructor'? 'For starters, don't push the gas so hard. You'll break it. Second, why did you come in with such crazy speed for the landing? Your landing was very weak, in my opinion. General evaluation, good.' Chkalov replied, 'I understand, I'll do better.' And he turned from me flashing a broad, satisfied smile. Chkalov quickly and confidently finished the required program and began his solo flights. When Chkalov performed his aerobatics in our brown Fokker C3, I never doubted in the young pilot's success.

"Chkalov, like many physically strong people, was kind and good natured with his comrades. They loved him. On the ground, he was a typical young man, broad shouldered, slow moving, unhurried. But like a volcano, there boiled in him a desire to erupt into the sky. In him was hidden a great strength and his character was completely revealed in flight.

"After Chkalov finished his training in our group, I wrote and sent to the command evaluation documents. 'Chkalov finished his studies with the evaluation Very Good. He was calm as a person and as a pilot. He catches on slowly, but he masters his requirements completely. There were no disciplinary problems."

Zhukov describes yet another episode: "One time during flight lessons, someone shouted, 'Hey, what's he doing! Look! Look!'

"I looked up. Someone in a fighter bi-plane, a 'Martinside', was performing aerobatics. He turned too sharply. The plane, almost standing on its wing, lost speed. It unexpectedly and quickly fell into a downward spiral. Unfortunately, it entered this downward spin at a low altitude. Everyone froze, afraid that the student pilot would be unable to correct his problem; he would not have time. Against the bright background of the sky, every movement of the seemingly doomed plane was terribly visible. Being twirled around in this rapid rotation, the pilot seemed helpless. Inexorably, with every passing second, the tragic meeting of plane and earth came closer. I glanced at that spot on the airfield where the crash would occur.... And suddenly, at some 300 feet above the earth, the Martinside broke its rotating rhythm and with a countering turn, slipped out of its downward spin.

"He pulled it out! Good man!' I breathed easier, and only just managed to reach for my cigarettes when again I froze at the unexpected: The pilot with his martinside, instead of coming in for a landing, again headed for altitude. Having, happily, just escaped death, he should have landed immediately, gathered his thoughts and looked over the plane for damage. Instead, he again gained altitude to about 1800 feet. And everyone watched as the pilot again, this time from the other side, sharply led the plane into a downward spiral — this time intentionally!

"The tension became intense as we watched again the dangerous spinning plane. And again, at the last minute, at the lowest possible altitude, he pulled his plane out of its spinning dive and swooped low over the field.

"Together with the others, I approached the Martinside. From his cabin, having calmly unbuckled his belts, Chkalov slowly climbed down. He jumped to the ground, and beaming happily to the mechanic, slapped the side of his plane. 'A g-o-o-o-d plane,' he told him.

"A 'good plane' or not, another time after Valery completed his aerobatic wing-over, barrel rolls, and dives in this same Martinside, he seriously damaged parts of the plane and wings. In spite of this, he successfully landed the plane. One can imagine the monstrous pressure on the wings performing these aerobatic figures, to say nothing of the pressure on the pilot.

"They say I was a strict instructor. It's true. There was no familiarity between my students and me. Our relations were good, simple, and friendly. We had many of them in our home, Chkalov among them. Valery, as the others, always addressed me formally, calling me Comrade Instructor or Comrade Zhukov. It was only on graduation day from the Moscow school that he came up to me and for the first time called me by my first name and patronymic. Looking me straight in the eyes and firmly shaking my hand, he said, 'Alexander Ivanovich, thank you!' That same day he from his heart wished me all the best in my life and in my career. And I wished him the same."

In May 1924, Valery Chkalov graduated from the Moscow school with a grade of outstanding and was sent to Serpukhovsk Advanced School for Air Combat and Bombing, headed by F. Astakhov. After talking with Chkalov, Astakhov assigned him to flight instructor M. M. Gromov.

Gromov says about Chkalov, "I remember Chkalov in my new group of students as a broad shouldered fellow with an unusually determined expression on his face. When Chkalov flew, it was apparent to an experienced observer that this was an especially talented person. He felt at home in the sky. He had an indominatable confidence in the success of any of his undertakings, even in the most difficult circumstances. He didn't know what it was to doubt his own strength and most important he could grasp and analyze situations on the fly. He was not only brave, but also daring and unusually assertive... At the decisive moment he had the ability to ignore extraneous events that might prevent him from reaching his goal.

All the strength of his powerful nature was concentrated in one direction—to success. The speed of his reactions matched the speed of his mind. He acted so decisively that really there was no time for doubt ... I would say that in his bravest decisions he reacted so quickly that a feeling of fear, or any kind of irrelevant thought, could not take hold."

Chkalov was always first at all of the stages of competitive practice air battles. It was in this school that he began to perfect flights at low altitude about which Aviation Marshal Astakhov later recalled. He finished this school in a month and half with a grade of outstanding.

It was Chkalov's marvelous memory and tenacious persistence that allowed him to master the necessary theoretical knowledge and practical skills leading him to his goal—to fly!

His desire to create, to hunt for some new way to fly an airplane, to fly like no one has flown before, was apparent in his character from the very first years in his flight schools. He said, "I can't overcome the passionate desire to constantly search for something new, for perfection, to constantly polish the technique of flying."

HOOLIGAN OR INNOVATOR?

In 1924, Chkalov was sent as a fighter pilot to Leningrad to the First Red Banner Fighter Squadron. This squadron was formed from the air groups, which had been commanded by P. N. Nesterov. Chkalov, following the innovative traditions of this creator of the death loop and master of aerobatics, was happy to consider himself a student of this marvelous countryman. "From this time I considered it the beginning of my independent journey in aviation," he said.

In the notes of the writer N. N. Boborov, who spoke with Chkalov in April 1937, that is, before his world famous flight across the North Pole to America, I found a surprising quote from my father, "Serving in the First Fighter Squadron, I learned all the good and bad habits that were to follow me in my flying career: The First Fighter Squadron taught me to fly; the First Fighter Squadron taught me to be undisciplined." Let's analyze what he means.

On August 14, 1924, 20-year-old Chkalov entered the First Fighter Squadron directly from school. At the time, the flight staff was considered the most experienced and, at the same time, the oldest.

Chkalov was the youngest of them all, not only by age but also by flight experience. Therefore, everything that the older pilots did he considered to be the ideal. He observed all the old traditions of this military unit. And these traditions were, to speak mildly, very unique. Father remembered that the first question asked him when he entered the unit was, "Have you received your salary yet"? It turned out there was a tradition: From the first salary, it is necessary to buy the pointed military hat. All the rest of the money had to be spent drinking. These fledgling pilots bought their hats for 3 rubles and 50 kopeks, and the rest of the money, 140 rubles, they spent on drinking. This was the military baptism father received in the First Fighter Squadron.

The First Fighter Squadron was the only military unit of its kind at that time. The flight staff was the first to master air combat, and Chkalov would perfect his combat and flying skills under their direction. After arriving at the squadron, he spent whole days at the airfield tinkering and fussing with his old airplane, the Nyupor 24 Bis.

Once when he was performing some particularly vigorous aerobatics, he came close to destroying the old plane. After a successful landing, the commander of the squadron, Ivan Ponfilovich Antoshin, received the following explanation from Chkalov, "Comrade commander, I know I broke the rules and I must be punished for it." He added, "I can't hold myself back. Understand. I've been in the air for less than a month." Of course, the explanation didn't help. He spent five days in the brig. After this event, however, they gave him a more modern plane, the Fokker D-7.

After several days, he asked Antoshin for a transfer to the Third Detachment headed by the outstanding pilot, Peter Leontievich Pavluchev. The main reason Chkalov asked to transfer was that the commander of his three-plane team, Moskvin, flew very little himself and gave Chkalov even less flying time. Chkalov also asked Antoshin to allow him to fly the plane, Vuazen. He thought the plane's characteristics were solid and reliable, and said that he wanted to use the plane to try to fly upside down. Antoshin fulfilled his first request. On the second, he suggested to the young pilot that he should carefully think through the possibilities of upside down flight in a machine with such little power. On that, the wise commander and the impatient young fighter pilot parted.

Difficult days began. The squadron began practicing air combat with flying targets. Chkalov did poorly. He "killed" only one target in four tries. In order to fly accurately, it was necessary to have a lot of practice, of which he had practically none. Under the direction of Antoshin, and true to his life's motto, he began to train at first with fixed targets and then against flying balloons. "Chkalov's dogged persistence and his desire to become the best air combat pilot surprised me. Not two weeks had passed before Chkalov had surpassed everyone in the squadron by "killing" more balloons through the use of his ring sight and his telescopic sight," remembered Antoshin.

Once Chkalov asked Antoshin to test him in air combat. This was a rather unexpected and daring suggestion, but Antoshin agreed, "Its difficult to recall all the encounters which we performed in this 'battle.' I remember some of Chkalov's shortcomings. I noticed his reactions against the 'enemy's' actions were late. Besides that, he flew too close to my plane, not observing the proper distance. But he commanded the plane exceptionally well, especially for such a young pilot, still a 'fledgling.'"

It was in this squadron that Chkalov performed his first upside down flight, and for which he was grounded for two days.

Chkalov quickly mastered his plane. He asked Antoshin to allow him to fly in all kinds of weather, even when the weather was especially bad. He wanted to be a good pilot, "better be a good chauffer than a poor pilot," he said.

This training in all kinds of weather allowed him to fulfill an assignment issued by the command of large practice maneuvers of the Baltic fleet in 1924. This episode has been well described in books by various authors and was presented in the film "Valery Chkalov" by the director, Michael Kalatozov.

During these maneuvers, Chkalov was given the assignment to fly over and drop a message bag on the battleship Marat. On completing this assignment in the most difficult of conditions, i.e., in heavy rain, thick fog, and flying close to the water while reading the names of the ships painted on their sides, Chkalov displayed the remarkable qualities needed in a military pilot: strength of will, persistence, feeling of responsibility for his assignment, excellent knowledge of his aircraft, and making exact calculations. He was the only one who successfully completed this assignment.

Under the direction of Antoshin, Chkalov served in the squadron until March 1925.

It was in this period that he met Olga Orekhova about whom I will write later. Valery Chkalov fell in love with another girl earlier, but this feeling didn't last and they separated. His first marriage also fell apart. I think meeting Olga Orekhova was a defining moment for the young Chkalov. He had now met a girl with whom he wanted to start a new life—but it wasn't to be. It seems to me that the emotional shock of his attraction for Olga left a defining imprint on many later events in his life in 1925 and 1926.

In May Commander Shelukhin was assigned to head the squadron. Our family archives contain his memoirs, which were never published since he so frankly wrote about the events of those years. Chkalov broke regulations and rules that at that time were not publicized, but today are of much interest and shed light on a series of events in his life.

A. I. Zhukov in his memoirs characterizes his former student as follows: "Chkalov could not adjust to doing anything halfway. Chkalov had a strong, healthy, expansive nature. He could not fly calmly following instructions. His strength and bravery pushed him to search for new ways of flying. As a fighter pilot, he knew deep in his heart that the winner in air combat would be the one who had mastered his plane as completely as he had his own body. He was constantly searching and learning in every flight he took."

The new commander was ordered to select the best pilots for a reorganization of the squadron, which was to receive new, more modern technology.

Out of 47 people, the new commander chose 31. Among the very best of the "old" pilots were Pavlushov, Korol, and Bogoslov, and from the young—Chkalov.

According to Chkalov, the squadron was resupplied with a new, faster type fighter, the Fokker D11. However, the plane turned out to be less than solid. The engine supports were continually breaking. The leadership decided to examine all the planes and it was discovered that the engine supports broke during Chkalov's aerobatics, much to the dissatisfaction of the firm that had supplied them the planes.

It was also discovered that Chkalov would damage the planes while breaking the rules of flight in his incomparable aerobatic exercises. For this he was sent to the brig many times. It was in this plane that Chkalov made his famous flight under the Troitsky Bridge in Leningrad.

Shelukhin remembered, "My interest in Chkalov was the result of the Leningrad military region's special forces' political department. The head of this special forces political department and the political deputy of

Chkalov's squadron demanded I either change Chkalov's basic psychology through a very strict educational program or take him to court and discharge him from the army. I had been told that Chkalov was a good pilot, but an extremely undisciplined person. He didn't want to follow orders, commands, or directions. Besides that, he was a negative influence on his comrades. They looked up to him as a leader. I asked specifically what he was guilty of. They told me that he maliciously disobeyed orders, drank too much, and was a negative moral influence on those around him."

The Troitsky Bridge Chkalov flew under in Leningrad, and spent time in the brig as a result.

Once Chkalov broke the rules by coming on duty while drunk. "I didn't want to part with Chkalov, writes Schelukhin. "I had examined his flight in the air and recognized his exceptional ability and techniques of flight. He understood the new technology and tactics of air combat. His most important qualities were a strong will, quick reflexes, and a cool head in difficult circumstances. Especially during aerobatic exercises and in landing, I noticed his quick and correct calculations. I recognized these qualities in the very first flights I took with him, and from that time I began to value Chkalov as an outstanding pilot. I flew with him, checking him out, sitting in the same plane and in separate planes.

"Having gained such an impression of Chkalov's outstanding flying ability, I decided to pay a great deal of attention to his re-education. It was necessary for me to release him from duty in the squadron and not give him assignments until he learned to follow the rules and fulfill commands and orders correctly."

Schelukhin had a long talk with Chkalov and demanded that he end his misuse of alcohol and the breaking of regulations, commands, and orders. Chkalov had behaved badly. For drinking while on duty, he was given 20 days in the brig. However, this strict punishment made Chkalov angry and on the same day he finished his 20-day sentence he again got drunk. Schelukhin, in his memoirs, explains the event, but does not indicate the exact date. It was perhaps this incident that was the cause of Chkalov being sentenced to one year. This was September 7, 1925, at a time when Chkalov was supposed to report to the airfield for group flying lessons at 3:00 p.m.

The sentencing document states, "… Chkalov appeared for duty at the appointed time in a completely inebriated condition. As a consequence, he not only couldn't fly, but he conducted himself in an unacceptable manner, shouting, creating commotion, etc. He attracted the attention of everyone present at the airfield.

"Having been arrested, Chkalov was sent home by automobile with the pilots Blaginym and Bogdonov. Again, Chkalov, en route, became very angry that he had been sent from the airfield and not allowed to fly. He loudly expressed his unhappiness by again shouting and gesticulating wildly. During a chance meeting with some acquaintances at a tram stop, he dramatically exchanged formal bows with them, all the time accompanied by these same cries and gesticulations. He again, of course, attracted the attention of all passersby.

"The above-mentioned actions by Chkalov have discredited the authority and the name of his commander and the Red Army, i.e., he has committed a crime and, therefore, the Commission has sentenced Citizen Valery Pavlovich Chkalov to one year of strict isolation and a deprivation of his citizen's rights."

However, taking into account that this was his first time in court, his youth, the fact that he volunteered to serve in the Red Army, and was from a proletarian family, they reduced his sentence to six months. He was demobilized from the army. This sentence was carried out on November 16. It is interesting that the testimonial about Chkalov, written on the 1st of November, was not signed by Squadron Commander Schelukhin, but by the head of the detachment, Korol.

Having spent four and one-half months in a correctional institution, Chkalov was released early and for several months was without work. He was then recalled in 1926 and sent to a unit that was based at the time in Gatchina near Leningrad.

Describing Chkalov as a fighter pilot and examining his professional activities, one must not forget about Chkalov the person. He was only 22 years old, and it was at this time that he wrote Olga Orekhovaya, "I love you, Olga, with all my heart. Life without you would be the beginning again of my downfall. Valery. P.S. I am very much afraid of this. If one's in love, he values that person greatly."

Chkalov speaks specifically about this difficult period of his life and Schelukhin writes about another Chkalov misstep. I want to dwell on this because in his heartfelt, honest admission to the commander of the squadron, Chkalov reveals that he does not understand the process of his own creativity, this process of hunting for the creation of something new in flight.

Any person creating something new, innovating, knows that during this period his thoughts will possess him and inexorably follow him. This thought is always with him, always in his head, even when he is doing something else or thinking about something different and only when the product of this creative process appears, when the thought finds material realization, will it leave the person with his creation. It seems to me this is how Chkalov created. Having thought of some kind of a new figure, he began to ponder the possibilities of its fulfillment. He would make the calculations, draw out the imagined figures, and think through its realization step-by-step. Only after this would he approach the performance of his imagined new figures. And only after he had repeated the figure in flight many times, whether he had accomplished it immediately or whether he had to work it out by parts or sections at a time, could it be combined in a completed and mastered flight pattern.

So what did Chkalov "honestly and frankly" admit to?

"Chkalov would begin to do his favorite figures—repetitious loops together with the assigned complex of figures necessary for the careful working out of the elements of air battle. Sometimes these loops, with the quick, repetitive pulling on the control lever, would turn into an "Immelman" figure. This very difficult figure was dangerous for that type of plane, and in particular for the Fokker D-11. This plane's engine didn't really have enough power to complete this figure, but Chkalov did complete it perfectly, however unexpectedly for him and the others. On completing the figure, he began to work it into the flight assignments that had been given him. This was his first regulation violation in the air.

"The second violation was on the ground. Comrade Chkalov took all the subordinates of his three-plane team to a beer hall and got them all drunk. This drinking bout ended in a drunken brawl. They got into a fight with civilian youths…

"I suggested to him that we have a heart-to-heart talk and that he frankly tell me what it is that persuades him to do these unacceptable regulation violations. Why did he, against regulations, against orders, and finally against common sense, as a commander of a flight team, allow such violations.

"He told me frankly: 'Comrade Commander, I have a very difficult character in the air and on land. In the air, I begin to feel part of the plane and the control system. I'm not satisfied with the usual flights; I want to do something new. It seems to me the plane could give more and it seems to me that I can take from this plane more than it's given up to this point.

'As a result, I get carried away. I begin to do those figures and those elements of combat, that are necessary, and the figure, which is more interesting to me. On the basis of this figure, I am able to create a new figure, very important for the elements of air combat. The Immelman figure allows one to quickly turn the plane 180 degrees and at the same time gain altitude. Altitude gives a tactical advantage against the enemy, and this thought was constantly troubling me.

'After taking off, I forgot that I was the commander of a team, forgot that I had to complete a series of exercises, and being carried away in that manner I rudely violated the regulations. After I landed and faced my comrades, I could tell that they were unhappy with me and my behavior, and I didn't know how to correct my mistake. I highly value my relationship with my comrades, especially with the mechanics. I decided that they would like me again if I invited them out to drink. I had no idea that it would end in a drunken brawl.'

"I understood that Chkalov, because of his youth, couldn't understand the serious consequences of his actions and the negative influence he had on his subordinates... From this came the obvious conclusion that Chkalov had been made commander of a flight team too early. It would be necessary to teach Chkalov ... I announced to him that I would be merciless. I would personally analyze every one of his actions. I would call him before me and severely react to any missteps ...

"Gradually, Chkalov began to recognize the unacceptability of his misdemeanors and gradually began to eliminate them. I searched in him for acts which I could encourage and which I could use as examples for others. When I began to present these examples to others, it made a very strong and positive impression on Chkalov.

"Before this he understood that in the squadron he wasn't receiving the authority that comes from respect because of his mistakes. The brig, punishments, scoldings, being called before the commander, depressed him deeply. I discovered this from letters which were shown me and in which he complained to his comrades and to his wife [Valery Chkalov and Olga Orekhova were married on February 27, 1927, auth.]. He was even thinking of quitting aviation and resigning from the military, that perhaps he couldn't succeed. This thought so depressed him that he began to lose faith in himself and his ability, but when I began to encourage him and use him as an example to others he immediately came alive. His mood changed and he began to more accurately fulfill his assignments.

"When I became convinced that he had begun to recognize his mistakes and properly assess them and when he began to eliminate those faults, I again appointed him commander of the three-plane team."

According to the evaluation given to the young pilot Chkalov by Schelukhin, he had all the qualities of a fighter pilot. He could carry the attack of air combat to the opponent. He could properly lead his subordinates and gain their respect. He was a leader in the air.

Once in a family circle Chkalov told about how he changed the tactics of air combat during a training flight. "It was often my responsibility as a fighter pilot to destroy the formation of reconnaissance planes. Usually I would fly directly into the head of the formation and cause them to scatter. One time, however, the 'enemy' gave me a categorical warning, 'This time, Chkalov, we're not going to give way.' This complicated the situation. If they fulfilled their threat, then a collision was inevitable. It was necessary to change tactics.

"I quickly took a place directly in front of the formation of reconnaissance planes and quickly did a barrel roll to the left. The 'enemy' was presented with a dilemma. They could crash into my plane or they could scatter. It was clear, of course, that after I had begun my barrel roll that I could no longer control the course of events, so it was the enemy's responsibility to choose between life and death. Of course, life won and the formation scattered."

The squadron commander used Chkalov's tactics introducing group flying strategies to young pilots. Schelukhin remembers, "Chkalov was the first to show examples of group action. He better than anyone in the squadron lead his group of planes. He taught the flying staff of the school very difficult and intricate group maneuvers for air combat and firing at fixed and moveable targets."

"Chkalov was the first to develop examples of close flight formation." remembered Schelukhin.

As Astakhov recalls, "I met Chkalov in 1926 at a reception for the chief of the Air Force. At this conference, there were several experienced pilots, including Chkalov, who gave reports on the evaluations of several Air Force units, from the point of view of practical pilots and crews of one and two seat aircraft, concerning flight in difficult conditions, how to fly through clouds, and fly blind. The fact that Chkalov was given such a responsible assignment spoke of the growth of his professionalism and technical competence. His report was accurate, grammatical, and persuasive. Chkalov's suggestions were well reasoned with very accurate conclusions. He had grown up, looked sharp, behaved in an exemplary manner, was disciplined, and in all ways made a very favorable impression."

From the experiences of the First World War and the Civil War, it was discovered that in order to bring a plane down it was necessary to strike it 15 times. The squadron had experience in firing practice against balloons, which moved only in the vertical and in no way imitated the actions of a plane. It was necessary to develop training methods against moving targets, against aircraft. Schelukhin remembers, "Chkalov was the best aide I had in my work. Not only was he personally the best shot, but he also helped me teach the flight staff.

"In 1927, in a visit to the squadron by Air Force chief Peter Ionovich Baranov, we demonstrated this outstanding method of firing. Pavlushov, Korol, Makarsky, Chkalov, and I demonstrated the results of this method of firing and scored an exceptionally high percent of hits. The average percent of hits per pilot was 62 in the squadron. Chkalov and Pavlushov scored 98%.

"In firing at ground targets and in the air, Chkalov's innovations and suggestions helped overcome difficulties and lead to new, successful methods of firing. Comrade Chkalov was considered an innovator in the squadron, constantly hunting for new methods for the use of a plane in battle. His suggestions and innovations and his untiring searching mind helped create a highly qualified, battle ready squadron, which allowed it to take first place in the Russian Air Force."

At the end of June 1927 Chkalov was sent to Lipetsk for an advanced aviation course. Foreign fighter pilots were based in Lipetsk at this time. At the conclusion of the course all pilots were to show their best methods of battle and the techniques they had learned in advanced aerobatics, maneuvering and firing. In these demonstration flights Chkalov took first place and won the admiration not only of the participants of the contest, but the leadership of the Air Force who were in attendance.

After returning, Schelukhin gave him an assignment to show the squadron's flight staff what he had learned at this advanced aviation school. Chkalov asked that he be allowed to fly as he wanted and Schelukhin agreed, with "great anxiety." Chkalov prepared three days for the demonstration. He looked over the plane himself, made adjustments, oiled and lubricated it, and checked all the bolts and joints. In this, of course, he was helped by his former work in the plane repair shop in 1919.

It should be noted that he always paid particular attention to the mechanical needs of his plane and his superiors noticed this.

The flight was completed on the Fokker D11.

Following is a very interesting description of this demonstration flight from the memoirs of V. V. Brandt, who was serving in this squadron at the time: "Gaining the necessary altitude, Valery Pavlovich performed a cascade of figures of advanced aerobatics, always as only Chkalov could do—dashing, accurate and precise. Everything was going well, the commander observed with satisfaction, but suddenly the plane began a sharp dive toward the hangar. The dive was accomplished with the engine going at full speed. The plane, with a roar, rushed at the earth, at the exact spot where the commander stood. Everyone watched in bewilderment as the plane streaked downward. At approximately 160 feet, he began to pull out of the dive, but the downward inertia, of course, continued. As a result the plane pulled out only a few feet above the earth so that Chkalov's head could be plainly seen in the cabin. He was looking straight at Schelukhin.

"In the next moment, the pilot sharply pulled upward with the obvious intention of performing a loop, but this loop was at such low altitude it was suicide! Everyone froze. Having gained about 470 feet and showing the observers his back, Chkalov smoothly and accurately turned the plane 180 degrees around a longitudinal axis, continuing the flight upward. The figure was an Immelman! And this at the minimal possible altitude! He confidently repeated this exact figure five or six times: A sharp dive with the motor at full speed, pulling out just above the earth, sharply creating the loop, and an accurate turn at an altitude of 450-600 feet.

"Having finished his program, Chkalov began his descent for landing, but here the onlookers awaited a surprise. Reaching the approximate boundary of the airfield, the pilot turned the plane upside down and continued gliding in. When only a few feet remained between him and the earth, he completed the turn and came in for an exact three-point landing. He had completed a slowed down version of the barrel roll while gliding in for the landing."

This demonstration of Chkalov's ended with him receiving 20 days arrest in the brig and 20 days grounding from the commander of the brigade, who had just arrived at the airfield at that moment.

Later, at the commander's question as to why he had done this, Chkalov answered that in battle conditions the pilot may be presented with a necessity for an emergency landing and this maneuver might allow him to land the plane without accident in many situations.

The Immelman figure on a Fokker D11 could be performed only by Chkalov. It couldn't be done by others, because the plane would fall into a spin. Chkalov showed not only the possibility of doing this figure in advanced aerobatics, but at the request of the commander, he described how he performed it. "At the start, I sit loose and as deeply as possible into the cabin so that my legs are capable of full motion. I give the gas all it will take. I then wait for the right moment and push the rudder bar to its maximum." This sounds relatively simple, but it obviously took serious analysis to work through the problems.

Evidently, he wasn't the careless daredevil that so many thought him to be. Before completing any new figure, there preceded a serious analysis of every movement of the pilot and the plane. Once V. V. Brandt saw father with a pencil working over some sort of drawing, seriously thinking out something. When asked what he was doing, Chkalov answered that he was thinking about how to do a reverse loop, but nothing was working out. The control surface would peel off.

His goal was to know as completely as possible the technology on which he was flying. This gave him the possibility to avoid accidents in the most unexpected situations. According to Brandt, there was the following episode: "Once flying in formation with a squadron, Chkalov's plane's engine suddenly stopped. Not losing a moment, Chkalov took the plane into a sharp dive, was able to restart the motor, caught up with the squadron, and, as if nothing had happened, took his place in formation. This should've been at least an emergency landing if not worse. The height was only 3,000 feet. Below were massive forests."

Yes, Chkalov could fly as no other, but to imitate him was dangerous, if not impossible. But this, of course, irritated the leadership and they in all ways possible tried to slow his advancement in the service. So he continued among the leading pilots, but with the added reputation of being undisciplined. However, when the question arose about participation in the November 7, 1927 celebration of the 10-year anniversary of the revolution, Chkalov was included in the list of participants. Yakov Ivanovich Alksnis, who had been appointed at the time as a deputy of P. I. Boronov, gave Schelukhin permission to allow Chkalov to participate. At Alksnis' request, Schelukhin told him that the most skillful fighter pilot in the squadron was Chkalov, who could demonstrate the highest skills in individual flight. Schelukhin, therefore, asked Alksnis to allow the pilot free flight at low altitude.

On November 8, at the central airfield in Moscow, an air show took place in which pilots demonstrated their achievements. Members of the government, diplomatic representatives, Air Force commanders, and pilots were present at this celebration. At Chkalov's request, he was given permission to perform advanced aerobatic figures at low altitude, but carefully!

A. I. Zhukov, his instructor at the Moscow School of Advanced Aerobatics, was present and noted how Chkalov's skills had grown in the last three years. He performed incomparable, classical aerobatics in the Fokker D11. Zhukov basically repeated what Brandt had described; only all the complex figures were performed at the minimal allowed altitude, 60-90 feet—and at full speed. This is how G. F. Baidukov described the scene, "Chkalov took off at full throttle, gaining speed, he turned the plane upside down over the hangar and for a short time gained more altitude. Then the plane completed the turn and headed for more altitude. At a height of 900 feet, he performed a wingover and turned into a steep dive at full throttle.

"It seemed something was wrong because the plane, with maddening speed, was flying straight at a group of onlookers, including members of the government. At only about 150 feet of altitude, the fighter sharply turned skyward. But the speed dropped so sharply that the plane dropped about 30 feet and from there, with a huge burst of speed, began a loop. At this altitude, it was impossible for a fighter to perform this loop and undoubtedly would crash. But Chkalov knew what to do. At a height of about 450-600 feet, he forced the plane to fly upside down, gradually gaining altitude, and, again, a wing-over, and like the first time, a roaring dive with the motor at full speed he again pulls out of the dive just above the earth.

"And then Chkalov climbs to a height of 300-600 feet, does two barrel rolls, approaches the ground so closely that the onlookers involuntarily shouted from fright. But now it seems the plane is gliding in for a landing, but...surprise! In front of the hangar the plane turns on its back and flies over them to the landing strip. It seemed to everyone that there was going to be a catastrophy ... but at a height of 60 feet the plane again turns as if guided by some automaton and not a human. The plane makes a perfect three-point landing on the exact appointed spot. After such a gripping flight, the airfield was flooded with cries of approval—hooray! "

The confidence of fulfilling all these figures at such a height was achievable only because Chkalov persistently and stubbornly trained in secret, flying 20-30 miles from the airfield and performing these figures somewhere over the forest. At these demonstration flights, Chkalov won first prize, which was awarded to him in the evening at the Bolshoi Theatre in Moscow.

In the order given by Defense Commissar K. E. Voroshilov, it was announced, "We give this monetary prize to the leading pilot, Chkalov, for the especially outstanding figures performed of advanced aerobatics." This prize was the first official recognition of Chkalov's flight mastery.

Astakhov, the head of the Serpukhovskaya Flight School, which Chkalov attended, and future marshal of aviation, who attended the Bolshoi Theater award ceremony said, "I would like to fly like Chkalov, but such people are few. They're unique. Of course, this is talent ... ! But it's impossible to depend on them. We need massive numbers of flight staff, who will prepare schools and specifically these kinds of pilots in time of war to protect our country. Masters such as Chkalov are needed to advance into the future. In the future, aviation will be presented with thousands of puzzles and problems, which only pilots like Chkalov will be able to decode or interpret. Its necessary to find and protect this type of pilot."

But after this admission, his fate didn't change. In July 1928, Schelukhin received appointment as Commander of the Third Brigade in Krichevitsy. By that time, his squadron in Gatchina had attained the highest battle readiness. It flew at night, took part in night combat drills, flew tight formations, through clouds, without instruments, and flew blind.

In April 1928, Chkalov was transferred to Bryansk to the 15th Aviation Brigade under the command of Lopatin. We know about this period of his life from his letters, which we will quote from later.

This period for him perhaps was the most difficult: far from home, from his family, his wife and son, who had been born on January 1, 1928. He was no longer with his friends in the squadron and without good instructors. As he said, "I'm not located in the right spot and not doing the right things."

Ferrying planes from Gomel to Bryansk, he led a group flying too low and flew into some telegraph cables and destroyed a plane. This was characterized as air hooliganism. Chkalov was grounded and he was sentenced to a year in the Bryansk prison. As Schelukhin remembers, "I was surprised at the rash and inexcusable actions of Lopatin and felt it necessary to write a petition to free Chkalov. The government did pay attention to it and I don't know if my petition helped or the other petitions helped him, but Chkalov was soon free." After 16 days, he was freed by order of the Central Committee of the USSR, but demobilized from the Air Force. I will quote two testimonials about Chkalov in 1927 and 1928 that are kept in the Podalsky Military Archives at the Ministry of Defense.

The first testimonial was written on May 26, 1927 by the commander of the First Red Banner Aviation Squadron, Schelukhin, "He has a strong will, but he has little self-restraint in his mutual relations with others, but lately he has been improving. He is rather young ... He is sufficiently politically developed and politically completely reliable. He is an outstanding fighter pilot. He will make a great commander of a team, especially in combat situations ... ." This testimonial by Schelukhin is supported in his article about Chkalov, which was written several decades later, a section of which I quoted above. It is now possible to evaluate the role Schelukhin played in developing Chkalov as a fighter pilot.

The second testimonial, dealing with the period between December 15, 1927 and October 1, 1928, and which was written after the accident, did not arrive in time for the trial at the end of October. "Comrade

Chkalov has a persistently strong will. He is energetic and decisive. He has sufficient initiative, but in practice it doesn't show. He exhibits little self-control during his time on duty. In complex battle conditions, he analyzes well. He loves to fly. He is a good pilot and knows his technology. He is skilled in the technique and practice of aviation. He is outstanding as a fighter pilot because he has qualities of courage and persistence in the air during flight.

"He is undisciplined, in the air and on the ground. He doesn't recognize any kind of authority. This is especially noticeable in his relations with his direct superiors. In the air … his actions border on hooliganism … His development is better than average. He has significant strength, endurance, and health. Morally, he is unstable. He can't be a leader because of his rude relations with his subordinates and his superiors. He is equally familiar with everyone while on duty. He drinks too much in all situations, which has led to him being late for his flights. Educational measures do not affect him. Social and political work does not interest him. He has not earned advancement in the service."

This testimonial was written on October 3, 1928. In addition to this testimonial being a bit illiterate, there is nothing said about those successes which Schelukin described, but, of course, Schelukhin was no longer in the squadron and, therefore, it was possible to write anything they wished—both truth and lies.

Perhaps this testimonial was written especially in order to get rid of Chkalov. In the course of his short life, he never changed his convictions and could not be persuaded to call black white. And even much later, while giving speeches at important conferences, he called things as they were and sometimes criticized his superiors and the leadership.

From a letter Chkalov wrote to his wife, Olga Erazmovna, "Yesterday I was in court. They tried me without witnesses, without defense, and in a closed meeting. I was sentenced to one year in prison … Today in a conversation with the military commissar of the brigade, he expressed great surprise at the sentence and tomorrow will go to Smolensk to petition to have the sentence removed … The commissar says they will save me for the Air Force no matter what … I feel no kind of guilt. If it had been someone other than Chkalov in this accident, there would've been no problem. I am a thorn in their side from which they want to be delivered in order that Chkalov will never expose their unjust acts with his evidence … ."

Chkalov was sent to prison on January 3, 1929. In prison he kept a diary, which is kept in the V. P. Chkalov Memorial Museum in Chkalovsk in the Nizhni Novgorod region.

PRISON DIARY

"When a person gets trapped in a stone enclosure, he ceases to be a person. I am a living being deprived of my freedom. When a person has his freedom, he doesn't value it. He may curse it, but only deprive him of his freedom and he will recognize that he has lost everything that is dear to him. He can't see people that he would like to see. He doesn't have the right to do what he wants to do and, most importantly, he can't love realistically, but only in his thoughts. There somewhere in the distance is a beloved person in freedom.

Diary:

Chkalov, Valery Pavlovich, worker in the peasant Red Army, senior pilot in the Russian Air Force, has been deprived of his freedom for one year and has entered the Bryansk Prison January 3, 1929.

Day One, January 3, 1929, Bryansk Prison. And so I am in prison. I arrived at 5:00 p.m. without a convoy and this is good. They put me in the white cellblock, cell #12. They put me with three other people. Komzvoda has been sentenced to six months for drunkenness. A sergeant has been sentenced to a year and a half for robbery and one citizen has been sentenced to a year and a half. The public is sympathetic. The general bitterness at having lost freedom unites people. My cell is small, but warm. As soon as I arrived, I started to read. I couldn't fall asleep for a long time last night. Thoughts about Lelyuska and Igor give me no peace. How are they in Leningrad? Poor Lelyuska dear, how you suffer for me. I feel this and my heart is sick. I can say sincerely that I am unfortunate in life and if it weren't for Lelyuska and Igor I would end my life. This is cowardly, but it is so.

Day Two, January 4, 1929: I got up early. I couldn't sleep. I had a headache. My consciousness is deadened. I'm beginning to understand the significance of being in this stone trap. Some day I'll get out of here. I've read everything here. Everyone has gone to work. I'll be alone here until 6:00 p.m. The boredom is terrible, depressing, and oppressive. I slept during the day. I woke up and they brought dinner. Dinner? This word sounds so nice at home, but here! It doesn't even pay to describe it. I sat, I lay down, I walked. Everything is boring. I'm tired of everything. Thoughts, thoughts about my wife, about my son, about my good, dear, beloved Lelyuska and Igor. One reflection, one thought, how are they? With this thought I go to sleep and with this thought I awaken. I wrote Lelyuska the first letter from the prison. Tomorrow I'll drop it in the mail. The day after tomorrow Lelyuska will read it and cry. Goodnight to you, Lelyuska. Our life is still in the future. Let this thought comfort you. If you only knew how depressing it is for me and how much I want to see you, to speak with you. The only thing that makes me happy in life is that I have my sweet Lelyuska, my wife, and I have from her a son. It seems I am going to go to sleep. Goodnight, Lelyuska. In my thoughts, I embrace you warmly.

Day Three, January 5, 1929: I got up early. I couldn't sleep longer. I didn't want to. I read the book "Communists" by Lebedinsky. I stopped reading. I'm tired of it. I walk around the cell, which is very small. I'm waiting for a longer walk outside, just to be in the fresh air. They brought dinner. Only a feeling of starvation can force one to eat this dirty, turbid slop, absolutely tasteless. I only eat a little bit, just enough to calm my hunger, then I can't eat any more of this slop. How I would love to eat the plainest dinner on the outside. But I well understand that there won't be anything better and I'm going to have to come to terms with this. The question, "why" sticks in my head and I can't get it out. I decided not to go on the walk because I decided to read more. Why walk under the gaze of these guards around this dirty yard. I'm reading the book "Island of Sunken Ships" by A. Belyaev. I just drank some tea, more accurate to say boiled water, with black bread. I finished the book, all 333 pages. I read it without stopping. Women are washing the corridor. They swear worse than men. It hurts my ears when women swear, but what can you do. This stone prison has its own rules and its own education. I've begun reading the book "Microbe Hunters," which describes the work of Levenguk, the discoverer of the microbe and life in a drop of water. Spallatsiani, an Italian, discovered how molecules multiply. Pasteur, Koch and other great scientists. I haven't finished reading. Tomorrow. Goodnight, my dear Lelyuska and Igorek. I kiss you warmly in my thoughts, beloved Lelyuska and Igorek.

Day Four, January 6, 1929: I got up early. Inspection. After the inspection, we got to wash. They called an inspector to the kitchen. They checked the produce and checked that the food was being served properly. The inspector checked the cells. Brrrr … not good. I could never stand so much time without work, without reading, and alone. Why is humanity so cruel to the weak? Better to kill them outright than to torture them and to produce more weak and useless people. I read a book, I finished two. I read in one gulp, I can't tear myself away. I was in the club, a small place, with a primitive projector. I watched the picture "Prisoners of the Sea." I then sat down and am finishing the book "Microbe Hunters," but my thoughts continually pull me to Leningrad, to Teryaev Street, building 21, apartment 28, to my Lelyuska and Igor. Sweetheart, don't be sad, everything will be all right. Only guard your health. Mine is getting worse with every day. I've lost weight, which is apparent even to me. I finished the book "Microbe Hunters." Yes, they were great people whose name every child knows. A man will never become humane without the support of those around him. I have lived just 25 years and am not satisfied with my life. These people lived 50-70 years and never received compensation for their work, but continued to do their thing and only after their death did humanity begin to value them. I'm a weak man, but I will make myself strong and useful for the struggle. Self-confidence is a good thing and so I will harden myself for the struggle in life. Going to bed now. Goodnight, my little, beloved Lelyuska and Igorek. I kiss you warmly.

Day Five, January 7, 1929: I got up at 6:00. Inspection. After the inspection, I went to sleep until dinner. After dinner, I wrote Lelyuska a letter. I'll send it tomorrow. Later I was called to the office to work and worked until 10:00 in the evening. I'm going to bed now. Goodnight, my dear beloved Lelyuska and Igor. Work has eased the boredom some, but the thoughts remain. Leningrad, Leningrad, where are you? I so want to go there, where my beloved waits.

Day Six, January 8, 1929: I got up the same as yesterday. Drank tea and went to work. I don't like the work, but what can you do. It's necessary to work. After evening tea, I again will go to work. Physical work is better than the work in this office. More so when one is not accustomed to it. After evening tea, I again went to work in the office and worked until 9:00 p.m. Afterward, I went to listen to Radio Leningrad. The

Marinsky Theatre broadcast Khovanshchina. Listening, I became depressed, so depressed in my heart. Dear distant Leningrad, dear Treyaev Street, dear beloved Lelyuska, Igorek. You were so close and dear to me, and at the same time so far and unreachable. It will be a long time before I see you dear Lelyuska and Igorek and I want to so much. I will read now. I have a lot of time and it's necessary to read. I'm reading the book "A Woman's Journey" by Patrick Mak. I will finish and go to bed. Goodnight dear beloved Lelyuska and Igorek and everyone. I embrace you warmly.

Day Seven, January 9, 1929: I got up at 6:00. I slept only two hours. I read at the beginning and then couldn't go to sleep. Listening to the radio from Leningrad upset me. It pictured reality and, as a matter of fact, I'm in prison. I went to work. Before dinner there was little work, so I just sat there doing nothing and looked at the street. It's a nice day, sunny, but my heart is heavy. I bought myself 500 grams of white bread. After dinner, I again went to work. For now I'm reading the book "Contemporaries" by Olga Forsh. Olga is the name of my wife. I love that name. It sounds of strong will, courage, and energy. I went to work. I came back at 5:00 to drink tea (that is, boiled water) and again went to work. After work I listened to a concert from Moscow and part of one from Leningrad. I'm going to bed now, but first I'm going to read "Contemporaries." Goodnight, dear Lelyuska and Igoruska. I kiss you warmly.

Day Eight, January 10, 1929: I woke up at 6:00, slept very little. Thinking about my dear Lelyuska and Igor doesn't allow me to sleep. I was at work at 12:00 when the commander of the 17th squadron, Voishitsky, came to a meeting and brought a parcel. I'm very grateful to him. He's going to Leningrad. What happiness! After the meeting, I ate dinner and again went to work. At 4:00, the chief of staff of the 17th squadron, Khatsrynov, the military commissar of the 17th squadron, and Muravev, the manager of the 44th airfield, came to a meeting. They had asked the head of the prison for this meeting and he agreed. How nice to know that somebody is thinking about me on the outside. I've become calmer as a result. The difficult thing is that when you're in prison and nobody comes to see you, you think that everybody has rejected you. I was thinking that I would be sitting here and no one would come. I want to thank them so much for coming. I've had a very good day as a result.

Now if I could only see Lelyuska, this would be the greatest of all happiness. I'm going to work again now. Its 6:00 p.m. I will work until 8:00. After that I went to listen to the radio, a broadcast from Leningrad. Poor reception, massive interference spoiled the concert. I then heard a concert from the Hall of Columns in the House of Unions (Moscow). The orchestra was under the direction of Andreyev. It's now 11:20 p.m. In spite of the fact that its night and I haven't slept, I don't feel like it. I will read some and then dream about Leningrad and Lelyuska. The thought about how she's doing there gives me no peace. Is she healthy? How is Igorushka? How do they spend their time? What's new in their lives? These are the questions that I constantly want answers to. I need very little now in order to be calm. I'm going to bed. Goodnight, my dear beloved Lelyuska and my dear Igoryushka, and everyone.

Day Nine, January 11, 1929: I woke as usual. I slept a little longer than yesterday, probably as a result of the meetings. I worked until dinner. I'm now having dinner, its 1:30. I found out that they want to take me from my office work and assign me to the club, but I don't know whether this is true. Then they want to use me as a lecturer on aviation and have me lead an excursion to the airfield with the personnel from the prison. That means I'll be free for a day or two. That's good. Now I'm again working in the office. I'm going to drink tea and then again work until 8:00 p.m. I worked again in the evening in the office and then went to listen to the radio until 10:00. I played chess and now I'm going to bed. Goodnight, dear Lelyuska and Igorek. I embrace you all warmly.

Day 10, January 12, 1929: I got up as usual. Went to work. There was a lot of work and I didn't even have time for tea. I just came back from dinner and I will write Lelyuska letter #3. But from her I haven't received even one letter, although I know that many have arrived. I'm so anxious to receive these letters. Maybe tomorrow I'll get them. After dinner I'll again go to work until evening. I sent the letter, worked until 9:00 in the evening, then listened to Radio Leningrad, my dear and distant Leningrad. I dream about soon traveling to Leningrad, to my dear Lelyuska and Igor, to break through these strong walls of this stone trap, but I will remain here. But at some point Lelyuska and I will live together in freedom. I really can't live any longer without Lelyuska. I'm going to bed. Goodnight, dear beloved Lelyuska and Igorek and everyone. I embrace you all warmly.

Day 11, January 13, 1929: I got up as usual. Went to work since even on Sunday I have work. At 12:00 the commander of the attachment, M. I. Andreev, came to see me. In spite of the fact that I've already had a meeting, they allowed him to speak with me. They want to make a fuss so they'll release me. He brought me two letters and a parcel of food. He's a good, kind comrade. The received letters have arrived at Bryansk 4-1. I was already a prisoner. Lelik congratulates me on the birth of my son and wishes us success in our future life and a quick return to Leningrad. Poor thing. She wrote these lines not knowing that I was already a prisoner in this stone trap. But that's all right, dear Lelyuska, I will soon be free and together with you. Zhorzhik writes me a letter in which he congratulates me with the New Year and with the birth of my son, and drinks to my well being and coming demobilization. Yes, Zhorzhik, dear good friend, I am already demobilized, but for this demobilization I'll have to pay with six or seven months in prison. But this doesn't bother me as much as the fact that Lelik and Igor are without means of support. Our financial situation also troubles me. Lelyuska has nothing and she so wanted to buy some furniture and some clothes, and I can't give her anything right now. This kills me. It bothers me so that I could provide for her well with my head and with my hands, but I don't have the opportunity because I'm sitting in this stone trap. And what for? If I don't behave according to my beliefs, then it's better simply to get rid of me and not try to change that which is rooted deeply in my blood. I'm not going to change my opinions and convictions. Zhorzhik, you write that I have to study. Yes, I agree, but I have to arrange it so that my study does not make us suffer materially. But I do want to study, very much. I will prove that it's impossible to play with people like me. It's necessary to deal with people like me. I'm going to work now. I'll work until 5:00. I've just come back to have a bite and will go back to work. I've just returned from work. Its 3:00 a.m. I worked from 5:00 until 8:00 and had only three hours sleep and again went back to work. You're already sleeping, Lelyuska, and my son sleeps. I wish you a calm, pleasant and restful sleep. I kiss you warmly, warmly. I'm going to have a smoke and go to sleep.

Day 12, January 14, 1929: I got up early. I only had three hours sleep. I wanted to sleep badly, but there is much work and I had to go. When I arrived at work they informed me that Orekhov from Leningrad was here. I was greatly alarmed. I thought that something must have happened at home. I worried until 12:00. At 12:00 Fedya came. He told me how things were in Leningrad and this made me feel better. He brought a package from Lelyuska and letters from everyone. It was a large packet and contained everything that I love. My dear, sweet Lelyuska so cares for me. Fyodor left and I went to work. At 3:00 they brought me two letters from Lelyuska and one from Moscow from Gessler and one from Klavdia Vladimirovna Navrotskaya. This has been a good day. I have calmed down. Gessler writes that in the next few days I'll be released. This is good. Right now I'm going to work. I will write letters to Lelyuska. I wrote Lelyuska a letter and K. V. Navrotskaya. I worked until 9:30, then listened to Radio Leningrad until 12:00. I'm going to bed now. Goodnight dear Lelyuska, Igorek and everyone. I embrace you all warmly.

Day 13, January 15, 1929: I got up at 6:00 and went to work. I didn't drink any tea; there was no time. Now its 12:00. I left work. I can't sit. My stomach hurts. It's probably from the package that Lelyuska sent. I went to work anyhow since there is much to do. At 5:00 chief of staff Khotsrynov and pilot Moshkin came and I was called to a meeting. It surprises me that they released me for these meetings in spite of the rules against it. Its good that they come and everyone is so calm. In the brigade they already know that Alksnis has raised a fuss in Moscow and they say that in a couple of weeks I'll get my freedom. I listened to Radio Leningrad. Today there was a good concert. A professor from the government philharmonic played the violin. Its 12:00 and I'm going to sleep. Goodnight, dear Lelyuska and Igorek. I kiss you all warmly.

Day 14, January 16, 1929: I got up as usual and went to work at the office. Later I went to work in the archives. From the 25th I'll again work there. It turns out that for eight days I have earned 5 rubles and 83 kopeks in the office. From tomorrow morning I'll work in the archives. There is no work there, I'll just sit the whole day. I finished at 5:00, went to my cell, awaited inspection at 7:00, and am now going to sleep. Goodnight, dear Lelyuska and Igorek and everyone. Kisses to all.

January 15-17, 1929: I got up and went to work, sat all day, and didn't do anything. Some prisoners came. We talked. Everyone told about how they ended up in this stone trap. I came from work at 5:00. I sat in my cell, talked to the prisoners. There is going to be another inspection. After that I'll go to sleep immediately. Goodnight, dear Lelyuska, Igorek and everyone. I kiss you all warmly.

Day 16, January 18, 1929: I got up as always, worked in the archives, slept. In the evening they informed me that a telegram had arrived and that I would be released right away. A telegram from Moscow! Hooray! I'm free. Tomorrow at 12:00. I will send a telegram to Lelyuska. Sleep calmly, my dear Lelyuska. I'll kiss you. Valery.

And so another page was written in the life of Valery Chkalov, who in two weeks would be 25 years old.

In this diary Chkalov wrote that, "If I don't behave according to my beliefs, then its better simply to get rid of me and not try to change that which is rooted deeply in my blood. I'm not going to change my opinions and convictions." With these words, he formulated his life's credo and perhaps predicted his future. His convictions and beliefs never changed. This hampered his career in the beginning of his life's difficult journey. He remained the same until the end of his days.

The 24 year old Chkalov held to his convictions about the training of fighter pilots when making his appeal to the military board of the Supreme Soviet written October 31, 1928, after the accident described above. I quote the following document because his thoughts are interesting today and have not lost their significance. "… To the facts of my earlier testimony I would like to add what's important and should be included in the various understandings of the characteristics of fighter pilot training. In my opinion the tendency in the army to maximize safety in flight is a mistake, especially in the training of fighter pilots. Fighter pilots must, in my opinion, be bold, daring, and with an absolute absence of fear and caution in flight. In combat with an enemy pilot one training to fly cautiously will be thinking more about his plane than about the enemy and, as a result, will undoubtedly be shot down by his opponent. This question is of crucial importance to the Russian Air Force. I very well know and understand the necessity to take care of military weapons and materials (aircraft are expensive), but at the same time to allow thoughts about this necessity to creep into the pilot's mind lessen the battle readiness of the fighter pilot. Considering these conditions in any future battle with an enemy aircraft, the contest will be uneven.

"This point of view is characterized by the command as hooliganism, undisciplined action. I have to add that in five years of daring and bold flights I have had only two accidents for which I am now sentenced to a year in prison. In my defense it's necessary to point out that on November 8, 1927, the Russian Air Force expressed their gratitude and awarded me a monetary prize of 150 rubles for 'brilliant achievement in the techniques of piloting.'

"The accident which I had in an old, poorly armed plane, the FD7, on the 15th of August has been characterized by the court as being caused by negligence and inattentiveness in flight, which resulted in my tearing into the telegraph cables and destroying an aircraft. Negligence and inattentiveness in low-level flight are unacceptable because flying at low altitude demands maximum attention and alertness. Flying into the cables at a speed of 90 miles per hour would mean sure death of the pilot. I have no desire to end my life with suicide. Consequently, we have on the one hand my mistake in which I failed to account for the presence of these cables at this spot and on the other hand my sight was affected by the fact that I had no sleep the night before and I didn't notice the cables.

"To characterize this as negligence is, of course, not true.

"To sentence me to a year in prison will deprive me of flight work which I very much love and am devoted to, and would also deprive me of the possibility of feeding my family (a wife and 10-month old infant who will be left completely without means of existence).

"Considering the above, and most importantly my sincere desire for continued work to atone for my mistake and personal faults, I ask the board of the Supreme Court to change the sentence to probation for any corrective length of time. I'm certain that I can atone for my mistake and most importantly I will be useful during an important time for the Russian Air Force."

This deeply patriotic document bears witness to the professional maturity of father and explains his innovative actions and desire to equip himself as a future fighter pilot with the techniques of flying necessary to allow him not only to bring down the enemy, but to be a survivor. Only 24 years old, his courage, I would say his reckless courage, allowed him to stand up for his views of fighter pilot training and education, which oppose the generally accepted methods of Russian Air Force training at that time. In this document, father pronounced some prophetic words: "I will be useful at an important time for the Russian Air Force." As a matter of fact, when Sigismunde Levanevsky's flight across the North Pole was cut short, and we had announced this flight to the world and showed our failure. The Chkalov crew saved the situation. Flying nonstop across the northern extremes of the USSR to Yakutia, Kamchatka, and landing near the lower reaches of the Amur River, Chkalov, Baidukov and Belyakov demonstrated to the whole world that the Soviet Union produced marvelous aircraft and well-prepared pilots, but more about these events later.

DEMOBILIZED AGAIN

From 1929 to the middle of 1930 Chkalov worked as a pilot in Dudergof, near Leningrad, as the head of a glider school. In addition, he conveyed passengers in a four-motor plane, the Yunkers, so they could see Leningrad from the air.

In Dudergof he was not only the head of a school, but also an instructor pilot. Among the students was Oleg Konstantinovich Antonov. Antonov was a student at the Leningrad Polytechnical Institute and a future famous designer of aircraft. Another student was Samuil Yaklovich Klebanov, a talented pilot, who in the Second World War was one of the first to bomb Berlin and died heroically during the Second World War.

Antonov remembers that Chkalov was very down to earth with the young students. He would pull the glider with them up to the top of the hill, take it apart, put it back together, and sometimes would raise laughter by lifting the light glider with one arm. I remember one photograph with Valery Pavlovich among a group of students carrying a glider on his shoulder, the OKA-3, with the students only supporting the wings. They flew on this glider, the OKA-3, which was designed by O. K. Antonov, and the Standart, built by P. V. Tsybin and O. K. Antonov.

Among these people, Chkalov felt at home. He talked about aviation and about flying. If a glider student made a mistake, Chkalov in the next flight would himself sit in the glider and, putting his cap on backwards, showed how it should be done.

It was in this period that Chkalov first participated in testing a light, one-seat plane, the LAKM, designed and built by activists of the Society of Friends of the Air Force, V. N. Smirnov and the brothers R. L. Zarkhi and V. L. Zarkhi. It's interesting that a woman, L. E. Palman, especially designed the engine of this plane. The propeller of the LAKM had two wooden blades with a diameter of 900 milimeters and the logbook is preserved in the V. P. Chkalov Museum in Chkalovsk.

Pilots V. P. Chkalov and A. K. Ioost completed 24 flights of about 10 hours and 15 minutes. Chkalov planned to fly from Leningrad to Moscow on this plane. He prepared for it, but unfortunately it was not completed because of an inadequate engine.

Chkalov didn't like the work in Leningrad. On one of his photographs he wrote, "A former military fighter pilot. I used to fly. Now I ferry a Yunkers. It's boring and sad to look at you Valery Pavlovich. You should be flying a fast plane, like a fighter. Oh, never mind. Have a ride passengers, enjoy." In August 1930 Chkalov left Leningrad.

Because of the intervention and support of the many people who knew him well, father was rehabilitated in the army and assigned to the air force as a fighter pilot. Among these people were M. M. Gromov and A. B. Yumashov. "We more than once having seen Chkalov in the air could not but be attracted to his unusual talents," remembers Gromov. "This forced us to turn to Comrade Alksnis, who decided to return Chkalov to aviation. Chkalov was born for heroic work."

In spite of the difficulties that accompanied Chkalov's work in the First Red Banner Squadron, the period of his life from 1924 to 1933 was the most creative. He created in his mind, and created together with his plane.

Chkalov substantiated theoretically, and practically proved, the possibilities of completing a whole series of new figures of advanced aerobatics not imagined by earlier pilots.

He worked out the ascending spiral and a slow motion barrel roll, the creation of which he worked on a long time, and performed the first four and five rotation barrel roll. He also worked out combat at low altitude long before the Second World War. The innovations Chkalov contributed to the technique of piloting include: performing figures of advanced aerobatics close to the ground, aerobatics at low altitude at great speed, engaging in air combat at low altitude, working out methods of combat on the vertical plain close to earth, improving the vertical maneuverability of aircraft, and hedge hopping flights. These innovations have all received general recognition. Hero of the Soviet Union, A. N. Serov, wrote, "Chkalov flew hedge hopping flights that many world famous pilots could only dream about."

Chkalov performed brilliant steep turns describing a closed, curved line on a horizontal plain. This figure was called a classical "virazh." He very much valued this figure as a warrior, "Being one with the fighter is crucial," he said. "He will win who more exactly performs this classical 'virazh.'"

Two-time hero of the Soviet Union, G. P. Kravchenko, wrote, "He deserves great praise for the fact that starting with the I-16 aircraft, all of our following fighter planes were able gain significantly more altitude with one vigorous revolution than earlier types of fighter planes."

Chkalov performed delayed action piloting. The outstanding test pilot, C. P. Suprun, remembers, "In several days he demonstrated to us the high art of advanced aerobatics in a fighter plane. We stood as if charmed. He performed barrel rolls, Immelman maneuvers, 'candles,' loops and spirals. Thousands of pilots performed figures of advanced aerobatics, but Valery Chkalov did them in an unusually artful manner. He flew freely, effortlessly. He completed his aerobatics beautifully, accurately, and artistically. Every figure he did his way. It was uniquely Chkalov's. Earlier, all these figures of advanced aerobatics were performed sharply, with energetic actions. Chkalov conducted them with his delayed action piloting. Even during the most complex figures, his plane would fly smoothly, as if in oil. Accomplishing these figures demands complete coordination of all the movements of the pilot and exact maneuvering of the plane. Chkalov performed these delayed action figures impeccably, forcing the plane to obey all the wishes of the pilot."

This very interesting uniqueness during the creation of figures of advanced aerobatics was noticed by A. N. Serov, "In him there lived the strong desire to master the new, the incomprehensible, to realize the unknown. If a new plane in the air completed something unexpected, but perhaps a noteworthy figure, this would be fixed in Chkalov's memory for a long time. Possessing quick reactions and quick wits, he would study this figure for a long time, remembering in what circumstances it occurred and then mastering it, changing it, enriching it, and creating a piloting work of art. Many original Chkalov figures were created in this manner."

All the experiments that Chkalov conducted in the air, all of his innovations and inventions, were subjected to one goal: to improve the quality of the military training of pilots, to prepare them for success in future air battles. And, really, remembers Hero of the Soviet Union, distinguished test pilot, M. L. Gallai, the ability to confidently, exactly and energetically pilot a plane skimming over the surface of the earth saved many of our pilots in the first very difficult months of the Second World

War, when practically all of the air battles took place with an overwhelming advantage in numbers of the enemy.

A. I. Zhukov remembers: "As a test pilot he knew deep in his bones that in air battle the winner would be the one who commanded his plane as freely as he commanded his own body and he stubbornly trained for this in every flight."

He hunted, probed and tested the possibilities of the plane and the pilot.

"That which critics, and at times even the friends of Chkalov, called air hooliganism," wrote Gallai, "was really just searching, hunting and groping for new possibilities of flight. Of course, in every search there were false steps, excesses, misses. But his basic 'willfulness' lay not in the thirst for sensation or in thrill seeking but in a wish to break through the standards to find new methods of piloting, to expand the possibilities of man having acquired wings."

Chkalov would fly between two trees, the distance between them being less than the wingspan of his plane, by turning the plane on its side. Once in a 40-minute period he performed 250 death loops. He flew under the Troitsky Bridge in Leningrad. He completed a ramming maneuver flying into the target plane with his propeller. The flight under the bridge was actually used during World War II by the pilot Rozhnov and saved his life.

Once after a 40-minute performance of aerobatics Chkalov found he couldn't lower his landing gear. By using his aerobatic skills he forced the plane to release the landing gear and saved himself and the plane. It was later found that the landing gear had to be completely replaced. Yes, A. N. Serov characterized Chkalov correctly: "Chkalov had the heart of an eagle and the mind of a scientist." Serov called him the best military pilot our country had long before the beginning of the war.

Russian Air Force Chief Aviation Marshal K. A. Vershinin, 10 years after Chkalov's death, wrote: "Chkalov rendered great services to aviation. He was not only a matchless pilot, an outstanding master of his profession, but the creator of a school of advanced aerobatics and a school for test pilots of new planes. He was the author of fighter aviation tactics and the creator of new figures of advanced aerobatics: an ascending corkscrew, upside down flying, and other figures. He proved the necessity of flying at critically low altitude. To Chkalov belongs the honor of creating a school of advanced piloting, creating better and more valuable pilots; for example, marvelous Russian pilots like Nesterov … ."

In 1972 at the 35th anniversary of the historic transpolar flight from Moscow across the North Pole to the USA, aviation Marshal A. A. Novikov wrote about Chkalov: "… He created new tactics in air battle. First, he worked out and proved the military usefulness of hedge hopping flights, which received general recognition. Second, he created many new figures of advanced aerobatics, such as the ascending corkscrew and delayed action barrel roll. Third, he worked hard on developing vertical maneuvers and brought them to perfection. Lastly, he worked out exact methods of air combat at low altitude. All of these Chkalov methods and accomplishments were widely practiced in the Second World War, which means they were vitally important."

FAMILY LIFE

I once heard the following words, "To be good parents is high art. You must create child psychological comfort in the home around the child." These words made everything clear for me. I now want to write about our family.

The psychological comfort which mother created in our family was quite exceptional. She was able to keep the image of father in the family. My younger sister, Olga, born several months after his death, never saw him, but she said she knew him as if she had lived her life by his side. In our family there were no scandals, no shouting, no cursing at children, no slaps on the back of the head, but there was the unquestioned authority of mother and her demands that we respected our elders.

Life was difficult for us because our only source of income in the family was the pension and there were many of us. Our mother, Olga Erazmovna Orekhova, was born on May 17, 1901 in St. Petersburg. Her father, Erazm Loginovich Orekhov, was a rural inhabitant in the area

Chkalov's father, Pavel.

65

around the village of Lugansk in the Slavyanoserbsky district. Her mother was Maria Karlovna Tulachek.

Erazm Loginovich Orekhov and Maria Karlovna Tulachek were married on June 2, 1903 in the Nikolayevsk Chernorechensk Church two years after the birth of their first daughter, Olga.

The 25 year old Orekhov came to St. Peterburg in 1896 from Lugansk where he was a student lathe operator at a steam locomotive factory and began to work as a lathe operator in the Baltic Ship Building Factory and from 1898 in the Primorsky Railroad where he occupied the position of a steam engine machinist and an assistant instructor for testing foreign steam locomotives. The documents show that Erazm Orekhov participated in building the armored train "Three Saints." Later he was the head of the steam locomotive workshop of the Primorsky line of the Finland Railroad. The last years of his life, as mother remembered, he taught young people lathe operated repair in the M. I. Kalinin factory. According to his children, he possessed a very good baritone voice, played the guitar, and was a large man. He was strong, with an open face, but had a very serious manner about him.

Maria Tulachek was born in Prague in 1878. Prince Peter Oldenburg, head of the Preobrazhensky regiment, sent her father, the musician, Karl Ioanovich Tulachek, to Russia in 1885 with his family, including the 7-year-old girl. Emperor Nicholas I had appointed Prince Oldenburg to military service in Russia. Karl Tulachek was appointed bandmaster of the Preobrazhensky regiment with which he sang solo baritone. Besides Maria, he had three sons. Emil (Alexander) married and stayed in Russia. His other two sons, Franz and Rudolph, returned to Prague. Maria was the opposite of her husband, Erazm: small in stature, frail, with soft movements and a quiet, calm voice.

The Orekhov family was large, six children — two boys and four girls. The oldest was Olga. When she was 12 her mother died. In 1914 Olga was left with five brothers and sisters to care for, the youngest of which, Anna, was two and a half years old. It was necessary to feed them, clothe them, and look after them. To Erazm Orekhov's credit he saw that all of the children received an education and four of his children received a higher education. In 1912, mother finished elementary school, and in 1916 the Petrograd Girls' School. In 1919 she graduated from the city's high school, majoring in humanities. She studied the following subjects: Russian, French, and German languages, history, geography, mathematics, physics, science, sociology, the history of work, art history, introduction to philosophy, astronomy, drawing, and singing. She also studied Latin, which mother demonstrated to us when we were in school, reading Alexander Pushkin's "Monument" to us in Latin.

In the spring after graduating from school in 1919 mother went to work in the office of the steam engine workshop. Life was difficult and they needed the money.

In the autumn of that year she entered the evening school at Leningrad University in the departments of history and languages.

The family was large and it was difficult for her father to support them. In 1920 mother began to work as a teacher in Childrens' Home #23 as they then called kindergarten in the 14th Soviet Workman's School. It was difficult to both work and study and, therefore, in 1920 she entered Leningrad University's A. I. Gertsen Pedagogical Institute, because they supplied her free lunches and a stipend so she was able to stop working.

In the fall of 1921, as a third year student, Olga Orekhova was invited to work in an evening school for older teenagers. This school had a very friendly and dedicated staff under the direction of Pavel Dmitrievich Sokolov, a progressive, creative person who helped many young teachers. For mother this was a marvelous school and her teaching experience there was so rewarding that she remembered it her whole life with gratitude.

In 1923 mother, while studying at the pedagogical institute, finished a one-year course in physical education at the Institute of Physical Culture. This gave her the possibility to work as a teacher of physical education during the summer months at children's summer camps. This allowed her to help the family financially. In 1924 she was allowed to work as a physical education instructor of the second level for the organization Spartok in the northwest region.

In 1925 mother graduated from the Gertsen Pedagogical Institute with majors in language, literature and economics.

In 1924 a life-altering event took place. In November she began to work as a member of a group in a cultural commission. Among the organizations tied to this group was the Leningrad Red Banner Aviation Fighter Squadron in which Valery Chkalov served.

Mother not only organized cultural work under the sponsorship of the squadron, but was an active participant in their programs. She was a member of a choir and participated in the institute's evening performances. "After a while," remembers mother, "I began to notice that often a sturdy, thick-set fellow in a summer suit would slowly open the door and carefully come in. Usually he would stand by the fireplace and listen to our songs. Sometimes I noticed how attentively he watched me. I didn't pay any attention to this. I simply considered that he probably was interested in me as a singer because I was usually singing the solo parts in the choir. This continued for about three months, right up until the new year celebrations."

A New Year's Eve party was organized on the last day of 1924. Mother sang love songs. The following is from mother's memoirs about the day that decided her fate: "The kind audience generously awarded me with applause. I noticed especially loud clapping coming from the side door. Glancing to the side I noticed that same pilot who often came to the squadron club where we entertained Red Army men. This time he was in a short, leather jacket and as he was clapping for me I noticed a broad smile on his face. Maybe from my 'artistic' success, maybe from the fact that this man was in the hall, but the nervousness that all day had bothered me suddenly disappeared. It was as if some kind of pow-

Valery Chkalov at 17.

erful wings possessed me, and my shyness disappeared. I sang a second love song. When the concert was over, the young man came up to me and, leaning down, introduced himself, 'Valery Chkalov.'"

They began to meet often and to make plans. Father had a dream about writing a book detailing how to fly and what kind of a person a fighter pilot should be, and he very much wanted mother to help him in this. These dreams were fulfilled only in 1935, when he wrote not a book, but an article, about how he sees a pilot and about what that pilot should know and be able to do. Thus, their friendship began. During one meeting on January 21, 1925 he gave her his photograph. At home she noticed that inscribed on the back was, "To the only one who can fulfill my life."

This inscription said a lot, but their relationship was about to change. My mother invited Chkalov home to meet my grandfather. The meeting did not go well. It left my grandfather worried that marrying such a man would not make her happy. As a result, they broke up.

If grandfather had not ended the relationship at this time, I don't think father would have acted as he did and be sent him to jail for that first offense. He would not have gone through a behavorial breakdown, which led him to write to mother that he needed her to prevent his moral collapse. But, as they say, you can't escape your fate. Mother and father accidentally met on a Leningrad bridge after a year had passed. After that, they never parted.

They were married on February 27, 1927, when she was not yet 26 years old. Father died December 15, 1938, when mother had reached 37 years. Mother and father lived together for 12 very difficult but happy years. They were years of great love, which, after father's death, mother carried with her throughout her long life. When Pavel Grigorievich, Chkalov's father, came to Leningrad to meet the Orekhov family and his son's bride, he said, "My Valerian is now in reliable hands. I am happy for him." For their first anniversary, father gave mother four volumes of Sergey Yesenin's poetry and wrote, "I will help you realize your dream of building your own large library." On the next page he wrote, "For our anniversary, to my small, sweet wife from your loving husband."

From 1927 to 1932 mother worked in the school. She was appointed the head of the academic program of that school, but after that academic year she left to join father in Moscow.

The first child, Igor, was born on January 1, 1928. This brought great happiness, not only to the Chkalovs but also to the Orekhovs, since father and mother, after their marriage, were living in the large Orekhov family. Father loved children and wanted to have at least six. In his letters to mother he was constantly asking how his first-born was, if he had started to walk, if he had started to talk, and, while he was alive, father took an active role in Igor's education. We still have Igor's school progress reports for two semesters with father's signature.

I was born on May 10, 1935, after two important events in father's life. On May 2, during an aviation parade, Defense Commissar Voroshilov introduced Chkalov to Stalin. On May 5, he was awarded the Order of Lenin.

Father was awarded this order together with N. N. Polikarpov. In his supporting document G. K. Ordzhonikidze wrote, "The builder and designer of aircraft factories, N. N. Polikarpov, is one of the most talented workers in our aviation. He has designed and built the I-15 and I-16 planes. Both planes, as is well known, have been accepted into our Air Force. Pilot V. P. Chkalov tests new fighter planes and is considered one of the best of our pilots. I ask that the Order of Lenin be presented to aircraft designer N. N. Polikarpov and to pilot V. P. Chkalov." This was father's first medal. Apparently, in honor of these events, which changed his life, they named me Valeria.

Igor Chkalov at 42 years. He ceaselessly worked to improve Russian-American relations. In his later years, he never tired of quoting from his father's speech, that Russia and America should live together in friendship and "With cooperative work decorate this ocean of human life."

Igor passed away July 10, 2006. He was very proud of being named an "Honorary Citizen" of Vancouver.

The third child, a girl, was born seven months after father's death, July 21, 1939. Mother named this daughter Olga. "I awaited this child's birth with heartfelt anxiety. She was bound to me by the life of Valery and was for me a savior."

Having to live through this tragedy, and carrying with her the heavy shock of the death of her beloved Valery, mother had a very difficult birth. She was taken to the hospital several times and again taken back the dacha, which was given to the family after father's death. Father's chauffer Phillip Ivanovich Utolian had become very close to the family after father's death. Mother was surrounded with the love and care of all of our family's friends. The sculptor Mendelevich, journalists Rodin and Rosenfelt, and the writer Panferov wrote to her at the time of Olga's birth, "We are here under the window, all four of us love you."

Olga was immediately taken to the dacha from the hospital. Many of the people who came to congratulate mother, were famous: actors, Alla K. Terasova and Ivan M. Moskvin; the sculptor, Isaak A. Mendelevich, whose monuments to father stand in Nizhni Novgorod and in Orenburg; the family of the Ambassador to the United States, Alexander A. Troyanovsky, and Consul, P. U. Borov; writers B. Galkin and F. Gladkov; and the widow Zinaida Ordzhonikidze.

We have saved the congratulations sent to mother from the factory where father worked and where designer Polikarpov was the head, "Dear Olga Erazmovna, the staff of the designer bureau of N. N. Polikarpov warmly congratulates you on the birth of your daughter and express our confidence that you will be able to raise and educate her to be a worthy daughter of her great father. We wish you the speediest recovery."

Our parents tried to instill in us a feeling of camaraderie and a kindness toward people, a love of work and justice, honesty and humility,

Valery Chkalov with his daughter, Valeria, named in his honor.

traits which both of them possessed in abundance. But they really educated us with their personal examples. "We built our family on general agreement and mutual understanding," wrote mother in her memoirs.

Mother successfully continued the education of her children that she and father had begun together. I remember a story mother told us about how they bought a grand piano. Mother sang well and our parents wanted their children to study music. It was only possible to buy a piano at that time in a second hand store. When they bought the piano and called a piano tuner to tune it, it turned out that the sounding board of the piano was cracked. They suggested to father that we sell the piano but he refused, saying he had been deceived and he did not want to deceive anyone else in selling it. This piano with the cracked sounding board served as an example of the character and honesty demanded by our parents. We all studied music and to this day the piano stands in our apartment.

I remember another episode. Someone told mother once that her children were good students in school and mother answered, "Why should they be poor students? They have all the opportunities to be good students." And, really, in spite of the fact that we lived only on a small pension, mother acquired for us a library with all the necessary books. Mother alone, having brought up her three children, and giving them the opportunity to receive a higher education, also raised Irina, the older daughter of her brother, Fyodor, who had lost his wife and two children during the war. She also raised the son of her youngest sister, Anna, Leonid, who lived with us until he was nine. All the girls finished school with gold or silver medals. Alexander, the son of mother's sister, Yelena, lived with us while he was studying at the G. G. Neigauz Moscow Conservatory. As you can see, our old piano was exploited to the fullest. Mother's sister, Aunt Zhenya, and our paternal grandmother, Maria Ivanovna, also lived with us.

I would like to quote the words of special Komsomolskaya Pravda correspondent, G. Bocharov, writing about Mary Hemingway. It's impossible to find words more appropriate to describe mother. "... Mary is one of those women of great men who know how to live on after they lose their men. She is one of those who after the death of their husband have found within themselves the strength to continue life and, no longer being the companion in arms of their husband, become instead the defender of his work and of him personally. She is one of those who, having given her husband faithfulness and tenderness, has found spiritual strength and fortitude and, relying on this strength of spirit and faith, can write about him and speak about her great friend with only the most faithful and warm words, words of genuine truth and enduring admiration. Such women fortunately are in no small supply among our contemporaries: Artensia Bussi d'Alende, Olga Chkalova, JoAnne Khara, Valentina Gagarina, Valeria Prischvina, Mary Hemingway ... ."

Mother herself had a very strong personality.

Having come to Moscow and not having the opportunity to work in an established position, mother joined in the social work of the wives of the factory where father worked by rendering assistance to the families in raising and educating their children. In 1936 she was a participant in the All Union Conference of Women and Economic Managers of Heavy Industry in the Kremlin, which was headed by Sergo Ordzhonikidze.

The Chkalov family, 1987. Valery's wife Olga, center, with great granddaughter Katya. Daughters Valeria, seated, and Olga, standing extreme right.

Mother and father were often invited to celebrations and ceremonies in the Kremlin. At one reception, mother said, father told her, "Stalin is watching you." Mother turned her head and saw how Stalin, having taken his wine glass, got up and came to their table. Approaching, he said to father, 'your wife is looking at me with reproach. She thinks I'm the one who sends you away, but it's not me, it's those others, those cutthroats over there, but I'll put them down. Let's drink to your wife."

There was another such incident after father's death. Mother and Valentina Serova, our marvelous actress, and the wife of the Hero of the Soviet Union, Anatoly Serov, who died in 1939, were invited to a reception. Suddenly, Stalin approached them. Taking them by the arms and turning to mother, he said, "You're a good woman; you remember your husband." Turning to Serova, "And you've begun to forget." Apparently, Stalin was well informed about the lives of the families of heroes.

Mother began her first official civic work in 1939, when she was chosen to be a deputy to the Moscow City Council. She continued to work as a deputy until 1950. Of course, she was acquainted with the work of a deputy. Since she was the main aid to father in his work, she read the voters' letters, looked over his correspondence, and prepared answers. But its one thing to be an aid to a deputy and another completely to be a deputy oneself. And she had us three children to deal with, and young Olga being only a year old.

The work was complicated further, because they wrote to her from everywhere. Letters came addressed simply Moscow, Kremlin, the wife of Hero of the Soviet Union V. P. Chkalov. They wrote about their problems and asked for help in freeing husbands, children and relatives from their tortuous prisons.

She worked in a school commission examining schools, children's homes, special schools, and decided questions of summer work for children and the work of pioneer camps. It's really impossible, but not really necessary, to enumerate all the problems decided by this commission.

Mother worked with the people. She decided problems of every day life: bettering living conditions, solving problems with registration of internal passports, housing, receiving pensions, and admitting children into sanitoriums, etc. In the beginning she received everybody in our apartment, in father's office, and only later in the building where we lived, they gave her a room where she could receive the public. She was able to fulfill most of the requests and, therefore, people came to her with all their problems.

Maybe she was able to do this because she was Chkalov's wife and maybe it was because of her general ability; specifically her ability to talk with people and to correctly refer their problems to those who could solve them. And, finally, it was because of her personal authority, which she had earned in the process of her work.

Mother, like father, was able to stand up for her opinions and to convince others of their correctness, only she did this more softly and quietly. Much later, even we children noticed the great respect others had in their relationship with mother.

When war started we left Moscow for Chkalovsk and then evacuated to Omsk. All of mother's sisters and their children came with us. So we had a Chkalov collective farm, as we liked to call it, when we lived in Omsk. Here, mother led a full life. She took an active part in helping families with men at the front. In 1943 mother was awarded a Certificate for Good Work by the Siberian Military Council and the Omsk Regional Military Committee.

Mother continued this work on our return to Moscow. She organized concerts in School No. 330 at which famous people, such as I. C. Kozlovsky and the young actress from the Vakhtangov Theatre, Yulia Borisova, performed. They performed free, of course. Tickets cost one ruble and all of the proceeds went to the purchase of school uniforms, supplies, and other necessary things for the children of those at the front and to those families with many children.

On April 19, 1942, in Moscow's Bolshoi Theatre, a meeting was held to promote the defense of children from the barbarity of fascism and Appeal to the Women of the World. The Central Committee of the Leningrad Komsomol organized the meeting. Nikolai Mikhailov, the First Secretary, asked mother to come to Moscow to participate in this meeting. The following people spoke: academician L. C. Schtin; the mother of the Hero of the Soviet Union, Shura Chekalin, N. S. Chekalina; poets S. Y. Marshak, and Alexei Surkov; Hero of the Soviet Union, V. S. Grizodubov, and others.

Mother opened this meeting. Olga Chkalova, educator, deputy of the Moscow City Council, was given the honor to be the first signatory on this Appeal to the Women of the World, which was officially accepted at this meeting. This appeal was signed by all the Presidium of this meeting, 77 people. The partisans, Yelena and Anastasia, who left immediately from Moscow to go behind enemy lines, also signed it, as did Worker-Stakhanovite, Zoya Usonova, and Hero of the Soviet Union, pilot Ivan Golubin.

I cannot enumerate all those who signed the appeal, but I will only say that beyond those who spoke, the following famous people also signed: writers Ilya Ehrenburg, Vilic Latsis, Vladimir Stavsky, Zinaida Ordzhonikidze, Rosa Dimitrova, and Lyubov Kosmodemyanskia, academicians Emelyan Yaroslavsky, and Alexei Speransky, poet Alexander Zharov, composer Dmitri Shoshtakovich, journalist Yelena Kononenko, Hero of the Soviet Union Yevgeny Fyodorov, People's Artist of the USSR Valeria Barsova, and scientist Alexander Vishnevsky, and many others.

In the 1950s, mother wrote many articles about the education of the new generation. The articles were published in the journal "The Family and School" and in foreign journals in various countries, such as Norway, Romania, Korea, and Czechoslovakia. For 16 years mother was a member of the editorial board of this journal.

In 1953 Stalin died. Representatives came to us from the regional party headquarters and said that our family had to stand in the honor guard by Stalin's casket, together with the regional party organization. That evening they said they were going to come for us. I was sick and at home, but they took me also. They left Olga at home since in the Hall of Columns it would be necessary to spend the whole night without sleep and we did not know when it would be our turn to stand in the honor guard. Late in the evening they took us with the regional delegation on buses to Revolution Square. Then we took the long journey by subway, transferred at Okhotny Road and exited the subway on Petrovka Street. The whole delegation from the Moscow Region had gathered at this entrance to Petrovka Street on the upper floor of a small but beautiful hall.

The whole hall was filled with funeral music. All of the chandeliers were draped with black material and, therefore, it was rather dark. We sat there the whole night. I would slip off to sleep and then wake up to the sound of creaking chairs when some delegation was called to take their turn. As it turned out, our family was never asked to stand in the honor guard by Stalin's casket. Why we were taken there I don't know.

There were no tears in our family about the death of this person, since in our family alone, two of mother's relatives found themselves in places "not so far away." One was shot in 1937. Of course, later they were all rehabilitated, but among the living the wound has never healed.

I remember well that after Stalin's death they began to let people out of the camps.They would make the rounds of apartments, some asking for clothes, some for food, some for money, some for a trip home. The door to our apartment was always open, and we lived near the Kursk railway station. We helped in any way we could. If we had baked pies or pastries, we gave them some. If there was no pie, we gave them a piece of bread. We gave away Igor's old coats and hats, since most of those who came were men.

In the 1960s, from the moment of the creation of the Pedagogical Society at the Academy of Pedagogical Sciences, mother was the permanent representative of the Department of Parental Society of the Central Council of the Pedagogical Society of the RSFSR. She was the initiator of uniting the Parental Society around the question of family education. She directly participated in the creation of the Peoples' Universities, and organized congresses and conferences of Parental Societies, together with educators and scientists in various cities of our country. Mother gave a speech at a conference in Leningrad on the theme "The Role of the School, the Family and Society in the Education of Children." She was a delegate to the Second Congress of the Pedagogical Society of the RSFSR with the right of a decisive vote. She gave presentations in Ufa, Saratov, Ekaterinburg, and Chita.

Mother took the preparation for these events very seriously and there were many meetings, as always, in our apartment. We were acquainted with the activists who made a huge contribution to social work with the goal of educating parents about raising their children.

Mother carried on a great deal of educational work in boarding schools, pioneer organizations, summer schools, and educating the young population in general by using the example of father's devotion to his homeland and his heroic life. We still have her correspondence with pioneer volunteers and detachments that carried the Chkalov name.

This was her constant work, which she carried on through the years. It was a second parallel life given to her beloved husband. In the 1970s and 1980s mother published books about father.

In 1971 mother was awarded the Order of Labor of Red Banner and, as was written in the presentation, "For many and productive years of education and social activity and for promoting communist education to the young generation." I think that this very short description of her life is appropriate: She earned this medal.

And there were still many more awards: from the Central Committee, from the Military Council of the Air Force, the Khmelnitsky Garrison, the Presidium of the Council of the Pedagogical Society of the Ukraine, and the Central Committee of the Pedagogical Society of the RSFSR.

On her 70th birthday the staff of the magazine Soviet Woman wrote her a letter in which they correctly reflect her essence and her spiritual reach, "We know and love you as a wonderful educator and social activist who passionately advocates the educational enlightment of parents, and as the faithful friend and comrade of the greatest pilot of our time, Valery Pavlovich Chkalov.

"All of your life you have devoted to planting in young hearts fervent patriotism, strength of will, persistence, and striving for success.

"The boundless generosity of your soul you have shared with people, and they pay you with love, they come to you for good advice — students, teachers, and parents ...

"Let your tireless energy never wane. Let your charm and warmth warm the people who need you so."

During all of this activity mother was able to help raise and educate her grandchildren: my daughter, Yelena, Igor's son, Valery, and Olga's daughter, Maria. She was unable to help educate Igor's youngest son, Alexander, but took part in the education of her great grandchildren: Ekaterina, Daria, and little Igor. And now Ekaterina has a small daughter, Ksenia. I have no doubt that mother would have loved her great great grandchildren as she loved her own children, grandchildren, and great grandchildren.

So let the wishes written to mother by Mark Lazarovich Gallai apply to our large family. Upon giving her his book, "The Third Measure," he wrote, "To dear Olga Erazmovna, with deep respect and many kind wishes, and to her whole family — down to the fourth generation."

Alena, Valerick, Masha, Sasha, Katya, Dasha, Igor, and tiny Ksusha, do you hear? These good wishes are for you all.

REVEALING LETTERS

When I look at a photograph of father at the height of my maturity, I think how impossible it would be not to love this person, and that to forget him also would be impossible. He radiated unusual masculine strength and at the same time tenderness. The features of his face were masculine with a kind smile.

There's a legend: an evil troll turned all people into walnuts and then cracked the walnuts into two pieces and scattered them throughout the world. And now every person is hunting the world over for his other half.

Mother and father were a happy exception, because they found their other half and were joined together. They fulfilled one another and this is apparent from the letters of their first years together.

In the book, "Our Family," among the excerpts of letters that father wrote to mother, published by A. I. Gertsin and T. N. Granovsky, there is the following: "You have given me a reason to live today. My life has become worthwhile and dear to me. You and my son are my life, my air, and my light. Our son is the link that connects our lives. You are that friend, comrade, who did not desert me in my most difficult moments and together with whom I can feel rested, morally and physically."

Mother did not want to publish their correspondence when she was alive; justifiably, considering the letters are very personal. Our family has decided to publish these letters in order to remind us of the positive moral principles and feelings of love that united our parents. We have mostly published the letters from 1928, since there were so many, and to publish them all would take another book. On one of the photographs of father many years after his death, mother wrote, "My dear beloved, how I miss you." The almost 12 years they lived together were not trouble free. Father worked in various cities, Gatschina, Bryansk, Moscow, Lipetsk. There was a large correspondence from those cities that covers several years.

August 16, 1926: (Olga Orekhova and Valery Chkalov were not yet married.)

"Valerick, I'm leaving today and must return on the 29th in the evening. In the evening I'll drop by to see Nura. She says that you are ill, have lost weight, and look bad. What's going on? Don't despair. Everything will be all right. I believe in you. You'll be the kind of person that I wish for. You can do a lot in this life if you only want to badly enough. Nura will miss me. And you? Well, get well, and be sure to write me about how things are going—only be honest."

March 30, 1928, 4:00 p.m.:

"Dear Lelyuska! I arrived safely in Moscow. I'll leave today from Bryansk, since I've made all the arrangements. I think they'll call me back to work in Moscow, but for the time being everything is going all right, but I do think I'll escape from Bryansk. Kiss little Igor. Greetings to everyone. I embrace you warmly. Valery. The train leaves at 10:00 this evening."

April 2, 1928:

"My dear Lelyuska! You can't imagine what a slum this Bryansk is. I've never seen a worse city in my life. There are two train stations. One is four miles from the city, the other about five. The city is located in the mountains. There is not one street that doesn't go up to the mountain or down into a ravine. The mountains are huge and the ravines are deep. The devils were playing with dice when they built this city.

"The commanding officers met me very warmly. The brigade commander even suggested that I live with him temporarily. I don't know how our relationship will develop in the future. Everybody's been waiting for me a long time. They all ask what took me so long to come. In general, Lelyuska, I don't know what to do. I may ask to be demobilized. I can't live like this. Alone here, I'll die of boredom. There's absolutely nowhere to go.

"Take care. I kiss you warmly. Kiss little Igor for me and write me all the details about how he feels and how he's gaining weight. Greetings and kisses to all. In the next letter I'll write more details. Well, take care and don't worry. I think I'm going to get out of this place. Warm, warm embraces, your Volyuska."

Some time before April 13, 1928:

"Hello, my dear Lelyuska! How are you? Are you tired … ? Well, now I'm writing you. I'm now thinking that Lelyuska has fed little Igor and is lying down to rest, and would be much happier if I were there also. What a pleasure it would be for me to hold little Igor.

"And here I am sitting in this damn Bryansk not doing anything and its impossible to run away. Impassable mud, boredom, an uncomfortable room, separation from you, all this is acting on me to the degree that I think I'm going to go out of my mind. I've become so accustomed to you, and to my son, whose cries I can't hear and I can't see the way he pesters his mamachka. I so love my little son. It'd be so wonderful if I were now in Leningrad. And why do they need me here? I don't understand. I won't be flying. I told them specifically. It's impossible to fly in such material conditions. It's damned impossible to live here and I'm going to tell them this directly when I go on vacation. I'm going to come for Easter, probably the 13th of April. Well, Lelyuska, don't pay any attention to my bad language and don't worry, everything will be all right. I will manage everything. Kiss everyone warmly for me. Give little Igor a tender kiss on his forehead. Take care. I kiss you warmly. Your Volyuska. Don't let Zhenya offend anybody."

May 11, 1928:

"Greetings, my sweet Lelyuska! Forgive me for not writing for so long. As soon as I arrived it was necessary to find an apartment, which I haven't done to this time. I'm staying with the brigade commander Kozyarev. How are you and son Igor? Bryansk is affecting me worse than the first time I came here. In a few days I'm going to visit the commission and I think that they'll give me a month sick leave. Then you and I will live together on the Volga at our place. I'm thinking I'll begin flying again from the 15th, but I think I'm not going to fly until the medical commission decides whether to give me a vacation or not and, if not, maybe I can convince them.

"Lelyuska, write me all the details from home. Is everything in order? How is your leg? When are you going to work?

"Take care of your other leg so you don't repeat what happened. Does little Igor cry much? Write when he begins to sit up and, in general, about everything new he does. And don't you worry, don't be nervous, and don't work too hard. Don't forget that all your nervousness affects not only you, but also little Igor. Then, Lelyuska, take care of yourself, please. Spend some time sewing what you need, and buy what you need also. We'll be able to save money later. It doesn't pay to skimp on what you need now. And, Lelyuska, take my suit and have it re-dyed black and then have it pressed so it looks nice.

"P.S. Greetings to Papa, M.I., and Fedya, Georghik, Yenya, Zhenya, Yurichka and all our friends.

"It must nice with you now, everyone together, someone to talk to, but here, oh! How hard. But it's necessary to fight and overcome. I embrace you warmly. Valery."

No Date:

"How are you Lelik? How are you feeling? How is my little son? Forgive me for not writing for so long. I didn't know what to do. I couldn't think of anything.

"It looks like now I'm going to get a month off. I was at the doctor today (he said that perhaps we can do something). Will know on Monday.

"I will write you right away. Lelik, I sent you 75 rubles, a postcard, and a letter. Did you receive from Vasileva 200 rubles? Or more accurately, 175 rubles? I asked Alexei to give you 25.

"On the 27th of May I have to go to a camp in the mountains, Gomel. In the early morning on Monday I'm going to go hunt for a landing field. I'm not going to fly myself and probably won't be flying for a long time, not until I receive permission from Moscow. The commission says my sight is not good. Come fall, whatever happens, I'm moving to Leningrad.

"Right now I'm serving in the brigade and the boredom is terrible. Yesterday I went to an operetta, but that didn't bring any satisfaction either. I wouldn't wish my worst enemy to live in this place. I'm looking forward to our trip to the Volga and I imagine how you're going to like it there. I'm writing this letter with breaks because people are coming to see me and that prevents me from continuing. Tomorrow or Monday I'll write you another letter.

"I've only received one letter from you, which I've read four times and I think that it's because Igor is preventing you from writing me a letter. How I'd like to be holding him now. Well, take care. I embrace you warmly, warmly. Kiss little Igor on his forehead and cheeks. Your Valery. Greetings to Papa, M.I., Fedya, Georghika, Lena, Zhenya, and Nyurochka. How are the girls doing? Are they studying or not? What's Zhorzhik doing? Tell him to write."

May 19, 1928:

"Hello, my dear Lelyuska and son Igor! I just received your letter. Lelik, you can rest easy. It's boring and with such boredom it would be easy to get drunk, but I've decided not to do that. Lelik, today I visited the commission and now on Monday there'll be a garrison commission and then I'll come after you in Leningrad. The weather here is good. It's very hot and I don't have a summer suit. I sent it to the tailor. I'm going to have to pay the tailor 10 rubles. I've had to repair two pairs of boots for three rubles each, six rubles in all, so I've had this unexpected expense. It's going to be necessary to cut back on my expenses, but this is all nonsense. Don't you worry. How are things going with you, Lelik? How's Igor? You don't write very much about him. Write more details. How is his behavior? Yes, and you don't write much about yourself either. But there's nothing to write about me either. I'm not doing anything. I'm hoping for time off, and that we'll be able to see each other soon. Well, greetings to everyone. I kiss you warmly, warmly. Your Valerick. Kiss little Igor on the forehead and cheeks.

"P.S. How are things with my suit? If you haven't taken it to be dyed, then please do so and then prepare it to be sent to me. Valery. May 22, 1928."

June 23, 1928:

"Greetings dear Lelyuska, Igor and Nyurichka. Yesterday I arrived at Gomel and immediately went flying. Today I made three flights. Gomel isn't a bad place, better than Bryansk, a thousand times. But it's still a lousy place. The command at the beginning was angry because I was late arriving from my vacation, but when I showed them the covering voucher they immediately understood. Lelik, today I sent you 20 rubles for expenses. Your letter, forgive me, I'm only sending now together with these letters. How have you settled in? How are you spending your time? How's our little son's chicken pox and how is he feeling? Has Alexei arrived? You write to Papa and I'll attach a message to him in my letter. Greetings to Papa, Mama, Guta, and Aleck. Write in detail about what's happening and write more often. How is Nyurchika feeling and have you gone swimming yet. I don't have anything more to write. In general my situation is not bad. Well, take care. kiss you warmly, warmly. Your Valerick. My address is Gomel, 15th Avia Brigade "

June 27, 1928:

"Greetings, my dear Lelyuska, Igor and Nyurichka! How are you and how are you spending your time? How is Igor and Nyurichka's health? How boring it is without you, if you only knew. I'm looking at a map now and I've become very depressed. Without you there's no kindness, no comfort, no feeling of satisfaction as there is when we're together. How happy I would be to embrace and kiss you and Igor and Nyurichka. How dear you all are to me. No, Lelik, I can't live alone without you. My work suffers. I am anxious. Yesterday I had a serious talk with the commander of the squadron. I handed in a request to transfer me to the intelligence department. The commander was not pleased. He called me to his office and tried to dissuade me and to convince me to calm down and not be nervous, that I would do well here. And today we had a very friendly conversation about work. Today I spent all day fussing with the airplane. I mounted a machine gun on it. I finished at 8:00 and now out of boredom I'm playing billiards. It's now midnight. I'll write a letter and bye bye. I wish you a good night.

"Right now you're probably feeding little Igor and he's being capricious. He doesn't want to be on your breast. Feed him from the bottle.

"Write me all the details. How is his behavior? What new things is he doing? I don't know what the future will hold, Lelik, but I think this fall I'll be in Leningrad. If not, I will resign and I've told them so. Don't you worry, and get well. I don't feel too well, but I can explain this by the boredom and the overwhelming wish to see you and my son and all my family. Take care. Greetings to Mama, Papa, Guta, and Aleck. Kiss Igor and Nyurichka for me and I kiss you 10,000 times. Your Valerick."

Before July 10, 1928:

"Greetings, dear, sweet Lelik, Igor and Nyurichka! I received your letter, Lelyuska and was greatly saddened. You're still not resting. What are you doing? I think you can hire a nanny in Vasileva who could watch after our son. I don't see any other solution. Lelyuska, the thing is, in my opinion, you're too shy to ask mother to help you with igor. You musn't be shy about this. After mother, you're the mistress in the house. Please write me all the details about how things are going. You write that Nyura is coming to Vasileva and, therefore, Guta has to leave. I'm going to write a letter to mother about this now and you tell Guta for me that she's not to think of leaving. The captain and his wife can go to hell, and please don't think about persuading Zhorzh not to come to Vasileva. On the contrary, invite him to come. How is Nyurichka feeling? You're not writing anything. For God's sake, write everything in detail. I live by these letters. And, Lelyuska, speak with Alexci, ask him to prepare Nyura for the divorce since they're living like that. Lelyuska, I'm tired and I'd like to go to sleep, but I still have to write a letter to Leningrad. I received a letter from Zhenya. A nephew has come to see him from Lugansk. I'm having a gold tooth put in front and three teeth filled. Take care of your teeth and don't forget to write about what Alexei is doing and how he's behaving himself. I'm not flying very often and don't want to. I have some sort of apathy. The planes are terrible and one has to be very careful in flying them. So I don't get any enjoyment out of the service here, only frustration. There is nothing in my work new to report. Everything is bad and I'm drawn to Leningrad to study further and to live together and not apart. I don't have the strength to continue living like this. I won't endure and I'm going to tell the command directly. Enough! I want to write Baranov a letter about the service and about the planes on which it is impossible to fly. Things are smelling of a counter-revolution here. You asked how I'm living. In my opinion, I'm not living, I'm just existing. I lived only at Leningrad, but not here. When you were with me everything was fine. I was happy, as you were with me. Well, now its after midnight. I'm alone. There's nobody here, nobody to say a word to, nobody to listen to. I dream now about how pleasant it would be to talk with you, to hold you close to me, and to feel that next to me was my life, my dear, beloved being. Write, Lelik, write often. Ask Nyurichka and Guta to write. Well, I kiss you all warmly, warmly. Your Valerick."

Before July 15, 1928:

"Greetings my dear, sweet Lelyuska, Igor and Nyurichka! I received your letter and am saddened that you're bored there. Lelik, you're not writing me anything. What are you doing? Describe your day from the early morning until evening. How is Nyurichka? Write about our son. Is he sitting up? By himself, or with help? Is he capricious or not? How is his chicken pox? Have his teeth cut through yet or not? You don't write anything about these small things. How much has he grown? How much does he weigh? Go and weigh him. You know how much I want to know all these things.

"Have you received my registered letter in which I sent your certification to Mama and Papa?

"How are you and mother getting along? Does father talk with you? If he does, about what? What about Guta? Has she come or not? If she's coming, then convince her for me that she must stay in Vasileva. How's Alexei? What is he doing and why are you afraid to talk with him? He'll listen to you, and you scold him if necessary. You shouldn't be afraid or shy of anything.

"I have nothing new to say. On Monday I'm flying to Mogilev and Bobruisk and then back to Gomel on the same day. I had them put in a gold tooth. It seems it looks all right. A wife of one of the mechanics has asked me to make her 40 pounds of jam. She's already paid me the money. It'll be ready tomorrow. On the 15th I'm going to telegraph you some money. I wish you were here. Without you there's not one bright moment. Without you my heart is heavy and everything bores me. If they don't transfer or demobilize me, I don't know what I'll do. Every day I feel worse and worse. Write more often, please. Your letters revive me. When I read them I feel that you're right next to me. And, please, write everything in detail. With whom are you speaking? Who talks to you? Describe our son to me. Does Nyurichka have a girlfriend? How are you getting along with her? I'm very interested in whether father talks to you or not and how he loves his grandson. And how is mother doing? I'll be very sad if Guta won't be able to live with us. Well, that's all I can write. Write greetings to father, mother, Alexei, and all the rest. I embrace you all warmly. Kiss my little son on the forehead. Your Valery.

"P.S. If you were now next to me, I would smother you in my embraces and kisses. I wouldn't give you time to say a word, but alas these dreams will remain dreams and it seems reality is far away. But I do love you more and more. I kiss you an infinite number of times. Your Valerick.

"I'm looking at your portrait now and thinking why can't it be alive?"

July 17, 1928:

"Greetings, dear Lelik, Igor and Nyurichka! Why have you not written? Don't you know, Lelik, how I feel when I don't receive a letter from you, not knowing what's happening to you or little Igor? Lelik, shame on you! You must write. I think it's easier for you to write than me. I've sent you more letters than you've sent me. This is the third letter in a row and I haven't received one from you. I sent a registered letter and also haven't received an answer. What does this mean? I'm getting very anxious and can find nothing to calm me down. You must write more often. Yesterday I flew from Gomel to Mogilev to Bobruisk and back to Gomel. The flight ended successfully, although during the flight I was alarmed. I hadn't flown 135 kilometers and some mechanical problems developed on the right side of the plane, which could have ended in a breakup of the plane, but everything turned out all right. On the 28th of July there's going to be a championship competition. I hope that you'll support me morally and will write more often. If not, I won't even be able to dream about first place. There'll be a prize of 150 rubles it seems. After our local competition there'll be a national contest. Whatever happens I've got to enter that contest. I sent you a telegraph with 75 rubles. What's new with you? How are you living? How's little Igor, Nyurichka, Papa and Mama? Who has come and how is everyone treating you? In the name of God, Lelik, write! I must get out of Gomel. Without you life here is terrible, monotonous, boring. Write me letters so that I don't become introspective. Sunday I was at the river and got sunburned on my shoulders and back, and today I got a haircut under the plane, so now I'm without hair, but it'll grow back. We have great weather here now. What's the weather like there? Have you rested or not? I want to know everything and calm down. I would pay much if only I could be with you and little Igor, but it's apparent I can do nothing. Patience, Cossack, no matter what happens, you'll never be the chief.

"Dear, kind, Lelyuska, write more often. Everything. Everything. All your thoughts and about little Igor, about Nyura and Papa. I await your letter with impatience. I embrace you warmly. I miss you and my son terribly. Valerick.

"P.S. Greetings to Papa, Mama, and all our friends. Valery."

July 18, 1928:

"Greetings, dear Lelik, Igor and Nyurichka! At last I received a letter from you. It doesn't make me too happy, however. Write me more in detail about what's happening. I'm so surprised that you feel a stranger there. This mustn't be. If necessary, then put them in their places. It pleases me greatly that Nyura answers as she should and as they deserved. There's nothing to be shy about. You're not living among strange people. And if someone doesn't like her, read my words to her, that she doesn't have to be their friends, and also tell her that she is right. And the captain's wife should be cut off more often. Tell Aleksei that this is his responsibility.

"In general I regret that I took you to Vasileva. We should've gotten a dacha some place near Leningrad. That would've been much better and I can see that we can't change these people. It's just going to be necessary to never go to Vasileva. We must demand more respect. And if I say that I'm going to come, these aren't just going to be words—I'm going to come. We'll have to invite them to Leningrad and show them how it's necessary to live and how they should treat people. In general, Lelik, it will make matters better if you take your problems and questions to Alexei. I'll write him immediately. I just sent you a letter in which I described everything I need from you. Write more often. I kiss you warmly. Your Valerick. Gomel."

End of July 1928:

"Dear Lelyuska, Igor and Nyurichka! I've just received two letters from you. The first letter is very painful for me because I'm in Gomel and you're in Vasileva. Lelik, I feel like a fish frozen in ice. I can do nothing. I curse myself for sending you to Vasileva, but what can be done now? This is your last trip to Vasileva and it will be mine also. Why didn't I take you to Gomel? Did you really ask me to go with me to Gomel? I'm bored and depressed. My health is failing only because I don't have you next to me. My health has worsened and I've begun to fly poorly. Without you I don't have the energy I have when I can look on my beloved one. I need you in my life as my bread and air, and I'm afraid. If my request for a transfer is not approved and you're not able to come to Bryansk, I won't be able to live. I don't have the strength.

"When I start to talk about a transfer, they simply don't listen to me. I need to receive an answer from you. If they don't transfer me out of

Bryansk, will you come to Bryansk or not? I need your answer quickly. I can't come after you. I thought I would be able to see the commission, but haven't yet been able to. The doctor says nothing will be forthcoming. He by himself can do nothing because he has very few acquaintances here.

"I really forgot that 7/24 is your name day, but good God forgive me. I'm in such deep depression that I could forget my own birthday.

"I see that you are reproaching me in the second letter. Your girl-friend's husband is very solicitous and attentive. Does that mean that I am not solicitous and attentive enough? This is painful for me, Lelik, very, very painful. I love you so strongly that no one could love you more. And, believe me, if it weren't for you, I couldn't live and if it weren't for our little son Igor, if he weren't with us, then for me life would end. You and my son are my goal in life. Advise me what to do and, believe me, I will follow your advice. I believe that they would probably take me to court because of the abrupt way in which I would fulfill your advice. You must know that I am suffering. Forgive me. And if you agree to come live with me in Bryansk, things won't be so bad. They've promised me two rooms in Bryansk in a government building … All the evidence suggests that the apartment question has been solved.

"Lelik, why haven't Igor's teeth come in? Pay attention! Its not good if they all come in at once later. First there should be two teeth on the bottom, then two on top, and in the 8th or 9th month there should be four on top and four on the bottom. Who's there with you at home now? Where's Guta? Write me about life at home in detail. Tell me when father's going to finish his work. I'll write him a letter then. Well, take care. I kiss you all warmly. Your Valerick.

"P.S. I so want to see you and little Igor, you can't imagine. I'll prob-ably cry like a baby from happiness when I see you and my little son. My spirit will immediately be reborn and I'll begin to fly again like I used to. I'm going to write a letter to Baranov now. I don't know what's going to happen. Well, I kiss you warmly, warmly. Valerick."

August 1, 1928: From Gomel to Vasileva

"Greetings, my dear Lelyuska, Igor and Nyurichka! I've just received two letters from you. I'm glad that Sonia is coming August 1st. Be sure to make friends with her. She's a good woman. You must go see her for sure. I don't know how I'm going to get you to Leningrad since my studies begin at that time, specifically maneuvers.

"I think, Lelik, that I'll ask Alexei to take you or perhaps Papa. You won't be too angry, will you, if I can't take you? I've received a letter from Papa and Zhorzhiik. What a good man Papa is. He understands me well. His letter had a calming effect on me and he says that he'll arrange everything. Everything will be all right. Yes, I believe him. I think everything will be all right. The only thing that bothers me now is how I'm going to get you to Leningrad. I will ask Alexei. No use writing me any more. I'm still feeling badly and will continue to until I see you. Yesterday I damaged an airplane. Terribly unpleasant, although the damage wasn't great, but for six years I haven't damaged anything. Now, all of a sudden, I have. It can be explained by my depression and condition. Well, no matter. This is all nonsense. Greetings to everyone! I embrace you warmly. Your Valerick. Write more about my son and in more detail. It calms me down. I'll write you another letter tomorrow."

August 2, 1928: From Lelyuska:

"My dear beloved Valerick, I received your letter today. You're very upset and write that you caused some damage. Valerick! Perhaps I'm at fault? Forgive me, my sweetheart! I'm suffering as much as you. But this is all nonsense, Valerick. It's just your self-respect that's suffering, or more exactly your ambition. Don't be so upset. It's not good to be under such stress. Such a strong man as you should be ashamed. I think you'll get hold of yourself. Isn't that true, Valerick? Forget that damage. Don't be so upset. Remember that I love you very very much and I regret those sad letters that I sent to you. They can be explained because of my fatigue and your absence.

"So tell me you're going to stop being so stressed, do you hear? Pull yourself together and you will again be happy. Enough of all that! Be thankful you're healthy and unhurt. Everything else is unimportant!

"You write that you can't come for us. Well, what can we do? We'll come alone. Papa can't take us because he has pressing work and he can't get a leave before the end of September, but Alexei is also working and it's doubtful he will be able to go. It wouldn't make any sense for him to go so early. We'll set out around the 22nd. Its all right, we'll come by ourselves. I just don't know where we'll be able to obtain a train that will go all the way to Leningrad as we did or whether we'll go through Moscow. I'll have to think about that. If we went by steamship against the current it would take even longer than it took us, but there would be only one transfer, and through Moscow there would be two transfers.

"I'll write now about our little Igor. Everyone says he looks like you. He does patty-cake all by himself. He can now pronounce Mama and Papa. Everybody is thrilled with him. Yesterday I weighed him on your scales. He weighs 22 pounds. He's an entertaining little fellow, but he still doesn't have any teeth. They say that's okay. Only he's become very accustomed to be carried and demands it all the time. I think, Valerick, that in Leningrad we'll have to buy a baby carriage. I'm feeling better now. I go swimming when the weather is nice, but I'm afraid to swim too far. Father wanted to swim with Igor, but I was afraid. I think that if you were here, maybe I would let you take him for a swim. You see, I'm a coward. Well, Valerick, I'll finish now. Forgive me, and don't be angry. I feel that its my fault that you're in such a depression and I feel very sorry about that. Take care of yourself! I love you very much. Lelyuska. I embrace you warmly"

Before August 15, 1928:

"Greetings, my dear Lelyuska, little Igor and Nyurichka! I received your letter. I just arrived from my maneuvers. I've caught a cold, a bad one, and have a bad headache as a result. But it's okay, it'll pass.

"Lelyuska, I can't say for sure, but I think that I'll be given a leave around the 20th of August, so I think I can take you to Leningrad. Everything depends on whether they will send us airplanes from the factory since we don't have enough. If they don't send them then I'll be given a leave, but if they do I'll have to fly in the local maneuvers. So expect a telegram from me. I terribly want a leave now since we still have nice weather and we could go walking, although I know your work starts soon. My heart aches for you, Lelyuska. You haven't rested. Although you write you're feeling better, I think this isn't true. You just want to make me feel better. My mood hasn't changed and it won't until I see you and my little son. But if they send the planes it'll be a long time before we see one another, probably it will be until November. Your letter says that our son is looking very good. I'm very, very happy. How is Nyurichka feeling? Just write the truth. You don't have to make me feel better. I'll feel better as soon as I see you and my little son. Greetings to everyone. I embrace you warmly. Your Valerick. Has Sofia arrived? Who's living in the house besides our relatives? Send your letters to Bryansk, 15th Avia

Squadron, from the 15th I'll be in Bryansk. Write. I kiss you warmly. Your Valerick."

August 18, 1928:

"Greetings, my dear Lelyuska, Igor and Nyurichka! I'm now in Bryansk and in a few days will leave for Vasileva. I've been held up a bit because I have to take care of some business here. Lelik, before my departure from Gomel, somebody robbed me. They took my linen, underclothes, shirts, including my satin one, towels socks, shoes, they cleaned me out! It's outrageous. I'll be in Vasileva around the 25th or 26th. Be ready and we'll leave immediately for Leningrad. I'm bringing 94 lbs of jam, which I think I'll check with my baggage in Moscow. I didn't send you any money, because you can bring some yourself, although I do think now I'll telegraph you some.

"And so I'm waiting. I'll soon see my dear, sweet Lelyuska and little Igor.

I kiss you warmly, warmly. Your Valerik."

September 24, 1928:

"My dear beloved Valerick! I've just received a letter from you and I'll answer it now. I feel so sorry for you. It occurs to me often that my bad luck is playing an important role. If I were with you, you would be calm and not stressed. You wouldn't have damaged your plane and not been summoned to court. I feel so bad, Valerick, because of that. When you wrote me from Moscow that it was possible that you would be in a research institute I made up my mind that I would abandon you no longer. Who is slandering you there again? My dear Valerick, I ask of you only one thing. Control yourself and be calm. Maybe everything will work out just fine. I'm so sorry I'm not with you right now. I would try to comfort you. And why wasn't I with you this summer? Why didn't I insist that I would go with you? If I'd been with you then none of this would've happened. But now don't lose your self-control and keep up your spirits. I will try never again to leave you alone.

"Papachka! Igoryok sends you his warm kisses. I had to spank Igoryushka a little. He was sitting in his playpen and asking for me to pick him up. I picked him up, but he wouldn't let me write. I've just given him to Nyura, but I don't know what to write to you in order to calm you down. It's good that you'll be talking personally with Baranov. But,

Valerick, I'm very much afraid that if you demobilize you'll continue to yearn for aviation because you're not an ordinary pilot. You're a person who loves his profession and loves to create. I don't know what to advise you. I only want things to go well for you so that you can work happily.

"Yesterday I saw Pavlushov and Makarsky. They asked about you. I told them only what I knew about you from your letters from Moscow. When will you be going to Moscow? Please write about this at length. What should I do to make your life easier? Just tell me and I'll do all I can.

"But I want to tell you one more time not to be so talkative and don't trust people so much. Its been clear for a long time that they don't want you in the Air Force and want to ruin you. They accuse you of saying things when you don't. They accuse you of doing things that you don't do. They say you drink when you're not drinking. They say things about you that are not true and never were. Don't be worried about me. I'm healthy and am not so tired. Igoryushka is also healthy and everything is fine at home.

"And don't lose heart. I think that this lie they made up about you will be uncovered and everything will become clear.

"Write more often and at length. Speak seriously with Baranov. I think that he'll understand you. Everybody sends you greetings and asks you not to be upset. Warm kisses, your Lelyuska. Zhorzhik will write you a letter today or tomorrow."

Undated:
"Greetings, my dearl Lelyushka and Igorek! I received your letter and am hurrying to answer it. Lelyushka, don't worry about me. I think that everything is going to end all right and, if not, then it won't be too bad. In general, there's no use being too angry. Only, for God's sake, don't be stressed about my situation. I don't need money. I'm getting along fine and am not worried, my dear sweet Lelyushka. I'm not going to lose weight, but if I do it won't be because I'm not eating enough or from some kind of unpleasantness. I will lose weight because you're not with me and my situation bothers you. That's the reason I lose weight. After all, the time is not too distant when we'll be living together, you, I and Igorek. It's very boring to be alone. There are times when I feel stressed and worried. Be with me, Lelyushka, and I will be happy, calm. I think that if Lelyushka was with me I would be calm, I would rest on her breast and

Lelyushka would caress me and create comfort and provide a place of rest from all of the misfortunes, cares and troubles of the day.

"Yesterday, Lelik, I was in the theatre and listened to a concert. There was a quartet, two basses and two tenors. They're a well-known quartet. They had to sing without a piano, which was very difficult, but they sang so well that I wanted to go back and listen to them again today, but I sat too long at the card game and didn't make it. I'm sorry I didn't hear them again because I've never heard anything like this. It seems they were singing with one voice. Their technique was marvelous and their choice of voices excellent. No one voice seemed to stand out above the others. If this quartet comes to Leningrad we must definitely go listen to them.

"There is absolutely no variety in my life here except for an occasional visit to a show. They show two new movies a week, some of which I've already seen in Leningrad. Only billiards seems to give me enjoyment. But in a couple of days they're going to close down for repairs. Well, stay healthy, don't worry, don't be upset. Try to improve your health. Greetings to everyone! Kisses to my dear, golden Lelyushka and Igorichka. Write everything about little Igor. Warm embraces, your Valerick.

"How are Nyurichka, Zhenya, Yelena, what are they doing? Write about how they're doing in school."

Around October 6, 1928:

"Hello, my dear Lelyuska and Igorek! I received your fifth letter and I've sent you five, maybe six, I'm not sure. Everything is as it was with me, but the future is not clear. Things seem to be leaning in my direction, however. If everything goes well here then I'll be serving in Leningrad or Gatschina. I'm not doing anything right now. There's no place to go in the evenings. I get together with friends and play cards, Preference, every day. That's all I do.

"My mood is rather hard to describe. Sometimes I'm bored, sometimes just apathetic. My mind is tired of all this and I can only think about you and about my son and how you're managing with school and with Igorek. Are you nursing him? If you are, then stop right away. Otherwise, he will nurse you dry. Feed him more solid foods. How are his teeth? What does the doctor say? On October 2nd he was supposed to be seen by the doctor. How much weight has he gained and how does he look? Write me all the details.

"I feel very sorry for Yelena, that she has had to feel the injustice of life so soon. But I suppose this was bound to happen sooner or later. But maybe it's all right. Sometimes I'ts better this way. Let her study next year in college. That's the best thing for her to do. When she receives a higher education her situation will change. She will better know her value and people will respect her. I'm very happy that Zhenia's going to school. You've not written anything about Fyodor, Zhorzhik, Nyura, and you haven't mentioned Papa at all in your letter. Write how everyone is doing. It would be well if they don't take Zhorzhik in the Army because his health isn't good.

"I don't know why you all look so calmly at the disintegration in the apartment. Is it really impossible that you can't tighten things up? You can call the doctor, who will say that such a situation is intolerable for a child. Yes, and I think something can be done to speed up the apartment's repair. It's sad that Mother's relatives are not living there. Our life is such that a child who grows into adulthood still wants a mother's affection and care and if he/she doesn't get it this person will be completely different...

"A person is worse than an animal, more fearsome and dirty. If a wolf attacks a person or some animal and satisfies his hunger he will not continue this behavior until he is once again starving. A person doesn't wait for hunger but acts in ways to be satisfied at all times and will do this always at the expense of others. And if someone interferes then he will not leave that person alone, but will hound him to death. Wolves will eat their own dead and this can be explained, but a civilized person, himself alive, will not allow another to live and this is unexplainable.

"Why do I write this? Because I'm one of those people who is not allowed to live how he chooses and they force him into a certain framework of life in which he is constricted and which he hates. I know myself. I know that I can do my work better than another, and others know this too. But in spite of this, my command gives the work to another and this person is my subordinate. And if, because of my character, I never attempt work that I don't know or know poorly, then these sweethearts, having nothing to do, will take on this work and imagine that everything is going smoothly.

"The leader of a wolf pack never makes a mistake in leading it, but a man, not deserving to be a leader, will never lead correctly, although it will seem everything is going all right. Well, this is philosophy. You know well yourself, Lelik, that people are animals on two legs.

"Take care of yourself and my son. Don't let him catch cold. I embrace you both warmly. Your loving Valerick.

"P.S. Greetings to all our friends. How is K.L.I. living? How is M. Tereshemkova? I received a two-room apartment here with a kitchen and bathroom, but have no furniture. You and I will have to get some furniture because I think it will be difficult to bring your furniture here. Write what you think about what we will do if we have to remain here. Again, I embrace you warmly. Your Valerick."

Before October 20, 1928:

"Greetings my dear Lelyuska and Igorek! If you only knew what I've been through these past few days. I received a letter from you today and I'm going to read it. I'm glad that everything is going well for you. I've had a nightmarish few days. You can't imagine what I've been thinking since I haven't received anything from you for the last two weeks, but I'm very glad that everything is going well. But only, please, don't wait so long between letters. Lelik, you wrote very little about our son. Has one tooth broken through, or two? How is he doing? Is he walking or not? Write me about him in detail. How much does he weigh? What does he look like? What does he eat? And how does he torment his little mama? Lelik, and how are you feeling? You wrote me nothing. You didn't even write me anything about Papa, how he's feeling.

"Please write more details in your letters. Why aren't you studying singing? I want you to study. What have you sewn for yourself? Probably nothing. No, Lelik, without me you never dress like you should. I have to be there to encourage you in this business. Take care of yourself, as you should, please. How is the piano playing? Without me, probably, you can't have it tuned. How are the repairs coming along? Why haven't you sent me a photo?

"Oh, how many questions I've asked you. How I want to go to Leningrad. Fall for me is the most difficult time of the year. I don't like it when life dies, leaves fall, constant drizzle, mud and slush, loneliness, bad mood, a heavy heart. Oh, how nice it would be to be in Leningrad with my small, sweet, dear Lelyuska. She would calm me, caress me. I so want your love. We would go to the theatre, we would argue about the theatre beforehand. Isn't that true, Lelyuska? Dreams, dreams.

"You write that Nyurichka wants to celebrate her name day. Put on a nice party for her. The girl has to understand that everybody loves and cares for her and would make her very happy and give her much enjoyment. You must let her be the hostess that day. I don't think it would be too difficult for us to spend 15 rubles to entertain her friends. If I were there I would arrange the party as it should be. I'll send her a gift on her name day. So, Lelik, put on a nice party for Nyurichka.

"How is Zhenya feeling? How does she like her courses? What's new with her and what is she thinking about? Do you speak to her about life? Probably not. You really need to talk to her and find out how she looks at life. And, Lena, how's she feeling? Have sports ended? What is she doing now with her free time? Is she going with someone? And with whom? You must be interested in these things. They don't have a mother and so you must be one for them. How is Fyodor? He's probably lost weight. Is he still arguing about politics? What's new in his life? I'd like to get a letter from him. How is he getting along with Musenka? When does he plan to defend his project?

"I got a letter from Zhorzhik and will write him, but I want to ask you. How are his relations with Gelma? Why is Zhorzhik depressed? How is his health? Talk with him, please. Gelma is not the only fish in the sea. His bad mood, I'm sure, is because of her. He needs to get a hold of himself. You need to pay attention to Zhorzhik and speak with him. How are Papa and M.I. doing? Do they argue a lot? How is Father feeling? He's probably tired. All my thoughts are directed to Leningrad. I like to imagine myself at the dinner table and seizing the appropriate moment pull Fedya into an argument about politics. Lelik, we have a great family.

"I very very much want to go to Leningrad, but now it's only a wish. I don't know when it will become a reality. Now I'll write about myself. I'll probably go to court this week. Today a brigade representative was here and I talked with him. He said nothing would happen to me. Please don't be nervous and don't be upset. Everything is going to turn out all right. I think after this they'll transfer me out of here.

"After I received your letter my mood is great. Tomorrow I'll send you money. I still haven't received my pay so I'm going to get it a day late.

"I received my military fitting and even broadcloth for an overcoat. Broadcloth is very difficult to get, but, in any event, there is a chance that I'll be able to buy at least a piece of dark blue broadcloth. Tomorrow I'm going to buy you a dark blue woolen dress and if there'll be enough money I'll also buy one for Nyurichka.

"I had to pay 10 rubles on a loan, three rubles, 50 kopeks for material for a summer suit, 40 rubles to a mutual aid fund, and I'm going to send you 75 rubles. And since this month I'm going to receive an additional 15 rubles I'll receive 170 rubles all together. I'll have 35 rubles left over. And since I'm going to receive 10 rubles from the loan then I'll have enough money, so don't worry. Buy little Igor a knit suit. You need a hat, shoes, and some other things. So you buy everything that you need. You don't need to sew me anything. You'll be able to sew everything in the spring when we have enough money. And you need to sew for yourself first of all. I think you must take care of yourself. If everything ends all right with me then in November I'll go to Leningrad on sick leave. I think that'll work out. My advice to you is don't be nervous, don't get depressed, take care of your health—its not great you know. If you're healthy then I'm healthy and happy.

"How is your appetite? Take care you don't catch cold. That's very easy to do now. Pay more attention to your health and your rest. How are things going in school? Have any of our friends decided to get married? When does Nyura expect the child? How is she feeling? How is she living with Volodka? My greetings to everyone. Kisses to all the family. I embrace you warmly, warmly. Kiss Igorushka tenderly on the forehead and cheeks. Take care of yourself. I love you very much. Your Valerick. I'm going to bed now. Its 11:00 Kremlin time. Goodnight my dear, small, sweet, beloved Lelyuska and Igorechek."

October 19 and 20, 1928:

"My dear Lelyuska and Igorechek! I received two letters from you, but can only answer them tomorrow. I can't answer them here. I moved to an apartment in a new building. There's no bed, no table, nothing. I can't buy anything. I've only spent one night here. Today I'm on duty with the garrison so tonight I'll be here in the duty room in the garrison. The weather is disgusting. Its been snowing for two days, but it melts immediately. I've been walking around the town. When I got back my boots were muddy from top to bottom. Its still unclear how my problems will be resolved. I expected results this week, but still haven't received any. I think that next week my situation will become clear.

"For the time being nothing is definite. I don't know what we're going to do with the furniture if it becomes necessary for you to come here. You don't want to take anything from home and we aren't able to buy anything and that will be apparent.

"Take care of little Igor. Take him on walks, only make sure he's properly dressed. Yes, and also take care of yourself. I'm going to fulfill the request of K. l and I. V. and pull you by the ear because your serious cough shows that you haven't been taking care of yourself and this is not good. You told me that you do everything you should and I wouldn't have to criticize you more, but your cough again demands criticism.

"Sweet Lelyuska, for God's sake take care of yourself. It's a great pity now that Naum and Clava's child died. Send them my greetings and consolation. How are things now in Leningrad? What are you all doing at home? I imagine you have just returned from school probably and have begun to wash the baby's swaddling clothes and you're carrying Igor in your arms. How good it would be to go now to Leningrad. We would live so well there and be so happy.

October 27, 1928:

"Greetings, my dear, good, sweet Lelyuska and Igorek! For me this is a day of great happiness. I have received three letters from you. Your letters for me are as valuable and necessary as water to a person lost in the desert. Your letters create in me a feeling of great spiritual rest and calmness. You ask me how things are going. In truth, Lelyuska, I still don't know a thing. On Tuesday, October 30, everything will be decided and I will write you then. I feel badly because I feel that you are hurting for me and this is very difficult for me. Forgive me for this, Lelik, that I've given you such stress, but I am not to blame.

"You say that everything will dissipate like smoke. Yes, I agree with you, but for that we need time. My spirit aches, it aches badly, badly. But in order to cure it I need time and to be able to look into my small, sweet Lelyuska's face and to be with all our family. My spirit and body were once strong and I'm now so weak. It's like night and day. It wouldn't pay for you to come here because, if everything ends well, they will transfer me and there is a rumor that it will be to Moscow. Yes, in no case will I stay here. I couldn't possibly live here, its so disgusting. My nerves wouldn't take it. Well, but we are still strong, so I'm going to stand up for myself and insist that they take me out of here. Lelik, you wanted to send me money. You don't need to. I have enough. You think so little about yourself, Lelik. You're too good natured and your life is all about care for others and not about yourself. Tell Zhorzhik that they don't sell fur coats here. Lelik, I will write to you next time about my conversation with this one person that you wanted to know about. I got a bed, so don't worry. I'm going to bed now. Tomorrow is Sunday. I need to give a lecture at the airfield to an excursion of workers. Stay healthy. Greetings to everyone. And describe Igorek in every letter. I so terribly want to see him. Warm, warm embraces, my dear, sweet Lelyuska, my life. Your Valery."

October 1928:

"Hello, my dear Lelyuska and Igorek! We'll soon be together. I can't answer about the documents because they haven't arrived. When they will come I don't know. I hope they come soon. I so want to get out of this place and not have to see this damn city, Bryansk. It makes me so depressed. I'm very glad that Igor is walking by himself around the apartment, only be careful that he doesn't spill something hot on himself from the stove. There's nothing else you have to worry about. I'm surprised he hasn't broken a plate. That would give him so much pleasure. I want to see him so terribly.

"What's going on with Zhenya? Your letter about her worries me. Talk with her frankly. Ask her what she needs and what she doesn't have, although I know the reason for her depression. It's because she wants to have nice clothes and she has none and she sees it's impossible to have them in the future. Neediness is an evil humanity suffers from. I'm going to try to do something for her soon. She needs shoes, she's worn out the ones she wears, and she doesn't have a nice dress. To have to wear one thing and one thing only bothers a person, and a person becomes so used to it, that it becomes disgusting. But maybe there are other reasons, Lelik. Go to her and tactfully find out all you can. There is a period in a woman's life when she doesn't have a man, though she needs one, and this influences her health. A girl begins to contemplate her life and create plans for the future, but Zhenya is secretive. She'll tell no one her thoughts if someone approaches her insensitively.

"Nyurichka is another type of girl. She thinks about and creates plans and dreams, and will tell everyone what she is thinking about. But not Zhenya. I am in complete agreement with you about Gelma. She needs to change and become part of our family. She needs to be very sensitive in order to make Zhorzhik happy. I wish Fyodor and Lena success, but warn Lena about a few things and convince her to bring him into our home as soon as possible so we can all get to know who he is as a person. How I would like to look him in the face. I would know and understand his intentions immediately. Well, be healthy. I kiss you warmly, warmly. Your Valerick. Kiss Igorushka for me and all the family."

October 1928:

"I received your letter and am very happy that everything is going well for you and that you can work in the school. Lelik, take care of yourself and try to cure your anemia. You need to go to the doctor. He will write you a prescription for arsenic. This will restore you and protect you from anemia.

"My situation is still not clear for the time being. I wrote a letter to Baranov and I am awaiting his answer. No matter what happens I think that they will demobilize me and then I will go to Leningrad in November. I think I'll be able to find work there. Let it only be for only 100 rubles at first. My mood is such that I don't care what happens as long as I can get to you in Leningrad as soon as possible. While writing these lines I received two more letters from you. After reading them I felt so happy that you were so perceptive and understanding. I'll try to be completely calm. You write that I will be sorry to leave aviation. Hardly, Lelik. It has treated me so badly that it has killed any love for it.

"Lelik, you shouldn't have changed your mind about talking with Gelma and Zhorzhik. If this marriage takes place Zhorzhik will be a very unhappy person, and you as an older sister must put your brother on the proper path in life. I don't have anything against Gelma personally, but as a person I don't especially like her idiotic character. And Zhorzhik is too good natured and will fall under her heel. In view of that, I'll probably insist on their divorce and that would be destructive. If not permanently, then at least for a long time there would be an open wound. We have to consider Zhorzhik's health. If possible, try to prevent this marriage until Gelma's character changes. Her character is temporary and when she matures her character will improve. So talk with both of them, but of course as diplomatically as possible. You're able to talk with people and smooth things over with them.

"Write to me about how Igor feels and everyone in the family. A few days ago, I found out the truth about me from one person. And even I became fearful because this person related everything that has happened to me in my life and what the future holds. I'll write you about this all later. I embrace you and Igorek and all the family warmly, warmly. Your Valery. Greetings to all your colleagues who know me in the school."

November 1, 1928:

"Greetings, my dear, sweet Lelyuska and Igorek! I was in court yesterday. They judged me without witnesses or defense in a closed session. They sentenced me to one year in jail. I appealed the decision to the Board of the Supreme Court and at the same time I'll write a letter to Voroshilov. Today I had a conversation with the brigade committee. It was very surprised at the sentence and tomorrow will go to Smolensk for an explanation and lobby for the repeal of my sentence. It'll be a month and a half before I receive an answer from the Supreme Court. The brigade committee says that no matter what happens they're going to keep me in the Air Force. But for that it's necessary that the sentence be dismissed, because after I serve my term in prison, according to the laws of the Revolutionary Court Martial of the USSR, I would have to take a very long leave, or more likely be demobilized. But since the command doesn't want to lose me, and although they themselves pressed charges against me in court, they now want to take my side and have the sentence repealed.

"Lelyuska, send me a telegram that says that you or Igor are seriously ill and they'll give me a leave for two or three weeks and I can come and talk to you about this. Don't be upset and don't grieve since we won't receive any final results for at least a month and a half. And, for God's sake, don't be angry with me. I am in no way to blame for such a sentence. I don't feel any kind of guilt and agree with what one commander here said. He said that if it hadn't been Chkalov in the accident then none of this would be taking place. That means to them that I'm a thorn in their side, which they want to get rid of so Chkalov will never come forward with evidence of their improper actions.

"Well, never mind. The thing that concerns more is your opinion of me. I can think of nothing else. Lelik, I await your sentence. My mood is such that I take no account of anything happening around me. All my thoughts are directed to one thing only and that is what will my Lelyuska say. Please write. It's been five days since I've received a letter from you. It seems everything is fine in Leningrad, but here everything is going badly. Today our little Igor is 10 months old. I so want to see him, to caress him. I need you so much now. I need you more than I have ever felt the need for bread, water or air. I need you more than all of that. One word from you can destroy me and a word from you can restore me and again allow me to believe in a bright future. I'm waiting anxiously for your answer.

"And there is one other thought that torments me: that Father doesn't understand what's happening as he should. He may assign all blame to me. Lelyuska, believe me. My guilt lies only in the fact that I wanted to be the best of the best pilots. I didn't want to be a very ordinary pilot, but wanted to be a fighter pilot who would always come out the winner in air combat. But if the Appeals Board rejects my appeal then I will never fly again, not even if there's a war. Separation from you for six months (because I won't be in prison any longer) will be difficult for me, not only because I won't be able to see you and my son, but because for this period of time I won't be able to send you any money. And this will torment me greatly. Lelik, write. I await your answer and telegram. I love you. I love you very very much. Is it possible that this could end our good life together? Oh! This is terrible and painful. Greetings to all our friends! For God's sake, don't be upset. We will know nothing for one and a half months. I kiss you and Igor warmly, warmly. Your Valerick.

"P.S. When will life return its good side to you and I? When I'm alone I don't believe it will happen, but when I begin to think that I'll be with you then it begins to seem to me that our life will be good. If it weren't for you I wouldn't have appealed to the Supreme Court. I wouldn't be waiting for a repeal, but I would've immediately gone to prison because it's not in my nature to ask for anything. Sometimes in me there grows a thirst for struggle, but if I don't meet with support it immediately dissipates.

"Lelik, in these last two days I've been transformed. Everything around me seems dark. I see nothing good, but only one large lie and obnoxious human thoughts and I think 'Is it really necessary that in the future I have to wear this mask of hypocrisy and kiss up to people, who I perhaps will not respect or agree with their lies and incorrect views?' But apparently it is necessary to be such a person. Otherwise, we'll never see a happy, good life. Well, all right, Lelik. In the future I'll make no decisions alone, but we together will decide how to live and what kind of people to be. I kiss you 10,000 times. I love you very, very much. Your Valuska."

November 2, 1928:

"My dear, good Lelyuska and Igorek! I just received your letter and I am writing you an answer straight from the post office. I wrote you the results of my court appearance yesterday. And I also wrote that you shouldn't be nervous or upset and I ask you once again not to be upset. You write that you're tired and not as tired as earlier, but that you feel worse. This is only because you're always thinking and caring about others. If you'll send me a telegram that you or our son is sick, then I will come home on leave. I think they will let me do that. In the telegram, write as follows: Your son is ill. Please come home. Or Zhenya is ill. Please come. You can sign the first text and Papa can sign the second one.

"So I await the telegram. God grant that everything will be all right with Nyura Razumovskaya. You write that she is going to give birth. When you see Alexei tell him that I couldn't get the broadcloth for him. Greetings to everyone. I kiss you warmly, my small, sweet wife and Igorka. Your Valerick."

November 28, 1928:

"Good day, Lelyuska and Igorek! I've just received word from the highest command. Everything has turned out well. I go to Bryansk today and await transfer to Moscow. So you need not worry. I'll write you in detail in my next letter from Bryansk. Greetings to everyone. I've been ordered not to even think about demobilization. I embrace you warmly, warmly. Your Valery. Don't forget to take care of yourself."

November 29 and 30, 1928:

"My dear, sweet Lelyuska and Igorek! You already know the results of my trip to Moscow. I'll now tell you everything that happened. When I arrived in Moscow I immediately went to administration headquarters. At the headquarters I met the commander of our region. I explained my problem to him and he immediately went to Baranov's aide. The aide called and asked to speak with me. After our conversation he began to speak with Baranov's deputy, Alksnis. When Alksnis found out that I was at headquarters and sitting in his aide's office he immediately ordered me to come see him. I went to see him Saturday evening. He cursed me out, appropriately, and said "I will transfer you to Moscow to the Scientific Experimental Institute and I will ask that the tribunal's sentence be repealed." I was ordered to come on Tuesday for the answer.

"I didn't see him Tuesday, but Wednesday instead. He told me that everything was taken care of, that I should go to Bryansk and not worry. Now I will await the transfer. The Leningrad factory Red Pilot asked me to work in their factory, but I don't think that'll happen because Alksnis said that I was still needed badly and he was going to squeeze everything out of me, but perhaps they'll release me since they need to test a plane there.

December 10, 1928:

"Greetings, my dear Lelyuska and Igorek! I received a letter from you two days ago, but I'm answering it only today. Lelyuska, I sent you 20 rubles. Give them to Guta or she'll have trouble making it until payday.

"I'll now answer your letter. And so: You say that I'm to blame for not receiving advancement in the service. You're right, but it's not because I don't want to work, but because I can't convince others to accept what I do. The answer depends on your understanding of the essence of the matter. Frequently my flying qualities as a good plane jockey prevent my advancement. If I were like everybody else I wouldn't fly like I do, and if I flew like everybody else, of course, I wouldn't be considered undisciplined. And so because my piloting stands out from others then it's necessary that it be eliminated. And so it's labeled air hooliganism, but they all would want that their pilots fly like I do and if they did, of course, this wouldn't be called hooliganism.

"And, further, where did you get the idea that they wanted to assign me as commander of the detachment? I don't know this. Now, about the transfer to Moscow. Moscow will be my last stop in the Air Force, since I want with all my strength to leave the Air Force and I'm going to do this at the first convenient moment. Because I'm not a communist, no matter how good my behavior, I'll not receive an advancement, because only communist pilots receive advancements. Yes, of course, this is true. So now you probably understand me correctly and not as you did before.

"As a fighter pilot my behavior was correct and in the future will be shown to be even more so. We as workers and peasants of the Soviet Union can't hope for support from the workers and peasants of other countries in the event of war. Our own workers and peasants will have to depend on themselves to defend the Union, as I will have to depend on myself in such an event. Therefore, I must always be prepared to the degree that I will always be able to shoot down the enemy and not be shot down myself. And for this it is necessary to train myself and develop the confidence that I will always be the victor. The victory will only go to the one who enters the battle with complete confidence in himself. I recognize only the kind of warrior who, in spite of certain death, will sacrifice his own life in order to save others. And if the Union needs such warriors then I am prepared to act in such a manner at any time.

"And now the most important answer. Why did you conclude that I don't like to fuss with Igor? I'm not to blame that he's not used to me and he's uncomfortable with me. You're to blame for this. As soon as I pick up Igor and you walk by or he sees you he doesn't want me to hold him any longer. It's my impression that if you wanted you could train Igor to adjust to me. Yes, I think this fault you're finding with me in this instance is because you're very, very weary of this life, but no matter. This will all pass and we will live together as we should.

"Lelyuska, fix your teeth. I'm sending you 15 rubles. We'll pay it back in three installments. How is it there in Leningrad? I'm glad that there is no mud here, but there's no snow either. I often go to the theatre. My mood isn't bad. I'm waiting for the transfer. Write about what new things Igor is doing. Greetings to all! Good health to you both. I kiss you warmly, my weary, small, sweet Lelyuska and Igorek. Your Valery.

"P.S. How are Fyodor, Zhorzhik and Alexei? How are things at home? Write more often and, most important, Lelyuska, take care of yourself and don't give in to depression or let yourself go. That would be very bad. Use every free moment for sleep and rest. Take up exercise with Miller's method. Then you will quickly restore your earlier delightfulness, happiness, and cheerfulness. Well, kiss everyone for me. Your Valerick."

December 1928:

"Greetings, my dear, good Lelyuska and Igorek! I received your letter and want to answer the questions that are bothering you. My financial situation—I have 30 rubles now and if they transfer me to Moscow in the next few days I'll have some more, so I think that I'm all right. You've taken your brown dress to the tailor and that's good. Take your black dress also. Don't worry about your shoes, you'll have them. As soon as I receive my advance, I'll send you money for your lacquered shoes. In general, I like it very much when you want to dress well. I like to see you dressed up. I'm glad that you're receiving a 12-day rest. This will strengthen you a bit. It's not necessary to watch Igor so close all the time.

Arrange things so that he doesn't drop something heavy or hot on himself. It's all right if he falls, it'll make him stronger.

"I think that I'll come in January for five to seven days, if I'm in Moscow at that time. Sergey Gessler invited me to Moscow to be his guest on the 22nd of December, but I can't go. I really don't know when I'm going to be in Moscow. It's tedious waiting for the results. I want to get out of here as soon as possible. I'm so tired of Bryansk. Send greetings to Nyura Razumovskaya. How's her daughter? I wish her a full recovery. It's good that you're wallpapering the dining room and Zhorzhik's room. Ask the girls about their room. It should also be done. It would be nice if you could wallpaper all the rooms. Lelik, if you have any money left over then from the 100 rubles buy yourself some lacquered shoes. Don't worry about the money. You're going to have all kinds of shoes. I need to buy some shoes. Well, all right, next time. Greetings to all! Be healthy. I kiss you warmly, warmly. Your Valery. Igorushka is probably very interesting now. If he's sly he gets that from his Mama. If he's daring he gets it from his Papa."

Undated:

"Greetings, my dear, good Lelyuska and Igorek! After a long break I received two letters together. I'm very sorry that we won't be able to be together for the New Year. The comfort you describe makes me want to be with you and leaves me with a heavy heart. I hope you meet the New Year happily and well, and no one must make you gloomy on that day. Give Papa my felt cloaks since I've received some new ones. These will keep him warm as he walks to work and his legs are not very healthy. Let him wear them every day. I'll get the boots myself. Stay healthy. I kiss you warmly. Your Valerick. Congratulate everybody for me with the New Year and with Igor's birthday. Take care. Valery."

December 31, 1928, 4:00 p.m.:

"Greetings to my dear, sweet, small Lelyuska and Igorek! Lelik, sweetheart, don't be surprised and don't be stressed. Apparently, in this life it's necessary that on the second of January I will go to prison. The command's intervention didn't help. Well, to hell with them. I wrote nothing about this earlier because I was afraid you would be upset and you're ill and already having a poor New Year. Now I know that you'll be suffering on my behalf, but I pray to you in the name of all that is holy don't ruin your health. You have a strong will and you can overcome all this. By May I will be in Leningrad and I'll be working at the Red Pilot. I've already obtained their agreement. Now all that's necessary is for me to sit out my time.

"Promise me silently, 'okay, Valerick, I'll endure all this with determination.' My mood is rather strange. I so want to be at this time in Leningrad. I'm imagining it's midnight in Leningrad and I'm sitting at the family table with everyone. Now I'm imagining how I suffered through your giving birth, how I was so nervous on January 1st and cried. I was afraid of the unknown, but such grand happiness I experienced on that first morning of January. I'll be with you on this memorable date. I'll think of nothing else but you and Igor. Well, Lelik, take care. I kiss you and Igorek warmly. Your Valery. Embrace everyone for me."

January 2, 1929:

"My dear, sweet and good Lelyuska and Igorek! I'm writing you as you can see on the 2nd of January. Today I'm supposed to be sent to prison, but because Baranov arrived they've allowed me 15 to 30 minutes to speak with him. What he'll say I'll include at the end of this letter or in the next one. Lelik, you said in the letter I just received from you that I should try if at all possible to be demobilized. I'll be demobilized, but first I'll have to sit out three or four months in prison. Dear Lelik, don't grieve and don't be upset. Although I have to sit out three or four months, on the other hand after this I'll be in Leningrad and nothing will be able to separate us. I'll find work and in the evening, with the help of loving support from my small Lelik, I will study and study seriously and persistently so that I will be able to prove that I can accomplish something more serious in life than to fly, and I'll be able to do it just as well as I was able to fly.

"So now the important thing is to sit out my time. It won't be so bad. The only thing that bothers me is your material situation and that breaks my heart. It really breaks my heart, Lelik. You write that if I was with you now you would embrace me and find comfort from all the misfortune and that I would gaze at you and at my son and would become much more calm than I am now. The thing that frightens me is that you're not well and that you will suffer for me and be upset. You'll lose weight and the blame is all mine.

"Lelik, don't condemn me. It's not my fault that I'm such an unfortunate man. My fault lies in the fact that I can't hide the truth and will speak it always, even when it harms me in the service. If you don't condemn me or scold me and remain more or less calm, then my time in prison will be a thousand times easier. After I get out, we'll together straighten out our life and, believe me, life will be much better and more attractive than now. I really feel now that I have a lot of strength in order to make life good in the future. I think that I'll be correct if I say that my future work on the ground will be better and more realistic than it was in the air, where in my opinion there is no future for me because of the disagreements and differing opinions. You, yourself, probably noticed this from my conversations with my comrades in the service. Write me letters to the old address and they'll forward them to me. Don't worry about me. In the next few days I should be given my discharge pay and I'll send you some, but keep enough so that I can improve the quality of food that I get in prison and after that I'll be in Leningrad with my small, sweet and good little wife. You are my atom that gives me energy for life. If it weren't for this atom, my life would be uninteresting and unnecessary. I have only you and Igor left to live for. I don't have a separate life. I don't live now, I exist and console myself that I'll soon be in Leningrad with my Lelyuska.

"Of course, you'll read these words with bitterness. Soon, Lelik, soon. This is the quickest way to get to Leningrad. It's the surest and the fastest, only three or four months. On the first of January, I was with you and Igor in thought and I thought only about you and how you looked. You were very clear. I saw you clearly, only physically I couldn't feel you. I felt your pain and torment, and remembered your face on that day when I was with you in the hospital room after Igor's birth. Your face told how you endured the severe pain and torment, but at the same time on your face was written a feeling of indescribable well-being, a feeling of motherhood, a feeling that you had just given the world a brand new live being whose future could present the world with colossal benefit. How happy I was that day, so contented, I wanted to cry out, to sing, to carry you in my arms. You gave me that which I live for today. My life seemed no longer dark, hopeless, and useless, but had changed into something different, good.

"You and our son, that's my life, my air, my light. Our son is the uniting link in our lives and you are my friend and comrade who doesn't desert me in the most difficult moments and together with whom I can rest, both spiritually and physically, and who comforts me and who herself can become comforted with me. Yes, Lelik, my heart has been transformed. I want very much to study. My self-respect has been affected very strongly. No matter what happens, I must prove my worth, what I'm made of. I will not ask for mercy from the world for myself, nor will I give any quarter. Well, take care. Don't worry and remain calm. You can do it, you're a strong person. I kiss you, my son, and everyone warmly, warmly. Your Valery.

"P.S. Did you give Papa the cloaks? How does he like them? Congratulate Fyodor for me and wish him happiness and success in life. Don't forget to think of yourself. You, yourself, came to the conclusion that its absolutely necessary, and don't let the bitter moments weaken your resolve. Greetings to everyone. I kiss you warmly, warmly. I want you terribly, your presence, your caresses, which so comfort me. Your Valerick. Life is cruel. Mankind is cruel.

"Only a dishonest person who has no self-respect or sense of self can live well in this world and who doesn't care whether his ruler is a fool or intelligent, but only whether he gets paid. It's stupid, not good. One has to be very careful in life and trust no one. Valery.

"Lelik, I just got through talking with Baranov. He said that he will speak on my behalf before the All-Russian Central Executive Committee and ask for a pardon. He doesn't want to demobilize me. He wants me to remain in the Air Force and to work again as a pilot. I'll still have to sit out a month. That's all right. The sad thing is they won't demobilize me. He didn't say where they're going to send me to work, so I don't know what the future holds. Well, don't worry, don't be nervous, stay calm. Everything will be all right. I embrace you warmly. Your Valerick. Write. I await your letters."

2nd Letter:

"Greetings, my dear, beloved Lelyuska and Igorek! I would very much like to know how you are and how you are spending your time. I haven't been assigned work yet and I'm sitting alone in my cell. The other three have gone to work. The boredom is deadly and more so since I've read all the books and they haven't brought any new ones yet. Lelik, how are things going? What's new in your life? I think about you all the time and I'm concerned about your situation, which I can guess, but I don't know for sure. For God sake, don't grieve. Everything will be over soon. One month or two months at the most. So I won't be able to see you for at least that amount of time and maybe longer. But after that we'll be together. It's only for this that I'm paying with my freedom. It's not so bad. Freedom without you for me is a poor freedom.

"At first I was afraid that I wouldn't be able to send you money. Now you can stop worrying. I've already sent you some and I have money, which I can take from the cashier at any time and send you, but I don't want to take it because it's a beginning for us. We now have a little bit put away and we can use this for a reserve for unexpected expenses.

"They've promised me work in Leningrad as soon as I get there, so I'm beginning to think that there can't be happiness without some unhappiness helping it along. I can endure any experience as long as I have my Lelyuska's support, but without that support I cannot. It would be better if they would assign me work. The time would go faster. When I write you a letter I feel much better. I can hear your answer and your comforting words. Everything will pass like smoke. Yes, Lelyuska, this will pass. We'll act so it will pass and we will create an interesting, good, needed, and useful life for you.

"I'm very sad that your letters will come to me only rarely and you can meet with me only two times a month. I don't want anyone to touch or read your letters. I so need your letters. I will receive them with such happiness and they will give me much support. A man just came and told me that they have assigned me to keep some sort of a diary. I'm keeping my own diary in which I'm describing everything I see here and experience. Lelik, write and tell me what Zhorzhik is doing. Has Fyodor found work yet? And how did they spend his graduation day? How are Lena, Zhenya and Nyura? What is Papa saying? And how is his health? And what new things is Igoryushka doing? Is he speaking yet or not? Write all the details.

"Oh, and I forgot, how did your hat turn out, the one from those we took to have redone? Take my hat to the cleaners and ask them to attach a new band if they can't turn over the old one. Lelyuska, don't lose heart. Take care of yourself and, as much as possible, try to cure your anemia. Dispel your sadness and grief. Just as after a storm there's quiet, after a powerful unpleasant spiritual experience a calm, happy, good life will follow. And so watch your health, be calm, don't lost heart, and don't complain about your fate. It doesn't pay any attention to complaints or expressions of gratitude, and asks only for an even temper and a stout heart. And you were such a person and can become one again at any moment if you just convince yourself that its necessary. In your small figure, there is all kinds of energy, which you have temporarily destroyed, but you only need to retune yourself, and this energy, strength, and desire will come flying out like powerful cords from a well-retuned grand piano. A person, in the final analysis, is like a grand piano which must be retuned when you hear it gives off incorrect sounds. And so you, Lelik, are like a fine grand piano, only you're out of tune and you need a tuner so you will again be that Lelyuska who I saw on the 1st of January 1925 on Stone Island. Well, take care. I kiss you and Igoryushka warmly, warmly. My beloved Lelyuska, I want you, your conversation, your caresses, your sensitive understanding. I kiss you warmly. Your Valerick."

January 12, 1929:

"Hello, my dear, beloved Lelyuska and Igorek. How are you doing and how are you spending your time? How are you feeling? Of course, badly. Is Igor doing new things? How is everybody else feeling? Your letters have gone to Bryansk and I haven't received them yet. They'll probably bring them tomorrow or Monday. I don't want others to read your letters; therefore, send them so the authorities won't see them. I'm working in the prison office. I have freedom to walk around the prison and they want me to be the head of a club, but I don't want to since I like working in the office, because I can meet with people as much as I like. The fellows come to me often. They haven't forgotten.

Baranov is appearing before the All Russian Central Executive Committee asking for a pardon for me. I don't know when the answer will come. It'll be at least a month before we get one. Only, for God's sake, don't be upset. When you need money, I will take it from the cashier and send it to you. Have you received the 120 rubles? I sent it on the 3rd of January.

"What's happening at home? In the evenings after work, I listen to the radio and sometimes broadcasts from Leningrad. Thoughts and dreams swim in my mind about how you're living there. How is little Igor? How is everyone? I'll be thinking how everything is nice there, comfortable. There is love, agreement, friendship, and help for one another, and I am not there. This is difficult. Lelyuska, your family is everything for me. Only in your family have I found kindness, care, respect, and love.

"Only with you and in your family, from the very first, I found everything that a person needs in life. It's so pleasant for me when I remember celebrating the New Year and Easter, all those preparations when the whole family is together and everyone is sitting around one table. And those Sunday dinners, when 15 or 16 people are gathered around the table. All the conversation and the arguments. How I would like to be there now. Today is Saturday, tomorrow is Sunday. Somebody is coming for dinner. There'll be arguments. Fyodor will undoubtedly become heated, loose his temper at Papa, and leave. Zhorzhik will wave his hand in disgust and leave also. Papa will be sitting there alone, but in any event trying to make conversation. Papa's a good man. I like him for his perceptiveness, for his kindness, and how he understands his sons and daughters. I've rarely seen fathers in conversations with their sons or daughters, and I've never seen a father who was interested in the lives and work of his son or daughter. But Papa is very interested and this is very pleasant when you see that your father is interested in your work. I don't need anything in life except the means to feed and educate my children and to live in Leningrad with my dear, sweet, beloved, small Lelyuska.

"Well, take care, don't be upset, and take care of yourself. And don't forget your teeth, and also your dresses. I kiss you warmly, warmly. Kiss our son tenderly, tenderly on the cheek and on the forehead. Greetings to everyone. I love you very, very much, Lelyuska. Your Valerick."

January 14, 1929, 4th letter:

"Hello, my dear, beloved, and good Lelyuska, and Igorek! I just received two letters from you. Thank you for everything, for your care and your advice, which I always follow. What Fyodor sent me only frightens me. This morning I went to work and they told me that someone named Orekhov arrived from Leningrad and that he left to see the prosecutor to get a permit to see me. Only just yesterday detachment commander Andreyev was unable to get one. I so often see my comrades here that it's uncomfortable for me, because the others aren't allowed such a privilege. I'm only supposed to see someone once every two weeks and in the last 12 days I've already had six meetings.

"I was frightened when Fedya came. I thought that something must have happened at home. I was very nervous until I saw him, but Fedya and your letter calmed me down, and, in addition, today I received a letter from Moscow. I'll send it to you. Toward the end of January I'll be free. Then I received a letter from Gomel from Klavdia Vladimirovna Navrotskaya (the one who made the jam). I'll send that to you also. If you want to answer her, then send it to Gomel, P.O. Box 25, A. I. Navrotskaya. I'll write her now. I'll answer her questions about why I'm in prison because of the accident and the court determined that I was inattentive, careless, and said that I didn't see the telegraph cable, which I should have seen, but I couldn't see it because the cable was invisible on the background of the sky.

"But my unwillingness to fly in Bryansk also influenced the decision. My relations with the authorities were strictly official here. There are some people now who consider informal talk after hours as work discussion—but for me, this is clearly comradely discussion. You write that I shouldn't trust my comrades. You're right in all these observations, but understand, Lelyuska, that a person wants comrades, hunts for them, and finds traitors. I'm the kind of person who would never do anyone harm and I thought that no one would do me harm, but it turns out not to be so. Now, although it's too late, I'll keep my mouth shut and hunt for comrades no more.

"You ask how much money I have left. 20 rubles and 200 at the cashier. I don't need anything here. I have everything. They bring me things and wash my clothes, so don't worry about me. Why did you wait so long before you stopped nursing Igor? You've become terribly thin. This I know. Don't save the money. Buy yourself shoes for sure or they'll be gone soon. Don't send me stamps, I have them. Well, take care. I kiss you warmly, warmly. Kisses to Igoryushka and everyone. Your Valery.

January 12, 1931:

"Dear Lelik and Igoryushka! I received a letter from Papa and got very upset. I don't know what to do. I'm sending the letter to you. Read it. I just don't have the strength to correspond with him. My vacation will be ruined. I had hoped in April to go to Kislovodsk and improve my health. Now I'll have to go to Vasileva. Lelik, send me my doublebreasted jacket or overcoat. I want to sell the jacket and send the money to Papa for his cure. My stomach for some reason or other is getting worse and worse. As soon as I have eaten some kind of meat I experience severe pain. It's been continuing now for the second week.

"My spirits are down because of Papa. Alexei's tricks aren't worthy of any kind of criticism. I don't know what brought this out, since up 'til now Father has been feeding himself and now suddenly he leaves home and goes to another house. I can't figure this out. Is it possible he can act this way all the time with a good conscience? At the moment, I don't want to try to figure this out. I'm feeling terrible and I want to calm down. I'm flying to Kharkov on the 14th of January. I flew yesterday and today. Tomorrow I'll prepare the plane for the flight to Kharkov. As soon as I return from Kharkov, I'll take up this business and find out what's going on. If you can get those galoshes, go ahead. Go to that store again and ask Zhukov. He'll get them for you. Tell him you're my wife. Well, take care. I kiss you and Igoryushka warmly, warmly. Your Valery."

February 19, 1931:

"Greetings, my dear sweet Lelyuska and Igorek! How are you? How's your health? How's Papa, M. I. And others? You hinted at the fact that you were ill, but with what you didn't say. Day after tomorrow, February 21st, I'll send you 100 rubles with a Marine pilot. I'll send you additional money as soon as I receive it from my test flights. My situation isn't bad. My health is also much better. Stomach hurts a little, but less so.

"I sent Papa a package. Yesterday I sent Volodya 100 packs of cigarettes. So it seems I fulfilled all my promises and can now rest easy. Now I need only to send Igoryushka a little suit and something for you. Lelyushka, our anniversary is coming soon. That day when I was a most happy person and I think I'll be that way until the end. I think that you and I will overcome all of our rough spots. You know what caused them. I want to congratulate you early on our anniversary. It's already been four years since the two of us became one. When I look at our four-year journey and ask myself whether I am happy, I can answer yes. I wish you happiness and health. I love you now and I loved you the first day of our marriage. I'll remember all the details of that day and will imagine how that day will be repeated. Now I'd like to ask you that question. Are you happy with our life together? Has it not been difficult for you these four years? Have you received what you wanted and what you were searching for? On February 27, I'll call you on the telephone to congratulate you. I have to fly a lot now, day and night. But that's all right. I'll manage. Write me all the details. Greetings to everyone. Tell Zhorzhik to add a note. Take care. I kiss you warmly, warmly. Your loving Valery."

April 1931:

"Greetings, my dear Lelyuska and Igorek! How did your operation go? Was it a success? Lelik, you write that you received the package, but what was in it you didn't say. I sent you cheese, caviar, stockings and socks. I sent Zhorzhik a belt and oranges. I forgot the rest. It seems that was all. So write me what you received.

"I can't thank you enough for going with me to see Papa. He was able at least to see you and his grandson before he died. After we left, all he could talk about was you, Igor and your family. He died on the 22nd of March. I received the telegram on the 24th, but the funeral was on the 25th and I didn't arrive until the 27th in the early morning hours to an already filled gravesite. If you only knew how difficult, painful and offensive this was for me. Mother was the only one home when he died. He asked her to seat him on his chair and there he died. He bowed his head and quietly, quietly died. He wanted to say something, but he couldn't. He could only move his lips and that was all. That was the end. Life had been taken from him. His life was such that you and I could scarcely have endured, full of misfortune, suffering and shock.

August 18, 1931:

How's Grandmother? Tell her that I'm glad that she's in Vasileva and I'll try to come see you all together. Write to Sonia and tell her to come and stay in Vasileva for the summer, that it would be foolish for her to stay in Kamavin. I think that because I've been working harder than what they expect of me, they'll give me a week's leave. You say you don't want to live alone any more. I don't either, Lelyuska. I don't want to live alone. I'm weary without you and Igoryushka. Rest as you should. Get well. I'll be sending you some produce soon.

"I kiss you and Igoryushka warmly, warmly. I want you very, very badly.

"Kiss everyone for me and write more often. And please forgive my late letters. I'm working to earn an extra leave so that I can see you and Igoryushka. Kisses. Your Valery. Two white moths have just flown in the window. These are my guests. Its 1:20 in the morning. Bye bye, goodnight, you're already sleeping. And tomorrow again to work, to teach people to fly. My commander just died in a crash."

January, 1932:

"Greetings my dear Lelyuska and Igoryushka! Why has it been so long since I've received a letter from you? Lelik, my situation with the apartment will become clear in the next few days. They promised to give me two rooms for sure. That'll be great. Lelyuska, my left cheek is frostbitten. I've been flying all this week and I'm terribly tired. They sent for me this morning, but I didn't feel well, so didn't go. Let them get after me, I don't care. Lelik, I bought you 12 meters of linen, a table cloth with 4 napkins and 2 towels. I think I'll buy two or three more tablecloths. So you see, we'll have table cloths and napkins. Lelyuska, it will soon be our anniversary and I terribly want us to be together on that day. I want it very, very much. If I can't come to you, then you must come to me for at least one day. I so want to see you. I awoke this morning thinking why it is that Lelyuska is not sitting next to me at this moment. I would smother her with kisses. Lelyuska, I just finished testing a plane these last few days and things will be a bit easier now. The work was difficult, and to top it all off, the weather was freezing. Flying at high altitude, the temperature dropped to –61 degrees. My hands froze badly, since I had to take notes at that altitude, but everything's all right. Everything ended well. There's only one day left of flying at high altitude and I'll be done.

"Tomorrow I'll begin receiving my vaccine shots. I've already written you about them. The vaccine will be ready and I'll go to the hospital tomorrow to get it. That will be the end of my carbuncles, but I do have three new ones. I kiss you warmly, warmly, your Valerik.

"Pass on my greetings to everyone, everyone. Smother Igoryushka in kisses for me. Write. I'm waiting to receive your letters.

March 1:

"Greetings my dear, beloved little son. How are you Igoryushka? Do you miss your papa, and do you mind your mama? Igorechek, you must mind your mama and don't misbehave. Don't weary your mama. Our dear mama is tired and she is alone without papa. I will come soon and look to see how my little son is doing. Is he minding his mama, and does he love her? How do you spend your time? Do you walk a lot? How are you eating? Well? Or are you misbehaving at dinner as before? How are you playing with Irochka? Are you fighting with her? You are older than she is and must love her and not fight. Instead you must protect her.

"And so, Igorechek, your papa hopes that his son will be a good, well-behaved boy. Take care, mind and love your mama.

Kisses,

Your papa"

June 17, 1932, from Moscow:

"Dear, sweet Lelyuska! I just returned today from assignment. I successfully completed the testing and the head of the Air Force presented me with "The Order of the Red Star" along and a 1931 Harley motorcycle with a sidecar. So you can judge by the award what important work I was doing. I'm very pleased with the award.

"Today I found out I was suppose to go to Leningrad on assignment, but since I just returned from an assignment, they gave it to another. What a pity! I so much wanted to be in Leningrad.

"Lelik, forgive me. I forgot to congratulate you on your birthday, but I was on assignment. Congratulations! I wish you all the best! Soon, soon we'll be living together and then everything will be all right. How is Igor? You haven't written anything about him. Lelik, they gave me two rooms, but I still haven't moved in. There is still no electricity and no sewage system. Lelik, as soon as you can get free from your work, come to see me. It's not a very happy place; so don't waste time, but come as soon as you can. If I had received that assignment in Leningrad, then everything would've been great. It was a three-week assignment. I would have been able to see how you were all living there and if everything was all right. Lelik, write me all the details. How are you doing? I think that if you come to see me, you'll stay.

"Write, take care, don't worry and don't be angry with me. I just can't do what you and I both want. I'm a military man and have to do what I'm ordered. Kisses to you and to Igoryushka.

Your Valerik

"I have some chocolate, but there's no one to send it with. I received the butter for May, but there's none for June. By the time I receive it, I think you'll already be with me. I want you! I want you very badly! Come as soon as you can. Your Valery.

"Pass on my greetings to everyone.

"Tell Zhorzhik about my award. He'll tell you what privileges come with it. The head of the Air Force is pleased with my work. They also gave an award to Anisimov, and regardless of the fact that they have slandered us repeatedly to Air Force' authorities, when he presented us with the awards, the Air Force Chief said, "These are two of my best pilots in the whole Air Force. This is your husband. And you're not happy with him.

"Kisses,

Your Valery"

CHAPTER TWO

Test Pilot For All Time

TEST PILOT AT THE AIR FORCE RESEARCH INSTITUTE

By decision of Red Army Air Force Chief, P. I. Baranov, Chkalov was returned to military aviation and commanded to work with a group of fighter pilots in the Air Force's scientific research institute in November 1930. At the time, he was located at Moscow's Khodynsky Field. This, in essence, ended his Leningrad life. During the summer in 1932, after mother finished her work at school, the whole family moved to Moscow.

Father tested heavy bombers as well as fighters at the institute. He flew the R-1, R-3, R-5, R-7, I-4, I-5, I-7, FD-X1, TB-1DI-3, VN-33, and the four-motored TB-3.

On January 21, 1931, Red Army Air Force Order #18 expressed gratitude to individual outstanding workers, Including pilot-instructor Chkalov.

The institute tested the planes of A. N. Tupolev. The TB-1 had a range of 950 miles; and later, the TB-3 with a range of 1600 miles. These bombers could strike deep behind enemy lines. However, they would have to be protected by fighter escort, and the fighters fell far short of the range necessary to carry out such missions.

In early summer, 1931, a pilot and designer at the institute, Vladimir Sergeivich Vakhmistrov, suggested putting two I-4 fighters on the wings of the TB-1. This construction would be called "самолёт-звено" or "link-plane."

The point of the construction was to allow the fighter to be fueled from the bomber's tanks. And, of course, while riding on the wings of the TB, the fighters would use none of their own fuel. As a result, the fighters' range would be doubled.

Deputy Head of the Red Army Air Force, Y. I. Alksnis, approved the project. Vakhmistrov invited Chkalov to participate in the creation and testing of this, "этажеркой" or "two-story plane", as it was also called. Vakhmistrov described Chkalov as follows: "Carefully observing his flights, meeting with him on the job, and after work, I became convinced that he was an outstanding pilot: innovative, bold, decisive and skillful. He was a marvelous comrade; one you could depend on in all situations."

In his turn, father suggested his friend, Alexander Frolovich Anisimov, one of the best pilots at the institute, as the second fighter pilot. Test pilot, I. T. Spirin, wrote a very interesting description of these two fighter pilots:

"These pilots were brave innovators in testing new fighter planes. Their flights always struck one with their daring, technical skill, and sharp perception of the qualities of the tested plane... On coming to the institute, they immediately took a leading position among the test pilots. Anisimov was an outstanding expert on the techniques of air combat. His maneuvers in practice engagements, and his figures, were surprisingly sharp, fast, and appeared to be easily done.

"Chkalov, it seemed, didn't cede anything to Anisimov, although when they engaged in practice combat, Anisimov almost always came out the winner. Aviation specialists admired their flights, and they taught a great deal to young pilots. Anisimov and Chkalov were given the most complex and most crucial testing assignments."[17]

These two pilots had much in common, relative to both their flying mastery and in their personalities. This allowed the possibility of flying complex figures in close wing-to-wing formation, as if they were tied together. Finding two such pilots, who could understand and sense each other's actions in flight, was, of course, highly prized by Vakhmistrov.

In November all the work was finished and it was now necessary to carry out this daring experiment to determine the fate of Vakhmistrov's idea and design. Nothing in the world had been created like this up to that time.

The first test of this "Link-Plane" was scheduled for December 3rd.

The release of the two fighters from the TB-1 bomber had to follow a definite process and order. First, the fighter pilot had to release the tail of his plane. Then the co-pilot of the TB-1 was to open the forward lock holding the fighter. After this, the fighter pilot could fly off the wing of the bomber. This system had been well worked out by the crew of the TB-1, which included first pilot, Adam Zalevsky, co-pilot, Vladimir Vakhmistrov, who was in charge of releasing the fighters, and Vladimir Morozov.

Just before the test, Vakhmistrov received an order from the project head to transfer the most crucial part of the process, the release of the fighters, to a new pilot. This pilot had not participated in the training and didn't know the process, as he should. As a result, Vakhmistrov had to sit in the plane's cabin and watch the test process unfold.

The new pilot, not knowing the proper releasing technique, mistakenly released the front lock on Chkalov's fighter before Chkalov released the plane's tail lock. The plane shot upwards, but its tail was still locked to the wing of the TB-1!

Vakhmistrov remembered: "Now we were to see what Chkalov was made of. In the few seconds he was given, he was able to twist his plane in such a way that he tore the back lock from its frame and was able to take off from the TB-1. Then, as if nothing unusual had happened, he flew in close to the wing "womb," and successfully completed the flight. In this way, Valery literally saved the project. Had there been an accident, continuing work on the "Link-Plane" project would have been impossible."[9]

In two weeks, on December 19th, Deputy M. N. Tukhachevsky, of the Revolutionary Military Committee, wrote Air Force head Alksnis: "This is an important innovation. We must analyze the flights of the TB-1 and TB-2 with a range of 550 to 800 miles in order to judge the effectiveness of this Link-Plane. The inventor must be rewarded."

For carrying out the successful test, four people were awarded "The Order for the Red Star" and given motorcycles with sidecars. But Chkalov never received his awards. What was it that prevented father from receiving his first well deserved and hard earned awards? In the best tradition of our society at that time, a denunciation was sent in against him. And what was the substance of this denunciation against Valery Chkalov?

Valery's father, Pavel Gregorievich Chkalov died in March,1931. Although he didn't leave a large inheritance to his children and wife, he did leave a home, orchard and all kinds of household goods, which he earned through his own labor.

The grown children with their mother, Natalya Grigorievna, decided to entrust the young Valery with the power of attorney over the inheritance, which was done and signed on March 27, 1931.

Later in this book I'll use documents that were published by V. T. Lukin, the director of the V. P. Chkalov Memorial Museum in the village of Chkalovsk. They were published in his book "Secrets of a Thousand

Years," also, in the work of G. Maximovich "The Story of the I-180 or the Secret of Chkalov's Death."

Comparing these documents with my father's letters I can see a very clear picture.

On April 11, 1931, the following document appeared, which I will simply call "The Denunciation."

An excerpt from protocol #2 of a meeting of factions of the Vasilevo Town Council, April 11, 1931 follows:

"Secret —

"Reported: Information from comrade Parnyakov about the credibility of V. P. Chkalov.

"Comrade Parnyakov says that after the death of Pavel Grigorievich Chkalov, a petition came before the town council from his sons, daughters and wife to transfer Pavel Grigorievich Chkalov' real and personal property to his son, Valery Pavlovich Chkalov, who at the present time is serving in the RKKA (Workers' and Peasants' Red Army). This transferable property, in particular, a house and other buildings and fruit orchard is a product of a nepman's wealth. Pavel Grigorievich Chkalov was a former steamship owner.

"This transfer of property to a Red Army man and Red Commander, Valery P. Chkalov, may lead him to be a capitalist member of the economy, but along with this, since he is a Red Army man, he and his family will be free of paying taxes. Incidentally, Valery P. Chkalov will receive unearned income from apartment rent and from the fruit orchard.

"Decreed: V. P. Chkalov is to be called from the ranks of the Workers' and Peasants' Red Army, as a son of steamship owner and as one who is attempting to enrich himself by receiving unearned income.

Comrade Parnyakov, secretary of the faction, is assigned responsibility for informing the political department where Valery P. Chkalov is serving.

Faction executive secretary, Parnyakov.[18]

We should also examine one other document, "Excerpts from Protocol No. 13":

"A meeting of the Gorodetsky Regional Special Committee on the examination of persons deprived of voting rights, from June 1, 1930, page 56. Chkalov, Pavel Grigorievich, a pre-revolutionary steamship owner. From 1920 to the present a worker in the Ulyanov-Lenin Shipyard.

"Page 57. His wife, Chkalova, Natalya Grigorievna, his dependent, resolved: Voting rights to be restored."

This decision about the restoration of voting rights was taken almost a year before the death of Pavel Grigorievich and the good name of Chkalov in the shipyard was restored, but the denouncer and perhaps an envious person, who himself was not able to work like Pavel Grigorievich, didn't stop there. If he couldn't get Pavel Grigorievich, he would go after his children!

Father, working at the time in the Red Army Air Force Research Institute, sent his mother-in-law the following document:

"Affidavit No. 795

From April 5, 1931

On this day Comrade Valery Pavlovich Chkalov, instructor pilot of the first unit, is a military service person in the Red Army Air Force Research Institute. His mother, Natalya Grigorievich Chkalova, is his dependent and on the basis of pages 85 and 86 it is decreed by the Military Central Executive Committee and the Soviet of Peoples Commissars from 23/IV 1930 Nos. 252 and 253 that his family will have access to the privileges of living quarters and be free of paying rent. As signed and sealed and confirmed on this day."

This document was to give privileges to Natalya Grigorievna, but the local authorities took them from her. I won't quote all of her official complaints and the answers she received from authorities. But during this exchange of letters, zealous authorities and several simple villagers who, for a long time, had been envious of Pavel Grigorievich Chkalov, and coveting what he had earned with his hard work, took everything from the home. They even took Natalya Grigorievna's dowry and once again assessed her an agricultural tax.

It is necessary to note that the Nizhny Novgorod Regional Political Committee did everything they could to restore justice. Following is its last decree:

"Decree No. 969. The Nizhny Novgorod Regional Political Committee Presidium August 20, 1931, concerning the elimination of the agricultural tax levied in the village of Vasileva.

No. 1. Considering that:

    a. The village of Vasileva having lost its recognition as an agricultural economy from 1929 is not liable to be taxed.

    b. The population is predominantly workers and service personnel (to 2000 persons) in the shipyard, who own private plots and livestock for personal use.

c. Gorodetskiy District Executive Committee of Soviets (RIK) violated the 30th statute: Regulation of agricultural tax for the year of 1931 – to reverse the obligation of an agricultural tax in Vasilievo town.

2. The head of Gorodetskiy District' Financial Department (RaiFO), comrade Puzyrev, who allowed an unlawful and unjustified agricultural taxation (on an individual basis) of the following households: N.G. Chkalova., N.I Shaposhnikov., A.M. Krasilnikov, A.I. Motina, V.A. Rubinskaya, as well as engineer A.P. Chkalov with immediate requisitioning and sale of their belongings, despite the prohibition by the District Financial Department (RaiFO), should have judicial proceedings instituted against him.

3. To cancel the individual agricultural taxation of the households listed in item 2 (…) and to return the requisitioned belongings (according to inventory) to the rightful owners."[18]

But there was nothing to return. Today, in father's museum, there are no original household goods, which belonged to his parents. The table, chairs, and other things in the house in 1936, had been ordered by father from the Ulyanov-Lenin factory.

So from the above, one can see how the authorities in Vasilevo dealt with the Chkalov family. And what effect did the denunciation have on father?

As long as the denunciation was still being investigated, father decided to leave it alone, since he was very busy continuing the work preparing for further testing of the Link-Plane project.

But 10 days after the completion of testing, a new testimonial turned up concerning senior test pilot, V. P. Chkalov, evidently requested by the denouncer:

"His general development is good. Politically, his growth is unsatisfactory, and he works very little to improve himself in this area. He is insufficiently active in the social life of his unit. He drinks hard liquor and demands too little of himself. The demands he makes on his subordinates are satisfactory.

"A feeling of responsibility for assigned work is insufficiently developed. He doesn't always complete his work and orders accurately. As a good pilot, he has worked out the techniques of flight well. Discipline on the ground is satisfactory; in the air, it is unsatisfactory. For breaking flight discipline, he has been warned by Air Force Chief, Alksnis, that he may lose his right to fly. His experience in testing planes is not satisfactory, and in this unit he is doing very little to improve. Knowledge of the mechanical parts of the plane and motor is satisfactory. He is able to point out defects. Knowledge of aircraft armaments is unsatisfactory. Knowledge of combat and formation flying, and organization of joint military actions is not satisfactory. Training in flying blind is insufficient (two hours). He has tested planes in high altitude flights. During 1931, he accumulated 235 hours of daylight flying time; 3 hours 40 minutes of night flight. In testing planes, flying assignments and bombing runs, he has had no breakdowns or accidents. He has experienced a forced landing due to motor failure — he landed successfully. He is unable to carry out research work and is not working to improve himself in this area. Military affairs are of little interest to him. He is healthy and satisfies the requirements of a pilot's responsibilities."

This "evaluation" of my father provided more than enough justification to refuse him the awards. I won't comment further on this description consisting of contradictions and not corresponding to reality. For example, "His experience in testing planes is not satisfactory, and in this unit he is doing very little to improve." In a testimonial from November 13 to the question "On what planes have you flown recently (indicate the specific planes)?" the answer was given, "I-4, I-5, I-7, Avia-VN-39, K-47, R-1, R-3, R-6, R-7, DI-3, TB-1, and FD-XI."

In spite of all this malicious nonsense, father continued to work in the research institute testing planes and preparing newly arrived pilots for their test flights.

CHKALOV MEETS BAIDUOV

It was in the Red Army Air Force Research Institute that my father met Georgy Filippovich Baidukov. They became great friends and Baidukov, although he outlived my father by many decades, remained true to this friendship. Georgy Filippovich described this first meeting as follows: "Our group of four novices gathered beside the large hangar of the institute. The summer evening was slowly fading away. Soon an authoritative voice rang out. 'Attention!" All persons on the airfield in spite of the darkness quickly gathered in ranks. The commander of the unit, calling off the pilots' names in order, gave orders concerning the conduct of that day's night flights. 'Comrade Chkalov! It is your responsibility today to conduct flights with pilots newly assigned to this institute. Evaluate their night flying skills and, if necessary, train them and then release them when you think necessary.' Chkalov replied, 'Very good, Comrade Commander! I will examine them and, when necessary, release them.' The commander then said, 'Carry on. There is your group.' The commander then indicated the group of four young pilots in which I stood on the left flank, slightly nervous, attentively listening to the commander's every word.

"Chkalov came up to us and with a low, rather husky voice asked, looking at me,

'What's your family name?'

'Baidukov,' I answered.

'How many years have you been flying?'

'Five.'

'What did you fly on?'

'On a Snooper [reconnaissance plane].'

'That's not the question. Did you fly on an R-1?'

'Yes, exactly,' I answered, slightly struck by the rude tone and the fact that he referred to me using the familiar, and not formal, form of you. And also his slightly noticeable Volga dialect.

'Well, why didn't you say you fly an R-1 observation aircraft? What's this nonsense about a snooper?'

"After a few moments pause, Chkalov added, 'Get in the plane; I'll come shortly. ' Chkalov disappeared not saying where the plane was or what its number was. We stood there, confused.

"I hurried to the planes in order to hunt out or more exactly to guess the plane that I was to take my examination flight in. Running alongside the planes, I tried to catch sight of Chkalov's broad shouldered figure in order to figure out where our plane was. I was darting in and out between the planes meeting other pilots. I ran up closely to one and called out loudly, 'Chkalov, report to the commander.'

"I thought up this phrase thinking that it was such an authoritative announcement I would hear the instructor call out. I ran into two pilots, and, repeating my earlier clever attempt, I suddenly heard that voice with the dialect. 'What are you bellowing about? To what commander?' It was Chkalov! I stayed quiet, trying to figure out how I was going to wiggle my way out of this stupid situation. 'To what commander?' the instructor again repeated the question. And feeling somehow awkward, he came up close to me and struck a match. Lighting it in my face, he burst out laughing. 'Baidukov, why so quiet?'

"'The sharp, severe features of his face softened a bit, but as the match went out all I could see was his silhouette—short, broad shouldered.

"'Have a smoke! Then we'll go to the plane.' Either he forgot that I had attracted his attention with a call for him to report to his commander, or he guessed my trick, and calmly continued the conversation: 'I'm going to be taking the young guys for a ride today....'

"'Let's go Baidukov... Well, get in the cabin. Your assignment will be a simple, circular flight.'

"'Yes, sir, comrade commander!' I called over the mechanic, and with the light of a lantern, carefully examined the landing gear and tail unit.

"Chkalov climbed into the plane and, sticking his head over the side of the rear cabin, whistled something.

"We had already completed the check up, and the mechanic whispered something in my ear: 'Be careful you don't mess things up. Chkalov doesn't like too much passion, take it easy.... But he can't stand timid flights, either.'

"I crawled into the plane's forward cabin, thinking over the advice of this simple hearted mechanic....

"'Comrade commander, I'm ready!'

"'Well, carefully taxi to your place, and then take off!' I heard the answer through the telephone.

"I asked permission to start... In just a few seconds, we were flying over the roofs of the hangers. The red flashes from the field's border lights momentarily made the plane's wings transparent. Through the canvas, the wings' ribs and spars could be distinguished. Was it the flash I saw in the calmly expectant eyes of the instructor, or was it the mechanic's advice, acting on me? Gently pushing the plane to gather speed, I put her into a steep upward turn. The plane, plunging into the darkness, turned sharply to the left with capricious zigzags. I carefully and slyly glanced in the mirror, where I expected to see signs of approval or condemnation for my actions. Completely unexpectedly, I saw the instructor's hand rise up in front of his nose with a forceful thumbs-up sign. After landing, Chkalov crawled out of the rear cabin and, hanging over the side, said:

"'Good, nothing I can comment on. Fly in the zone and practice what you think you need to by yourself. I don't need to work with you any longer.'

"'Yes, Sir, comrade commander!'

"'Well, what's with this "comrade commander"? Simply call me Chkalov. You're also a commander and an instructor and test pilot just like me.'

"'OK, comrade Chkalov, I answered, smiling.'

"'And what do I call you?'

"'Georgy.'

"'That means I'll call you Yegor, like we call our people on the Volga. Well, get going, Yegor, but don't fly too far. I still have to fly with others on that plane.'

"…So in this dark summer night, over a Moscow airfield, I became acquainted with this bird-man, who was to enter Russian history as an aviation legend. His relationship to me as an instructor was to change, and neither he nor I could foresee that our future fate would draw us closer and closer with each passing year as our lives would make us very dependent on one another."

One of father's "students" was Peter Mikhailovich Stefanovsky, who also described his first meeting with him:

"I met a typical representative of an all-round test pilot before my first flight on a TB-1. We met on the airfield. Stocky, thickset, in a quality flight suit of fox fur, he met me with a friendly smile spread over his broad, weather-beaten face. After he listened to my formal report concerning my arrival and being placed under his command, he waved his hand in the direction of the plane and said, 'Crawl in. Enough already with these formalities.'

"This was Valery Pavlovich Chkalov. In flying circles they spoke of him then as an extremely independent, but outstanding pilot, regular guy and marvelous comrade. I somehow immediately trusted this first instructor of my heavy bomber flight education. This type person will teach you everything he knows, and not scold you or blow up over insignificant details. He won't send you to the authorities if you slip up somehow. And what possible slip ups is it possible to make on this plane? You lay the route, set the speed, follow the course, and correct for wind drift.

"…We took our places in the cabin. Chkalov, as if by the way, asked:

"'Fighter pilot?'

"'Fighter pilot.'

"'Then let's go.'

"Valery Pavlovich sat calmly behind the controls, as if he were having a cup of tea.

"'This is going to be easy,' I thought. 'Nothing to worry about. A bomber is stable in the air, no sharp turns, no somersaults, like some hawk….'

"Completely unexpectedly, however, the plane took a sharp downward turn. We were only at about 900 feet, not more. Flawlessly completing several figures, Chkalov sharply lifted the plane's nose, smoothly reduced speed and then took the plane into a steep dive. What's he doing, the devil! The earth was rushing closer! I looked at my instructor with anxiety and anger. We were not on some fighter plane! And he was calmly going about his business.

"The ground was coming at us fast—not more than 150 left…The little wooden homes were rapidly growing very large, and seemed to be rushing at us. Only seconds left—and….

"The motors gave a roar, the plane jerked upward, easily turned about and settled into horizontal flight.

"I was confused. A bomber? With such maneuverability? I looked a Chkalov with admiration.

"'You get it?' He asked, smiling broadly. I nodded my head in agreement.

"'You take it.'

"'Now?' The instructor had already left the controls.

"'Well!'

"We were at 900 feet. I made an equally sharp turn, then lifted the plane's nose, smoothly let up on the gas, and with Chkalov like energy threw the plane into a dive. It seemed it wasn't the plane hurtling downward, but the earth racing to meet us. We were at 450 feet, then 300 feet… Now! The plane, as if on springs, broke its downward flight and shot upwards.

"'Good!' Valery Pavlovich shouted his approval with that Volga accent. 'You got it. Go in for a landing.'

"After a second landing, Chkalov got up from his commander's seat, and his face again broke into that broad smile.

"'You can take it yourself now. There's nothing more for me to do here.'

"So began my career on heavy bombers. Preconceptions about these bombers had now been stripped away. I trusted these huge machines, learned to love them, though they didn't always return my affection.

"During my long career in the air, I experienced many close calls. Many times the earth came up inexorably to meet my crippled plane. It was in moments such as these that I always remembered the 'christening' Chkalov gave me. Flying with Chkalov opened the door to a serious career in aviation, to a boundless sky, and sharply changed my flying fate.

"I would permanently remain a military test pilot."

In February 1932, in the Russian Air Force Research Institute Order No. 52 was issued, "… I commend the especially outstanding quality of work by test pilot Valery Pavelovich Chkalov of the 1st Permanent Detachment of the 2nd Squadron … I award Comrade V. P. Chkalov with a camera. Signed by Institute Director Buzanov." Perhaps this camera was intended to replace the promised medal and motorcycle.

In the winter of 1932, P. M. Stefanovsky remembered an incident when a foreign delegation came to the institute; Italian generals of aviation, to whom the possibilities of our technology were to be demonstrated. Stefanovsky was to demonstrate the bomber TB3 but there was no one to demonstrate a fighter, since Anisimov was on assignment and Chkalov was sitting in the brig. Finally, the director decided to free Chkalov early. "After some time, my crew," remembers Stefanovsky, "began preparing for the flight. With fur flight suits, high dog fur boots, helmets in our hands, parachutes thrown over our shoulders, and not hurrying, as was the habit with typical bombadiers, we ambled toward our TB bomber. Suddenly, we saw an unexpected sight. With a parachute under his arm, an unbuttoned flight suit, carelessly drawn up fur boots, and with wide, quick steps, Chkalov caught up with us. 'They gave me an amnesty. But the head hancho says the next time he gets a chance he's going to tack on another two or three days' Adam Iosifovich Zalevsky loved Chkalov and valued him highly. Therefore, he ruled him with an iron hand and gave him no quarter.

"Our guests smiled ironically … but a bit early. At the assigned time, we both started our motors and taxied into position.

"Valery was all impulse, uncontrollably striving ahead, striving to get into the air. If he'd had wings, he'd have left us on the spot and rushed into the sky. It was at this moment I saw him vividly; recognized his many-sided talents—this Volga warrior with his expansive soul, his valor, his unquenchable thirst for flight, his indomitable striving to accomplish something unusual, something unique.

"Chkalov understood that today he could go all out. Completing figures of advanced acrobatics at minimum altitude was his ace in the hole. But only today, during the demonstration flights. Tomorrow, during the usual working regime, they not only would not praise him for such flights, but punish him, by throwing those three days in the brig at him that the head man promised.

"At the assigned time, we started our engines and took off, straight from our parking spots. In order not to hinder Chkalov in performing his vertical aerobatics, they suggested I work at about 300 feet. Therefore, I wasn't able to see the figures Chkalov was writing in the sky. Anyway, my own situation demanded my full attention.

"The flight was coming to an end. Was I really going to have to land without doing something special? And what if….? My hands seemed to be drawn to the engine control levers. Two of the engines fell silent; their propellers froze. On two motors, I flew over the heads of the foreigners, took a tight turn and came in for the landing.

"Chkalov followed right after.

"After the flight, Valery and I were presented to the head of the delegation. He was amazed:

"We've traveled all around Europe and America, and we've never seen such quality aviation; both your planes and the mastery of your pilots."

This evaluation of flight mastery was given by the head of the Italian delegation, which thought very highly of the accomplishments of their own military air force.

This high evaluation, however, didn't hinder the authorities in sending Chkalov to correctional facilities at a special service school, after having given another testimonial denunciation, not significantly different from the first.

It's possible that the following order, issued by the Red Army Air Force Research Institute's aviation brigade on April 26, 1932, was a delayed reaction to this denunciation:

"Pilot instructor, V. P. Chkalov, First Detachment, 2nd Squadron, during four months in 1932 committed a series of serious undisciplined acts.

1. For not fulfilling orders of the squadron, January 7, 1932, through unauthorized flight on the bomber TB1. Penalty: 5 days in the brig.
2. For not fulfilling Air Force orders concerning instruction of flight staff on new types of planes, which led to the catastrophe of March 26, 1932 of pilot Albensky on the plane I-5. Punishment: 5 days arrest by the director of the Research Institute. [If there was a catastrophe, then 5 days arrest would have been very little.]
3. For damaging the TB1, #651, March 29, 1932, during the process of taxiing from the parking area to the airfield. (An official reprimand by the squadron commander.)
4. The breaking of flight discipline by flying across the airfield during general flight time, April 2, 1932, at Moninsky Airport and completing aerobatic figures at low altitude. Punishment: 5 days arrest by the director of the Air Force MVO.
5. This list of punishments over such a short period of time demonstrates the extreme undisciplined nature of pilot Chkalov.

"My many reprimands and disciplinary punishments had little effect on Comrade Chkalov.

"I consider that such behavior is incompatible with the responsibilities of a detachment commander. For the intolerable breaching of flight discipline, I dismissed Comrade Chkalov from his responsibilities in the detachment. Aviation Brigade Commander Skrobuk."

Well, what can one say, having read this document? How can one forget the camera given to Chkalov in February for an "especially outstanding quality of work"? In two years work at the flight institute, Chkalov completed more than 800 test flights, mastering the technology in piloting 30 types of planes.

On April 23, 1933, father was transferred to the Red Army reserve; that is, for the third time he was discharged from the army. Perhaps the authorities again decided to distance themselves from the restive, anxious person, who, with a cascade of figures of advanced aerobatics, uncovered the qualities or hidden defects of tested planes, which included heavy bombers.

So, again, Chkalov was left without work. However, the director of Factory No. 39 offered work to Chkalov as his test pilot at the factory.

FACTORY TEST PILOT

So it turned out that Father was still able to use his skills, knowledge, experience, and mastery of advanced aerobatics. During his short life in the air, he flew more than 70 types of planes. He gave life to the I-15 and I-16 planes designed by Nikolai Nikolaevich Polikarpov.

It was only due to the well-coordinated work of Polikarpov and test pilot Chkalov that allowed the I-16 to be accepted by the Air Force. Without them, this plane would have been sent to the aviation graveyard as Hero of the Soviet Union A. A. Turzhansky noted. "It would have been sent there as an unsuccessful attempt to design a completely new type of monoplane fighter with retractable landing gear." It's difficult to say whether Turzhansky was correct or not, but this plane fought in the skies of Spain and faithfully served on the front during the Second World War.

It seems it was no accident that brought these two people together. They understood each other very well. One could say that they fulfilled one another. Many of Polikarpov's planes were a success after Chkalov tested them in flight and found their defects, which the designer could then eliminate. Nikolai Nikolaevich Polikarpov was one of the best designers of fighter planes of that time. His design ideas exceeded the technical possibilities of our factories.

So who was this Nikolai N. Polikarpov? He was born on July 8, 1892. He graduated from the Petrograd Polytechnical Institute in aviation courses in 1916. He then worked at the Russell Baltic railway car factory where, under the direction of I. I. Sikorsky, he participated in the creation of the plane "Ilya Muromets" and designed the fighter plane "RBVZ." He then went to work in the factory "Duks" where, until 1923, he headed the technological department.

In the spring of 1923, Polikarpov created the first Soviet fighter plane, the I-1 (IL-400). Also under his direction in that year, the reconnaissance plane, the R-1, was created. In 1927, he created the fighter "I-3" and in 1928, the reconnaissance plane R-5 and the training plane U-2.

In October 1929, Polikarpov was accused of "participating in dangerous counter-revolutionary organizations," arrested, and sentenced to death without a trial. In December, without a rescission or a change in the sentence, they sent him to the "Special Design Bureau" (ЦКБ-39 ОГПУ), organized in the Butyrsky Prison, and then transferred to the V.

R. Menzhinsky Moscow Aviation Factory No. 39. At this factory, together with D. Grigorovich, in 1930, they redesigned the I-5 fighter, which was used in our Air Force for nine years.

In 1931, the OGPU board sentenced Polikarpov to 10 years in a labor camp, but after Stalin, Voroshilov, and Ordzhonikidze saw a demonstration of the I-5 aircraft piloted by Chkalov and Anisimov, it was decided to reduce Polikarpov's sentence to probation. In July of that same year, the Central Executive Committee of the USSR granted amnesty to a group of people that included Polikarpov. It was only in 1956 that Polikarpov was posthumously rehabilitated. In the 1930s, Polikarpov created the I-15, I-16, and I-153 fighter planes, which formed the basis for Soviet fighter plane aviation during the pre-war years. Toward the end of 1938, he designed the I-180 fighter and then in 1939 and 1940, the biplanes I-190 and I-195. The design project for the new I-200 fighter plane was transferred to a newly created design bureau under the direction of Artem Mikoyan. Between 1938 and 1944, Polikarpov designed a series of military planes, the TIS, VIT, SPB, NB, and others. N. N. Polikarpov was a deputy of the Supreme Soviet of the USSR from 1937, held a doctorate in technical science, was a laureate of two Stalin prizes of the USSR, was a Hero of Socialist Labor, awarded two Orders of Lenin, and an Order of the Red Star. N. N. Polikarpov died on July 30, 1944 from stomach cancer.

On December 31, 1933, Chkalov tested a new fighter, the I-16, which had never yet been flown. After this began the slow, laborious and detailed work necessary to bring this plane on line. Following are several excerpts from the diary of the work done on the I-16, in which father participated:

"...A circular test flight was completed without landing gear retraction. Pilot Chkalov.

"A test flight was completed with the purpose of testing landing gear retraction. Pilot Chkalov.

"The landing gear could not be retracted. Four releases and retractions of the landing gear were completed in order to discover the reason excessive force was necessary to raise the landing gear in flight.

"The testing on the ground of the landing gear retraction mechanism was completed. Seventeen retractions and releases were completed. Cylinders were installed. Adjustments were made to the electro signaling devices. Test flights were completed to the test landing gear retraction mechanism in flight. Pilot Chkalov.

"Releases worked with pauses. Signaling worked poorly."

And so, day after day, Chkalov, test pilot Vladimir Kokkinaki, and the whole factory staff, worked to carry out the testing necessary to bring planes on line for the air force.

At a May 1st parade, in 1934, Chkalov demonstrated the I-16 to Moscow. The new, fast fighter swept over Red Square, delighting the crowd, then rushed upward and disappeared.

Working as a factory test pilot, father was often present at a new plane's development. Head engineer, Z. I. Zhurbin, said he stood out due to his perceptive observational abilities and his unusually quick comprehension of new construction. Zhurbin writes:

"The plane was still in its construction stocks. Following accepted procedures, barely stopping, we passed by the stocks where they were installing the plane's landing gear, and proceeded to the place where they were assembling the fuselage. I here began to speak of the construction of the undercarriage and landing gear. He interrupted me and continued the description himself. I asked him: 'How did you know that?'

"'Well, we just passed by the stocks,' he answered, laughing."[4]

It's well to remember, he had a marvelous memory, including the visual. Besides that, his experience as plane assembler from 1919 through 1920 always helped him.

"Testing planes, I still would not be stopped by risk, but it would be a risk of a higher order – genuine, sober-minded risk, cautious, cool-headed," my father remembered. Now his main thought was to save the only copy of this new fighter.

Chkalov not only tested planes, but also "taught" them to fly. And to do this, it was necessary to eliminate all the defects found during the testing process.

Several pages of his detailed evaluation of the testing of the I-16 in the process of a descending spin has been saved. At the end of the evaluation, he wrote the following: "All the spins were carried out in accordance with the developed program and instructions of department head, Comrade Iliushin. During all spins, mentioned above, there was no tendency to flat spin. If not given a foothold, a plane won't spin, but makes a steep spiral. In a spin though, on pulling the lever more toward you, the speed of rotation does increase. The sum total of failures was 75."

This was father's everyday work. He tested the VIT-1, (a new type of anti-tank fighter plane), and the I-17.

But there were test flights, which could've easily ended in catastrophe. The pilot's life, in these situations, hung by a thread.

It was April 10, 1934, and having finished the testing of a new plane, he started to come in for a landing. The landing gear, however, refused to lower in place. Gathering speed, he began to perform figures, which would help shake loose the landing gear. The struggle for these two lives—his and the plane's—continued for 40 minutes. He would dive from high altitude at extremely high speeds, then shoot upwards in a rising spin. He completed figure after figure, sometimes in the process experiencing seven Gs of gravity. During the completion of some figures he blacked out; his forehead struck his knees; he momentarily lost consciousness. And finally—success! The landing gear released. Below, emergency vehicles had gathered on the landing strip. But they weren't needed—father had averted a catastrophe.

One winter, while testing a ski plane, one of the skis was torn off. At slow speed, he artfully landed the plane on one ski, not allowing the possibility for the plane to bury itself in the snow nose first. The plane did flip over, however, but the pilot remained alive.

Two years later, in 1936, a similar event occurred while testing the ANT-25 before his famous transpolar fight. Stefanovsky was a witness to the event and described it as follows:

"When I ran up, the plane with its thin wings, and huge wing-span, was circling at very low altitude... After one more circle, the plane began its descent for a landing on one wheel. Smoothly, seemingly with complete calm, the plane lowered itself toward the earth. It was now hovering just a meter and a half above the grass covered landing area. One wing was sharply tilted toward the side with the released wheel; the other was correspondingly tilted upward. We froze. The speed began to lessen; the plane lightly touched the ground and began to run on one wheel. The speed now lessened yet more, it appeared almost stopping, and when the ailerons stopped moving, the second wing gently lowered onto the grassy cover.

"Our surprise knew no bounds, when we saw that the plane had not in the least been damaged. The landing had been accomplished with the delicate touch of a jeweler."[9]

In 1934 and 1935, newspapers still had not written about him. Only the factory paper, "Menzhinets," published his portrait. He still was not known to the world.

The first serious publication about father turned up in the newspaper "Pravda" on May 4, 1935, and on May 6th Pravda published a long article, "Flight Testing." The article was published because on May 5th, the design engineer, Nikolai N. Polikarpov, and test pilot, Valery P. Chkalov, were awarded the Order of Lenin. This was his first significant award. By decree of the Central Executive Committee of the USSR, the following was written about Polikarpov: "For outstanding service and the creation of high quality designed aircraft." The following was written about Chkalov: "For many demonstrations of exceptional daring and courage while testing newly designed aircraft."

This was official recognition of the service rendered by test pilot Chkalov and was to change the course of his life.

U.S.S.R
People's Commissar
Of Heavy Industry
Moscow, Nogin Sq.

N 200-25 IV 1935
To be sent to the
Central Committee

Designer of aircraft factory No.39, comrade N.N. Polikarpov, is one of the most talented of our aviation workers. He designed the following planes: I-15, I-16. Both planes have been added to our armory.
Pilot V.P.Chkalov tests new pursuit planes and is considered one of the best pilots.

I ask that the designer of aircraft factory No.39, N. N. Polikarpov, and pilot V. P. Chkalov be awarded with the Order of Lenin

Sergo Ordzhonikidze

CHKALOV MEETS STALIN

This was preceded by one other no less important event in the life of father when, on May 2, at Central Airfield, Defense Chief Voroshilov introduced Chkalov to Stalin. It is there that Stalin made the statement to him that later became famous: "Your life is more valuable to us than any aircraft."

A photograph of Chkalov with Stalin was published on May 4th in Pravda. It was at this airfield that pilots demonstrated advanced aerobatics to the Soviet leaders. Father participated in these aerobatics, completing his favorite figures, of course, at very low altitude.

J. V. Stalin, G. K. Ordzhonikidze and V. P. Chkalov on Frunze Air Field. May 2, 1935.

In the Kremlin, in the Hall of Facets, there was a reception in honor of the best pilots and aviation designers, which Chkalov and Polikarpov attended. The First Heroes of the Soviet Union had been invited, along with well-known flight instructors and masters of advanced aerobatics. Among the invited was Alexander Ivanovich Zhukov under whom father studied at the Moscow School of Advanced Aerobatics.

Zhukov remembers that, "When I entered the Hall of Facets, everyone was sitting around tables and Peoples Commissar Sergo Ordzhonikidze was speaking. I wanted to go to the place where pilots were sitting, but I was politely asked to sit at the side, almost at the end of the hall. Kokkinaki, Vodopyanov, Slepnev, and other well-known pilots were sitting in the front. Chkalov, to whom was paid special attention, was sitting next to the government leaders' table. Sergo Ordzhonikidze raised a toast to the Communist Party and to the powerful wings of the fatherland and warmly noted the selfless, honorable work of Valery Chkalov. For Valery, my comrade, all were raising their glasses. I was so pleased!

"Chkalov stood up, pale from excitement, and pronounced some heartfelt words of gratitude to our people and to the work that created an impressive culture of aviation. Chkalov was full of happiness and stood very handsomely by his table during his ceremonial moment. I felt very sharply then and understood that his goal had not been the achievement of personal glory. He wasn't thinking of himself, but gave himself completely to his Soviet homeland. He raised his hand suddenly, drawing the attention of the crowd. The hall became silent. Chkalov's words rang out clearly, and surprised me. It seemed to me, here, in this Hall of Facets, they resounded with special effect.

"'Students are praised because of their teachers. And if they speak well of me, they are speaking well of the one who taught me to fly. And my dear instructor in the Moscow school is here. You know him. He is Aleksandr Ivanovich Zhukov...'

"And Valery Pavlovich pointed to me.

"Applause rang out.

"I was confused, but somebody elbowed me in the side and forced me to stand. As in a quickly running film, I saw separate sharp frames — Valery's smiling, happy face, Sergo Ordzhonikidze affably waving his hand, the happy faces of familiar pilots, Mikhail Gromov saying something warm and good.

"How, at this moment, personally for him full of such special significance here in the Kremlin, would he remember about me? How did he find me among the throngs of people? He studied with me only three months and that was a long time ago. The questions came fast, feverishly.

"Now, after many years, I can find only one answer. Chkalov was thanking everyone who, in a comradely way, was helping him become the person he became. For this it's necessary to have a large heart, and Valery Chkalov certainly had that large heart."

Yes, father really did have a large, kind heart and was an unusually modest person. He always mentioned and thanked everyone.

After the transpolar flight in 1937, he spoke at various meetings and always spoke of the members of his crew — about his friends, and nothing about himself.

Brigade Commander Shelukhin, who father served under in the 1st Aviation Squadron at the end of the 1920s, was present at one reception in Georgy Hall in the Kremlin. He recalled: "When I got up from the table, I observed that Chkalov noticed me. Then I saw how he filled his glass, picked it up, and started to leave the table. I thought, 'Is he coming to me?' Truthfully, I have to admit that I wasn't prepared to meet with him and hoped that he was going to meet someone else, but I noticed how he was boldly coming straight to my table. I thought: 'Chkalov is now a famous person. Is he going to remember those times when I took repressive measures against him, when I sent him to the guardhouse?'

"Approaching me, Comrade Chkalov, with a friendly smile, announced that when he saw me he immediately hurried to meet me: 'I saw in you the very best friend, an educator,' he said, 'you put me on my feet, you set me in the right direction. I only now recognize how valuable your instructions were, so I want to drink to your health.'" Father never forgot his teachers.

Chkalov in 1936, a favorite of Stalin, was named Hero of the Soviet Union. Baidukov, Belyakov, and Voroshilov, Stalin's Minister of Aviation, to Stalin's left.

Father's work at the factory was not limited only to testing planes. He participated in the life of the factory, where he created a flight school. He said: "In order to know how to build a plane, it would be useful to know how to fly." He taught the workers of the flight station and the workers in the assembly plant, the designers, including the head designer Polikarpov, as well as the engineers of the factory. They all learned to fly the U2 trainer in all kinds of weather, how to take off and to land on any landing field. They even learned to perform his favorite low-level hedge hopping flight.

As an experienced fighter pilot and test pilot, he was drawn in to work in the commission that examined plane crashes. The following people served on one such commission created by the decision of the Politburo of the Communist Party in 1935: Alksnis, Kokkinaki, Chkalov, Levanevsky, Tupolev, Kharlamov, Polikarpov, Ilyushin, Piontofsky, Filin, and others.

He also participated in meetings conducted by the Party and the government with military pilots.

There is a shorthand record of a meeting that took place on June 7-8, 1936, to which Polikarpov, Gromov, Chkalov, and Kokkinaki were invited. The subject concerned accidents in the Air Force and stated that many accidents were linked to the performance of advanced aerobatic figures and especially with the ability to pull out of a descending spin.

Chkalov: I consider that air force accidents are the responsibility of leadership.

The Voronezh brigade of comrade Sokolov, which has not had an accident in four years, is an example. Why? Because he has conducted 1800 exams of his staff, 800 of them at night, and he has checked each of his subordinates approximately 10 times.

Who is a pilot who has just finished school? He is still an infant, who needs to be carefully watched for the first five years.

I just happened to run onto a statistic, true, from the Polish Air Force, where they compiled statistics concerning aviation accidents among pilots who had flown for 1, 2, 3, 4, and 5 years. They found that pilots who had flown for 4 or 5 years had the most accidents. Why? Because as the pilot begins to feel his mastery of the plane, he becomes overconfident and starts to take chances. The percentage of accidents begins to fall after the fifth year, but not my much.

The Voronezh Brigade Commander was able to go four years without an accident in his command, because he constantly checked his pilots and didn't allow any carelessness. He watched his flight staff carefully and really educated his personnel.

Another reason is a lack of sufficient care: sometimes a sick person flies; he becomes dizzy during this spin and crashes, sometimes even after the spin has actually stopped. For example, the R-5 (plane). It takes skill to make it spin. So why does the pilot crash? Because he didn't learn to exit the spin, or he was sick and got dizzy after making just three turns, and couldn't tell North from South.

Comrade Peoples Commissar, Voroshilov, emphasized the descending spin, and was saying that most get killed during these spins. I'm a civilian and I agree with comrade Voroshilov. Now about aerobatic figures. Is it necessary to learn aerobatics? Of course, it's necessary. And not only the figures we perform today; we need to improve our aerobatic figures, comrade Stalin.

Stalin: That's easy for you to say. We don't have many such pilots as you.

Chkalov: There are pilots that fly better than I. There are a lot of them.

Stalin: How many? 100? 200?

Chkalov: Those 100 or 200 can each teach five others—that's a thousand.

Stalin: We need five thousand.

Chkalov: Each one of that thousand can teach five—there's your five thousand. (Laughter).

Our personnel can solve the problem. Take the Northrop plane. What's good about it? It was built by good people, by qualified workers. If we built planes using workers of the sixth or seventh rank, you wouldn't have planes with even one defect.

If you have an accident, it means you didn't learn your job. If you readjust like I suggested, you'll be able to fly and nothing will ever happen. But if you continue to work as you do today in the factories, then you're just going to be burying aircraft.

Comrade Lopatin spoke about speed—150 kilometers per hour. That's not right. We can only go 105 kilometers per hour today. And the load has been increased to 117 kilograms, but don't forget that in a year the landing capacity will be 130 kilograms.

Alksnis: We're not going to have any Chkalovs in our Air Force. If you try to drive a car 130 kilometers per hour and you make a turn, you'll be killed.

Chkalov: We'll land safely.

Alksnis: We've seen how you land.

Chkalov: In any event, we have to prepare our pilots to handle such speed. If we don't teach them now, then no matter, in a year we'll run up against the same problem. Industry has left us behind. The Ministry of Defense can't become familiar with all aircraft: not all of the pilots can fly the I-16.

Alksnis: If we do produce planes that reach 160 kilometers and hour, there won't be anyone to fly them.

Chkalov: What you mean by 160? 130. Now, while you're mastering fighter planes, understand, the speed will soon be 600. We were late with the I-16, we were left behind.

From the seat: The I-16 plane is defective.

Chkalov: Why? My plane is in good condition.

From the seat: The gas tanks break away.

Chkalov: Inspect them yourselves, check the belts. In 1934 you supposedly mastered the plane, but still said that it was not safe. Stop blaming people. Start studying the equipment, when you're familiar enough with it, there will be no defects in your work. I know the I-16 planes very well. I fly them. I won't have such defects.

Voice from the audience: You're Chkalov, that's why.

Chkalov: Young pilots have to learn more than I did. I think that the instruction in the unit courses of combat training and military preparedness have to be redone in many departments.

A last comment—how to help our commanders in their work. I suggest that, unfortunately, we've worked very little with our commanders and from this stem all of our misfortunes. Our commanders are extremely overloaded. They don't have time to prepare for the flights each day and it's difficult to find a solution to this problem. But find one we must. The commander must be able to work more with his units. Instruction from the center must help the commander master his flight details better than at present.

Secondly, we must strengthen them with good staff. If a commander doesn't have a good staff leader, he is pulled down by a thousand details and, of course, his main responsibilities slip from his hands. This question about staff is extremely important and it must be solved.

We need navigators, and I believe that there is not one in the Air Force who couldn't be turned into a pilot. They are very important and must be reserved for work in the staff.

Voroshilov: There is a suggestion today to end the conference in order that tomorrow we'll be able to open the session at 2:00 p.m., but before 2:00 it would be desirable if a small commission would meet, preferably from the comrades who spoke here today. They could develop practical measures, which could then be read aloud to us and we could add new suggestions or, if the measures have been worked out well, we could accept them as written. Any objections? So ordered.

Comrade Alksnis and all of the comrades who spoke today, and also … the civil aviation comrades—Gromov, Chkalov and others, should take part in the work of this commission. Are there objections? So ordered.

So ended the first day of this important conference at which father showed himself to be no longer a boy, but a man. It should be noted that his emotional, substantive speech received a warm response in the auditorium.

But I quoted from this excerpt of verbatim notes with a different goal. If you analyze father's speech, it becomes very apparent that he was speaking with confidence because he knew the problem, criticized his leaders, and gave suggestions. In his speeches, father was already expressing his old thoughts about special preparation for fighter pilots. He expressed his point of view on providing active help to the commanders in the preparation of their flight staff. He expressed his thoughts about the raising of the qualifications of workers in factories. All this he said frankly in spite of the presence of highly placed Soviet leaders in the hall.

This was the essence of Chkalov. He spoke frankly and to the point. I think that he also behaved this way earlier, pointing out the defects of the leadership, giving suggestions about how they should be working. Perhaps it was this character trait, which called forth the negative evaluations and the wishes of the leadership by whatever route possible to get him out of their hair. It seems to me that the confidence he expressed in his speeches came from the fact that he was describing life as he saw it in his own units, the units in which he served.

Gradually, father was drawn into the political life and his authority grew. Already in November 1936 he was brought in as a member of the newly created soviet under the leadership of the main administration of the USSR's civil aviation and confirmed by the Politburo of the Central Committee of the Communist Party. Besides father, the following leading pilots were brought into this soviet: Hero of the Soviet Union I. T. Slepnev, M. M. Gromov, M. V. Vodopyanov, V. S. Molokov, C. A. Levanevsky, G. F. Baidukov, and also the pilots V. K. Kokkinaki, V. I. Chulkov, N. P. Shebanov, A. G. Shirokova, P. E. Timashev. In March 1938, father was selected member of the Soviet of Aviation under the Defense Department.

In February 1938, he was a member of a commission created by order of the Commissar of Defense and the Commissar of Defense Industry and under the Chairmanship of Mikhail M. Gromov. It was Gromov's job to decide the question of the future production of a huge air ship of the "Maxim Gorky" type. The members of the Soviet Politburo had decided to have such a plane produced and to name each one after a Politburo member.

The commission came to the conclusion that the planes already produced and standing on the airfield of factory #124 in Kazan, were outdated and couldn't be rationally used. The commission therefore considered it necessary to immediately stop production of this plane.

Father was also a member of a commission devoted to the design and production of aircraft at the new Zhukovsky Central Aerohydrodynamic Institute in Moscow (CAHI) and again worked with Gromov and Kokkinaki.

Chkalov and Gromov participated in commission work, which had been assigned by the Defense Commissar and by the Commissar of Defense Industry. It directed them to examine the quality of work being done in factory #21 in the city of Gorky. They were to check pilot knowledge of equipment, piloting techniques, and flight test methods of the flight staff.

I mentioned only a small part of the work in which father took an active part. It should be noted that while working as a test pilot, Chkalov with his friends Georgy F. Baidukov and Alexander V. Belyakov were preparing for distant flights, which they would successfully complete in 1936 in their flight to Udd Island (now Chkalov Island), and in the first transpolar flight across the North Pole to the USA in 1937. After the first long distance flight, Chkalov, Baidukov, and Belyakov were each officially awarded the title of Hero of the Soviet Union. Both of these long distance flights brought them worldwide fame.

More about these long distance flights later, however. I would like now to describe in greater detail the profession of test pilot and look at it through the eyes of Gennady Ashotovich Amiryants, a leading Ph.D. specialist at CAHI, who in his book "Test Pilots" describes in detail these representatives of the profession, including our famous countrymen Artseulov, Gromov, Chkalov, Kokkinaki, Garnaev, Gudkov, Nazaryan, Tolboev, Volk, Kvochur, and many others. G. A. Amiryants turned out to be a marvelous psychologist. He very perceptively and with much feeling described the special characteristics of the members of this wonderful, but extremely dangerous, profession:

"A test pilot is a link in a chain of creation of one of the most developed of contemporary machines, a very unique link. In what does its uniqueness lie? In its people—they are one of a kind... They are unique because of the high level of skill they developed through extensive training. They risk themselves, placing the safety of their plane above their own. Of course, they recognize this and others have spoken of it …

"There is no doubt that an actively working test pilot views life differently than ordinary people, feeling themselves immortal and not imagining the possibility of a sudden end. More understable, perhaps, is the thirst of the best pilots to feel not only the beauty of this high art, but of the simple beauty of the every day, easily destroyed world. The test pilot chooses for himself this difficult to achieve and completely original role of a pioneer. This role is best fulfilled by those who are best prepared and most talented and understand the significance of the natural creative process hidden in the recesses of their consciousness. The best professional test pilots, first of all, have been given a gift of nature. In addition, they have the knowledge gained by having flown a lot, and of having studied the experience of many, many pilots.

"In all of history, there have been such people and there will continue to be such people, who without any rationale and in spite of everything will take on the role of pioneer."

Cosmonaut K. P. Feoktistov was undoubtedly correct, when he stated the following about the work of test pilots: "They have, in my view, the most dangerous work. Not every one, and not during every flight, but, over all, they work in the most "costly" of professions. Not all of its practitioners by far, live to collect their pensions."

Leading test pilot, V. G. Pugachev, the creator of the advanced aerobatic maneuver now called the Pugachev Cobra, on answering a question concerning what is most difficult and dangerous in his profession, had the following to say: "I can say with complete confidence that everything in flight testing is difficult. But what is especially significant and difficult in general, is the fact that one is testing a plane that has taken years of work to develop and is the only one in existence. Being a pilot on that plane is a huge responsibility. And what is most dangerous? As soon as the plane leaves the earth, a special, definite danger descends."

The first person in Russia to take a plane into a descending spin and to come out of it successfully was K. K. Artseulov in 1916. "If you remember," notes Amiryants, "the strictly theoretical explanation of the nature of a spin was given by scientists only 20 years later, so that before this discovery by Artseulov, practically all the pilots who fell into a spin died — and Artseulov performed his historical flight without a parachute (there were no such things at that time). One was especially struck by the intelligence and bravery of this man."

In 1924, A. I. Zhukov, test pilot for factory no. 1, was given the assignment to fly the first Soviet fighter, the I-1 (the first in a series of planes called the IL-400), designed by N. N. Polikarpov.

But Artseulov had tested this plane in 1923. At that time, the plane quickly left the landing strip and sharply ascended. Test pilot Artseulov could not level the plane out and, at a height of only 50-60 feet, the plane made a pancake landing. It struck the earth so hard that the pilot was severely wounded. The plane was almost completely ruined. The whole flight lasted only 21 seconds. Artseulov refused to test this experimental plane of Polikarpov's for a long time, of course, considering it too defective and dangerous for testing. Test pilots have a special feeling for danger.

After the reasons for the crash were descovered, the plane was redesigned and, in the spring of 1924, Zhukov was assigned to test it. They expected high speed, high altitude, and good maneuverability from this plane.

The first test flight Zhukov performed was normal and after that began the detailed, complicated finishing work. On the I-1, Zhukov set a record for altitude, 24,000 feet. The plane demonstrated outstanding speed. It was, however, unstable in its handling and Zhukov was worried they would not be able to bring the plane out of a spin.

On the next test, Zhukov took the plane into a spin. The plane hurdled down, spinning. Zhukov attempted to bring the plane out of its spin, but it refused, continuing to rapidly rotate.

Zhukov's thinking remained clear. Suddenly Zhukov felt a strong pressure on his foot and when the plane's nose rose slightly, he pushed the pedal with all his might and forced the flight lever forward. The rotations suddenly stopped. The nose rose again and the plane began a sharp downward glide. It then smoothly glided down into a landing on the airfield.

The finishing work on the plane continued. In accordance with the government test program, Zhukov was to make the final test flight. In summarizing the plane's behavior while performing various aerobatic figures, Zhukov came to the conclusion that the plane could not relialbly exit from a downward spiral.

Though he made this report to the facory's director, it was decided to continue testing, but with a different pilot, Mikhail M. Gromov.

It was June 23, 1927. Gromov was ordered to wear the newly invented parachute, which had never been used to that time by anyone in our country. Gromov took the plane into a slow, protracted downward spiral, which unexpectedly turned into a strange, never before experienced spin — the so-called flat spin. Gromov tried everything in order to save the plane, but nothing worked. The plane crashed, and Gromov became the first person in our country to successfully use a parachute and saved his life in the process.

The I-1, however, was lost. As a result of much further testing, it was considered too dangerous for flight and the Air Force refused to accept the remaining 30 copies.

Chkalov wrote that, "The determination of a plane's tendency to enter into, and its ease of exit from, the downward spiral is the final and most significant stage of testing."

It wasn't until 1938 that test pilot, V. V. Rastorguev, successfully worked out a method for exiting the flat spin.

Among contemporary aircraft, there are some, which enter a downward spin with difficulty and exit it easily — but there are others. It's not by chance that test pilot Yury Garnaev considers the spin even today to be the most dangerous problem to confront test pilots. Research into the spin performed in aerodynamic tunnels and its theoretical analysis does not always provide full and reliable information. Therefore, the final evaluation concerning the tendancy of newly designed contemporary planes to fall into, and to exit, a spin is left to the test program and the test pilot.

In June 1940, test pilots, Suprun and Stefanovsky, tested the LaGG-3 in a government-testing program. Suprun, a leading test pilot, was convinced that his fighter was unstable in flight and landing it was dangerous. He took this information to the engineer and said, "Landing this piece of work, say what you will, is like kissing a tigress: its dangerous and provides absolutely no pleasure." Suprun was a witty fellow and could be very exact in his expressions, and he hated to write reports.

Chkalov many times tested planes with problems of retraction and release of the landing gear. A crash landing is inevitable without a landing gear. Landing on one wheel also would mean destruction of the aircraft. Father remembered one incident with a faulty landing gear. "In my flight, the landing gear would not release. It was later discovered that the latch, which secures the landing gear was separated from the cable and prevented the wheels' release. The situation was hopeless. Since the latch was located in the center of the fuselage, approximately at the base of the steering mechanism, I couldn't reach it with my hand.

"Not wanting to destroy the plane, I decided to increase my altitude and fly away from the city. I unbuckled the safety belts and crawled into the center of the fuselage in order to reach the latch. Having gained an altitude of 6,000 feet, I left my seat and allowed the plane to free fall in any way it wished and crawled to the center of the fuselage to get to the latch. Feeling it with my hand, I opened it and in that open position I pressed hard with my foot. I crawled back out of the fuselage, sat in the seat, brought the plane to level flight, and lowered the landing gear. In this operation, I lost 1,200 feet. The plane during this time was falling erratically, but I was able to land the plane successfully."

In 1933, a documentary film crew from France came to Moscow to make a documentary entitled "The Aviator." The film was to be about an ace—an aviator of advanced aerobatics and of whom there was no equal in the world. The French considered that pilot to be Alexander Frolovich Anisimov, who headed the fighter group for the Army's Air Force Research Institute.

Anisimov was the best friend of Valery Chkalov, although he was seven years his senior. Alexander Anisimov and Valery Chkalov were born to be pilots. But each of them possessed their own special flying characteristics—brilliant, with matchless ability.

In order to record Anisimov's performance on film, the French had signed a contract in the USSR the year before, but now in Moscow the Air Force Command reneged. "Anisimov is forbidden at the present time to demonstrate flights, but we will fulfill our promise by supplying you with another pilot." The French film representative, Louis Chaubert, vigorously opposed this action. As a result, the air command allowed Anisimov to perform several demonstration flights on October 10, 1933. For his flights, Anisimov chose the I-5, a light, maneuverable fighter with a top speed of about 200 miles per hour. He had tested this plane himself and he loved it.

For the cameras, Anisimov worked at an unusually low altitude, with a program so intricate and risky that the French film operators, who were experienced at filming various head-turning aerobatic tricks, at times forgot about their filming and stared with open mouths in dumb-founded admiration.

When the I-5, close to the earth and camera crew, roared into a steep climb, the wind from the propellers swept the thin, tall Louis Chaubert off his feet; his hat was blown from his head and never found. But the film representative was not offended. In the evening after the first day of filming, he presented the pilot with a Swiss watch with his personal monogram. They asked Anisimov to give them his Russian leggings. On the second day, Anisimov was to finish work with the film crew.

Chkalov arrived at the airfield when Anisimov was performing his third dive for the camera. He watched as Anisimov pulled the plane from its dive and went into a half loop in which the plane at its apex turned on its head with its wheels pointing skyward, prepared to complete the Immelman figure, but Anisimov's plane, exiting from the top of the loop, froze in the upside down position and started falling rapidly. Chkalov broke into a run, seeing nothing but the I-5 falling straight down with its wheels pointing upward. "Pull out, pull out! Hit it with your leg, hit it with your foot, hard! Your foot!" cried Chkalov, gasping for breath, beside himself.

But the plane did not even begin to turn on its wing, but crashed on the landing field in the same position, with the wheels pointing skyward.

The Accident Commission concluded, "The catastrophe occurred because the foot pedal of the steering mechanism broke, which, of course, made it impossible to right the plane at such low altitude." I think that this film still exists, taken on October 11, 1933, which captured the death of our remarkable pilot, Alexander Anisimov.

Even in our time—1995—from Amiryants' book: "At the 38th annual Le Bourget Airshow, test pilot Anatoly Mikhailovich Kvochur demonstrated the MIG 29. After performing some impressive figures, the barrel roll, sharp turns, loops, and the famous 'bell,' the audience was stunned by the most simple, ordinary horizontal flight at a height of little more than 300 feet, but at an extremely slow speed, much slower than was allowed ordinary pilots. At a certain point, the pilot was to start his engine at full power and begin from essentially zero altitude to a sharp vertical climb. Unexpectedly, however, the plane's nose simply rose a bit, started to fall off to the right, and, in three or four seconds, the plane took a very unnatural position: very close to the earth with its nose pointing downward.

"On the flight field, thousands of observers held their breath. In the course of seven seconds, an event occurred which was later described as a miracle. At that extremely low altitude, about 270 feet, the pilot catapulted out and the plane crashed at a spot free from observers. A sharp explosion was heard and the crowd saw the parachute open over the falling pilot. Rescuers were at the plane in a minute. It's unbelievable, but no one was hurt.

"Kvochur was asked at CAHI what he thought and what he felt in a second, a minute, an hour, a day, and a month about the accident after the engines refused to start in that demonstration flight at Le Bourget when he was forced to catapult out. Anatoly Kvochur answered,' A second after the first indications of the engines' refusal, I was relatively calm and there was no indication there would be an accident. I was firmly convinced that the engines would start and I would be able to pull out of the problem and perhaps no one would notice it as a close call.

"'Later I felt disappointment, and a sense of responsibility: Disappointment because this happened to our plane at such a prestigious air show. Responsible because it happened with me as the pilot. A second after the fall, I felt great happiness and surprise. In a minute, when the plane was burning and the rescue workers were near by, I shook my arms and legs and recognized I would live, but probably not very well, considering I was the pilot. In an hour? After an hour, I was feeling much better. In the hospital, in Paris, I saw some girls and realized I would live, and that perhaps life wouldn't be so bad after all. After a day, they released me from the hospital and I realized I could walk—that I was walking. It was at about this time that I recognized an internal psychological challenge—the need to fly! In a week, this need strengthened. In a month, however, some doubts began to arise, but they turned out to be short-lived.'"

The outstanding test pilot, Yury Garnaev, tells of how he exited a burning, falling helicopter just seconds before it exploded. The door had wedged shut and Garnaev had to crawl along a norrow passage to the escape hatch, and, as luck would have it, something caught on his flight suit. By the time he freed himself from the plane and his chute opened, he was only about 600 feet above ground. The next day, when they were discussing what they had just lived through, the fear involved, Garnaev stated: "There was no fear. There was simply no time to be a coward. The fear came later, at night, as I was tossing and turning in bed."

The flight test pilot V. Nazaryan tells about was one of his first on the Yak-VVP. Before taking off, Nazaryan felt an unusual jolt. It turned out the pneumatic left landing gear was severely damaged. On hearing the news, ground control began a lengthy search for a solution. Finally, in his earphones, he heard his call letters and an order: "Two—fifty! It will be necessary for you to fly over the firing range and exit the plane!" Surprised, Nazaryan demanded the order be repeated. A very firm voice replied: "Valya, don't worry about the plane. The order is simple. Fly into the zone and jump! All emergeny crews have been alerted!"

Nazaryan flew into the rear of the firing range, turned on the automatic pilot system and performed several other preparatory actions, necessary for catapulting free of the plane. When the time came, Nazaryan pressed himself hard against the back of the catapulting seat, closed his eyes and pulled sharply on the appropriate lever. Instead of the expected jerk and following tornado, there was only the feeling that something strange had happened. He opened his eyes and saw a light on the cabin panel. His chest belt had pulled tight as it was supposed to, but the firing mechanism, which was to propel the pilot and his chair high into the air and safely over the plane's tail fin, which was necessary to release the parachute, had failed.

The firing charge could explode at any time, including at a most dangerous point. He lowered the undamaged part of the landing gear, most importantly, the forward section. All his attention and anxiety were concentrated on one thing only: that the plane not flip onto its back. But this was really out of his control.

During the most crucial seconds, Nazaryan recalled how he was the one who had taken similar bad news to the wives and children of his friends. Much of his life flashed through his mind. But it was as if the plane decided to take pity on its pilot, came down on its broken landing gear…and slid to a stop …successfully! A deathly silence ensued. A silence Nazaryan says he has never since experience. It was unbelievable! But his ordeal was not over. Shutting down the system, he prepared to leave the plane. This was extremely dangerous, since the firing charge could explode at any moment, catapulting him into the air and probable death. He carefully disconnected his chest belts, then his leg belts, then, with extreme care, crawled over the plane's side…and jumped free!

He was asked later, "Were you frightened?"

"Of course," he answered. "It was a very frightening situation. Fear is a natural reaction of a man to the unknown."

I have quoted these excerpts from Amiryants' book in order that the pilots themselves, having miraculously escaped death, could explain how they felt; what they were thinking; and, in those final, crucial seconds, what they did to try to save themselves.

Representatives of this dangerous profession often experience a premonition of danger. Nazaryan, as he was striding along his cruiser's deck to his Yak-VVP, for this first attempt to take off with such a short run, suddenly felt this foreboding feeling. It's possible that Chkalov felt such hesitation, as he was about to test the experimental I-180, which eventually cost him his life. Doubts overcame Nazaryan, but the plane had gone through such lengthy and successful preparatory work... But most importantly, the government had entrusted to him what it considered a significant testing program.

K. K. Artseulov refused to test a Polikarpov designed experimental plane. Garnaev refused to test a plane, taking off from the ground on skiis. They both considered several of the designer's decisions as being mistaken and too dangerous for the test pilot. But when the plane's creator insists on flight-testing, they did not want to transfer these tests to anyone else, knowing that the probability of failure for others would be greater than their own. Both of these pilots came within a hair's breath of death.

Valery Chkalov wrote: "Through my own special mistakes, I felt out the correct and only route a pilot can and must take: He should risk himself and his plane only when absolutely necessary and only in the interests of testing objectives."

Always after a catastrophe we conjecture for the pilot, give our opinions about what he did and what he must have been thinking. But worst of all is when we censure him, not having been in his situation. This is what happened to Valery Chkalov and to his plane, the I-180. But more about this later.

"The best pilots," continues Amiryants, "are surprisingly versatile and talented people. They are a part of that spirit, that code of life, of actions — unwritten, but created and imbedded in the fate of many test pilots. They include not only the great, the legendary, but also those not able, perhaps, to become the best; and, in any event, they make their considerable contribution as representatives of this prestigious, mysterious, barely attainable phenomenon—test pilot.

They are phenomenal, not because among them there are no weak people and, certainly, not because they are all honorable, selfless, and sinless. No, of course not, that's far from the truth. But, basically, at their core, these are people of the first order, and they are more modest, perhaps, than the people of any other profession. Their best examples are genuine knights, not only in the sky, but also on earth, which is just as difficult."

M. L. Gallai very correctly identified the main quality of the test pilot profession: "As distinct from the contribution of artists, writers, and composers, who are obligated to be unique, the contribution of test pilots makes sense and has the right to exist only in the event that it will not be unique, but repeatable, reproducible."

Valery Chkalov said that, "A plane doesn't recognize the authority of anyone who doesn't strictly observe the laws of flight."

Faith in the reliability of the test pilot is absolutely necessary to all who follow him.

Danilov recounts the following: "At the beginning of 1928 I was transferred from being a reconnaissance pilot to a fighter squadron. Saying goodbye to my R-1, I entered the fighter plane hangar. The commander gave me the right to choose any plane I wanted from those that were free and kept in reserve. It was difficult for me to choose; I couldn't decide which plane was best.

"Unexpectedly, Valery Chkalov entered the hangar. We greeted each other and shared the news of the day. Realizing that I was trying to choose my plane, Valery Pavlovich told me that in the next few days he would be leaving the squadron and, therefore, advised me to take his plane. Smiling, he added, 'You can rest easy. She'll hold up well.' And he struck the wing's cantilever with his fist and directed my attention to the opposite wing. It was repeating exactly the vibrations of the first wing. In such a simple way he demonstrated the hardness and strength of those wings. 'On this plane,' continued Valery Pavlovich, 'I flew pretty well and gave it quite a work-out.'

"And so I chose Valery P. Chkalov's plane. After making several get acquainted flights, I received an order to fly into the advanced aerobatics performance zone. During my effort to complete these figures, acceptable for an experienced fighter plane, but difficult for a beginning pilot (barrel roll with two turns), the plane's tail began to slip and float. There was enough altitude, but I have to frankly say that I felt a bit ill and a thought flashed through my mind: Is this plane going to hold up? Will it right itself? And directly after that thought, another: It'll hold up. After all, this was Chkalov's plane. And, really, after a few seconds, the plane regained its equilibrium. Again, and this time with more confidence, I repeated the earlier failed figures, taking my mistake into account. And as long as I flew this plane after that time, I never lost confidence in its strength and stability because it had been tested by Chkalov.

"… During the whole of my long life in aviation, I often met with those who flew fighter planes that had been tested at various factories by Valery P. Chkalov. These pilots always believed in their planes, which received their start in life from the intelligent hands of Valery Pavlovich."[4]

HOW IT ALL BEGAN

Russia and aviation cannot live without each other. The bond is almost mystical. The reason is not only because of the vastness and expanse of our country, its endless space, but also because from ancient times our roads have always been poor or non-existent. The absence of roads is a Russian tradition. How do you build a road from the west to the east, across the endless Siberian taiga, through swamps, across rivers, over mountains, and through the forests of the far east? How do you get to Nikolaevsk on the Amur River, by the Sea of Okhotsk. Getting to the farthest reaches of our country is possible only by airplane or helicopter. That is the only way to tie them to the center, to make them active participants in the life of our country. The huge expanse of Russia with her geographic and geodetic uniqueness makes our homeland in essence an aviation power.[1]

In the search for harmony and perfection in the Russian man, aviation plays an essential role. This is probably why the enigmatic, romantic, incomprehensible Russian soul has turned the airplane into an almost cult-like object. In something like 10 hours, you can be in Khabarovsk. And as you fly over our tremendous expanse, the soul is paralyzed with enchantment from the perception of the immensity of our homeland, from its beauty, seen through the window of the airplane.

In 2001 I was again fortunate to be on Chkalov Island, about which I'll write more later. I would like now, however, to write of the miracle I

1   From the Western borders of Russia to its Kamchatka Peninsula, Russia covers 11 time zones.

witnessed on the flight. We flew toward the east and saw a rising sun. It was so beautiful I spent the whole night without sleep.

The plane flew over clouds at the usual altitude of about 30,000 feet. The horizon began to turn rose colored, then crimson, and suddenly, somewhere beneath us in the clouds, our heavenly body, the sun, appeared. It hadn't, it seemed, fully awakened, and didn't shine with its usual intensity. It appeared as an orange ball, swimming in clouds. It was still small, a bit larger than a soccer ball, and seemed so defenseless—this powerful, enigmatic, heavenly body, earlier worshiped by our ancestors. I looked down on this miracle, with eyes wide open in amazement. I forgot all about my camera, not taking my eyes off the sun in fear I would miss that moment when it would awaken and shine in all its glory. It slowly rose higher and higher, and became larger and brighter with every minute. Suddenly it burst from the clouds and shone in all its glory—a new day had begun! Now where, and how else, could one see such beauty?

The Russian field of aviation has never known stagnation. Many indicators show us this is so, and even to this day we have no equal in the world. At the same time, undoubtedly, the 1930s was a golden era in the development of our national aviation. Even today, the non-stop transpolar flight from Moscow across the North Pole to America accomplished by the crew of Valery Chkalov, Georgy Baidukov, and Alexander Belyakov on the plane ANT-25 is considered a break-through to the 21st century, as was the world record for distance across the North Pole established by Mikhail Gromov, Andrei Yumashev, and Sergei Danilin.

The more a country is subject in history to fateful events, the weightier its contribution seems to be to mankind's more glorious achievements. It was in this spirit that the triumphs of our great countrymen brought the people of Russia and America closer. It is possible to relate to the history of one's country in different ways. But the fact remains: Only world powers have the wherewithal to accomplish such deeds.

THE BIRTH OF THE ANT-25

It was in the 1930s that the design bureau headed by Andrei Nikolaevich Tupolev worked on the creation of a plane destined to set a world record for distance. It was identified by the letters RD (record distance) or the ANT-25. In 1931, our aviation industry created a new motor, the M-34, which gave Tupolev the base on which to build a plane to achieve record distances. On the basis of his early calculations, Tupolev was given the green light to attempt the construction of such a plane. According to his calculations, CAHI could build this plane with the following characteristics:

Flight weight	11 tons
Flying time	80 hours
Flight distance (theoretical)	8,000 miles
Flight distance (practical)	7,500 miles
Crew size	3 persons

The Soviet government, having heard a report from the head of the Russian Air Force, Y. I. Alksnis, about the design of a plane for long distance flight, December 7, 1931, passed a decree about the construction in CAHI of a special single engine plane that would break the world's long distance record. The plane would be designed by Anton Nikolaevich Tupolev and be named the ANT-25, using his initials. There would be just two planes built and the new Soviet motor designed by A. A. Mikulin, the M-34R, with a projected range of 8,125 miles. CAHI would guaranty a distance of 6,000 miles without reduction gear and 6,500 miles with the reduction gear. The plane was to be completed by the summer of 1932; that is, in approximately six months. Such was the decision of our government.

The above figures were determined by the fact that in 1931 the world record for long distance flights was 5,041 miles and was set by the American pilots Boardman and Pollander on the plane "Bellanka Peacemaker" from New York to Istanbul. Therefore, the projected plane was to provide a guarantied distance of 6,500 miles.

The work proceeded in three directions: the creation of the plane, improving the parameters of the motor (that is, the creation of a record producing motor), and the construction of an appropriate landing strip, which we didn't have at that time.

However, it was only on June 1, 1932 that the creation of the new plane began, which, in spite of the decision of the government, stretched into 1933. On June 13, 1933, the plane was completed. Anton N. Tupolev said, "The building of this plane was a bold adventure." There was much new in this plane:

- A new retraction mechanism for the landing gear was installed.
- It was the first plane to use disc wheels.

- A very bold decision solved the problem of fuel storage. Fuel was poured directly into the wings of the plane, which had been built in the form of cisterns, which filled the role of gas tanks. Each cistern placed inside the wings was divided into impenetrable partitions in separate compartments. The fuel was fed to the engine in a special sequence.
- The wingspan was to be the longest in the world at that time, just short of 112 feet. At first the wings were covered with corrugated Duraluminum. All planes in the 1920s and 1930s were built this way. The corrugated form gave the wings their strength. But such wings actually slowed the plane since the powerful wind flow from the engine produced resistance and required more fuel to cover each mile. But since the time allowed to build the plane had already been extended, there was no possibility of rebuilding the wings. The solution they found was a stroke of genius. They covered the corrugated wings with a tightly drawn, light canvas cover.
- A new Soviet motor, the M-34, was installed in the plane, which produced 750 to 900 horsepower and produced fuel economy unheard of at that time (on the average, 202 liters per hour instead of the 222 to 230 liters per hour used by foreign aircraft).

The whole plane was built from Russian materials.

On June 14, 1933, the plane was transported to an airfield. It took its first flight on June 22. So a new, unique plane was born on that date, having been completed, essentially, in one year's time.

And what should one say of inspiration and enthusiasm? To bring to life such a surprising creation of the human mind in so short a time, and with the rather low technological level of production equipment then available, could only be possible with the enthusiasm and inspiration of the people involved; with a high level of devotion and love for their work.

Having built the first plane in August, 1932, CAHI began construction of a twin, second, ANT-25. When the second ANT-25 was finished, it differed from the first only in that it had a reduction gear installed and a different steering mechanism. Eventually, both planes were identically equipped.

On September 1, 1933, M. M. Gromov completed several test flights on this second, twin, ANT-25, and made a series of comments to improve streamlining the plane. As a result, the plane's wings and tail assembly were covered with a light and tightly drawn canvas. The whole plane was given several coats of lacquer and the front edges of the wings and the propeller were vigorously polished. This elaborate finishing work extended well into 1934.

As a result of this work, the ANT-25 had an advantage over foreign planes. Its flight weight was 24,200 lbs., as opposed to 16,720 lbs of the record holding French Bleriot Aircraft. Its speed was 164 miles per hour, compared to the 140 mph of Bleriot. It was concluded that the ANT-25 could cover the distance necessary to set a new world distance record.

Commander, M. M. Gromov, pilot-engineer, A. I. Filin, and navigator, I. T. Spirin, set a world record for distance in a closed circle flight on September 12-15, 1934, in the second ANT-25.

On September 12, 1934, at 8:00 in the morning, the plane took off from a new cement runway at Shchelkovo Airfield. The basic planned route was a triangle, from Moscow to Tula to Ryazan and back to Moscow. A second triangle was planned in case of bad weather, and was also staffed with observers.

On September 14, due to worsening weather, the crew was given an order to fly to the south and to continue the triangle in the Kharkov region. On September 15, 1934, at 11:00 a.m., the plane landed in Kharkov, having covered 8, 274 miles in 75 hours.

The Gromov crew had broken the world record of 7,067 miles set in March 1932 by the French pilots, Bossoutrot and Rossi, in the Bleriot 110. For this flight, Mikhail M. Gromov was awarded the title of Hero of the Soviet Union.

This was the first christening in "battle" of the ANT-25. It was now necessary to break the distance record in a straight line, which was established in August 1933 by the French pilots Codes and Rossi, having flown from Paris to Rayak, Syria, 5,657 miles in 76 hours on the Bleriot 110. Two different routes were suggested for the possible record-breaking flight in a straight line, Khabarovsk to Dakar (the west coast of Africa), 9,000 miles, or Moscow to South America.

Fate, however, was to decide differently.

LENANEVSKY'S FAILED TRANSPOLAR ATTEMPT

On January 19, 1935, Hero of the Soviet Union S. A. Levanevsky, who had participated in the expedition to save the people trapped on the steamship Cheluskin, wrote a letter to the editor of Pravda in which he suggested completing a non-stop transpolar flight from Moscow to San Francisco in 1935. He wrote, "The goals of this flight would be as follows: First, to establish a long distance record in a straight line. Second, to make the first non-stop flight across the North Pole. Third, to establish the shortest route between two important and large world centers. Fourth, to research and map the unknown areas of the North Polar Basin. Fifth, to demonstrate the achievements of the Soviet aviation industry … ."

It was suggested that Levanevsky take the route from Moscow "straight along the meridian [approximately 37 degrees] to the North Pole and from the Pole along the meridian [approximately 122 degrees] to San Francisco. The approximate distance of the route would be 6,500 miles. The distance from Moscow to San Francisco across the Atlantic Ocean is approximately 9,300 miles. Across Siberia and the Pacific Ocean is 12,000 miles."

This was a daring and risky proposition since the North Polar region was completely unknown. Attempts to master it had usually ended in failure. No one had yet flown across the North Pole.

It should be noted that in 1914 a Russian naval pilot, Lieutenant Yan Iosifovich Nagursky, was the first to fly a plane in the skies of the arctic.

In the summer of 1914, the steamship "Pechora" sailed from the port of Alexandrovsk-on-Murman with a hydroplane, the "Morris Farman," on board. The plane only weighed 990 pounds and could carry only 600 pounds. It had a motor with 70 horsepower and could fly only 65 miles per hour. The Pechora landed an expedition on the shores of Novaya Zemlya Island.

Together with mechanic, Yevgeny Vladimirovich Kusnetsov, Nagursky completed five flights, and spent about 11 hours in the air, extending at one point to 65 miles from shore.

Later, Nagursky described his flights: "The equipment I used was most primitive. There was no cabin. Over us hung an unknown sky; an unknown wind was blowing in an unresearched arctic airflow… To fly in arctic regions, though difficult, is very possible.

"Aviation in the future will be of great service in the study, description and mapping of oceans, lakes, and rivers….

"Past expeditions attempting to reach the North Pole were unsuccessful, because they underestimated the strength and endurance necessary to traverse thousands of miles of arctic territory filled with many barriers and in the most difficult of situations. Aviation, allowing for a tremendously fast method of movement, is the only solution to this problem."

Considering the seriousness of such a transpolar flight, the government took strict control of its preparations. It passed a series of resolutions: January 26, 1935: A Resolution of the Politburo of the Central Committee of the Communist Party; February 28, 1935: A Resolution of the Soviet of Labor and Defense. Both of the resolutions called for the ANT-25 to complete the transpolar flight in July, 1935.

Levanevsky's suggested project was sent by People's Commissar, V. V. Kuibyshev, to the famous polar explorer, O. Y. Schmidt, for evaluation. Schmidt sent his evaluation in a letter to the Soviet of People's Commissars on February 2, 1935.

Schmidt's conclusions were negative: "…The basic idea of the flight, apparently, is to demonstrate our aviation, because future international flights will be going not over the pole, but along the shore of the Arctic Ocean. This route won't be much farther, but more convenient and safe, since by 1936 we will have prepared and equipped it with support stations and personnel….

"…In case of success, of course, this flight will demonstrate the achievements of Soviet aviation, although the world press will not likely write much about it. But in the case of very possible misfortune, an exceptionally difficult situation would arise. In talking to comrade Alksnis about the flight, he informed me that he believed the flight had a 50% chance of success.

"In the event of misfortune, we won't be able to limit ourselves to merely ascertaining that Levanevsky didn't arrive at his destination, but we will, apparently launch an all-out effort to save him, or, at least, find where he went down.

"On the whole route, not only over the Arctic Ocean (north of France Joseph and Shpitsbergen Islands), but on American islands and in north Canada, there are no radio stations, let alone aircraft. The hunt for Levanevsky in case of a forced landing or accident will be an immeasurably more difficult operation than the rescue of the Cheliuskin survivors (from their camp to Vankarem was 100 miles and the closest base to a

Levanevsky misfortune would be about 1,300 miles)[2]. It would be necessary to organize an air operation on Canadian territory and in places much less populated than our Chukotka. This would be both technically and politically very difficult. Our icebreakers cannot overcome the "polar pack" of especially hard ice, which covers the whole central part of the Arctic Ocean (north of 82-85 degrees).

Due to these reasons, if the probability of the success of Levanevsky's flight is 50%, then the probability of getting help to him in case of an accident is close to zero.

A failure to help a downed Levanevsky would not only be a loss of a great pilot and hero, but a huge moral blow to the USSR in the eyes of the whole world.

I, therefore, believe it my duty to speak out against Levanevsky's proposed flight in its present form."

The letter was rather sharp and frank. I quoted from it specifically in order to help the reader understand the difficult political and physical conditions of the proposed flight. In his letter, Schmidt suggested a less risky route for the establishment of the long distance record, specifically: Moscow-Bering Strait-Alaska-Seattle-San Francisco.

The resolutions were passed, however, and preparations for the flight began. Red Army Air Force Chief Alksnis was given full responsibility for the technical preparation of the plane for the flight. In his February 17, 1935 report to Alksnis, Levanevsky suggested preparing two crews: navigators V. I. Levchenko and A. V. Belyakov, pilots G. F. Baidukov and V. M. Gurevich. Baidukov and Levchenko were included in the main crew.

Levanevsky chose the second ANT-25(2) for the flight. That is, he chose the same plane that Gromov in 1934 set a world long distance record in, flying in a closed circle. The plane was to undergo a series of changes and improvements, according to Levanevsky.

---

2   In July 1933, the first polar expedition along the Northern Sea Route was undertaken. Toward the end of the journey, the steamship Cheliuskin drifted into the Chukotka Sea, which was filling with ice. The ship was not an icebreaker and, in February 1934, was crushed by the freezing ice and sank. The crew and the scientific personnel left the ship, but were stranded on the ice. Soviet polar pilots made a desperate rescue effort to evacuate more than a hundred adults and two children from the shifting ice field. Seven pilots, who were later decorated as Heroes of the Soviet Union, accomplished this rescue mission.

Following are some of the changes in the ANT-25(2) that made it different from the plane that broke the world record in 1934: the ailerons were rebuilt, a new steering wheel was installed, wing radiators were removed, there was a new water tunnel radiator, a new system for heating the cabin, equipment for heating the carburetor, a three-bladed metal propeller, new strengthened wheels, the plane was recovered with canvas and painted, the cabin was warmed with a special upholstery.

The motor supports and steering mechanism were re-built, and new oil and fuel tanks installed. A new instrument panel with new instruments was installed in the cabin, and the portable radio transmitter was mounted and placed differently. Air cylinders were installed in the plane to keep it afloat in the event of a forced landing on water.

One can say with assurance, that CAHI, under the direction of Tupolev, had very carefully prepared this ANT-25 for its dangerous and difficult flight.

By May 5, 1935, all the plane's improvements were completed. On May 23rd, Levanevsky completed his first two flights. On July 9th, began a long 17hour training flight. The plane took off from Shchelkovo Airfield at 3:30 A.M., intending to fly from Moscow to the Berents Sea and back to Moscow. Poor weather conditions, however, forced the plane to change routes, which covered 2000 miles: Moscow — Beloserye — Moscow — Kupyansk — Slavyansk — Moscow.

As a result of all the testing, it was determined that this plane's flying qualities had much improved over the 1934 model. The estimates now were: Distance improved by 7%; Altitude by 265 feet; average speed by 8%.

Such positive estimates convinced them to allow Levanevsky, and the ANT-25(2), to begin his proposed flight across the North Pole to America on August 3, 1935, at 6:05 A. M.

In a letter to Stalin from Defense Commissar, K. E. Voroshilov, dated August 3rd, he mentions Levanevsky's take off, and notes that the weather was "disgusting"; constant rain, sometimes turning into cloud bursts. Among those at the airfield to watch this historic departure were the American Air Attaché, Feymonvill, Bullitt[3], and 12 foreign journalists.

And what was the goal of this flight? Perhaps it was to establish a

---

3   Valeria Chkalova is referring to William C. Bullitt, first American Ambassador to the Soviet Union, 1934-1936.

long distance record in a straight line, but in the documents I found, there was no mention of its registration with the FAI.

After only four hours of flight, at 10:20 a.m., a radiogram was received from the crew: "Oil pressure is falling, reasons unknown." At 10:40: "Oil is leaking from the system."

After 10 hours of flight, and having flown to the Berents Sea, Levanevsky decided to turn back and land in Leningrad due to the severe oil leak from the drainage tube of the active oil tank. However, the plane was forced to land in Krechevitsy in the Novgorod Region. During the landing, a fire broke out from the accidental ignition of a landing flare, and damaged the plane's right wing. On August 5th, repairs were completed and the plane took off for Moscow.

The contemplated, grandiose, polar flight ended in failure.

The minutes of the meeting of the Politburo of the Communist Party, August 20, 1935, contains the following: "Concerning cancellation of comrade Levanevsky's 1935 flight: In view of the fact that repairs of the oil system have been delayed, and time has run out, comrade Levanevsky's flight for this year has been postponed."

But the possibility of completing the world's first flight over the North Pole was very seductive; therefore, Defense Commissar K. E. Voroshilov authorized that a proposal be discussed and presented to the Politburo concerning the organization of a flight from Moscow over the North Pole to San Francisco in 1936.

O. Y. Schmidt was authorized to write an announcement to TACC representatives containing the official government point of view concerning the failed flight. This had to be done, because Levanevsky's flight was rather widely known throughout the world, and as a result the Soviet Union was put in an awkward position.

The official view was a follows: "...Technical experts, after having examined the plane, established that the plane had no construction defects, however, they found several inadequacies in the working oil feed system. The commission confirmed the crew's decision to terminate the flight of aircraft, "USSR 025." CAHI, in the course of several days, eliminated the insufficiency of the oil system after which Comrade Levanevsky completed a series of successful test flights.

"Weather observations continued unabated over the USSR and America. From these observations came weather forecasts that indicated the impossibility at the present time to again plan for this important flight. Also, the middle of August is the latest possible time for flights across the Pole. Fall is the time of extreme difficulty for polar aviation in general, and for such a flight as this especially...

"The only decision left for us was to postpone the flight of Comrade Levanevsky until the summer of 1936."

This article was sufficiently convincing and scientifically based.

On December 28, 1935, Levanevsky wrote a letter to Stalin that could have significantly influenced all future flights across the North Pole on the ANT-25.

In this letter, Levanevsky expressed his point of view concerning the reasons for his failed flight: "From the moment of the postponed flight, there will be five months. The perspective for a flight in 1936 is not clear. Relative to the failed flight of 1935, there were rumors spread by several people that the crew supposedly became afraid and threw the oil around, etc. Its characteristic that before this these people also spread rumors that we were engaging in unnecessarily hazardous adventurism, etc.

"With complete confidence, I assert that this is a lie.

"Concerning our 'cowardice,' during the time of the plane's testing, there occurred several catastrophic events in the air. For example, the support stabilizers broke, from negligence, due to the fact that in place of 14 rivets they had installed only six. However, after a forced repair, we again took to the air in spite of terrible weather. Even the head of CAHI announced that the plane had never been tested in such conditions.

"Relative to our 'throwing oil,' after our landing at Krechevitsy, it was discovered that the oil in the active tank was only slightly more than half full; the loss of oil continued until the moment of our landing. Concerning the charge of 'adventurism,' all opinions about the impossibility of the flight relative to navigation and high altitude atmospheric phenomena failed, since a series of observations completely supported the proof I presented to my critics in 1935.

"This, of course, does not speak to the simplicity of the flight. If there hadn't been any difficulty in it, I wouldn't have asked you to examine the project and, concerning its difficulty, enough has been said. I consider the reason for the failure of the flight in 1935 to be: the careless attitude toward the preparation of the plane from the leadership of CAHI. The government and the Commissar of Heavy Industry ordered them to finish the plane by a certain date, which they failed to do; in addition, work by the construction staff was poorly thought through.

"From the history of preparations of significant flights, we have the example of the American Lindberg. His head engineer stood over his drafting desk in the factory for 36 hours. However, in CAHI, the head engineer, if he was interested in the progress of the plane's preparation, would ask questions, not knowing the significance of this or that key element. It's enough that the CAHI's main designer was only once in the plane, and that was after the forced landing at Krechevitsy. Defense Commissar, comrade Voroshilov, who has many other duties, studied and understands each of the plane's key elements in more detail.

"To all the questions concerning the reliability of this or that system, there was always one answer: The plane had just flown 75 non-stop hours. However, if we speak of "the oil issue" – in 1934 the tanks were filled up with castor oil, which didn't foam. After return from Krechevits to Moscow, they were 'thinking' from August 6 to 14 at CAHI and then discovered a problem with the diagram of the oil circuit. However, this problem wasn't solved, and it was decided to fill the tank 2/3 full and to pump the oil out and back while in flight. Thus, in CAHI they decided on a substitute technique with an unskilled laborer, whose only role during the flight was to pump the oil using a wobble pump. For this, CAHI suggested taking a fourth man on board.

"Having reported the above to you personally in a letter (although very short) about the reasons for the failure in 1935, I turn to you, comrade Stalin, with a request to assign the start of the flight to be in May, 1936. (Navigational conditions will make the flight possible from the last 10 days in April. I believe the atmospheric conditions in May will be essentially no different in comparison with the summer months.)

"What will be necessary to complete the flight in May, 1936?
1. To immediately begin creation of a well thought out oil-feed system and to evaluate the function of other systems and accessories in low temperatures.
2. Since I'm asking you to assign the flight for May, it would be desirable to once again examine the atmospheric phenomena in the Arctic during the winter months for important analysis concerning the probable meteorological conditions during

166

spring and the first half of summer. It is intended that the R-6 aircraft complete a flight from Moscow to Franze-Joseph Island in February or March for this purpose, about which I have in detail informed Defense Commissar, comrade Voroshilov.

"I turn to you directly, since, in spite of the fact that I have made every effort to contact the head of the air force, I have been unable to speak with him, even by telephone. I've heard, it's true, that comrade Alksnis is involved in some project he's put together; but, even so, a decision is necessary so that I may begin work. On the eve of my flight, many shook my hand and wished me success. I understand, of course, that this related to the project, which I was to complete, and not to me personally. And now I have managed to arrange a meeting and report, again, not about me personally, but about the project, which apparently interested them.

"I know, comrade Stalin, that only with your help will I be able to complete the flight during the first half of 1936; of course not because people will shake my hand or wish me a happy journey, and not for any personal interests. My only interest is to fully justify the words you spoke to me on June 21, 1934, in the Kremlin.

"A flight over the pole is completely realistic; of this we have no doubt. The crew is prepared to complete this mission no matter what."

What are we to make of this letter? CAHI's head engineer; chief designer, Topolev; and even Air Force Chief, Alksnis, received copies. It's difficult to know how to explain it.

At a Politburo meeting, February 11, 1936, the question of Levanevsky's flight was discussed. Stalin reacted to Levanevsky's letter as follows: "We will refuse the persistent request by Hero of the Soviet Union, comrade Levanevsky, for a decision to complete a transpolar flight in 1936."

Such a decision was understandable, since it would have been necessary to prepare very carefully for this flight; a second false start would have been unacceptable. But could there have been, perhaps, other reasons?

O. Y. Schmidt brought forth a suggestion, approved by the Politburo, to construct a radio meteorological station on the ice in the region of the North Pole in 1937.

It's interesting that the Politburo's February Resolution spoke of the necessity for CAHI to reconstruct the two ANT-25s in 1936. However, according to the resolution, they designated them to be used in training for the Levanevsky flight. Levanevsky himself was recommended to study the flight conditions over North America (Alaska, Canada, Greenland).

It's necessary to quote another point made by the February Resolution, because it would pre-determine the events of 1937: "The Administration of Aviation Industry is directed to take to the Defense Commission in one month's time a concrete proposition concerning the improvement of the existing type of long distance aircraft (ANT-25), or the creation of a new plane fully capable of long distance flight, to be completed no later than March 1, 1937."

So what were the consequences of this resolution? The existing ANT-25s were rejected by Levanevsky, and since there was yet no other plane capable of the flight, Levanevsky's flight across the North Pole was postponed another year.

And how did the Administration of Aviation Industry react to the Politburo Resolution? On March 31, it sent a letter signed by Tupolev to USSR Chairman, V. M. Molotov. Tupolev's answer is an example of citizen bravery: "...I inform you that there are located at CAHI two planes with long distance capability, prepared and fully equipped, with everything necessary for the flights. To use them for distance training and endurance tests, one must assume, would be irrational, since their exploitation for training would make them useless for completing the long distance flights.

"I therefore consider that for training flights, it would be best to use planes prepared by factory #18, and save the CAHI planes for the completion of long distance flights. To build a new plane in 1936 for setting long distance flight records would not be possible, in view of the work load the government has already assigned to CAHI. The question of building a new plane in 1937-38 can only be decided with the approval of the government for CAHI's work plan for 1937."

Andrei Nikolaevich Tupolev had done all he could to decide the future fate of his creation—the plane created for long distance flight, the ANT-25. Now everything was up to the pilots.

So how did things stand on February 11, 1936—the day the Politburo passed its Resolution?

1. The "persistent request" of Levanevsky to fly across the North Pole to America was rejected.

2. The two specially created planes by CAHI, the ANT-25s, were rejected as defective, and proposed only for training flights.

3. A decision was made to create a polar station on the ice of the North Pole region; and, in this way, obtain the necessary weather and climate information, which would make the future flight more easily accomplished and safer.

4. The decision to improve the existing planes, the ANT-25s, or create a new plane capable of extreme long distance flights would be made not later than March 1, 1937.

They were given only one year again to create a new plane.

That meant the next storming of the North Pole could not occur sooner than 1937.

A TRIUMPH OF SOVIET AVIATION

In the middle of the 18th Century, the great Russian scientist, Mikhail Vasilievich Lomonosov, wrote the following prophetic poem:

"Russian Columbuses, scorning their gloomy fate,

Among huge ice floes, a new route to the East they take,

And our great nation finally reaches the American State."

Could it have been our Soviet pilots that Mikhail Vasilievich was speaking about two centuries ago?

Sixty seven years ago, July 20th, at 5:45 a.m., a single engine plane designed by A. N. Tupolev, took off from Shchelkovo Airfield (now named V. P. Chkalov Airfield). This was the same ANT-25(2) plane Levanevsky flew, and then rejected, after his ill-fated transpolar attempt in 1935. It now had a new crew: Valery P. Chkalov, Georgy F. Baidukov, and Alexander V. Belyakov, which, again, set the plane's course to the north.

The crew was to complete a non-stop, long distance flight along the following route: Moscow — Kharlovka — Victoria Island — Franz-Joseph Island — the Kara Sea — North Land Island — Cape Cheliuskin — the Laptev Sea — Tiksi Bay — Petropavlovsk-on-Kamchatka — Aleksandrovsk-on-Sakhalin — Khabarovsk — Chita.

At an August 10, 1936, meeting in honor of Heroes of the Soviet Union, V. P. Chkalov, G. F. Baidukov and A. V. Belyakov, Defense Commissar K. E. Voroshilov said: "There's no doubt that this great achievement, this triumph of our pilots, is the first stone in the foundation

ANT-25 before takeoff, 1937.

of that majestic building, which will be built from new and even more wonderful achievements and triumphs by the people of our great homeland."

Their non-stop flight was the first, after Levanevsky's failed attempt to complete a flight over the North Pole to America in 1935. It should be noted that this flight marked the beginning of the marvelous 1937 flights of Chkalov and Gromov crews, which brought them world-wide fame, and our country a reputation as a world aviation power.

But from where did this new crew come? And how was the route determined?

Georgy Baidukov, Levanevsky's copilot on his failed mission to cross the Pole to America in 1935, considered that the single-engine ANT-25, in spite of its earlier failure, could complete the flight to America. Baidukov and Chkalov had met in 1931 at the Air Force's Research Institute, and Baidukov introduced this marvelous machine to him.

Chkalov test flew the ANT-25, gave it a positive evaluation, and joined Baidukov in his opinion of the plane's potential. A new crew was formed: V. P. Chkalov, G. F. Baidukov and navigator, A. V. Belyakov, with whom Baidukov was acquainted earlier. Not wasting any time, this brave troika began immediately to work out the details of a plan for a trans-polar flight.

At the beginning of 1936, Chkalov, Baidukov, and Belyakov wrote to the Commissar of Heavy Industry, G. K. Ordzhonikidze, with a request to complete a non-stop, flight over the North Pole to America.

These pilots didn't know about the Politburo Resolutions concerning Levanevsky and his request, which were secret and only declassified and made public by me in 1998-1999.There was no tie, or friendly relation-ship, between Levanevsky and his co-pilot, Baidukov, which became clear in his letter to Stalin, May 22, 1937. We'll speak of this later.

At one meeting of the Central Committee of the Communist Party, Ordzhonikidze took the pilots to see Stalin. The following is what Chkalov said about the meeting: "During the break, we approached Sergo Ordzhonikidze and asked him about the fate of our project, the long-distance flight. 'You guys just can't sit still,' laughed Sergo. 'All you want to do is fly. Okay, I'm going to take you to see Comrade Stalin.' The door opened and Stalin came in smiling and asked, 'What's going on here? What do you want, Comrade Chkalov?' 'We ask for your permis-sion, Iosef Vissarionovich, to complete a flight to the North Pole.' Stalin answered in a joking way,'Why do you need necessarily to fly to the North Pole? Nothing seems to frighten pilots. They're used to risk. But why take a risk unnecessarily?' Then, in a serious tone, he explained, 'Little is known about the conditions for flight across the North Pole,' and then, quiet for a while, and looking at us closely, Stalin unexpectedly added, 'Here is your route, Moscow to Petropavlovsk-on-Kamchatka.'"

This is how "Stalin's Route" ("Сталинский Маршрут") came to be painted on the sides of the ANT-25. Later, the route was changed a bit. The crew suggested a "northern variant" route, with the goal of testing the plane's capabilities in arctic conditions, and from a desire to fly over unmapped and unexplored expanses of our country, where not one plane had flown or landed before. This route, then, was determined by Stalin in the Kremlin, and was later made official.

Why did Stalin turn down the pilots' request about a flight across the North Pole to America? Possibly, the failed attempt by Levanevsky, which 12 foreign correspondents had witnessed and about which all of America knew, played a role. Having advertised this flight, the country was in a difficult position.

This time, therefore, the flight across the North Pole would have to be completed for sure, and there would have to be very careful preparation of the crew and the plane. And also, perhaps, this flight was supposed to play a particular political role in the Far East, showing our eastern neighbors our aviation preparedness.[4] And so the decision was accepted, the route finalized, and serious preparations for the flight began. The ANT-25(2) was to be the plane prepared for the flight.

June 14, 1936, Aviation Industry Head, M. M. Kaganovich, issued an order in which the main responsibility for the preparation of both ANT-25(1) and ANT-25(2) was given to the Deputy Head of the Department of Experimental Testing and Development at CAHI, E. K. Stoman. A ground and support crew was created of workers from CAHI, the Ordzhonikidze and Aviaprebor Factories and others. Department Head, V. I. Chekalov, of CAHI, was put in charge of this ground/support crew.

Valery P. Chkalov was made plane commander and given the responsibility of training the crew on both ANT-25(1) and ANT-25(2), as well as working out itinerary details and navigational preparations for the flight.

On June 15th Red Army Air Force Head, Y. I. Alksnis, issued an order that the Red Army Air Force Research Institute also would be responsible for training the crew on the ground and in the air, and for determining preliminary astronomical calculations for navigational purposes. Meteorologists were invited to help with the preparations.

The crew was put under medical observation, supplied with food, oxygen, and other special supplies to be used in case of emergencies.

On July 14th, the Soviet of Labor and Defense issued a decree titled: "Concerning the Non-stop Flight of Long Distance Aircraft, ANT-25."

In the decree, was the following: "1. Organize in July, 1936, a long distance, non-stop flight on the ANT-25 aircraft to cover the following intinerary: Moscow — Victoria Island — Franz-Josef Land — North Land-Nordvik — Tiksi Bay — Petropavlovsk-on-Kamchatka — Aleksandrovsk-on-Sakhalin — Khabarovsk — Chita."

The crew was officially recognized as: Commander, V. P. Chkalov, test pilot, Factory #39; Co-pilot, G. F. Baidukov, test pilot, Factory #22; Navigator, A. V. Belyakov, flag-navigator and 1st rank military engineer.

4   Japanese aggression in the Far East, which included action near Soviet borders, had reached its zenith by 1936

The overall preparation and organization of the flight was assigned to the Deputy Commissar of Heavy Industry and Aviation Industry Head, M. M. Kaganovich, and to Aviation Industry Deputy Head, A. N. Tupolev.

The complete flight route was broken down into separate sections, and each section was given to someone whose responsibility it was to take care of any problems which might develop during the plane's flight over their area. So from the moment the plane entered the Tiksi Bay area, for example, all airfields were put on alert in case of a forced landing, and meteorological services and all communications were put under the command of Soviet Marshal Bliukher, of the Far East Army.

Y. O. Schmidt, Head of the Central Administrative Board of the Northern Seaway, was to get help to the crew in the event of an emergency landing in the area from Franz-Josef Land to the Kolyma River. The NKVD (Central Administrative Board of Frontier and Domestic Guards) was to secure help if there was a forced landing in the Kamchatka-Sakhalin region.

Commander of the Northern Flotilla, Fleet Admiral, Dushenov, was to give help during the plane's over flight of the Berents Sea; and Pacific Ocean Fleet Commander, Fleet Admiral, Viktorov, was to secure help in the Sea of Okhotsk Region.

On the same day the Soviet of Labor and Defense passed their decree, July 14, Chkalov, Baidukov and Belyakov were invited to the Kremlin to see Stalin. The meeting began with M. Kaganovich, Alksnis, Tupolev and Chkalov in attendance. The conversation lasted 35 minutes and also included Communist Central Committee members Molotov, Voroshilov, Ordzhonikidze and L. Kaganovich. They discussed the flight and the itinerary altered by the crew, and expressed their best wishes in parting.

The flight was planned to begin July 20, 1936, at 3:30a.m. According to notes sent to Stalin by the Deputy Commissar of Internal Affairs, comrade Agranov, the flight was delayed due to late fueling, and also, because "when the plane was taxiing down the runway for take off, the wheel bolts on one of the wheels came loose. The wheel had to be changed."

The plane finally took off at 5:45 a.m., July 20, 1936.

The first radiogram from the crew was received 25 minutes after take off, and then every hour thereafter a communication was sent home. At 11:10 a.m., the following radiogram was received: "Everything is in order. We're located over Onega. For two hours we've flown over clouds at an altitude of 6000 feet. The weather is changing now. The crew is feeling fine. Greetings."

At 10:10 p.m., the plane was flying over Franz-Josef Land.

The flight began to experience difficult meteorological conditions. At 2:10 a. m., July 21, the crew met their first cyclone.

At 4:15 a.m.: "Everything is in order. We're going around the cyclone."

At 5:10 a.m.: "...We're flying blind, turning from our route and heading for Tiksi Bay."

At 6:25 a.m.: "For five hours we've been fighting clouds and flying blind. After this long period of flying blind, we're re-orienting ourselves."

So ended the first 24 hours of flight. It covered the first difficulties of the crew. After several hours, they sent the following radiogram: "Everything is working well. We crossed the Lena River at 12:42 a.m. at an altitude of 13,200 feet. Today has taken a great amount of energy from the crew in our battle with the Arctic. Ice formation on the plane has forced us today to lose much time and fuel.... We've become convinced of the Arctic's insidiousness and the difficulties it has in store for us...."

The government's interest in this flight, after Levanevsky's failed attempt, can be judged from a telegram the crew received at 7:30 p.m., July 21:

"Aircraft ANT-25. To Chkalov, Baidukov, Belyakov.

The whole country is following your flight. Your triumph will be a triumph for your Soviet homeland. We wish you success and firmly shake your hands.

Stalin, Molotov, Ordzhonikidze, Dimitrov."

A rough copy of the telegram, composed by Ordzhonikidze with corrections by Stalin is preserved in our country's archives.

In a radiogram sent July 22nd at 5:20 a.m., Belyakov wrote: "...Thunder and lightning prevent us from hearing well." This was the beginning of the second very serious testing of the crew and plane.

At 8:15 a.m.: "Atmospheric discharges, hearing poorly. We can't receive Yakutsk. Only fragments come through. We'll make landing near Chita. The Khabarovsk—Bochkarevo beacons are working."

At 10:10 a.m.: "(Fragments from Yakutsk) Inform us (static) what kind of weather expected in Khabarovsk period after (static)."

However, because of poor meteorological conditions, zero visibility, heavy clouds and fog and ice forming on the plane, the crew was forced to change course and head for Nikolaevsk-on-Amur (river).

At 10:30 a.m.: "From Nagaevo. Everything is in order. We're changing course to Nikolaevsk. We'll land at Khabarovsk."

At 12:30 p.m.: "The ANT-25 is fast losing altitude... ice is forming, heavy fog. According to the beacon, we're heading toward Khabarovsk."

At 2:20 p.m.: "We made landing near Nikolaevsk..."

What happened to force the crew to decide to land?

From a telegram by Marshal Bkiukher, sent to Gamarnik and Kaganovich on July 22nd at 10:30 a.m., it's apparent the meteorological conditions in the Petropavlovsk and Aleksandrovsk region were very bad: thick, low-hanging clouds and fog. From Aleksandrovsk to Khabarovsk, there was nothing but clouds and fog to an altitude of 6000 feet. "In the Sikhote-Alin Mountain Range, which reach to approximately 3000 feet to 4,500 feet in places, the plane dangerously lost altitude in the clouds. If the weather doesn't worsen, I contemplate a landing no earlier than Bochkarev. In the interest of future safety of the flight, I suggested to Chkalov that he change the plane's course at Petropavlovsk and fly to the northern end of Sakhalin Island, then along the Amur River to Khabarovsk, since there is an army airfield at Komsomolsk on the Amur. Since the weather in the Bochkarev region is better, and is expected to continue to improve, the plane will be in the Bochkarev area approximately at 4:00 a.m. local time, July 23rd, and is expected to land. Everything on the plane is working well, and communication with it is constant. The plane was over Petropavlovsk at 6:00 a.m. Moscow time, when we received its last communication."

From Bliukher's telegram, it's apparent he changed the plane's route due to dangerous meteorological conditions. However, the crew was unable to fly to Bochkarev. From communications of the Head of the Special Department of the NKVD, it's clear that due to the bad weather, the plane could not reach Khabarovsk, because it was running out of fuel. They were to make a nighttime landing and take off again in the morning.

Soon, an order was received from Ordzhonikidze: "I order you to terminate the flight and land at the first opportunity."

From the crew's last message: "The weather in the Sakhalin and coastal region has turned out to be extremely treacherous. To fly under the clouds over land has proven to be impossible. After flying at essentially zero altitude over the sea for some time in conditions of rain and fog, we decided to try to fly through the clouds to a high altitude. According to the weather reports we had received by radio, the cloud cover extended to 1,800 feet. We gained altitude flying blind and at a height of 7,500 feet, we had still not broken through, and the plane began to ice up, leading to dangerous vibration, knocking and shaking. Fearing the plane would break apart, we decided to return again to the water, and entered the Tatar Bay region flying at an altitude of 45 feet above the water in a strong wind. Due to the plane's icing, the crew was forced to land on Udd Island. During landing, the right landing gear sank in the beach sand; the right wheel broke and flew off.

"The plane was in the air more than 56 hours at an average altitude of 1,200 feet; ten of those hours we were flying blind. After leaving the European land mass, the crew was able to see the earth not more than 5 or 6 hours."

Ordzhonikidze's order to land immediately, the heavy rain and dense clouds, forced the crew to land the plane on July 22nd at 2:20 p.m., on the shore of tiny Udd Island. V. P. Chkalov landed the plane.

Baidukov, in an article published in the newspaper, "Soviet Russia," in 1986, very emotionally described this most crucial moment of their difficult flight: "The first island we approached was Kevos—with almost inaccessible cliffs; the second, Langr—with a large village and factory, was also not good. The third island, Udd, was spotted with holes and gullies full of water, a few small cabins, and, for some reason, chosen as the spot to land by our commander. He shouted: "Yagor, drop the landing gear! Watch on the right! I—the left! Sasha and Yagor—into the tail!"[5]

"We secured contact with the radio station, understanding that the chances for a successful landing were close to zero. All hope was on the commander, and on the area's name: Bay of Happiness.

"And, really, Valery Pavlovich was born to be a talented pilot: the plane touched down softly, a three point landing—the left and right wheels and the tail assembly. Then—an unbelievably sharp braking, a powerful blow, and the ANT-25 stopped; literally buried in the sand and earth.

"...Oh, how fortunate we were to have Chkalov's skill at landing in the most unusual situations!... It seemed that to land in this place was

[5] Sasha and Yagor are nicknames for Alexander and Georgy.

impossible—full of saucer-like ravines filled with water; large rocks and bolders everywhere, one of which wedged between the wheels and tore one off."

Following is a letter from Fetinya Smirnova (an island inhabitant) to her mother: "…I hurry to tell you, mamasha, that a big plane, called an ANT-25, has landed on our island. At first we thought it was a foreign plane that was forced to land here, and our fishermen, Chistiukhin and Stepikov, set out in a boat to inform the border police. How we laughed later, when we found out that they weren't foreigners, but famous Soviet pilots, Chkalov, Baidukov and Belyakov. My husband and I, dear mamasha, were very happy when they accepted our invitation to stay with us. They lived the whole time with us in our apartment."

In this non-stop flight, the crew covered 5,860 miles in 56 hours and 20 minutes. The plane successfully held up for the duration of this very difficult flight.

This was the second triumph for the ANT-25(2), after the world distance record in a closed circle set by Gromov in 1934.

The courageous crew, with this flight, completely justified the work of designer Tupolev, and all crew members were awarded the title of Hero of the Soviet Union. Chkalov, Baidukov and Belyakov were also awarded the Order of Lenin, numbers 3050, 3051 and 3052, with the corresponding diploma certificate, Hero of the Soviet Union. In a Resolution, passed by the Central Executive Committee of the USSR, it was written: "For completing the heroic, non-stop, long distance flight on the route: Moscow—North Arctic Ocean—Kamchatka—Nikolaevsk-on-Amur, in the exceptionally difficult conditions of the Arctic and unexplored regions of the far North, and for demonstrating outstanding bravery and mastery during the flight…"

In 1939, the Golden Star was created for Heroes of the Soviet Union.

The first to receive Hero of the Soviet Union titles were those who rescued the passengers of the steam ship Cheliuskin, and were awarded the Golden Stars in the following order:

Lyapidevsky, A. V. – Golden Star	#1
Kamanin, N. P.	#2
Molokov, V. S.	#3
Levanevsky, S. A.	#4
Slepnev, M. T.	#5

Vodopyanov, M. V.   #6

Doronin, I. V.   #7

Levanevsky, however, died in 1937 and never received his Hero's Golden Star. To this day the Golden Star has not been claimed by anyone and so it can be assumed it has been awarded posthumously.

M. M. Gromov received Hero's Golden Star #8, having been awarded, as I've already written, the title of Hero of the Soviet Union for setting the world record for distance flight in a closed circle in 1934.

In 1939, father was no longer with us, so Hero's Golden Star #9 was awarded to Alexander V. Belyakov; #10, to Georgy F. Baidukov; and #11, awarded posthumously to Valery P. Chkalov.

According the Director of the Regional Museum of Nikolaevsk-on-Amur, V. Yusov, the island inhabitants of Udd, Langr, and of the Petrovsky Spit, proposed the change the names of their islands and spit to Chkalov, Baidukov and Belyakov. However, the government decided not to rename Petrovsky Spit, but to change the islands' names.

On August 13, 1936, the Politburo of the Soviet Union passed a resolution to change the names of islands Udd, Langr and Kevos in the Sea of Okhotsk's Bay of Happiness, to Chkalov, Baidukov and Belyakov.

But the ANT-25(2)'s journey was not yet completed. It still remained to construct a usable flight runway made of logs in order to return to Moscow.

Military personnel sent to the island by Bliukher, and island inhabitants built the runway. Twelve thousand cubic meters of logs were brought to the island for the construction. The logs were laid on the ground and a layer of thick planks placed on top. The runway was 164 feet wide and 1,640 feet long.

While the pilots were living on the island, it was transformed. Portable radio transmitters tying it with the capital appeared, as did electrical, mobile field stations and small factories, where from morning till night they sawed logs for the runway. And, of course, there had to be correspondents and film operators present. Local residents looked at themselves in amazement on the screen in movie theaters.

And while they were building the runway, the flyers spent much time in Nikolaevsk-on-Amur speaking to groups of citizens in the Regional Drama Theater. They spoke to all groups, including to the regional Presidium, in their high-topped fur flight boots, since they had no street shoes.

On July 23rd, a seaplane, the SH-2, brought Commander Shestov, of the Frontier Air Force Unit, to the island. He brought good news—an important telegram:

"Nikolaevsk-on-Amur

To the crew of the ANT-25

Chkalov, Baidukov, Belyakov

Accept our heartfelt greetings and warm congratulations on successfully completing a marvelous flight.

We are proud of your courage, bravery, endurance, cool-headedness and masterful skills.

We have presented a petition to the Central Executive Committee of the Soviet Union in order that you each are granted the title of Hero of the Soviet Union, and that as a financial award, the plane Commander, Chkalov, be granted 30,000 rubles, and pilot, Baidukov, and navigator, Belyakov, each be granted 20,000 rubles.

Accept our firm handshake,

Stalin, Molotov, Ordzhonikidze, Voroshilov, Zhdanov"

The decree officially awarding the title to the pilots was signed the following day, July 24th.

I don't believe it's necessary to describe the impression this telegram had on the three crew members. Baidukov remembers they were shaken to tears, since they had no idea they would earn such high praise from their country.

That same day, Chkalov, in the name of the crew, sent the following answer:

"Dear Comrade Stalin

The crew of the ANT-25 thanks you and the government for such a high tribute.

Taking off from Moscow, we named our route after you: 'The Route of Stalin.'

The crew is in good spirits and is prepared for the most distant flights. We'll inform you of our take off for Moscow from Khabarovsk.

Nikolaevsk-on-Amur

Chkalov   July 24"

From a letter by F. A. Smirnova:

"…Everyone on the island was very pleased with our guests—so sincere, down-to-earth, good humored. And when the greetings to the heroes from Stalin came to the island and they were read to them, Valery Pavlovich and his comrades came close to crying from happiness. The night before their departure we hardly slept. We were preparing our heroes for their journey. When everything was ready, Chkalov came up to me, took my hand, and said, 'Goodbye, Fetimya Andreevna. I wish you happiness. I don't know how to thank you.' And he added that I should study, 'Now,' he said to me, 'nobody is left behind in life.'"

The day before departure, Baidukov showed their hostess, Fetimya Andreevna, the ANT-25. She was very surprised at their "flying apartment." "We absolutely must change the name of our island," she said before they took off. "Or build a monument on the place where they landed," said her husband, Master Trades-man Tyn Min-bei.

On August 2 at 1:40 a.m., taxiing along the wooden runway, which had just been completed, for 900 feet, the plane lifted into the air from the island Udd. Chkalov waved the wings of the ANT-25 to say goodbye to the islanders and then followed the route Khabarovsk, Chita, Krasnoyarsk, Omsk, Moscow, for a victorious return journey.

The pilots never forgot the help given to them in building the long runway, and soon the inhabitants received gifts: men received rifles, women received domestic goods, and several families received phonographs with records.

Tupolev, Belyakov, Chkalov, Baidukov, before flight to Udd Island (now Chkalov Island).

In an article printed in the newspaper Pravda on August 14, 1936, Valery P. Chkalov evaluated the results of his flight, "The ANT-25 flew nonstop from Moscow to Udd Island, 5,860 miles, in 56 hours and 20 minutes. On the return journey, Udd Island, Khar-barovsk, Chita, Krasnoyarsk, Omsk, Moscow, the plane was in the air 48 hours and 25 minutes, having flown 4,794 miles. In sum, this flight of the ANT-25 was in the air 104 hours and 45 minutes, covering a distance of 10,653 miles. To this it is necessary to add the training flights before the start of the flight, which took 55 hours. Therefore, the motor and all of the plane's parts worked without needing any repair (and received no complaints) almost 160 hours. One can justifiably speak of the outstanding quality of the plane's design in general and of the motor group in particular. The crew of the ANT-25 expresses its deepest gratitude to Andrei Nikolaevich Tupolev, design engineer P. O. Sukhom, engineer E. K. Stoman, mechanic V. I. Berdnik, and flight staff head V. I. Chekalov, to the whole collective of designers, engineers, and workers of CAHI, engineer designer A. A. Mikulin, workers of the factory Frunze, and to all the comrades who created this marvelous machine on which we were able to successfully complete the great "Route of Stalin."

The high reliability of designer A. A. Mikulin's motor, which worked over all these days, was greatly valued by the leaders of heavy industry. On August 9, 1936, Heavy Industry Commissar Sergo Ordzhonikidze issued Order No. 1311, which said, "All the motors of the 'M-34 type' will carry the name of designer Alexander Mikulin."

"New motors of the type will be designated 'AM-34.'"

MOSCOW MEETS ITS HEROES

On August 10th, all Moscow prepared to meet their heroes. It was a national holiday, a national celebration. The streets of Moscow were decorated with red flags, green garlands, and posters with the words "Greetings to our beloved heroes!" Several hours before the plane arrived, two thousand fresh flowers and ten thousand pots of flowers were sold to Moscovites. Today these numbers surprise no one, but at the time it was very impressive. Mama rode to the airport with three bouquets of roses for the three friends—for the three heroes.

About 4:00 p.m., all knew that the plane was approaching Moscow. An honor guard of 12 planes took off to meet and accompany the red-winged ANT-25 in its approach and victory circle over the capital. They also accompanied the plane to its landing at Shchelkovo Airfield.

The government, represented by Stalin, Ordzhonikidze, Voroshilov and L. Kaganovich of the Central Committee of the Communist Party, was meeting the crew and, therefore, had assigned 4:50 p.m. as an exact time for the plane to arrive in Moscow. The crew didn't know Stalin and others would be meeting them, so the assignment of a time puzzled them.

As soon as the plane landed, Baidukov and Belyakov jumped from the plane, in order to lighten the plane and make taxiing easier. At this time automobiles approached the plane, from which the Central Committee members exited the cars with Stalin at their head. Seeing this from the cockpit, father also left the plane and jumped to the ground. This was the only time government leaders would meet the crew directly after landing at an airfield.

Working Moscow prepared its gifts for its heroes: The candy factory, "Bolshevik," made chocolate ANT-25s for the crew; the Markov Factory made blankets portraying the ANT-25; porcelain tableware and dishes turned up with images portraying the red-winged beauty.

Young people from the Irkutsk Region made up the following "частушка" or clever little song:

>I will embrace Baidukov,
>I will shower Chkalov with kisses,
>I will entwine Belyakov with a scarlet ribbon

A game was also created, "THE ANT-25," which was played by "kiddies" of all ages. One of those games was picturesquely described by the writer Samuil Yakovlevich Marshak:[6] "…Yesterday I met them (Chkalov, Baidukov and Belyakov) in Leningrad. All three of them. They were obvious pretenders. I listened to their conversation and was very surprised when I had heard them calling each other with the glorious names of hero-pilots.

- Listen, comrade Chkalov!

- What's that, comrade Belyakov?

The pretenders had been sitting on the fence in Lesnoi, waving their arms and legs and exchanging short notes between them:

6 Marshak was a very popular translator and children's poet. Among his Russian translations are William Shakespeare's sonnets, poems of William Blake and Robert Burns, and Rudyard Kipling's stories.

- "Where are we now, comrade Belyakov?"
- Above Petropavlovsk, comrade Chkalov.
- So drop a streamer! Are you sleeping?

The oldest of pretenders was about 9, the second one was the same age or a little younger, but the youngest – "Baidukov"– was just 6. The fence was their plane, there was no engine, but it was perfectly imitated with the drumming of three pairs of heels on the side of the fence. I watched the work of "the pilots" for a while until their successful landing on Udd island.

Children play – the same legend. Grown-ups tell their legends, but children describe them in live action – in play. It's good, when great heroic actions become the content of their play."

Our whole country's youthful generation played "Cheliuskin Survivors," "Chkalov Crew," and "Gromov Crew," games in the 1930s. These were the heroes of their time, and the heroic fetes of these Heroes of the Soviet Union were used as examples to educate the country's youth.

The writer, Nikolai Ostrovsky, sent his greetings from Sochi, which was printed in the newspaper "Komsomoskaya Pravda" on the day of the plane's arrival: "To three brave people with nerves of steel and the passionate hearts of eagles, who, to the glory of our country, rose on powerful wings to unattainable heights, I send my warm greetings and admiration."

People's Artist, Antonina Nezhdanova, wrote: "…I join my humble voice of sincere admiration and excitement to the powerful national greetings to Chkalov, Baidukov and Belyakov, and also to Tupolev, great masters of their profession, who have written a golden page into the history of our aviation."

Hero of the Soviet Union, Mikhail M. Gromov, in his salutation, "A Flight Unequalled in the World," wrote: "This was an exceptional flight, exceeding all previous long distance flights, both in a straight line and circular. The flight of the 'ANT-25' — this is an achievement, the equal of which the world of aviation has not seen."

And truly, the flight crew of Chkalov, Baidukov and Belyakov eclipsed the world distance record for non-stop flight set by the French pilots, Kodos and Rossi, who in 1933 covered a distance of 5,657 miles, traveling from New York to Riyak, Syria in 70 hours.

The brilliant fight by the Soviet aviators prompted a wide response in the world's press. The famous aviator and aviation designer, Louis

Bleriot, who completed the historical 1909 flight from France to England through la Manche, said: "This flight will carry great significance, since it was accompanied by lengthy, exemplary preparations, and was completed in extremely difficult conditions. The Soviet pilots chose their route, carrying them over completely unexplored regions. They themselves chose to battle the most difficult circumstances, instead of choosing an easier route to set their record.

"I was happy to become acquainted with Tupelov, the designer of the ANT-25 monoplane, and hope to see him in Paris during the coming International air show in November."

The famous English aviation industrialist, Fairy, announced that, "Chkalov's flight adds still one more triumph to the long list of marvelous technical achievements of Soviet aviation. It is necessary to command the highest mastery of piloting and exceptional endurance in order to fly almost 6000 miles non-stop miles in such difficult conditions. On the other hand, it would have been impossible without access to a marvelous aircraft and not less marvelous engine. Professor Tupolev, apparently, has created still another new, successfully designed aircraft. Any country could be proud of people like those who have moved Soviet aviation forward."

USA: "It was truly one of the most outstanding flights in the history of aviation. It demonstrated the possibility of long distance non-stop flight, and will serve to better aircraft construction in many countries, in order that new planes will be produced with adequate power and fuel capacity to accomplish similar flights."

The significance of this flight for the Soviet Union was great. The country's leadership equated it in significance to the action of two field armies. Soviet pilots had demonstrated the strength and power of our aviation to our Eastern neighbors, especially to the Japanese, with whom during this period our relations were strained. It took the pilots 56 hours to cover almost 6,000 miles along the northern border of our country to the mouth of the Amur River, and 48 hours—and 5,000 miles, from Khabarovsk back to Moscow. The ANT-25(2) aircraft was completely rehabilitated.

At the same time, in August, 1936, CAHI began preparing the first ANT-25(1) for a flight to cover the following route: Moscow—turkey—Greece—the Mediterranean Sea—French West Africa (across the Sahara desert)—the Atlantic Ocean—South America (Brazil). It was to set another record for non-stop long distance flight in a straight line. Hero of the Soviet Union, Mikhail M. Gromov, was appointed commander; co-pilot was A. B. Yumashev, and navigator was S. A. Danilin. The flight was to begin September 25, 1936.

The flight start date, however, was postponed to 1937, due to Brazil's refusal to accept the Soviet Plane. Foreign Affairs Commissar, Maxim M. Litvinov, in a letter to G. K. Ordzhonikidze, wrote: "I sent you a coded message from Washington concerning Brazil's refusal to accept Gromov's plane, in which I earlier had no doubts. If a landing is necessary in South America, then the closest point would be French Guiana…." Gromov, however, refused to fly to French Guiana.

On August 21, 1936, an order was sent to the Head Administration of Heavy Industry, in which the Commissar of Heavy Industry, G. K. Ordzonikidze, was to be responsible for preparing and sending the ANT-25(2) to take part in a Paris air show, November 13-30. The Chkalov crew, which had flown the plane non-stop to Udd Island, was also commanded to attend the air show.

RUSSIA SHOWS AMERICA ITS PLANE

To describe how events unfolded in the preparation for the flight across the North Pole to America, it is necessary to make several references to resolutions and decrees passed by the Politburo of Communist Party's Central Committee. At that time in our life, only the Politburo, which represented the real leadership of our country, made important decisions. In addition, I would like to introduce the reader to documents, which laid for more than 60 years on archive shelves, many of which were declassified only in the 1990s. I believe these documents will be of interest to those specialists who are trying to resurrect a truthful chronology of the historical events of that time.

As I have already written, Levanevsky rejected the ANT-25, and the Politburo decided to send him to America to formally accept new planes we had purchased. It was also recommended that he study conditions for a flight to North America.

Levanevsky returned from this assignment in a hydroplane purchased from the Vultee Aircraft Company, with several stops on an itinerary along the Pacific Coast of the USA to Nome (Alaska), across

Chukotka—Uelen—Schmidt Spit—Tiksi Bay—along the Lena River to Yakutsk, across Olekminsk, Kirensk on the Angara River and, farther, to Krasnoyarsk. At Krasnoyarsk the plane's water skiis were replaced with wheels before flying to Moscow, landing at airfields along the Aeroflot route. On August 5, 1936, Levanevsky took off from Los Angeles. The distance covered was 12,000 miles.

The flight had not yet been completed, when the country's leaders received a letter, delivered by Yanson, about the significance of the flight, and a request that a meeting with Levanevsky be organized at the highest level. This petition/letter instigated a whole series of Politburo resolutions.

In one of the resolutions, September 10, 1936, the Northern Sea Route Administration was assigned the responsibility of organizing a meeting with Levanevsky and Politburo members. The Resolution stated: "For new major successes in developing a Northern Air Route, Hero of the Soviet Union, comrade Sigismund Aleksandrovich Levanevsky, already possessing the Order of Lenin and the Order "Red Star," will be awarded the Order of the Red Banner of Labor. Navigator, comrade Viktor Ivanovich Levchenko, will receive the Order of Lenin." It was also recommended that Levanevsky's flight be published, so that the people would recognize its significance.

On September 14th, Stalin sent the Levanevsky crew a salutary telegram with the following contents:

"To Hero of the Soviet Union, pilot Levanevsky, and to navigator, Levchenko, brotherly greetings to the brave sons of our homeland. I congratulate you on the completion of this historic flight.

I warmly shake your hands.

J. Stalin"

On September 16th, the Politburo passed a resolution naming the electrical line from Sverdlovsk to Solikamsk, "Hero of the Soviet Union Levanvsky."

I believe this was the second time a living Hero of the Soviet Union was so honored. The first, was naming the three islands after Chkalov, Baidukov, and Belyakov.

On October 10, 1936, the Politburo again issued a resolution ordering comrades Levanevsky, Pobezhimov and Chechen to the USA to formally receive three purchased planes.

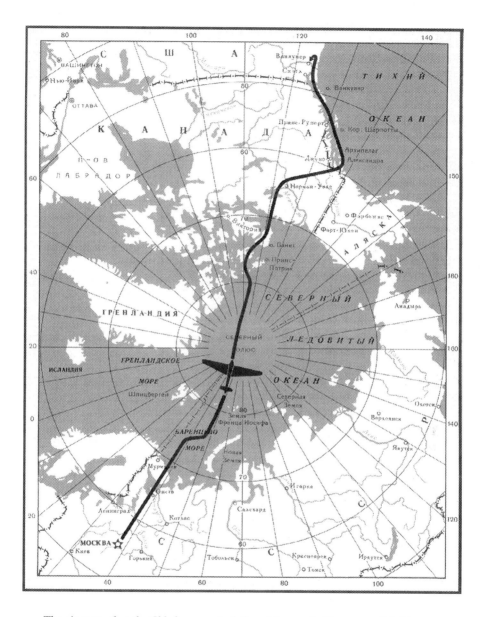

The air route that the Chkalov crew took from Moscow to Vancouver, Washington, over the North Pole in 1937. Flying time was 63 hours and 16 minutes.

I found very interesting documents in the economics archives. The documents were discovered in the safe of Defense Industry Commissar, M. L. Rukhimovich, after his arrest. They were plans of record flights, which were to be established in 1937.

One document was dated January 17, 1937. In a section of the plan titled, "Distance Records, Flights and Routes," the first point was recorded as, "Flight Across the North Pole." In a column titled "Crew," Chkalov, Baidukov and Belyakov were listed by the Defense Industry Commissariat (DIC); Stefanovsky, Yumashev and Spirin were listed from the Army Air Force. In the same document, a flight across the North Pole was indicated for V. K. Kokkinaki in a DB-3 aircraft.

Nothing was said in this document concerning a flight across the North Pole by Gomov or Levanevsky. I believe nothing was said about Levanevsky, because he represented another agency. Gromov had decided to establish a distance record by flying to South America. At this time, he was not interested in a flight across the North Pole to America.

Let's examine how events changed these plans.

In 1937, Levanevsky and Chkalov, having asked permission to fly across the Pole to America in 1936, received some pleasant news. A decision had been made to send an expedition to establish a station on the ice near the North Pole during March and April of 1937: From the Politburo Resolution: "In order to fulfill the February 14, 1936, Resolution, we direct the Northern Sea Route Administration (comrade O. Y. Schmidt) to organize an expedition to the North Polar Region during March-April to establish a polar station on the ice." Due to poor weather, however, the expedition did not get started until May 21, 1937.

In attempting to discover the chronology of events of that time—preparations for the flights, and the time they occurred—I began to work in the Moscow archives. My research in the archives was successful. I found several letters relating to the flights over the North Pole to America: two from Defense Industry Commissar Rukhimovich, and one from Gromov to Rukhimovich.

Rukhimovich wrote to Stalin in his first letter, dated February 13, 1937: "Heroes of the Soviet Union, comrades Chkalov, Baidukov and Belyakov have come to me for permission to complete in the current year a non-stop flight from Moscow over the North Pole to San Francisco (USA)...

"The ANT-25 aircraft is completely ready at the present time for long distance flight. More favorable weather is forecast for the North Pole and all along the route during the second half of April.

"I ask for your agreement in principle to organize in April of this year a non-stop flight from Moscow to San Francisco across the North Pole."

It wasn't until April 2nd that Gromov, in his letter to Rukhimovich, expressed his desire to fly across the North Pole to America: "I ask for your support concerning a decision to allow me to attempt to set a world long distance record in a straight line. The route: Moscow, across the Arctic to San Francisco, and further into California, until fuel is expended.

"The pilots in the crew, Gromov, Yumashev, and navigator Danilin, are fully prepared for the flight.

"…It's desirable to complete the flight during the second half of April."

It's possible to draw the conclusion, on the basis of this Gromov letter, that he was rejecting the long distance flight to South America, which the government had postponed to 1937, in favor of an attempt to set a record over the North Pole to America.

In Rukhimovich's second letter to Stalin, dated April 4th, he writes about a third crew — the Gromov crew, which also asks for permission to make an Arctic flight:

"Comrades CHKALOV, BAIDUKOV and BELYAKOV have placed the question of a flight across the North Pole many times before comrade Sergo (Ordzhonikidze).

"They have now again presented us with this question.

"GROMOV, YUMASHEV and DANILIN just yesterday came to me with the same request.

"In both situations: the plane is the ANT-25; the route is Moscow — North Pole — San Francisco; the flight would take place April 20-25, and both announced, 'both the plane and the crew are fully prepared to make the flight.'

"Since I am not a supporter of such a flight, I consider it my responsibility to ask you to examine this request by comrades CHKALOV, BAIDUKOV and BELYAKOV and GROMOV, YMASHEV and DANILIN."

I would like to direct your attention in Rukhimovich's letter, to: "the plane…(is) fully prepared."

Tupolev, the main designer of the ANT-25, acting on comments of the Chkalov crew following the 1936 flight, had begun preparing the ANT-25(2) for a flight over the North Pole.

On January 31, 1937, Tupolev issued directions to the Head Administration of the Defense Industry Commissariat: "For the purpose of preparing the aircraft ANT-25(2) for flight in cold climatic conditions...

1) Heat the oil in the main tank. 2) Re-do the cabin heating system, ensuring heat from the bottom section of the cabin... 4) Install an autopilot in the aircraft.

Make all improvements and test them before April 1st of this year in low temperatures...."

In March, Tupolev issued more directions, in which he asked for alterations of the two ANT-25s' motors: the AM-34R, series RD #22, 25, 41, 42. An air-vacuum oil-heating pump was installed for the autopilot. Lengthy testing (200 hours) of new fuel, oil, and wiring for the autopilot was carried out.

Time passed, and the Chkalov crew still had not received an answer to its letter. Unable to bear the absence of a decision concerning their request to complete a transpolar flight, Chkalov, Baidukov and Belyakov wrote a letter to Vororshilov April 22, 1937. I would like to quote it in full, since I'm sure the readers are not familiar with it.

"Please forgive our persistence. We are turning to you for the second time concerning the question of a flight to America from Moscow across the North Pole. It's necessary for us to do this for the following reasons:

1. There are rumors of a proposal by America to create a regular air service across the Pole (as a result, there is a premise that Americans will soon make the first flight and our three-years of conversation about it will remain only conversation).

2. Other crews (Levanevsky, Gromov) don't demonstrate the persistence necessary to accomplish their intentions, only sending announcements of their desires to the Commisariat. Levanevsky, not waiting to be called by the government, has departed for Murmansk.

3. The plane that Levanevsky is counting on (the Bolkhovitinova) in this year cannot be used for the flight since, in addition to its alterations, it will demand a great deal of time for testing (the plane has not yet made a long distance flight).

4. There are rumors from responsible workers...that Levanevsky will not be making the flight.

5. There are unhealthy relationships between the candidates for the flight across the Pole. Levanevsky, claiming to have an absolute

monopoly on the given flight, acts pretentiously in his relationship to others and in no way will he agree to join any other crew. Besides all this, he, as earlier, has a poor opinion of the ANT-25 aircraft and also of the leadership of the aviation industry. He himself is relying on prepared American technology and looks down on our aircraft construction and the capabilities of our planes and people.

"All of these reasons taken together create in us an extremely poor impression—that people involved in such an important undertaking allow their egos to determine relationships and, therefore, not give opportunities to others and do not allow the government to correctly evaluate the situation.

"As is clear to you, Kliment Yefremovich (Voroshilov), we are among the ardent supporters of this flight, but we, as we said in our last conversation with you, will allow any combination of crew, disregarding our own ambitions. None of the others have acted in this manner. Not wasting time, we insisted that our ANT-25 aircraft should quickly be repaired and altered as a result of the defects found in our last flight. The plane is now ready and it remains only to break in the new motor. Consequently, no great expense, anticipating millions, will be required for the fight on the ANT-25, since the plane is essentially ready.

"Second, this is a very good time for the flight, now that the North Sea Route Administration's expedition is heading to the North Pole and is now at the 82nd parallel. The expedition can be used for meteorological services, and also in the event of a forced landing. So here also, there is no requirement for additional material expense. Later, however, additional expenses will be a required condition.

"In view of all the above, we ask you, Kliment Yefremovich, to go to the government with a supporting petition for a decision concerning the flight of the ANT-25 as soon as possible. Our crew needs not more than 10 days for a final preparatory flight, i. e., enough time to receive permission from Canada and America for the flight. We are now in training, and our plane, the ANT-25, is ready for its final inspection flight.

"If you decide differently (insistence on a new plane and expecting Levanevsky's return), then the earlier mentioned possibilities will prevail: only the month of August will remain, and the time for appropriate weather will have passed—the flight will have to be cancelled. And worse, the Americans may use our hesitation and be the first to fly over the Pole.

"In our opinion, no one should be ashamed to show the Americans any of our planes, including the ANT-25 (contrary to what Levanevsky believes), if only our Soviet plane would fly there and demonstrate its stuff. No one is going to condemn us for a first flight. In the future, the flight can be repeated on a more modern aircraft, when one is developed.

"Forgive us our stubbornness and persistence. For these flights we have sacrificed often and much (for example, Baidukov has sacrificed a valuable goal in his life—study in the Air Force Academy). And, therefore, I'm sure you understand why we so ardently desire to complete the flight over the Pole.

The crew of the ANT-25, "The Route of Stalin"
Test pilots Chkalov, Baidukov"

It's clear the pilots demonstrated persistence, and they were right. They'd been thinking about completing this flight for three years and time was inexorably passing by.

On April 25th, Voroshilov wrote to Stalin, enclosing the pilots' letter, requesting a decision concerning the transpolar flight: "Comrades Chkalov and Baidukov literally give me no rest. They demand a decision about their flight over the North Pole to the USA. I'm sending you their note and ask for your decision."

And how was the third crew preparing for the flight? Gromov, Yumashev and Danilin had announced their desire to fly across the North Pole to America in an April 2nd letter to Rukhimovich.

On May 5th, Yumashev wrote to Alksnis with a request to allow him two independent flights as crew commander of the ANT-25 with the purpose of setting world records. The contents of this letter shed light on the developing situation and on several events, which took place during 1936 and 1937:

"Beginning in 1934 and in accordance with your order, I prepared and trained on the ANT-25 aircraft for the completion of record distance flights.

"The completion of this flight has been postponed from year to year for one or another consideration; so, for example, in 1936, the flight to South America was put off due to Brazil's refusal to receive our plane on its territory, and Hero of the Soviet Union Gromov's wish not to fly to French Guiana.

"On the basis of my petition, please allow me, as commander of the crew, to fly the route to Guiana, since the government has already approved this flight for 1937.

"Early in 1937, Gromov, as crew commander, and of which I was a member, sent an application to Defense Industry Commissar, Rukhimovich concerning our desire to complete a distance flight across the North Pole to San Francisco. To this time, we have not received an answer to this application, and Gromov has decided not to persist in receiving an answer to this question.

"Realizing that time is passing, and that further procrastination will result in the inability to use our plane this year to demonstrate the accomplishments of our aviation technology, I ask for your support in petitioning the Defense Commissar, Marshal of the Soviet Union, comrade Voroshilov, to allow me, with pilot Chernovsky and navigator Danilin, to accomplish the following:

1. To fly in May of this year, in a closed circle within the USSR, a distance of 6250 miles, during which a new world record for both distance and speed will be established.
2. In June—to break the world's record in a straight line and the international record in a broken, line along the route: Moscow—Iceland—New York—Mexico—for a general distance of approximately 6,900 miles.

"I can't give you an earlier report, since comrade Gromov was depending on flying one ANT-25, and comrade Chkalov is counting on flying the other."

In this last phrase of his letter, Yumashev indicates that Gromov is no longer planning to fly the ANT-25 and, therefore, he asks that he be allowed to use it to complete his proposed fights.

Alksnis sent a letter to Voroshilov with the following request: "I ask for a decision concerning the Yumashev petition." On May 16th, he sent it to Stalin and Molotov.

On May 22nd, Levanevsky also wrote a letter, but he wrote it straight to J. V. Stalin:

1. Immediately upon my return from the USA, I began a search in accordance with your directive, to find a multi-motored plane for the completion of the planned 1935 route over the North Pole.
2. The most appropriate aircraft found for this goal is the D. B. A., produced by Factory #22, and is designed by aircraft designer

BOLKHOVITINOV. He guarantees a range of 7,000 miles, and demands 1.5 to 2 months to complete its preparations.

3. Having turned for confirmation of the above-mentioned figures to Deputy Defense Commissar Alksnis, the Head of Material Security, comrade BAZENKOV, did confirm the figures, which were sent as a report to Defense Commissar, Voroshilov.

4. To this day the question remains an open one, apparently due to the lack of clarity concerning the operations of the North Polar expedition.

"Based on your instructions, that in the event I needed help I should turn to you, I ask for your permission to make the flight with the same 1935 crew (LEVANEVSKY, LEVCHENKO, BAIDUKOV) and direct that the D. B. A. aircraft be prepared.

"I would be please with an opportunity to relate to you the details of the preparations personally. I should not need more than 10 minutes."

Hard to believe! Levanevsky, it turns out, hadn't spoken with the members of his own crew, at least not with Baidukov, who, working closely with Chkalov, had completed the last long distance flight and had written for permission to fly across the North Pole in the single-engine ANT-25 aircraft.

Unable to contain themselves, Chkalov and Baidukov at about this same time again wrote to Stalin, realizing only he could give permission for the flight.

There is no date on the letter, but it carries a stamp: PB #49 p.313. It was attached to documents presented to the Politburo at its meeting on May 25th. The letter must have been written then, sometime between April 25th and May 24th, after the letter to Voroshilov:

"Not having received an answer from the government concerning the flight over the North Pole, we remain at this time in the dark and are living only with hope.

"We were recently summoned to meet with you, but all the comrades were unable to attend, therefore, comrade Molotov said we would be summoned again.

"Today, of the three crews summoned by the government, only one is available. Comrade Gromov lies seriously ill in the hospital. Comrade Levanevsky, according to several sources, has decided to fly immediately to Rudolf Island.

"Apparently, it will not be possible to meet with all the candidates for the flight over the North Pole. Therefore, we have decided to appeal to you with a request to give us a final answer. It will be very difficult for us to spend the summer in a state of anxious waiting.

"In addition, the time for favorable summer weather has begun to wane, and the time necessary to prepare for the flight is getting short, but the remaining conditions for the flight are much better than last year.

"The expedition on Rudolf Island, with all its technical equipment, will make the ANT-25's flight much easier, and our crew has already prepared it for the flight. We ourselves, not losing hope, are training in all our spare time.

"If we receive a decision soon, in the next two or three days, we could take off by June 15th.

"We anxiously await your answer.

"Test pilots V. Chkalov, Baidukov"

As can be seen from this letter, three crews had been selected for a flight across the North Pole, but the goal of each wasn't clear at this time. If one recalls the goals Levanevsky set in early 1935, there would have been enough for all three:

1. A non-stop flight across the North Pole.
2. Establishment of a long distance flight record.
3. Research and mapping of the unknown areas of the North Polar Basin.

From Chkalov and Baidukov's letters to Voroshilov and Stalin, it was clear that their crew was preparing for the proposed flight with great care. Together with Tupolev, they had prepared the plane and were constantly training on it.

The serious pressure put on the government by Levanevsky, Chkalov, Baidukov and Yumashev, demanded a decision. What would they decide, and who would be chosen to make such an important flight?

Unexpectantly, on May 25th, S. A. Levanevsy, V. P. Chkalov, and G. F. Baidukov were summoned to the Kremlin to meet with J. V. Stalin. The meeting lasted 1 hour and 55 minutes. After some time, M. M. Kaganovich and Y. I. Alksnis, were also surprised with a summons to the meeting. They discussed the coming flight. In his introductory remarks, Chkalov said that the crew was prepared for the flight on the single-engine ANT-25, and showed the plane's proposed route on a map.

On the way home after the meeting with Stalin, Chkalov and Baidukov had a conversation, which Baidukov later related to author Y. Kaminsky:

"Listen, Yegor (Baidukov)," Valery Pavlovich suddenly said. "Suggest to Sigismund (Levanevsky) that he fly with us across the Pole to America as a fourth crew member."

"In what capacity?"

"As the commander. It would fulfill his dream! Hurrah for Levanevsky! Only warn him we'll be flying the way we think necessary."

"Chkalov was not a vain man, and I understood he had thought this through sincerely.

"I attempted to dissuade Levanevsky from his venture with the DBA and gave him Chkalov's suggestion."

"Georgy, you know me well. I have a hard character — I've already said I'll never fly on Tupolev planes...."

Such a conversation is altogether possible, given the content of the letters of these pilots to Voroshilov in which they wrote: "...But as we said in our last conversation with you, we'll accept any combination of persons in the crew. We are not overly ambitious."

On that very day the Politburo passed a resolution: "Concerning Long Distance Flights." Probably, when they had been summoned to meet with Stalin, the decisions about the flights had already been made.

So what had the government decided?

The Resolution stated: "1. Allow Chkalov, Baidukov and Belyakov to complete a non-stop flight, Moscow — San Francisco, across the North Pole (on the ANT-25 aircraft)."

The flight was assigned for June-July. The Resolution also indicated the following: "Order comrade Chkalov and the crew, in the event of some problem or danger in the flight, to land before reaching San Francisco in one of the cities of Canada or North America."

The second point of the Resolution said: "Allow Comrade Levanevsky to complete a flight over the North Pole on the DBA aircraft (Bolkhovitinov), and assign the flight for July-August." Responsibility for organizing both flights will be assigned to 'The Four; comrades Rukhimovich, M. M. Kaganovich, Alksnis and Yonson.'"

Since the Chkalov and Levanevsky flights were mentioned in one set of documents, one government commission was created to oversee them.

In one of my conversations with Georgy Filippovich Baidukov about the Chkalov and Gromov crews and their flights over the North Pole to the USA, he said to me: "But why do they speak of two flights, they should speak of three." I finally understood what Baidukov was thinking on examining government documents in which I found that Levanevsky was the initiator of the flight over the North Pole to America in 1935, and for this flight there were three candidates.

And so, the first and second crews allowed to fly across the North Pole to America were determined. Chkalov's crew included Baidukov and Belyakov, Levanevsky's crew had yet to be named. The Chkalov crew was to fly first; Levanevsky was to fly a month later, apparently because his plane was not yet ready. Gromov durng this time was in the hospital, and, therefore, there was no mention of a third crew in the Politburo Resolutions.

There is a series of declassified official documents I found with very different information concerning preparations by the Chkalov and Gromov crews for their flights over the North Pole, which I'll discuss later. There is different information also in a book written by G. Ruznichenko, devoted to the life and accomplishments of M. M. Gromov, and in the last book written by Gromov himself, and published after his death.

On July 12, 1937, the day his flight over the Pole began, Gromov published an article in the newspaper "Pravda": "…On the day comrades Chkalov, Baidukov and Levanevsky were received by Party and government leaders, I was in the hospital and to my very great regret, though invited, could not attend this marvelous discussion. After I recovered, I asked to be received in the Kremlin, and to be allowed to fly over the Pole to North America.

"The request to be received was granted. On June 10th, at 7:00 p.m., comrades Stalin, Molotov, Voroshilov, and Mezhlauk received me. Comrades Alksnis and Rukhimovich also attended the meeting.

"They asked me, 'What do you propose?' I answered that I wanted to fly across the Pole to the USA. In the ensuing exchange of opinions, comrade Stalin and Voroshilov supported my request. After a discussion of various details of the flight, a decision was made: The flight would be allowed."

After their meeting in the Kremlin, the Chkalov crew began hurried preparations for the flight—it was already the end of May. By order of

Defense Industry Commissar, Rukhimovich, two planes were prepared for the flight—the ANT-25(2), and the ANT-25(1) as a reserve.[68]

For accelerated preparation of the planes, a grounds crew was assigned. V. I. Chekalov, Head of CAHI Department Eight, was responsible for all technical and mechanical problems as well as testing. Chekalov had also been head of the staff, which oversaw the 1936 flight to Udd Island.

CAHI Fourth Section Head, Kharlamov, was ordered to prepare Chkalov's plane, the ANT-25(2), securing final testing in the air by June 12th. He was to prepare the ANT-25(1) by June 20th as a back-up, and to install an autopilot in it.

Further events unfolded as follows: The Politburo issued still another resolution on June 8th: "Comrade Chkalov's Non-stop Flight."[69] It stated that, "The allowed non-stop flight will adhere to the following route: Moscow—Franz Joseph Land—North Pole—North America." The crew would consist of Heroes of the Soviet Union: crew commander and test pilot V. P. Chkalov; copilot and test pilot, G. F. Baidukov; navigator and engineer of the first rank, A. V. Belyakov.

A government commission was created to organize the flight. Defense Industry Commissar of the USSR, M. L. Rukhimovich was to chair the commission. Other members included: Deputy Defense Industry Commissar of the USSR, M. M. Kaganovich; Deputy Commissar of Defense and Red Army Air Force Head, Commander Y. I. Alksnis; Deputy Head of the North Sea Route Administration, N. M. Yanson.

The Commissariat of Defense was to carry the responsibility for securing communications with the flight. The Main Meteorological Administration was to help with meteorological services, preparation of airfields and radio stations along the route of the flight within the territory of the USSR.

M. M. Kaganovich was obligated to obtain registration with the International Federation. The USSR's reserve fund released 1,000,000 rubles for flight preparation, and also $150,000 in foreign funds.

The Resolution's 12th point stated: "Instruct all the above mentioned organizations to finish their technical and mechanical preparations, and the flight staff, meteorological services and communications to finalize their preparations in time for a June 12th departure date."

Note that the take-off date for the Chkalov crew was June 12, 1937.

In the archives, I found a letter dated June 8th from M. M. Kaganovich to the Central Air Club concerning the registration of Chkalov's flight with the International Federation. The letter indicated June 13th as the date of the Chkalov crew's departure. In a June 9th letter to the same organization, Kaganovich wrote of the necessity to "communicate with the national Aviation Association of the USA."[70]

On June 6th, Baidukov wrote that their plane, the ANT-25, was badly damaged.[71] An "I-5" aircraft, piloted by Commander Bazhenov, Head of the Air Forces's Scientific Research Institute, while gliding in for a landing, caught its landing gear on the right wing of the ANT-25. As a result, a huge hole was torn in the plane's wing.

A preliminary examination showed that the accident was serious and it would be necessary to disassemble the plane and ship it to the factory. But specialists from Tupolev's department convinced everyone that within a week the plane could be test flown. And, actually, by June 14-15, the repairs were completed.

There are two possible reasons, according to a Politburo resolution, for the postponement of Chkalov's flight from the June 12th date: Weather forecasters determined that June 18-24 would present the most favorable weather conditions for the flight, and the plane was damaged.

In a June 12th telegram to Washington, it was stated that the Chkalov plane's departure was postponed due to weather conditions.

The next Politburo resolution of June 10th, confirmed S. A. Levanevsky's crew: copilot, B. G. Kastanaev; navigator, V. I. Levchenko; flight engineer, G. T. Pobezhimov; and second flight engineer, N. N. Godovikov.

On June 11th the Politburo considered Defense Committee questions.

In a separate point, it was stated, "Confirm the following decision of the Defense Committee: Comrade Gromov's flight from Moscow — North Pole — USA should occur simultaneously with the crew of comrades Chkalov, Baidukov and Belyakov."[72]

However, the word "simultaneously" is used only in this resolution and was placed there, I believe, at Gromov's suggestion. In all the documents I quote from later, these two flights are separated in time, and the crews are mentioned as starting not less than two weeks apart.

On June 11th, M. M. Kaganovich wrote the Central Air Club a letter with the following contents: "After receiving seven requests from Hero of the Soviet Union, M. M. Gromov, I ask that you officially register his application, and secure the possibility of recording a record. Approximate flight departure will be sometime after June 19th.

"I ask that you choose the sports commissar to officially register the application for the place (Shchelkovo), and together with engineer STOMAN, the place and order of the sealing.

"The sports commissar must obtain for himself a barograph case, procure a place to locate it on the plane (it will be severely overloaded), and attach it securely...."[73]

As can be seen from the above letter, a new date for the Gromov flight has appeared—"after June 19th."

On June 13th, Rukhimovich issued an order to the Defense Industry Commissariat concerning Gromov's flight: "The mechanical and technical preparations for training flights must be ready by 6/15, and the plane must be ready for its flight by 6/25."[74]

The above order makes clear that the Gromov crew's flight was assigned for June 25th.

It wasn't until June 19th that the Politburo passed a resolution answering Rukhimovich's request for money to organize the Gromov flight: "For the organization of the flight of Gromov, Yumashev and Danilin, following the route Moscow—North Pole—USA, the USSR will release from its reserve fund 1,000,000 rubles and 100,000 dollars to be distributed by comrade Kaganovich."

A telegram from the Head of the Central Air Club of the USSR to AVI-ATION—OTTOWA, dated June 22nd, states: "Between June 26th and July 5th, the "Soviet ANT-25 aircraft with the crew of Gromov, Yumashev and Danilin, will fly from Moscow to the USA over the North Pole."[73]

So here the Gromov flight is assumed to begin no earlier than June 26th.

The Chkalov crew, because of the weather, had its date of departure postponed by decision of the Politburo, to June 18th, at 4:05 a.m., from Shchelkovo Airfield.

Mother recalled: "We wives did not know the exact day of departure and, in general, as I remember, we were forbidden to appear at the start. But not seeing them for a long time and not having any information, I broke my promise, and on the evening of June 17th I went to Shchelkovo. Only there did I find out they would take off at dawn. The desire to see them was very great. Someone wanted to inform Valery Pavlovich about my arrival, but I was against it. I sat near the airport almost till dawn, but remembering our agreement, I didn't see him off. I went home.

"We wives, of course, didn't sleep that night—nor did we sleep the following nights, until our pilots landed in the USA."

So three Soviet pilots, Heroes of the Soviet Union Valery Pavlovich Chkalov, Georgy Filippovich Baidukov, and Alexander Vasilievich Belyakov, were the first in the history of aviation to begin a successful non-stop transpolar air route over the North Pole to America. They were the first to lay the shortest route between two world powers—the USSR and USA—and also the first to join two continents by this shortest route.

From Moscow to San Francisco across the Pacific Ocean was approximately 9,375 miles; across the Atlantic Ocean, about 7,500 miles; over the North Pole, 6,000 miles.

Their route passed the following points: Moscow—Kola Peninsula—Barents Sea—Franz Josef Land—North Pole—Melville Island—Banks Island—Pierce Point—Queen Sharlott Islands—Vancouver.

The flight ended June 20th with the landing of the ANT-25 aircraft in Vancouver, Washington at Pearson Field, a military airfield. This was a great peaceful accomplishment of Soviet aviation. We were very proud of it!

All pilots in the world of that time dreamed of flying over the North Pole; but to complete this flight, to fly over "the roof of the world," to conquer the inaccessible Arctic, took bravery, courage and daring, which this marvelous troika was the first to demonstrate. They fulfilled their marvelous mission—carrying on the wings of their plane the honor of their people, in spite of the most difficult flying conditions.

Famous polar explorer Amundsen, who attacked the Arctic many times on foot and in the air, had this to say about it in his diary: "How much unhappiness you have brought to humanity through the many years; how much deprivation and suffering you have dealt us—oh, the infinite white spaces! But, on the other hand, you have known those who were able to put their foot on your unbowed neck—those who were able to throw you powerfully to your knees…"[38]

The American polar explorer Robert Peary, gave the following laconic description of this Arctic "roof of the world": "The North Pole—a place on Earth where time does not exist—where there is only one day and one night a year. There all heavenly bodies move horizontally to the Earth, and one Polar Star is seen overhead. There only the south wind blows. There is no north, no east, no west."[38]

Yes, the Pole—the border of two hemispheres, and after the Pole begins the region between the North Pole and the shores of Alaska and Chukotka; the so-called "Pole of Inaccessability."

This infinite, inaccessible white silence has claimed many of our brave pilots and caused untold suffering.

And so the flight, that grandiose conception, which history had produced no known equal to that time, began at 4:05 a.m. Moscow time (1:05 a.m. Greenwich time).

From Georgy Filippovich Baidukov's diary:

"At 3:00 a.m. Greenwich time, the accompanying plane, piloted by Dedyulin, performed a farewell circle and left. The second accompanying reconnaissance plane continued to escort us for some time, then, before reaching Cherepovits, it too turned back.

"We are now alone."

From the very first hours of the flight, the weather began to make itself known. A radiogram sent by Belyakov at 12:32 p.m., announced: "I can't hear you. We are located at latitude 68, longitude 38. Altitude 7,500 feet. Flying between two cloud layers."

At 5:30 p.m. an event occurred which caused the crew considerable anxiety. Near the Navigator's sight hatch oil was discovered, which had flowed into the fuselage. If you remember the first attempt to fly over the North Pole to America by Levanevsky in 1935, then this oil leak should dictate a return home. Baidukov wiped up the oil using a sack turned inside out, in order to determine whether the oil was still leaking. The oil did not reappear, so the anxiety subsided. Apparently, the oil meter was not working, and oil had splashed out.

At 7:13 p.m., June 18th, the following radiogram was received from Belyakov: "We are located approximately at 76 degrees longitude and 44 degrees latitude. We are flying around clouds. There is no problem with the oil. The motor is working fine. It's cold. We are heading for Rudolf. We'll set course on the beacon."

At 8:13 p.m., "Everything's going well. Latitude 78 degrees, 10'; longitude 51 degrees. We're flying blind. Altitude 13,400 feet. Light icing."

The real difficulties were still to come. Their first anxieties and difficulties began well before they reached the Pole. A cyclone caught them over the Berents Sea. In his book, "Polar Route," father wrote about it: "It became completely dark. On our left was a solid black wall. I sharply changed course and took the plane to the right. But the approaching cyclone was inexorable. It seemed purposely to carry clouds to the right, blocking our way. I tried to go around them. Our course was to Rudolf Island; our altitude 13,125 feet. It was cold in the cabin. The temperature outside was 24 degrees below zero.... It came time to change pilots. Baidukov crawled toward me. We changed. I didn't leave my spot, and pumped pressure into the anti-icing container.

"Yegor, that amazing master of flying blind, bravely flew into the cyclone wall. Everything disappeared from our field of sight. The plane, enclosed in clouds, began suddenly to be covered with transparent ice. It began shaking and quivering.... Pushing the lever wide open, Baidukov managed to stop the icing on the propeller. But the surfaces, the stabilizer, the antennae, were still icing up quickly."[75] Only after reaching an altitude of 13,450 feet, did the crew finally escape the cyclone's embrace.

Flying around the solid bank of clouds, the strong northwest wind of 35 miles an hour, and the plane icing up, forced the pilots to lose three hours before reaching Franz Josef Island. They had to work in plane cabin temperatures of eight degrees below zero, Celsius. In the flight log book, Belyakov wrote: "An over expenditure of two hours." This meant an over expenditure of fuel—300 liters (83 gallons).

They were forced to fly around another cyclone beyond Franz Josef Land. This detour cost another hour and 25 minutes.

On June 19th, at 4:15 a.m., Greenwich time (7:15, Moscow time), the plane passed over the North Pole, over "the roof of the world". But huge clouds hid the Pole from the pilots. Only after 15 minutes could they see the boundless ice fields.

Ivan Dmitrievich Papanin, head of the first drift-ice research station, "North Pole," wrote the following in his diary:

"June 17, 1937.

"...It was about 12:30 a.m. when Krenkel arrived (Ernst Teodorovich Krenkel, Hero of the Soviet Union, one of four researchers on the "North Pole" station – auth.), and told us that in 2 hours Chkalov would take off from Moscow on his flight to America. I feel happy for him and his crew. One would hope that everything will go well for these guys, and that they'll be able to complete their important historical effort.

June 18.

"From Rudolf Island they said that Chkalov took off at 4:00 a.m. We agreed that Ernst would get some sleep, since he has to work all night. After resting a bit, Ernst sat by the radio. They say they can hear Chkalov's plane very well. He'll soon be approaching Rudolf...

"At 10:00 p.m. Ernst announced that the Rudolf Island beacon was working for Chkalov's plane. Zhenya (Yevgeny Konstantinovich Fedorov, Hero of the Soviet Union, young scientist, researcher for Central Arctic – Auth.), every three hours sends a weather report to the plane and to Moscow.

"Tonight is lost for all of us; no one wants to sleep — we're all eagerly following Chkalov. Maybe he'll turn toward us; fly over us — though it's doubtful Chkalov would want to make such a detour....

June 19.

"An unusually tense day. All night long Ernst sat by the radio follow-ing Chkalov's flight. At 5:00 a.m., he dropped in at the tent and told us Chkalov was located half way between Rudolf and the Pole. We got up. After some time, I heard a plane's motor and cried out: 'A plane! A plane!' Zhenya rushed outside — there was nothing. But he soon ran back, and shouted at me through the door: 'Yes, it's Chkalov, but I can't see the plane! Nothing but clouds!' I can plainly hear the motor....'

"Everyone jumped up. Thousands of damned clouds. When it doesn't matter, the sky is clear, but now, at this most important moment for us, clouds hide everything. We so hoped Chkalov would see our station and at least throw us a newspaper, or, perhaps, letters from home. We waited with such anticipation!

"The motor's roar became quieter and quieter. It continued on to the north. We were so excited it's difficult to describe....

"The motor's sound died away. Ernst said: 'Dmitry, let's start the emergency communication system. There's no wind, and the storage bat-teries are down. I'm afraid we might let the Chkalov fellows down — we're their last Soviet communications point. We'll be able to hear them for a long time....'"[3]

Again, the pilots were alone. Now ahead of them was the Pole of Inaccessability, about which father had written: "Only a great literary artist would be able to adequately paint, with the words of our rich Russian language, a picture of the eternal ice in the great, severe Arctic."[75]

The next two cyclones caught the plane off the Melville Islands and over the McKenzie River, forcing the plane away from its planned route and to an altitude of between 16,800 to 18,700 feet. It also caused them to use up much of their oxygen.

The cloud wall of the third cyclone rose to a height of 21,300 feet. The plane flew for an hour at 18,700 feet through solid clouds at a temperature of 30 degrees below zero. The whole plane was covered with a centimeter deep layer of white ice. This porcelain-like icing is considered the most dangerous, because it is unusually hard and will hang on for up to 16 hours. The struggle with the cyclone brought on a catastrophic situation: They ran out of anti-icing liquid for the propeller; a threatening vibration seized the plane from nose to tail; pipes and tubing froze; there was no water in the engine-cooling system. And, of course, the drinking water in the rubber sacks froze.

In order to cool the motor, they mixed tea from their thermoses and some water still unfrozen from the center of the rubber sacks with urine the pilots had been collecting to present to doctors for analysis on their return. This "devil's brew" saved them from catastrophe.

They had lost three more hours and were running out of oxygen. But they were confident they could continue the flight. Father evaluated the situation this way: "In the stubborn, difficult struggle with the cyclone, we lost much time, much fuel, and even more physical strength, but we were still the first to fly this route. History will not condemn us."[75]

Such is the Pole of Inaccessibility, with its treacherous surprises. And under the wings of the ANT-25, stretched the lifeless, unexplored, and unconquered expanses of Northern Canada.

The fourth cyclone caught the plane over the valleys of the McKenzie River and forced the crew to fly at an altitude of 20,000 feet. They tried to use as little oxygen as possible, because they had decided to fly over the Rocky Mountains. The last of the oxygen would be used up in that effort. Severe physical fatigue gripped them all. Their hearts beat rapidly. Now the pilots were exchanging places every hour. Blood was flowing from father's nose. The oxygen was gone, so they had to descend to 13,100 feet, where they suddenly saw water beneath them. They had reached the Pacific Ocean.

And now across the Northern America to the south.

The successful landing took place in the city of Vancouver, at 4:20 p.m. Greenwich time (8:20 a.m., Sunday, in Vancouver – jvf), had traveled 5,288 miles and been in the air 63 hours and 16 minutes. Special Pravda correspondent, L. Khvat, "chasing" the pilots, traveled eight days from Moscow to New York: two of those days by train from Moscow to the French port of Havre, then five days on the fastest passenger ship in the world at that time, the Normandie, across the Atlantic.

The head of Vancouver's military base, General Marshall, kindly invited the pilots to stay in his home, a three story house, where they could rest and catch up on sleep after three sleepless nights crossing the Pole.

Our Ambassador in America, Alexander Antonovich Troyanovsky, flew to Vancouver. He remembers what great difficulty he had in waking the pilots, who were sleeping as if dead. In the next room, he was surprised to find what appeared to be a complete clothing section from a department store: suits, shirts, socks, shoes. It had all been brought from Portland.[7] The Americans didn't ask to be paid for these things, only requesting that the pilots loan them their flight suits and some equipment for a few days, so that they could be displayed in their store windows in Portland. This was great advertising for them.

7 The store was Portland's downtown Meier & Franks.

But Father was bothered the whole time, because they hadn't paid for their clothes. He had no understanding at all of American business.

After the pilots had dressed and greeted the General and his family, journalists and film operators descended upon them. A radio broadcast was organized so that all America could hear a conversation with the pilots.[8]

By this time, telegrams had been received from Stalin, Roosevelt and Hull.[9] So began their first day in America.

Americans were so excited and impressed with the flight, that there was no effort to spin the facts of the flight or distort the words of the pilots. The attitude of the journalists characterized the attitude of the average American to the Soviet Union at that time. America met them warm heartedly and with enthusiasm.

Chkalov was asked to say a few words from the Marshall House balcony to the film crews and the radio, which he did brilliantly. He always knew what to say and how to say it. Troyanovsky remembered: "There was never a time when Chkalov stumbled, hesitated, or couldn't find the right word. Always, in every situation, he found the appropriate expression. He possessed a marvelous tactful personality in his relations with people, and with some sort of internal sensitivity, he found the right tone. Not once during his whole stay in America did he display any kind of roughness."

It's interesting that Americans found Chkalov's voice very pleasing, and that this voice was the voice of a real Russian. Everyone seemed to have this opinion.

8 The national broadcast was on NBC.
9 The author is referring to U.S. Secretary of State, Cordell Hull

In his speeches, he always tried to emphasize the significant roles played by Baidukov and Belyakov.

Evaluating the work of the crew on this most difficult of flights, father wrote: "They say that we three have very different characters. It's difficult for me to judge. Perhaps it's so, but one thing is sure: we work well together. We know each other; we know each person's strengths and weaknesses — and what's especially important, we trust each other. This trust, which was strengthened during our first joint flight, has helped us."[75]

Pilots' reception in San Francisco.

In aviation it often happens that the copilot has a better command of this or that element of flying than does the plane's commander. This was the case in Chkalov's crew. Copilot Baidukov, who had attained the highest rank of test pilot, was one of the best, if not the very best, master of flying blind at that time. A large part of the route from Moscow over the North Pole to America passed through thick clouds and cyclones. In such conditions, it was necessary to fly by instruments alone — to "fly blind." During these periods, Baidukov flew the plane.

There's nothing surprising in this. Any plane commander, having a copilot like Baidukov on board, would give him the responsibility of such flight. But to pass the right to land the plane on American soil to the copilot, was surprising, and could only be suggested by the commander.

Chkalov let Baidukov land the plane in Vancouver — in America — and in this way showed his respect for the skill of his copilot.

Not every commander, on his own initiative, would underscore this fact before his listeners. But Chkalov did — and not just to his close circle of friends, but to the whole world. With this fact, he began telling his story of the flight to the gathered correspondents of the largest newspapers and telegraph agencies in America.

The political, business, and scientific communities in America, and of the whole world, evaluated the significance of this flight very highly.

June 20, 1937, United States President, Franklin Roosevelt, greeted the Soviet pilots with a telegram sent to USSR Ambassador, A. A. Troyanovsky: "I learned of the successful completion of the first non-stop flight from the Union of Soviet Socialist Republics to the United States with great satisfaction. The skill and bravery of the Soviet pilots, in accomplishing this brilliant, historical achievement, deserves the highest praise. Please, pass on to them my warmest congratulations."

On June 21st, the crew sent a telegram to our government from Portland: "We were extremely happy to receive your greetings, and happy together with you and our people at another achievement of Soviet aviation. "Stalin's Route" has been established. We have fulfilled our government's assignment, in spite of the complicated and difficult conditions encountered during the flight."

The daughter of Admiral Peary, the discoverer of the North Pole, Maria Peary-Stafford,

Valery Chkalov hands over the ANT-25 barograph to verify his nonstop flight across the North Pole. Courtesy of Pearson Air Museum.

wrote the pilots a congratulatory telegram: "My father predicted that the next person after him would fly to the North Pole in a plane. But even he could not imagine the huge triumph of bravery, courage, and skill, which these young people demonstrated."

The famous French pilot, Rossi, said: "I give this crew their due. Its flight proves that the people who make up an aircraft's crew not only possess an elevated feeling of duty, but surprising courage. I suggest that this flight is a victory for the Soviet Union, which brings honor not only to the crew, but to the workers who built the plane. I admire these three Soviet pilots and wish them success from the bottom of my heart in all their future flights."

The famous scientist, Arctic explorer, and President of The Explorers' Club, Vilhjamur Stefansson, telegraphed Ambassador Alexander Antonovich Troyanovsky: "In the name of the members and the Presidium of the Explorers' Club, I have the honor to congratulate you for completing the greatest achievement in the history of aviation and in the history of Arctic exploration. Explorers of the world bow before Chkalov, Baidukov and Belyakov, and also before your government for its wise and consistent support, which over the course of several years, it has provided for Arctic exploration.[76]

After the Gromov crew completed the second transpolar flight, Stefansson organized a dinner in their honor at which he expressed the following marvelous sentiments: "...For more than 2000 years, man has known that the earth is shaped like a ball, but has acted as though it were cylindrical in form. Soviet explorers, pilots and navigators, have proven that the earth is shaped in the form of a ball, not only from east to west, but from north to south. The transpolar flights show that we live in an epoch of deep change in human understanding."

Moscow newspapers in 1937 printed information about a Committee formed in Vancouver called the Moscow—Vancouver Committee and headed by Mr. Henry Rasmussen. The goal of the committee was to erect a monument at the landing site of the ANT-25 to honor Heroes of the Soviet Union, V. P. Chkalov, G. F. Baidukov and A. V. Belyakov—pioneers and conquerors of unknown expanses of the Arctic, and creators of a new air route over the North Pole to America.

The source of this information were letters sent by the Governor of the State of Washington, Mr. Clarence Martin; Vancouver Mayor, Mr. John

Kiggins; Moscow — Vancouver Committee Chairman, Mr. Henry Rasmussen; and Messrs. Thompson, Campbell, and Richards to USSR Foreign Policy Commissar, Maxim Litvinov.

Mr. Rasmussen, in a letter dated July 26, 1937, wrote: "We citizens of Vancouver and the State of Washington, residing at the end point of the first in history transpolar flight across the North Pole completed by Soviet aviators, express to these heroes and to the people they represent, our sincere congratulations on their achievements…

"They (Chkalov, Baidukov and Belyakov – auth.) accomplished a triumph, which has exceeded all others in the history of aviation. But in a broader sense, their victory over the unexplored Arctic turns out not to be their victory alone, but a victory of a people united for the attainment of a specific goal. The plane, which allowed them to cross the world's last frontier, is the product of the unity of the intellect and hands of the Russian people. The equipment and experience, which guided them during this fearless flight, was the result of lengthy planning and research. Their triumph was Russia's triumph.

"To properly recognize the USSR for the achievement of completing this flight, the inhabitants of Vancouver propose to erect a monument in imperishable stone and bronze, in order to make eternal and preserve the memory of this first air victory over the 'roof of the world.' We plan to erect a monument approximately on the spot where the now famous ANT-25 was parked after its historical flight…"[77]

So decided the Americans in long-ago 1937. Life, however, and especially the Second World War and Post War Period, put an end to the plans of Vancouver's citizens.

But true to their intentions, Vancouverites raised this monument in 1975. A Chkalov Transpolar Flight Committee was formed. Members of the legendary crew, Georgy Baidukov, Alexander Belyakov and Valery Chkalov's son, Igor Chkalov, attended the monument opening. The monument embodies a bridge over the North Pole between two continents — Europe and North America.

Every year Vancouver citizens lay flowers at the monument and arrange a meeting. With this act of friendship, another page in the history of Vancouver was written. Henry Rasmussen wrote about it as follows:

"…The wheels of the ANT-25 first touched earth at a place already considered historic. The plane was parked just a few steps away from the place where civilization in the Northwest USA began, and very close to the birthplace of water and land transportation to the Great Northwest.

"The first schooner in the Northwest was built on the shores of the Columbia River, the first steam ship was launched and the first plane took off..."

This flight has brought our peoples, and the cities of Vancouver and Chkalovsk, my father's hometown, closer together, and has created kind feelings in the hearts of all the participants and their descendents.

On June 21, 1937, the Associated Press published an article with a speech by Soviet Ambassador to the USA, A. Troyanovsky: "The flight was non-stop... It is only a beginning. This huge achievement by the pilots can be compared to the triumph of Lindberg. These three pilots were already famous as 'Heroes of the Soviet Union.' Now they can be considered heroes of the world."

In his letter, the Chairman of the Moscow — Vancouver Committee, Henry Rasmussen, was correct when he noted that this legendary flight was the result of serious and thoughtful preparation by the crew.

On the day of the plane's landing on American soil, June 20, 1937, The New York Times wrote: "...Today's flight by Chkalov, Baidukov and Belyakov, has to be evaluated more deeply than simply an effort to break the world's record for non-stop flight. This flight appears to be preparation for the establishment of a regular transpolar airline between the United States and the Soviet Union.... Their arrival in America is perhaps the first step on the way to organizing air postal, freight, and passenger travel in the shortest possible time."

Supporting the idea of establishing a regular transpolar airline between the USSR and the USA, Vancouver mayor, John Kiggins, in his June 29, 1937, letter to Maxim Litvinov, wrote: "...I want to propose to you the establishment of a commercial airline across the Arctic. We have all the resources necessary here to receive your planes..."[78]

On June 21, 1937, "The New York Times" wrote: "...The magnificent flight from Shchelkovo Airfield to Pearson opens up a new field of air exploration, and exhibits powerful support for the theory, long advanced by Stefansson and other experts of the north, that an air route to the east will cross the Arctic. Heroes of the Soviet Union have written a marvelous page into the history of aviation."

In a conversation Valery Chkalov had with the governor of the State of Oregon, Charles Martin, also printed in the June 22, 1937, "New York Times", Chkalov said: "We collected a mass of scientific material. During the course of the current year, we'll study this material. Then, when the right time comes, we'll again attempt to cross the Pole and this time land in New York."

The Baltimore Sun" wrote on June 21, 1937: "...The goal of the current flight by the Russian pilots consists of an effort 'to turn into reality the old dream of uniting America with the USSR by an air route over the North Pole.' They accomplished this with their flight, which turned out to be marvelously done due to their careful preparations, scientific exactness, and the skill and daring of the people who participated in it. This flight, of course, will occupy a much greater place in history than any other of the registered flights, which set records, because it was really the "first" flight to establish a new air route.

"In their huge, single-engine monoplane, the Russians not only flew over an unknown route, but came up against conditions, the character and actions of which, aircraft and people to this time could not have experienced, but only guessed at. The pilots themselves consider that their flight first of all carries political-economic possibilities established by this shortest air route between the USSR and America'...."

The journal "Soviet Russia Today", in the lead article of the July 1937 issue, gives the following evaluation of the Chkalov crew's flight:

"In these days, when war clouds are gathering, this great flight raises the spirits of all peoples. It unites two continents. A new tie between the Soviet Union and the United States has been established. Let this flight bring both peoples closer together and unite them in an effort to conquer nature for the benefit of mankind; let it unite their strength in an effort to change a world at war into a place of peaceful existence."

At a reception in honor of the Soviet pilots at the Waldorf Astoria Hotel in New York City, organized by the "Explorers' Club" and the Russian-American Institute, June 30, 1937, and under the chairmanship of Dr. Vilhjamer Stefansson, Chkalov, in his speech, said:

"Twenty years ago, my country became what it wanted to be. We sing songs about our homeland. In one of them, very popular at present, there are two lines:

'We love our homeland as a bride,
And care for her as a kind, endearing mother...'

"In this song, the composer has expressed the wishes and feelings of 170 million people. The flight across the North Pole was achieved not only by three pilots, but also by the whole Soviet people. In our three hearts, we carry to you the hearts of 170 million people...

"No cyclones, no icing on our plane's wings, could stop us, since we knew we were fulfilling the wishes of our people to deliver their friendly feelings to the people of America....Please accept the sincere and friendly wishes from 170 million Soviet people, which we bring to you on the wings of our plane."[3]

During this evening our three pilots were asked to sign a huge globe. The routes of expeditions and flights of other famous people had already been inscribed on it, such as Amundsen, Nansen, Lindberg, Byrd, and other explorers. I have drawn your attention, dear reader, to these old newspaper excerpts, in order to remember and to show you how America of that time reacted to this flight, about which Vilhjamur Stefansson said would be remembered for centuries.

Celebration of victory is a fine affair, but at home work waited. And our three pilots, already by June 26th, received a telegram from Rukhimovich: "Are you planning to stay long in America? We think it would be well if you returned to Moscow in a week or two. The people are anxiously awaiting you."

From America on June 27th flies an answer to Rukhimovich: "Your telegram is not clear concerning departure from America. We consider it makes little sense to leave before the departure of the plane.[10] We ask your permission to acquaint ourselves with the aviation technology of America. They are showing us more than usual and we should take advantage of that. A month will be necessary.

"We ask permission from the government for each of us to acquire a 'Buick' automobile."

On June 28th, the pilots received permission to remain in America "until the end of July, but not longer," and also received permission to buy automobiles.

And then began the endless invitations to various firms, factories, organizations, and societies. Unfortunately, there was not enough time to go everywhere and visit everyone who sent an invitation, so Troyanovsky wrote a standard polite reply, signed by the three pilots, and sent to the various addresses.

10 The ANT-25 was disassembled and shipped back to Russia.

Father was absolutely amazed on a visit to the Ford factory, and laconically wrote on the cover of a Ford advertisement, "To the Genius Ford. V. Chkalov."

Personal glory was not the goal of father's flight. "We undertook this "Stalin's Route" flight for the glory and well-being of our homeland, and not for any personal glory," he said. "Millions of unseen threads tie Baidukov, Belyakov and me to our Soviet people, and the tie helped us achieve victory. As fuel feeds the motor of our plane, our hearts are nourished by the wonderful strength sent to us by our homeland.

"My life belongs completely to our fatherland. When and where it is necessary, I will be ready to defend with my blood, the great happiness won by the millions of people living today a truly humane life."

He whole-heartedly loved his homeland and his people.

And when their crew, during an excursion, was on the 102nd floor of a New York skyscraper, Chkalov wrote the following words on a record: "Greetings to you, our wonderful homeland. From here, from this 102nd story, we see your outlines. Hello, Moscow! There still lie between us thousands of miles, and many hours of travel.

"We've seen half a world during this time, but my heart longs to return to you."[3]

When he was asked what he remembered most in America, Chkalov answered: "Yearning for my homeland."

This boundless love for his country, with his courage, humility, and daring, defined him perfectly. Speaking at meeting July 26, 1937, before Moscovites on the Byelorussian train station square after his return from the USA, Chkalov said: "…We fulfilled our assignment for the homeland, but we will not rest with this. We are already thinking of new, even more grandiose routes." His dream was to fly around the "globe."

Returning to their homeland, Chkalov, Baidukov, and Belyakov sent greetings from Paris to Moscow — their capital: "We — your sons — and to you, our mother, belongs the honor of our achievement. We are returning to you for rest and inspiration, for new work and new efforts. Because only you, Moscow — the true cradle of everything new, proud, and ennobling, will lead mankind forward.

"Greetings to you, Moscow, from a not too distant place! We will meet you soon!"

GROMOV'S FLIGHT

Yes, Troyanovsky was right, when he said that the flight was only the beginning in the conquering of the Arctic and the North Pole by Soviet pilots.

And what followed?

Among the enthusiastic responses to the Chkalov crew's flight by several American newspapers, was the thought that such a flight would not be repeated soon. The second flight, by the crew of Gromov, Yumashev and Danilin, not only proved to the world that the success of our pilots in mastering the transpolar route was no accident, nor done for personal enjoyment, but established a record which remained unbroken for nine years.

'The Gromov crew awaited decisions about the assignment of control points in Canada and the registration of the flight for the establishment of a world record. On June 22nd, the sports commission asked the Aviation Association of Canada to receive a sports commissar in Edmonton and the National Aviation Association of the USA to receive sports commissars at the place of the plane's landing.

From documents of VAAAN USSR[11] concerning the registration of the Chkalov and Gromov flights, it became apparent to me that after the Politburo passed its June 11th resolution dealing with the Gromov flight, the goals of the two crews had been determined. The Chkalov crew was to fly first across the North Pole, as first proposed by Levanevsky. The Gromov crew was to establish a distance record in a straight line.

From these documents it can be seen that the Chkalov crew was not assigned specific points to fly over, sports commissars were not assigned specific points in the route, and there was no registration for the expected long distance record. Therefore, if the Chkalov crew had flown farther than Vancouver and broken the then established world record for distance, it would not have been registered. The Chkalov crew, therefore, could land at any point in the USA, as had been written in the Politburo's decision.

There is a letter from the head of the Central Air Club of the USSR addressed to Gromov,[73] indicating specific registered points over which Gromov's plane was to fly. There are also telegrams from sports commissars dealing with Gromov's flight over these registration points.

11 A voluntary association formed to assist the Army, Air Force and Navy.

These preparations for registering a world record to be set by the Gromov crew demanded a great deal of time.

In a book by G. Reznichenko[79], and repeated throughout the press recently, it has been claimed that the Gomov flight was to have taken place simultaneously with the Chkalov flight, and that the reason it did not, was because the motor from Gromov's plane had been removed and placed in Chkalov's plane just before the Chkalov crew took off. The documents I have found prove this to be a baseless claim.

In the newspaper "Soviet Aviation," June 20, 1957, Baidukov wrote: "Having analyzed our flight, we quickly sent our conclusions to the flight staff in Moscow, suggesting improvements and changes to be made to Gromov's plane, its motor, equipment and supplies. This was very important, since the Soviet government considered our main goal to be reconnaissance and research over the new route and a study of the plane's qualities in Arctic weather. A second ANT-25 and crew, which included Gromov, Yumashev and Danilin, were being prepared to follow us over the same route.

"Taking our experience and advice into account, M. M. Gromov's crew eliminated unnecessary supplies, which allowed them to increase the amount of fuel to give them approximately 315 additional miles. They took three times as much oxygen and anti-icing liquid for the propeller."

The Chkalov crew sent these suggestions to make sure that a new record would be established.

A few words about the motor in Gromov's plane. The goal of Gromov's flight—the establishment of a world distance record in a straight line—demanded a large mount of fuel, or to greatly economize it during flight. Therefore, a motor was installed in his ANT-25, which would use the same fuel he used to set the world distance record in a closed circle in 1934. Aviation General-Colonel, V. V. Kovalenok, writes: "The new fuel Chkalov used could not be economized at high altitudes, since the carburator would begin knocking. The engine installed in Gromov's plane allowed fuel economizing at high altitudes and increased the plane's long distance capabilities."[8]

It's interesting that in the Archives of the President I found a letter to the Central Committee of the Communist Party from inspector Batarol, who had been appointed by the Main Inspector Commissariat of the Defense Industry to oversee the preparations of the flights, which confirms V. V. Kovalenok's thoughts. The inspector writes that the

"Ekstra 100" fuel at high altitudes produces "loud knocking and is dangerous for the engine. Comrade Gromov himself insists that they give him another fuel..."[81]

Taking the Chkalov crew's advice, Gromov took additional fuel, and increased his supply of oxygen, which allowed him to fly over cyclones at high altitudes and not change the plane's assigned course. All measures were taken for the establishment of a new distance record.

The Gromov crew took off July 12, 1937, at 3:21 a.m. Moscow time and began their flight. They finished it on July 14th in southern USA in a small city, San Jacinto, having flown 6,343 miles in 62 hours and 17 minutes. Their established distance world record in a straight line (class "C") will be forever carried in the record books of the International Aviation Federation. The flight heroes were awarded the medal of de-Lavo.

Umansky, an advisor to the USSR Ambassador in Washington, sent the following telegram: "The landing, in spite of the absence of an airfield, according to witnesses, was brilliant. The mood and health of the crew couldn't be better. However, there was a serious leak in two places forming a large gas puddle." The fuel leak forced the crew to turn back and land.

On the day they landed, the crew sent a telegram to Stalin: "The crew expresses its loyalty, love and gratitude for the trust you have shown us. We dedicate this flight to you, the great leader of our people. Gomov, Yumashev, Danilin."

And this crew didn't escape difficulties and the testing of their metal. Beginning at Franz Josef Land, the plane flew over fog and thick clouds. It cut into a cyclone at about the 85th-86th parallel, fighting through clouds at high altitude flying blind. The plane exited the cyclone in the region of the North Pole.

E. T. Krenkel interestingly described the crew's flight over the North Pole: "This time Papanin energetically prepared for the plane's over flight. He opened a can of paint and the three of them painted two bright yellow circles on the ice field. Each circle had a diameter of about 450 feet. The circles were drawn so that the pilots could more easily find their camp, since among the hummocked ice fields, huge cracks and open water, the tents were very difficult to find, especially in such gloomy, bleak weather.

"At 2:05 a.m., with deafening loudness, the plane's signal burst through: 'Greetings to the Arctic conquerors, Papanin, Krenkel, Shirshov, Fedorov! Aircraft O-25 crew, Gromov, Danilin, Yumashev.'

"Fedorov prepared the formal document, which had to be sent to Moscow. From there, it had to be sent to the International Aviation Federation, proving the plane had passed over the North Pole. I was sitting by the receiver; the other three left the tent, listening, watching.

"The weather this time favored us—there were high clouds, so the plane could fly under them. But the waiting was long and tedious—and no plane appeared. Four men, smeared with yellow paint, finally, with hanging heads, realized there was no use waiting any longer. According to information, which I discovered by radio, it was clear: the plane crossed the Pole along the island meridian, and we were located significantly to the west."

Approaching the Rocky Mountains along the 120 meridian, the plane crossed them in thick clouds and heavy rain. They began to ice up, which forced the crew to sharply change course and head for the Pacific Ocean. The remainder of the flight was carried out in heavy fog and thick clouds all the way to Los Angeles.

Morris Tores, Secretary of the Central Committee of the French Communist Party, sent Stalin the following telegram: "The Central Committee of the French Communist Party requests the Central Committee of the Communist Party of Bolsheviks to extent warm greetings to heroes of the air, comrades Gromov, Yumashev, and Danilin, who have broken the world's distance record, and with a sweep of their wings over the North Pole, have connected Moscow with the United States of America. They have covered Soviet wings with new glory, which has already been of such service to science and humanity. Torez."

After their flight, the pilots were allowed to visit a Sikorsky Aircraft factory, but were not allowed to see a new high-speed fighter plane, as telegraphed by Umansky.

In honor of the Arctic conquerors, receptions and processions were organized: On July 28th, in New York, a celebration with aviation science leaders; on August 2nd, an expansively planned celebration in Philadelphia, with a procession through town and a meeting before 5000 people.

THE LEVANEVSKY CREW'S TRAGEDY

Umansky sent a very interesting telegram from Los Angeles to Stalin, Molotov, Rukhimovich and Potemkin:

"In spite of the fact that the Gromov troika is traveling in still higher political circles than did the Chkalov crew, we're sure that a third flight, not establishing a record, and again along the western shore, would receive a rather tepid reaction. Beside that, the second half of July and the beginning of August is a time of constant fog and low clouds, not only in Alaska, but also all along the coast. I consider the following options very reasonable:

a) Fairbanks—Dawson—Edmonton—Denver (the most important political-economic center of the mountain region in the USA). In this option, the Canadian and American Rocky Mountains are spread out to the east.

b) Fairbanks—Dawson—Edmonton—Chicago or New York. Corresponding meteorological services and communication ties are possible to arrange.

"Gromov insists that the flight to Alaska would be extremely risky. It's difficult to know in advance whether Fairbanks would be closed, and the plane would be running out of fuel. A most dangerous situation. He himself had no suggestions to offer."

This telegram shows the general unease everyone had concerning the third flight—i.e., the flight planned by Levanevsky.

On July 31st, the Poliburo issued a resolution concerning the Levanevsky crew's flight on the DBA (N-209) plane from Moscow over the North Pole to the USA. The resolution speaks of the Foreign Affairs Commissariat receiving permission to fly over the countries affected by the route; the release of 2,500,000 rubles and 75,000 dollars in foreign currency.

Everything was ready for Levanevsky's flight, but the Politburo's resolution hadn't made clear its purpose. Perhaps it was to show the whole world that Soviet pilots could conquer the North Pole in any type of aircraft, and also create economic ties between the USSR and the USA with this shortest possible route.

The four-engine N-209 on which Levanevsky was to fly was built in 1935 in Factory #22 and had flown more than 160 hours in preparation. Loaded with fuel, the plane weighed 35.5 tons. At that weight, the plane had a range of more than 5,300 miles. The plan was to fly the following route: Moscow – Arkhangelsk – Rudolph Island – North Pole – Fairbanks. Then from Fairbanks they were to fly to Edmonton (Canada), Chicago, and New York, with stops in Edmonton, Chicago and New York.

On August 12th at 6:15 p.m. Moscow time, Levanevsky took off on his flight: Moscow – North Pole – USA.

At 1:30 p.m. the next day, the plane had reached the North Pole. After passing the North Pole for a distance of somewhere between 75 and 125 miles in the direction of Alaska, contact with the crew was lost. The last radiogram from them was received at 2:35 p.m.

I would like to quote from a letter dated September 21, 1937, from the head of the scientific-technical development and discovery department of the Central Committee of the Communist Party (CCCP), comrade Bauman. He sent his letter to the Chairman of the Government Flight Organization Commission for USSR – USA flights, M. L. Rukhimovich. I was struck by its contents:

"According to material received by the Science Department of the CCCP, the CAHI party organization indicates that in the process of preparing for the Levanevsky flight on the N-209, there were a series of mistakes made, which could in some way or other cause the flight to fail.

"CAHI's extensive experience in the preparation of aircraft for long distance flight was not applied to the preparations for the flight of the N-209, although the time allowed was a very short two months. Chaotic conditions were noted in the preparations: weighing the plane was turned over to technicians; therefore, it was only at Shchelkovo Airfield, that it was discovered the plane's flight weight had increased by two additional tons; there was no reliable oversight by responsible technicians during preparatory work on the plane, etc.

"During preparations it was discovered they had chosen the wrong wheels, since the wheels they chose were designed to support 18 tons and the plane weighed 35 tons. The propeller assembly was not assigned to first class workers, and they didn't pay attention to the advice of engineer Pogossky (a participant in the preparation of the ANT-25) about the necessity to change propeller assembly.

"In addition, it turns out the crew did not sufficiently study the plane's equipment, nor provide for the proper relief of the navigator and radioman. They didn't foresee the long periods of time they would be flying through clouds. In the opinion of specialists, for such a difficult flight through Arctic conditions, which awaited the N-209, there should have been not less than 30 hours of training flights—there were only 10.5 training flight hours...."[82]

It should be noted that early in June, government Commission Chairman, Rukhimovich, issued a Decree, which stated: "The flight across the North Pole will be made on the first copy of the plane designed by comrade BOLKHOVITINOV, which has logged about 200 hours of flight."

It was recommended that before the flight over the North Pole, there should be training flights within the Soviet Union. After these flights, the motors must be changed, and then about 20 more hours of training should be logged before the transpolar flight. Only after this, and depending on the results of the training flights, would the commission issue a resolution allowing the completion of the transpolar flight.

I'd like to quote from two more documents: Information from the head of the 11th section of the Department of National Securty(NKVD), Yartsev; and a letter to the Central Committee of the Communist Party from inspector Batarol, of the Defense Industry Commissariat's Main Department of Inspection.

Yartsev's information stated: "According to obtained material, the failure of the LEVANEVSKY flight was the result of unsatisfactory technical preparation of the "N-209" aircraft, and, to a well known degree, the abnormal relationships among the crew before the flight.

"...Several times during training flights, as a consequence of vibrations, tubing was loosened and cracks developed in the exhaust system. Insufficient cooling of the radiator, overheated from the motors' exhaust system, threatened to burn the tubing walls and ignite the fuel. POBEZHIMOV saw this defect and told the workers of Factory #22, where the plane's preparations were taking place, but they didn't take his advice. The flight staff almost eliminated participation by the crew in the plane's preparations, and the Polar Aviation Administration busied themselves primarily with purchases of consumer goods for the crew.

"...According to information from the intelligence services, the probable reasons for the fight's failure are a break in the fuel line due to obstruction, which was observed during training flights, but not eliminated, and then exacerbated by Arctic atmospheric conditions.

According to the same information, the absence of communications with the aircraft, apparently, was due to the destruction of the portable radio transmitter during a forced landing. The radio was placed in the navigator's cabin in the nose section of the plane, which in this instance was much more vulnerable and not in the tail as usual."[83]

The second part of the letter is very interesting, where it speaks of the crew's morale. I'd like to quote from it to show the conditions in which these people lived and worked, when everything was listened to, everyone was watched, and all was reported to the authorities. They even reported conversations, which took part in Levanevsky's apartment:

"Confirmed information shows there was disagreement among members of the aircraft's crew. Levanevsky 's haughtiness caused dissatisfaction...

"On July 21-22, Levanevsky expressed doubt concerning the success of the non-stop flight on the accepted route. To questions about the design qualities of the plane, Levanevsky alleged that he hadn't studied the plane.

"Those who clashed with Levanevsky indicate that Levanevsky poorly understood the new aircraft on the day of his departure, and relied on the experience of Kastanaev... In the Administration of Polar Aviation, there are recorded conversations that the flight was needed more by Levanevsky, than by the country."

In a second letter concerning the Levanevsky accident, dated August 21, the following was written:

"The organization was very poor. Frolov, the lead engineer of the N-209, and design engineer, Bolkhovitinov, did not have experience in preparing a plane for such a flight. They themselves worked day and night, but poorly led...

"Comrade LEVANEVSKY, the plane's commander, spent little time at the airfield, didn't know the N-209, and had never taken off with a heavy load.

"...The crew never flew at high altitudes with oxygen, and, therefore, was insufficiently trained in its use. They also trained little for night flying and for flying blind. Levanevsky didn't know the plane's preparation schedule and refused to turn it in, i.e., he didn't come for testing.

"...Wheels were installed on the plane without testing their ability to support the plane's weight of 35 tons... They decided to strengthen them, but testing never occurred, which could have caused problems during a forced landing.

"... On July 22-23, 1937, I reported all the defects to the NKVD."[81]

It's possible to conclude from the above letters that neither the plane nor the crew was prepared for the flight.

In August, September and October, a vigorous search was conducted for S. A. Levanevsky's plane. A series of Politburo resolutions was passed; one of which, from August 14, confirms a plan of action in the search for the N-209:

"The icebreaker "Krasin," located off the shore of Chukotsk Sea, is to immediately set out for Schmidt Cape, take three R-5 aircraft on board with their crews and fuel, and leave for Cape Barrow. From there it is to sail to the north as far as ice will allow (hopefully to the 74th degree), where it will serve as a base for R-5 flights."

Hydrographic ships were mobilized for additional bases from which to prepare flights. Three TB-3 aircraft were prepared for the search under the command of comrades Vodopyanov, Molokov, and Alekseev and took off for Rudolf Island. Sikorsky and Douglass planes set out for Dickson Island.

The search, however, did not bring success. It wasn't called off, though, until March 1938.

The result, then, of this last flight across the North Pole to America, ended with the death of wonderful pilots and navigators, and with the death of Hero of the Soviet Union, Sigismund. A. Levanevsky.

Schmidt's letter, written in 1935, proved to be prophetic. To find Levanevsky's plane in the endless expanse of the Arctic, turned out to be impossible. And Americans, also, took an active part in the search of Levanevsky's plane.

In memory of the marvelous pilot, the Nikolaevsk Navel Flight School was given his name, as was the icebreaker, "S. A. Levanevsky." Many streets in our country also bear his name.

In a conversation about Levanevsky with the newspaper "Pravda," Chkalov said: "He was a great pilot... To him, and not to me, belongs the idea of a flight across the North Pole... You often write that the sky subjugates the brave. I would add the tenacious and the stubborn. Such was Sigismund. Only death could keep him from his goal. The sky will continue to demand from us a high price..."

And what did conquering the North Pole in 1937 bring our country? Two marvelous flights from Moscow across the North Pole to America.

The first crew of V. P. Chkalov, G. F. Baidukov and A. A. Belyakov, established a route across the unexplored spaces of the Arctic in the single-engine ANT-25 (2), designed by A. N. Tupolev. The plane had a Soviet built motor designed by A. A. Mikulin. The flight demonstrated the achievements of our aviation technology and skills.

The second crew of M. M. Gromov, A. B. Yumashev and S. A. Danilin, showed the world that the first flight over the North Pole was no accident. The main achievement of the second crew was the setting of a world long distance record in a straight line, and the establishment of a Class "S" record on a single-engine plane, the ANT-25 (1).

So these flights demonstrated our country's aviation achievements, and showed to the world that Soviet pilots in a single-engine plane, containing much new technology, could conquer the most inaccessible spots on our planet, including the North Pole and the Arctic.

The political, business, and scientific world of America, and of the whole world, thought very highly of these two flights. In the city of Vancouver, on the landing spot of the ANT-25 and its crew, a memorial complex has been created, which includes a monument. A Chkalov Committee was formed, which is still active today. In the city of San Jacinto, where Gromov landed his plane, they have also erected a monument.

After the Chkalov and Gromov flights, the famous polar explorer, Viljamur Stefansson, wrote: "On the monument raised to them by humanity, must be carved the words, 'Judging by the world's routes of communication before them the world appeared cylindrical. They truly turned it into a sphere.'"

The future fate of the ANT-25 has a curious history.

On September 21, 1938, the Soviet exhibits Commissar to the New York World's fair, G. Tikhomirov, sent a letter to the head of NKOP Administration, S. I. Belyaikin, with a request to prepare Hero of the Soviet Union M. M. Gromov's ANT-25(1) for shipment to the USA for participation in the New York World's Fair during the summer of 1939.

On December 10, 1938, the Deputy Commissar to the exhibits, Zarubin, sent a letter to the Leningrad Director of Factory #23 NKOP:

"Factory #23 is authorized to prepare aircraft NO-25 for demonstration in the Soviet Pavilion in the New York World's Fair. It will be shown

as the plane on which comrade Gromov flew, therefore, during preparations, it will be necessary to make the following changes:

1. The whole aircraft must be painted one color: steel-gray.
2. The propeller hub red.
3. On both sides, along the center section, a red line extending the
   length of the fuselage from the front to the tail fin.
4. In place of NO-25, write NO-25-1
5. Paint the inscription, 'Route of Stalin' on the sides.
6. Of the special equipment, leave the oxygen instruments, the sun
   compass, and the radio equipment.
7. It's also necessary to change the mounting of the instruments on
   the instrument panel, for which we have sent you photos of comrade Gromov's instrument panel.

"The packaged plane should be sent to New Port by 12/25/1938. The
steamship leaves December 26-28, 1938.

On December 19-20, Hero of the Soviet Union, comrade Danilin, will
arrive to examine the aircraft."[84]

From this very interesting letter, it follows that an ANT-25 was sent to
the exhibit in New York, only for some reason, they sent the ANT-25(2),
which Chkalov flew across the Pole and not the ANT-25(1), on which
Gromov set the world's distance record in 1937. So, as it turned out, the
plane displayed in New York, Chkalov's ANT-25(2), was the same plane
which had been displayed in the Paris Air Show of 1936.

Why was the decision made to re-paint the plane? And why was it
not possible to send Gromov's plane to New York?

On December 15, 1938, Hero of the Soviet Union, V. P. Chkalov, died
while testing a new fighter plane. On December 20th, the government
passed a resolution to send Chkalov's plane to the New York World's
Fair; i.e., the ANT-25(2).

It's difficult to say whether they had time to make changes to this
plane or not. After the New York exhibit, the plane was sent to
Vladivostok and then to Moscow. Toward the end of 1941, the ANT-25
was sent to Pravdinsk, to a railway station not far from Chkalovsk in the
Gorky Region. The plane, in its disassembled form, was loaded onto four
railway flatcars.

The war had begun in June 1941, so the flatcars were in demand and
had to be quickly unloaded. The Director of the V. P. Chkalov Museum in

Chkalovsk, E. M. Boev, with the help of workers from the Balakhninsky Paper Factory, unloaded the cars in three hours, but then the question arose: how to get the plane to Chkalovsk?

The motor, wheels, and tail section, were carried on carts. The plane's center part and two wings were carried to Chkalovsk by barge with the coming of spring.

This is how Boev described the event: "The young sleigh-driver, sitting on the copilot's seat of the fuselage, and holding the reins in his hands, was proud and happy.... and didn't realize, perhaps, how comical this whole process appeared: Part of the fuselage was on the sleigh with its red inscription, 'The Route of Stalin,' with a silver background and the red parts of the tail section contrasting more brightly still. In front, the unattractive old horse was slowly pulling the sleigh, diving into potholes and ravines—all this on the background of hoar-frost covered bushes along the banks of the Volga...."[85]

From this description, it's clear that Chkalovsk did indeed get the plane Chkalov flew over the North Pole to America, the ANT-25(2).

And what was the fate of the ANT-25(1), which Gromov planned to fly to South America, and, in 1937, flew over the North Pole to America, breaking the distance record earlier set by the French? This plane, unfortunately, was used for target practice and destroyed.

And so now, this unique one of a kind exhibit, this famous aircraft, the ANT-25(2), has found for itself an honorable place in the museum in V. P. Chkalov's home town, where it now decorates a hanger on the shore of the mighty Volga River.

The huge, red-winged ANT-25, which came floating in over the Interstate Bridge (which surprised the piloting Baidukov through the mist and forced him to gain altitude), surprised Vancouver and the world by landing at Pearson Field.

The plane was one of only two designed by Andrei Nikolaevich Tupolev for the purpose of setting records. After following the advice of the Chkalov crew, such as tripling the oxygen supply for higher altitude flight, increasing anti-icing liquid, and eliminating life rafts and other supplies, the second plane with Mikhail Gomov as Commander, broke the distance record by flying 6,300 miles to San Jacinto, CA, three weeks later.

The ANT-25, with its 112 foot wingspan, dwarfs planes on Pearson Field after its 63 hour 16 minute flight from Moscow. They had flown over 7,000 miles, but "only" 5,288 miles in the "straight line" distance required to break the French record of 5,657 miles. Head winds and cyclones had forced them off course. But, as the author points out, their assignment was to be the first to fly nonstop over the Pole to America, not to set a distance record.

The ANT-25 was headed for San Francisco, but due to head winds and cyclones, ran out of fuel. The crew decided over Eugene, OR, to turn back to Portland. The huge, enthusiastic crowd at Swan Island reminded them that Lindbergh's plane and the clothes off his back were torn asunder by excited crowds. They felt Vancouver's military Pearson Field would provide more "discipline."

Сталинский Маршрут *(Stalin's Route), inscribed on the plane's fuselage in 1936, refers to the route Stalin drew on a map directing them to fly from Moscow to the Petropavlovsk on the Kamchatka Peninsula in that year. It was to prove whether the plane and crew could fly over the Pole to America. In a near catastrophe, they were forced to land on a tiny island in the Sea of Okhotsk. Chkalov, Baidukov and Belyakov were named "Heroes of the Soviet Union" for their accomplishment. Each has an island in the Sea of Okhotsk named after them today.*

Taken minutes after landing at 8:22 AM Sunday morning, June 20, 1937 at Pearson Field, Belyakov, Chkalov and Baidukov had to be happy just to be alive. They had flown 7000 nonstop miles in a cramped, freezing cockpit for 63 hours and 16 minutes, enduring high altitude nose bleeds, spinning compasses, forced course changes, dangerous icing, over-heated engine, frozen drinking water, and lost radio contact. The danger was highlighted, when on August 13, 1937, their countryman, Sigismund Levanevsky and five crew members in a four-engine N-209 aircraft disappeared shortly after crossing the Pole.

A huge crowd from Swan Island and Portland came streaming across the Interstate Bridge to see the strange plane and the crew the whole world had been following and talking about, since their June 18 departure from Moscow.

After being fitted for suits by a Portland Meier & Frank's tailor and a night's rest, the pilots enjoy breakfast in the Marshall house. From the left, Belyakov, Ambassodor Troyanovsky, Gen. Marshall, Chkalov, and Baidukov. They were later taken to J. J. Padden in downtown Vancouver for raincoats.

Chkalov, Belyakov and Baidukov being photographed before entering The Waldorf Astoria Hotel; in New York prior to a nationwide radio broadcast.

Son Igor, Chkalov, and his wife Olga, enjoy the adulation of a Moscow parade in their honor after his history making polar flight to Vancouver in June, 1937.

Moscow gives their heroes a welcoming parade on their return from America. July 26, 1937.

Gen. Marshall and Chkalov having a laugh at a picture of their afternoon "breakfast" at Gen. Marshall's home the day before.

Valery P. Chkalov with General George C. Marshall.

233

At a military parade in Vancouver in honor of the Chkalov Crew.

Crowds lined downtown streets as the three Russian transpolar fliers came to Portland from Vancouver to spend the final three hours of their visit in the Northwest. They had just arrived at the Portland Chamber of Commerce bldg. for a luncheon in their honor as this picture was taken.

CHAPTER THREE

Chkalov Lived Only 34 Years

DEPUTY TO THE SUPREME SOVIET OF THE USSR

Father was extremely popular. He was famous even in the most distant corners of our country. His love of his homeland and of his people was boundless, and it was apparent in all his actions. At every event, in speeches, in articles, he remembered the great Russian people.

During his flight to America, Belyakov describes the following event: "Due to poor weather, we couldn't communicate. Our wireless radio was out. Chkalov wrote Baidukov a note as we flew over Banks Island: 'Yegor, we've left all danger behind us, but since Sasha (Belyakov) is not receiving anything—he says he can't hear—probably, they can't hear him either. I think they're in a panic at home.'"

What was Chkalov worried about? About himself? About the danger? About the difficulties ahead? No, he was thinking about the anxieties and concern of his people back home.

The love of his country and his people were most important in father's life.

And the people paid him with their love. He received more than 190 telegrams from various corners of the country asking him to run as a representative from their region. Some of the regions from which he received such requests follow: Bashkir, Buryat, Mariysk, Chuvashsk ASSR; ASSR Volga Germans, Oiratsk, Tatar Republic, Altai Region, Krasnodar, Kazakh SSR, Nikolaevsk, Sverdlovsk, Orenburg, Kharkov, Odessa, Volynsk, Kurgannsk, Tambovsk, Voronezh, Vladiir, Zhitomir. From the following cities: Tashkent, Yerevan, Vladivostok, Baku.

Many requests came from small cities and villages, i.e., directly from the people, without encouragement from any campaign.

Father wrote an interesting letter to the Gorky (now Nizhni Novgorod-jvf) election commission, which was preparing the region for elections to the Soviet of Nationalities of the Supreme Soviet of the USSR:

"I feel deep gratitude for the trust of the voters who have put my name forward as a candidate to the Soviet of Nationalities of the Supreme Soviet of the USSR.

"The Central Committee of the Communist Party has instructed me to remove my candidacy in other cities and to vote in the Gorky Political Region—and to this I have agreed."

For father, the end of 1937 was marked by significant events. On December 18th he was elected Deputy of the Soviet of Nationalities of the Supreme Soviet of the USSR from Gorky Political Region #15. Of 2,578,218 votes, father received 2,547,885. Only 22,895 voted against him, and 7,538 votes were declared invalid.

In his biography, written in both Russian and Chuvash languages for the voters, was this very colorful description: "…Who is this Chkalov? He is the son of the Great Russian people… Among his comrades, he distinguished himself with his daring, courage and fearlessness. No bird can compare with Chkalov and his flying machine. Falcons and eagles, folding their wings, fall as if a rock from the clouds to the earth. And Chkalov can do the same. But Chkalov can also fly "on his back," with wheels overhead, turn over on his wing in a barrel roll, and head over heels in a "Death Loop." In one 45-minute period, he spun head over heels in the air without stopping until he had completed 250 Death Loops. And this not even an eagle can match."

A very graphic and convincing picture for every voter.

Father took his responsibilities as a deputy very seriously. His acquaintance with the voters began during the campaign. On November 21st, Chkalov traveled to Gorky and gave a talk on the radio.

During the 20 days leading up to the election, father spoke before the voters 72 times. Simple arithmetic shows that he must have averaged three or four presentations a day.

He traveled through 16 regions of Gorky Province and five regions of Chuvashaya and spoke before Gorky voters 18 times. In all, he spoke before 630,000 voters.

Leonid Aleksandrovich Kudrevatikh, of the "Gorky Commune," accompanied him on all his travels and wrote that he possessed yet another remarkable talent—he was a marvelous campaigner: "At meetings and gatherings, he not only told of his flying experiences—and this he was forced to do at the insistence of his audiences—he also spoke as a future deputy, relating directly to the potential voters. Whether speaking to students or teachers, factory or farm workers, he always found the appropriate words for his audience."[86]

Father began his campaigning in the northern regions of Gorky Province. He traveled by train and by automobile along the beat up Russian roads. People came to meet this future deputy from neighboring villages and hamlets, and there were some who traveled dozens of miles in order to see and meet with their Deputy.

A telegram arrived from the Central Executive Committee of the Chuvash Republic: "We have received many inquiries from factory and farm workers, who want to see you very badly. We ask you in the name of the whole Chuvash people, to meet with our voters." So father traveled throughout the whole of Chuvashaya, in the southern regions of Gorky Province, in order to meet with its people.

There were some very touching scenes, as people would gather at train stations to meet with Chkalov, if only for a few minutes. Father would give short speeches directly from the platform at the back of the train.

These many trips and speeches nevertheless tired father, and in spite of colds and a bad cough, he would never cancel them.

"But we, who accompanied Chkalov," remembered Kudrevatikh, "didn't risk suggesting to him that he cut short his trip and return to Gorky. We knew that he attached great significance to his meetings with the Chuvash people and looked forward to them… It was difficult for him give his speeches in the freezing weather, so it was decided that all gatherings where he was expected to speak would be held in enclosed areas. But at noon in Kanasha, there were 12 thousand people waiting in the square to hear him speak. The temperature had plummeted to 30 degrees below zero. What to do? We tried to find a way out. It was suggested he meet with the most active supporters in a club. Chkalov, however, went to the square. The meeting lasted more than an hour. Chkalov didn't limit himself just to words of gratitude and thanks, but gave an enthusiastic spirited speech."

And that's the way he spoke at all his stops. When Kudrevatikh asked him to at least wear a hat in the freezing air, he answered, "No, I'm speaking to the people!"

After these trips, father often commented, "These people are great! Russians are strong! Could someone really contemplate defeating such a people?!"

And to the measured sounds of the train's wheels, father would quietly sing his favorite song:

"Along the street the snow storm swirled,

And in that storm my sweetheart strolled."

Mother said he had a pleasant baritone.

And so began his many-sided activities as a Deputy. I'll just mention a few examples, since to describe them all would be impossible, and from these examples his relationship to the voters, and most importantly, his respect for the individual will be apparent.

In the Gorky Automobile Factory, production stopped because parts were not arriving on time from factory suppliers. Father wrote an open letter to the factory's lead suppliers with a call to "make every effort to fulfill and over fulfill the demand for supply parts for the Gorky Automobile Factory and create a sufficient supply for the normal production of automobiles." This open letter hit the target, as they say, and normal production proceeded.

After attending a performance at the regional drama theater, he went backstage. On seeing the wretchedness of the actors' restrooms, the dirty equipment and props, to which, unfortunately the actors had become accustomed, he asked the director to clean things up and bring order to the theater.

"The next time I'm here I'm going to check up on you," he said, and, of course, that's just what he did. As a result, he achieved major repairs to the theater.

He helped a group of medical workers to receive funds to build a children's hospital in the city.

Father helped to finish the construction of two community clubs in the Chkalovsk Region — at a peat factory, Chestoya, and in Katunky.

Now he was flying to meetings with citizens in a U-2 plane, loaned to him by the government.

Sixty years later, an elderly man showed up in our house — Safa Asfandyarovich Asfandyarov, who, as an 11-year-old boy on July 20, 1938, attended a citizens' meeting with Deputy Chkalov in the village of Urga. He told how Chkalov visited several peasants in their log huts, and showed interest in their lives, customs and the uniqueness of these Tatar families. He asked them to tell him their problems and difficulties and what they were particularly unhappy about.

Safa Asfandyarovich, himself a native son of Urga, devoted much time to educating the village's young generation about their famous fellow-countryman. He convinced the village to name its high school, "V. P. Chkalov."

During his year as a Deputy, father received more than 300 letters from his constituents. Each request was fulfilled, and every letter received an answer. Of course, mother helped him in this effort.

In order to communicate with the voters, he used the press — especially newspapers, which published articles describing the work he accomplished.

Father was also elected a member of the Gorky City Council and the Regional Party Committee. He never missed a meeting of the Gorky City Council or Party Conference, which were for him very significant events. He was often in Gorky, traveling there for holidays and when on vacations — and when he did, citizens would always feel free to approach him.

Chkalov did much as a Deputy for automobile and motorcycle racing. They would ask him to be the head judge at competitions.

The first competitions took place in February 1938 in Gorky. He took time to acquaint himself with the assigned race routes, especially with its difficulties and risky sections, saying that: "It's necessary to care for what's most important, most valuable — i.e., every person. Races are no joking matter, and carry no small amount of danger to the lives of these sportsmen."

This gave him the possibility of speaking to the participants with knowledge. In his final words to them before the race, he said: "Comrades, the road you'll be taking tomorrow will be a difficult one. You'll meet sharp rises and falls and curves. Deep snow will be a significant barrier, and at times an icy road. Overcoming all this, and racing against time in order to win, you mustn't forget that the race must proceed without accident. No one wants you to risk your life, and you must remember this well. Race boldly, but with a clear head… In a crosscountry race we evaluate how well you've prepared yourself and your machine and how well you understand its mechanical aspects. We need sports drivers who are technically educated; who know how to work their way out of the most difficult of circumstances."

At the next All-Union Competitions, devoted to the 20th anniversary of the Lenin Komsomol, Chkalov was again invited to be the head judge.

He decided to prepare himself even more seriously for this race and encouraged the use of only Russian made motorcycles. He said, "I look at you, brothers, and I'm disappointed. You're a brave people, tough. You have the strength to set many records, but you're racing on foreign machines—"Harleys," "Indianas," and others. You should take an example from us pilots. We long ago refused to fly foreign planes, and haven't done badly. Think about this…think about it well."

In order to solve this problem he placed before the cyclists, father worked to overcome many difficulties and technical problems. Many factories in Leningrad and other cities improved motorcycle construction and studied carefully the quality of their product.

The time came for a serious testing of what had been accomplished in a very short period of time. The competitions were scheduled for September in the city of Kiev. More than 200 of the best cyclists from Tashkent, Fergana, Tbilisi, Baku, Akhangelsk, Vladivostok, Novosibirsk, Kharkov, Odessa, Moscow, Gorky, Leningrad, and other cities came to Kiev.

Both factories and the cyclists themselves produced many fine machines for this race. Taganrog's Nikolai Shumilkin, on a motorcycle he built himself, broke the previous year's record set on an imported machine.

This was a huge victory. In an article, "The Road to Militarizing Sport", father wrote: "Earlier, we did not cultivate automobile and motorcycle racing. We had neither the machines nor the car or motorcycle racers. But our country has grown stronger. Industry has grown tremendously. We now produce our own cars and motorcycles, and our own courageous racers have appeared.

"There are now only a few enthusiasts, but thousands of car and motorcycle racers are growing up and mastering the skill in the large and small cities of our country."

From the memoir of Tatyana Viktorovna Federova, Deputy Director of Urban Development and Hero of Socialist Labor:

"Valery Pavlovich had a many sided personality. He was first of all a patriot. He devoted his full talents, withholding nothing, to his country.

"Chkalov read a lot. He loved classical and contemporary literature. He had many friends among authors, performers and artists. They loved him and invited him to their opening nights and new productions. They gave him books, and not because he was famous. It was simply because he had interesting thoughts about what he observed and read. He didn't suffer fools gladly, and didn't stand on ceremony if he would encounter a hack. Extremely honest in his work and with his friends, he demanded the same from others.

"Chkalov was constantly studying, and forced his comrade pilots to do the same. He didn't accept excuses such as, 'But we never graduated from college... ' He cut such people short with, 'What a pity. Every person has to study in this Soviet time. Today education is honored, not the shovel. It's time to forget the story that our fathers gulped down shchi using bast (birch strip) sandals. This story wasn't contrived by them, but was made up about them. They ate shchi with spoons. True, wooden spoons, but the shchi they served then was as hot as fire. I don't like people who don't work; and I don't like technology that doesn't work.'

"...In August, 1937, the Department of Urban Development hosted an evening in the Conservatory's Grand Hall. Along with other leading workers, I had been elected to the Presidium. The hall was overflowing. The speakers were taking their turns. Suddenly everyone rose from their seats in a burst of applause. Valery Pavlovich Chkalov had entered the hall! Embarrassed with such a reception, he asked everyone to continue. Taking me by the hand, we sat down together.

"I carefully kept a photograph which was taken that evening of Valery and I, and which was very dear to my heart. To me, that photo seemed the best of all that I had seen.

"In a later meeting with Chkalov, he joked:

'Tanyusha, have you seen our photograph? We're sitting together as if divorced?'[12]

"He congratulated me warmly, so happy that a young Komsomol girl 'from the back country' had been elected a Deputy to the Supreme Soviet of the USSR.

"I was proud, and am proud today, of his comradely relations with me and with his friendship.

"Valery Chkalov loved young people...

"He once said that knowledgeable people should more often visit schools to meet with young people. 'Tanya, let's write an appeal to that effect and have a group of Deputies sign it.' That's the way he was: No sooner said, than done!

"Valery Pavlovich and I sat in his home office. There were many books; everything was modest, simple, and comfortable. Chkalov loved

12 In the picture they are facing away from each other with serious expressions on their faces.

241

his home. We were writing when Olga Erazmovna came in. She moved our writing material to the edge of the desk and said:

'Take a rest and drink a little tea.' She placed two beautiful cups with steaming tea in the desk along with a little bowl of strawberry jam. Valery Pavolovich joked:

'Well, if we're going to drink tea, Olenka, don't be stingy, bring us some more jam—and make it cherry. And you come and join us.'

"We drank our tea, and then back to work. We wrote our Appeal and in several days it was in the newspapers. It was signed by V. P. Chkalov, I. M. Moskvin, T. V. Fekorova, I. I. Gudkov, and N. N. Burdenko. The sponsorship began—or more generously defined—a tutoring program of older, more experienced persons with the young generation was begun."[87]

A PERSON IS KNOWN BY HIS FRIENDS

"Talented people are usually attracted to one another, and are enriched in the process of mutual communication. On the other hand, they wither without this creative contact; and become too engrossed in themselves," wrote mother in her book. Father couldn't live without his friends. His expansive nature, unusual spiritedness, kindness and sincerity in relations with others attracted many, and convinced them to join his circle of friends.

This circle of friends was very wide and varied: the singer, Ivan Kozlovsky and popular pilot, Mikhail Vodopyanov; poet, Vasily Kamensky and writer Fedor Panferov; writer, Mustafa Sabirov and sculptor, Isaak Mendelevich; journalists Isidor Rodin, Mikhial Rozenfeld, Ivan Rakhillo; and young urban designer, Tatyana Fedorova. And, of course, Georgy Baikukov and Alexander Belyakov, members of the famous Chkalov crew.

This rather lengthy list is only a small portion of his circle of friends.

Gallai described very well the love Chkalov's friends had for him: "They loved him most of all not for his generally acclaimed courage and bravery. And not for his piloting skills or contributions to the development of the Air Force—it's possible to name pilots who possessed more contemporary technical skills, and who contributed no less to the progress of aviation. They loved him for his humanity, for his well-developed feelings of comradeship, for his large and generous heart...."

Father was drawn to talented people, and thirsted for heart-felt, sincere communication with them. His originality, and the ability to understand and evaluate what he observed and heard in a very interesting way, attracted them to him.

"In 1936 Chkalov's name was on everyone's lips... From that year, Valery Pavlovich made friends with many of the leading actors and artists of the capital... Gradually, a close group of friends with which Valery Pavlovich found common language grew. In this group, in addition to Moskvin and Klimov, was the sculptor, I. A. Mendelevich, his brother, the master of ceremonies, A. A. Mendelevich, and bibliophile, N. P. Smirnov-Sokoskiy. Often Alexei Tolstoy and Demyan Bedniy joined the group, and although Chkalov was the youngest among them, conversations were always "on an equal footing." The actors and writers were surprised this young, but world famous pilot, knew literature, theater and the fine arts, and could so sensibly critique and discuss the various expressions of our country's artistic life."[88]

After father was no longer with us, these friends remained friends of the family during both the happy moments and the sad moments of our life.

On January 1, 1939, on Igor's birthday—just two weeks after father's death—the doorbell unexpectedly rang. Of course, no guests had been invited; the family was in deep mourning. Opening the door, mother saw I. A. Mendelevich; People's Artists of the USSR, I. M. Moskvin and M. M. Klimov; the writer, A. S. Novikov-Priboy; and the Head of Government Publishing, P. I. Chagin. Loaded down with gifts, these friends had come to congratulate us on the New Year's holiday and Igor's birthday.

In 1956, Khrushchev renamed the city of Chkalov into Orenburg, which was published in newspapers with the statement that it was done due to "many requests from workers". In the late 1990s, when I was searching the archives for information about the life and work of my father, I didn't find any of these "many requests". I did find a letter, however, from the citizens of Orenburg, written in 1939, requesting that the city's name be changed from Orenburg to Chkalov.

In 1956, while studying in the physics department of Moscow State University, a paper with the name change was hung on the reader-board. Some notes were also typed with the heading, "Who was bothered by the dead Chkalov?"

There was a negative reaction to this name change, and everyone waited for a follow-up action. Our family was also puzzled by this name change and was living under a great deal of tension. December 15th was approaching—the day father was killed. By established tradition, this day every year, and especially years ending in '00 and '05, friends of the family gather in our home. The number of guests is limited only by the size of our table; which, of course, is added to and lengthened. But this year, even that did not help.

One of the first to come on December 15th was Ivan Semenovich Kozlovsky. He rang the doorbell and when it opened, he asked, "Do you have guests?" Behind him stood performers, whom he had brought in order to organize a concert. He wanted on this important day to make up for the tactlessness of our government.

The friends of our family were always with us. On father's memorable days, not only the people I've already mentioned came to see us, but others also, such as: Aviation Marshal, Astakhov; pilot-cosmonaut, Georgy Beregovoy; three-time Hero of the Soviet Union, I. N. Kozhedub; Hero of the Soviet Union, test pilot, Georgy Mosolov; pianist, G. G. Neygauz; and fathers old friends, Tselebeev, Turzhansky, and many others.

Most of our family friends are no longer with us, but we will always remember them with heartfelt warmth and sincerity. We will pass on these memories to our children, grandchildren and great grandchildren. The names of good people must forever live among us. The longer we preserve their memories, the longer kindness, warmth and love will exist on this planet.

POETS OF THE AIR

It's difficult to say, and under what circumstances, father and Vasily Vasilievich Kamensky met. But poet Vasily Kamensky was a pilot at heart; pilot Valery Chkalov was a poet at heart—they extended their hands to one another and remained friends forever.

Poet Kamensky was born April 18, 1884, on the Kama River near Perm; father was born 20 years later on the Volga River in the village of Vasilevo 65 miles from Nizhni Novgorod. Vasily Vasilievich and father spent their childhood among steamships, barges and rafts. Little Vasily became an orphan at age four; Valery lost his mother at age six. In 1904—the year of Valery's birth—Vasily Vasilievich began to write articles for the regional newspaper, "The Permsky Krai." They both began their working careers early.

Vasily Vasilievich first became captivated by aviation in 1911. He became a professional aviator and flew commercially in various Russian cities. It was he, who first used the Russian word "Samolet" to describe the airplane.[13]

Poet Kamensky fell in love with aviation, about which he wrote in a marvelous story: "The Airplane and First Love." Following is an excerpt from this story printed the journal "Oganyok" in 1911 under the title: "Study of a Pilot: Aviator Vasily Kamensky." It beautifully characterizes the soul of a person who has fallen in love with flying.

He was 27 when he took his first solo flight: "With the sacred trembling one feels with a first love, I purchased that spring a Bleriot Airplane, rented a hanger at Gatchina Airfield and hired a mechanic. For about 10 days I commuted to Gatchina, and observed very carefully the flights of the military flight school. I watched then again and again, drinking in and becoming accustomed to the sights and smells of the scene. I listened to the pilots and took careful note of everything I heard and saw.

"I entered my hanger and approached the plane as a groom would to his bride: with awe and joyful endearment; with happy hopes for the future. I lightly touched the resilient, quivering wings with love and care.

"I was offended, jealous, when the mechanic was sometimes not sufficiently delicate in his handling of the apparatus. I became seriously angry if someone called my Bleriot by the familiar "Blerioshka."

"I would look at my winged treasure for hours, and with passion think: Here is my wished for happiness, my reality, my real love—the first, bright, warm, and huge love...for an airplane.

"Damn! Really! In these sunny, spring days, I distinctly and deeply felt this first great love for my marvelous bird. And one thought: that very soon, on this bird, I would rise noisily into the sky, filled me with boundless happiness.

'And I will fly!' I proudly cried to the heavens.

"At last I decided... I got up at 4:00 a.m., pulled the plane onto the field, got in, started the motor, and quickly taxied along the ground... My God! How I shook from excitement. After half an hour taxiing around the field, I finally pulled the lever toward myself, and my dragonfly jumped into the air for the first time.

13 The literal meaning of "samolet" in Russian is "self-flier."

"My eyes were wide open, and an ecstatic smile of happiness was frozen on my face. Everything seemed light and happy, from this unfamiliar feeling, but a bit terrifying too. That whole day I felt myself a young god, and somehow couldn't believe that on the earth they still hadn't solved the most simple question about the meaning of life..."

Yes, only a poet can so perceptively understand and feel the beauty of a first flight.

Vasily Vasilievich Kamensky preserved this love for the sky, and for the wonderful profession of pilot, his whole life. After writing his novel in verse about pilots, "Power," he dedicated it to Valery Pavlovich Chkalov.

The novel was published in 1939, after father's death, and was presented to mother with a wonderful inscription and poems: "To the infinitely charming and infinitely wonderful Olga Erazmovna, from the depths of my soul and the fires of my heart." July 26, 1939.

The poems:

"I see beautiful dreams
In real life...
And during every
Exciting meeting,
I speak to you in
Unclear speech,
In this blue evening
Of flooding spring."

When Vasily Vasilievich completed his first flight in 1911, father was 7 years old and making the trip each day by himself to the village school.

Father's acquaintance with the airplane was less romantic. Here is what he wrote about it:

"Sometimes planes flew over the village. I rarely saw these planes, which seemed like fantastic birds to me at the time. On hearing the motor, I would forget about my work and jump out of the stoke-hole. Black all over, bathed in sweat, I followed the plane as it disappeared over the horizon. I then would let myself down again into my "scorching hell," dream of flying, and believe the dream would never come true...

"I saw my first airplane in Nizhni Novgorod in 1919. It was a seaplane, rocking gently on the waves and attracting a lot of attention.

"I looked at this never before seen bird; fell in love with it's lacquered surfaces, with the shiny metal motor parts, and admired its beautiful, sharp lines...and dreamed of flying in it.

"But really, was it just to me alone, that this plane seemed to be a fantastic bird, easily skimming over the Volga, over fields, over forests?"

However, father's route to aviation was more difficult than it was for Vasily Vasilievich. Father's love of aviation led him first to the Fourth Kanavinsky Aviation Park, and then to aviation schools: Yegorevskaya, Borisoglebskaya, Moskovskaya, Serpukovskaya.

The Yegorevskaya Pilots' Theoretical School followed the teachings of the same Gatchina Military Aviation School, about which Kamensky wrote in his story.

Father completed his first solo flight at age 20 at the Borisoglebskaya School.

What was it that drew these two very different, yet very similar people together? It was, of course, the love of flying.

Vasily Vasilievich flying career ended after an accident, from which it took him a long time to recover. Father's career ended when he died testing a new fighter plane, the I-180, December 15, 1938.

Following is a letter Vasily Vasilievich wrote to mother on New Year's, a few days after father's death. He was living in Tbilisi at the time.

"Infinitely dear Olga Erazmovna, in these hours approaching the New Year, I would like to extend to you across the Caucuses Mountains a hand of friendship, and in memory of the legendary warrior of the heavens, Valery, your closest and dearest friend, and the friend of our nation's peoples, and the friend of all humanity.

"Fortunately, we are all one inseparable, loving, Soviet family — your grief is our grief; your feelings are our feelings; your tranquility is our consolation.

"Life continues.

"You were the friend of a great hero, which means you must, heroically, bravely observe the life around you. You have marvelous children, and forever will have devoted, faithful friends.

"What is our life–
    A passing flock of Days
Doves into wonders.
    Today you're blossoming

Radiant with youth.

And leave for heaven tomorrow.

"Such is life. Suddenly something unbelievable happens, something unexpected—and its name is life.

"I wrote the above poem long ago, after I'd been a pilot four years (and barely left whole after an accident). In order that I not lose heart, I composed this hymn to life, understanding the full danger of the flying profession, of the tragic event, which could happen to anyone at any time.

"And we all know this, see it, and even foresee it.

"Valery was just such a great 'knight without fear'; one who accomplished amazing victories in the name of our wonderful, boundless, genius homeland.

"Valery was a hero of the Soviet land and lived as poet lives his poetry; as an eagle, a master of his profession.

"How could one forget that spring evening at your home? (You remember, when we 'dined' with Levanov almost till morning.) He, Valery, tenderly embraced me, and placed a Strause waltz on the phonograph. He said that he also created waltzes in the sky and that he would take me up with him so he could prove it.

"Only a poet with another poet could think and speak this way; turning life into art.

"It was no accident Valery loved art so deeply, and tied his mastery and interest of poetry and music with his life in the sky. He, himself, was a legend.

"And when you and he would come to visit me in the summer, and we would fish and hunt, he would say that we should get an accordion, take a raft down the river, sing and read poetry.

"A great poet of the air lived in these dreams.

"He was very interested in my future novel in verse, 'Courage', and gave me much unforgettable advice, which I used.

"I have dedicated the novel to Valery.

"The book is being printed now and I will bring the first copy to you, Olga Erazmovna, our charming friend, our poetic love, our golden heart, and dear soul-mate.

"I know there is no word to console you in these difficult days; as there is no strength for you to be inspired to turn this whole tragedy into a Heroic poem—belonging to art.

"Chkalov is a legend of the people. You also love art very much, and understand well that it is truth. A legend!

"I, a poet, during the three years I was writing the novel 'Courage', used the name Chkalov as an example of greatness when uplifting, fantastic bravery and inspiration was demanded by the poetic scope of my work. It inspires us to victories, to marvelous achievements, to pride, to willful courage.

"I would like to see you in this wise steadfastness, as if you exist in this legend, as a heroine with your epic children.

"Life continues — every morning the sun rises — and life is wonderful, miracles abound, there is much sadness, and much happiness, and much that is unexpected. This is life.

"We all create the legend of life.

"And we must all be prepared to meet every test.

"We still live and breathe the clear blue sky of art, and we continue to love as long as the heart beats. In addition, our children grow and blossom and we wait with impatient interest to know what they will become.

"Let this new 1939 year bring you peace and pride — pride that you have been able to remain at the elevated level of the heroic woman, about whom we poets write.

"And we, your and Valery's friends, infinitely loving life and all of you Chkalovs, have still more deeply strengthened this love, this sacred feeling of boundless friendship, this admiration for those glorious bursts of Chkalov expansiveness and achievement. And we will triple our mutual energy in order to create a more perfect life.

"And therefore, my dearest, charming Olga Erazmovna, I wish you happiness and good health.

"You, of course, are in no mood to listen to a poet, and I mustn't dare to hope for an answer to this friendly, sincere letter. But if you do happen to find a spare minute, I would be rapturously grateful for several lines acknowledging that you have received and read my letter.

"Please pass on my greetings to Levanov.

"Here, in Tbilisi, I'm writing a book about Mayakovsky. And I am thinking about a play 'Chkalov.'

I kiss your hand,

V. Kamensky

December 28, 1938."[3]

At some point, mother wrote: "Artistic people were attracted to him, and he had many of them as friends. Apparently, there is some kind of natural law of attraction among generally talented people. Communication and friendship among them enriches them."

Probably, these two unusual people were drawn together by the power of their creative work, by their talent for creation.

Vasily Vasilievich Kamensky was a poet, artist, writer and dramatist. He bagan his creative career as a poet of the Futurist School and as an artist. From his pen, came the novel, "Stenka Razin"; the poems, "Yemelyan Pugachev," Ivan Bolotnikov," The Partisans"; the books, "Summer on the Kamenok," "Life With Mayakovsky," and many, many others. In 1913, he invented an amphibious air-cushion vehicle and demonstrated it in the Kama River in Perm.

Valery Pavlovich Chkalov was a fighter pilot and test pilot, as I've already written. He created figures of advanced aerobatics: such as the rising spiral, and the slow, controlled barrel roll. He was the first to complete a four and five rotation roll, and worked out and completed figures, which could be used in combat—one, an attack, while flying upside down. Innovations Chkalov introduced into the technique of flying, include performing advanced aerobatic figures at low altitude, and skimming very close to the ground—hedge hopping—and combat at very low altitude.

Hero of the Soviet Union, Anatoly Serov, struck by Chkalov's flying artistry, said it could be compared with the art of a great actor, artist, or musician. He created in observers an unusual feeling for the beauty of his flights, which consisted of a constant cascade of aerobic figures logically following one after another. Chkalov was one with his plane, and it submitted to him, faultlessly expressing his will. He created wonders in the air.

The famous pianist, Emil Gilels, wrote: "Chkalov completed, or, more accurately, created his flights as great composers and artists create their works— passionately, and with inspiration."

Chkalov created a beautiful waltz in the sky. Charmed observers would follow his masterful flights in complete silence, not taking their eyes off the process of his skillful creation.

Yes, Chkalov really was a poet of the sky.

So the heavens gave birth to two talents, giving them the means to express themselves in various ways.

FROM A MEMOIR BY I. S. KOZLOVSKY

"This was a surprisingly versatile person; and, as a singer, I was surprised at his ability to understand and feel music so deeply. He loved opera very much, and he loved expansive folk songs. He often attended symphonic concerts. In America, amid all the noise, excitement, and hullabaloo following his flight from Moscow to the USA over the North Pole, Chkalov found time to obtain recordings of a Rakhmaninov concert, in which I preformed, and a Beethoven symphony.

"The more I met with Chkalov, the more I recognized the interesting qualities of his character. This fascinating personality attracted to himself the most varied of persons, and his understanding of art made him a favorite of actors, musicians and artists.

"Chkalov had a truly Russian nature: expansive, generously gifted, with an open heart reaching out to others.

****

"We exited to the street.

'Who is going where with whom?' Chkalov's cheerful question rang out clearly.

'I don't have far to go,' I said.

'Please, please! You can ride with me with ease,' joked Valery Pavlovich.

" Since we had discussed earlier who had what kind of car, Valery Pavlovich suddenly, half joking, half seriously, apparently knowing my passion for sports and for cars, and attempting to be businesslike, announced:

'Buy my car from me; I'll sell it!

"Although I wasn't especially convinced that a sale and purchase could be accomplished in two or three minutes, I did know that his car was first class. Apparently it had been a gift. He had arrived in this car and perhaps he had several, I didn't know.

"But Chkalov won over my hesitancy and curiosity.... And so we're standing in front of this car.

'Here, take it!'

'How much?' I asked.

'No, first take a look. Don't raise the price, okay?'

251

"I was quiet. Since it was, possibly, December 12th or 14th, and I was in my singing outfit, and wrapped up to my very nose in a scarf, it was obvious I couldn't freely continue the conversation. And he was standing there, as they say, with his soul wide open.

"Our conversation reminded one of a discussion between a cheerful, excited person and a deaf-mute. Someone observing from distance, would have thought it rather funny. Valery Pavlovich would say something quickly and loud, and I would try to respond with gestures.

"Suddenly, decisively, and very businesslike, he approached the car, raised the hood: as if to say 'Look, the motor.' I explained with gestures that the quality of a motor, in my view, is determined by its sound, not its appearance.

"And he, with the determined look of a real Nizhni Novgorod salesman, slapped the car with his hand:

'A beautiful car! Agreed?'

"I shook my head up and down, as if to say, 'Okay, agreed.'"

'But that's irrelevant. You judge correctly.'

'How do we make the sale, with a down payment, or not?' I said, forgetting this once about my 'singers' decorum.

"It was evening. The streets were brightly illuminated next to the Moscow Hotel, where the conversation took place. It was snowing lightly, with soft flakes circling down, playfully, covering the surface around us. We both stood covered in snow. From underneath his white hat, I saw an intense look.

"After an anxious pause, underlining still further the whole significance of the moment, Chkalov came up very close to me and said:

'And can you sell it?'

"And with a facial expression, I indicated: 'What, exactly?' He, understanding my answer, continued:

'Your voice! You won't sell it, I hope. Just like me, I can't part with this bird! Get in, it's better that I just take you for a ride!'

"And in two days I was at his funeral. I sang by his coffin: 'Who will tell me; who will calculate—how much life I have remaining....'"

Friendship with I. A. Mendelevich

Father had a very close relationship with sculptor Isaak Abramovich Mendelevich.

At first, Mendelevich was interested in father's face, which seemed to him to be created for sculpting. As an artist-physiogmonist, he drew a marvelous word-portrait of father, psychologically analyzing his character: "His face was especially distinctive, perfect in size and form. It was very expressive: the forehead showed great strength of will; almost always lying over his forehead was bright , soft hair; a strong nose; sharp features from his nostrils to his lips; sharply outlined lips and prominent chin. His eyes require separate treatment: they seemed to have good distant peripheral vision. His eyes were set in a way that reminded one of the eyes of a powerful bird. These curious, lively eyes, surrounded by premature wrinkles, intently studied a person. Chkalov, observing, wanted to find the essence of his conversation partner."

Father sat for a sculpture by Isaak Abramovich. They had even agreed that he would come to pose for him on December 15, 1938, after he had test flown a new fighter plane. The meeting never took place.

Father often visited Mendelevich's work shop, and since it was located in his home, he became acquainted with his wife, Anna Lvovna. Later, mother met the family, and so began a long friendship, which continued long after father's death.

In our home today, in father's office, stands a bust sculpted by Mendelevich. There is a photo of father, taken for Isaak Abramovich's work, when father was unable to pose for him. The likeness of the sculpture to the photo, and to father, is amazing. This was confirmed by me, when the whole family went to the Mendelevich's for one of father's sittings. I wasn't yet three years old, but to father's question, "Who is that?" I answered without equivocation, "Papa."

We have saved a small plasticine figure, sculpted by Mendelevich, which I asked him to give me when mother and I visited them sometime after the war. This fragment of a monument to father, sculpted by Isaak Abramovich, was to be erected in Moscow near the Kursk Railway Station.

Unfortunately, this monument was never erected in Moscow, in spite of a decree to do so issued by the Soviet of People's Commissars of the USSR. It is said that Moscow's chief architect objected, because the monument's head would be higher than the roof of the Kursk Station. Whether true of not, this monument was taken to the city of Chkalov (In 1957, "according to the wishes of its workers," the city changed its name back to the original Orenburg.), where it today stands on a high bank of the Ural River.

Isaak Abramovich, this marvelous sculptor, created two busts in white marble, of Chkalov and Gromov, which were shown at the USSR's International Exhibit at the World's Fair in New York in 1939.

By the wall of the ancient Nizhni Novgorod Kremlin, overlooking the Volga River, stands a magnificent statue of Chkalov, which was erected in 1940. Aviation Minister, Shakhurin, the statue's creator, Mendelevich, friends Baidukov and Belyakov and, of course, mother attended the opening.

A STORY BY F. I. PANFEROV

Father had warm, friendly relations with the famous Soviet writer, Fedor Ivanovich Panferov, whose works we studied in school.

He attracted Panferov with his inborn energy, his constant efforts at perfection, his wish to better himself. Panferov went with him to visit his home in Vasilevo, invited him and mother to his plays, and was very interested in and valued their opinions.

Once father invited him to the airfield. Following is what Fedor Ivanovich wrote about it. Chkalov begins:

"You know Polikarpov. Our artist-inventor has created such a machine... You'll be awe struck!

'What are you talking about?

"I'm testing it today.

'Listen,' I interrupted, 'why risk your life? The country needs you for more important things. Let others test them; you just fly them.'

"Valery Pavlovich was so offended; I began to feel uneasy myself.

"What are we? Heroes, or some domesticated bull calves, tied to a stall chewing our cud?"

At the airfield:

Valery Pavlovich approached his plane slightly swaying, as if he was afraid of frightening her. His nostrils were quivering, and it seemed he was about to shout to this pug-nosed bird:

"Hey, you! Beast! Tell me, are you going to submit to me or not? Will I be able to rein you in?"

And he smoothly separates the plane from the earth... Separates it, and, like lightning, disappears over a thicket of small trees; then, in a few seconds, he is flying directly over our heads. Then again, and again. Suddenly, he takes off with a roar to the other side of the field, but...what's this? The plane suddenly begins swinging back and forth. It plunges down; then up—then, suddenly, after lifting its nose, plunges down into the woods. A column of dust rises; a whirlwind of torn leaves.

People rush to the place of the fallen plane.

Among the bushes, scattered about, lay the remains of the pug-nosed plane. Not far away on the ground, lay Valery Pavlovich, a stream of blood flowing from the back of his head, which he held firmly in his hand...

A tragedy had occurred: the motor's cylinders began to break up. The pilot, having lifted the plane's nose, then plunged down into the small woods...

Polikarpov said:

"In such a catastrophe, the pilot's death is inevitable.

"Here Chkalov's mastery saved him..."

ALEXEI ALEXEEVICH IGNATIEV

Mother remembered that once father returned from work and told her: "Today a count is going to visit us."

"What kind of count? And where did you find him?" asked mother.

"You'll see," was the answer.

"Soon the doorbell rang and in came a tall, stately man. It was Alexei Alexeevich Ignatiev, the author of the book, *Fifty Years of Construction*. He had been a government military agent in France during the First World War in 1914 and lived in France. Father met Ignatiev at the Soviet Aviation Exhibit in Paris in November, 1936.

A. A. Inatiev remembered:[3] "I knew Valery Pavlovich from November 16, 1936 until the day of his death. For me, Valery Pavlovich, this young Russian pilot, was a Godfather, as strange this sounds. He found me when I was a civilian; we met when I was free. I had served in the People's Commissariat for International Trade for 10 years and had been appointed commissar of our Soviet pavillion at the aviation exhibit.

"Once a French Aviation Marshal came to our exhibit, looked at our small fighters, and said:

'Are these the kinds of planes you're sending to Spain?'[14]

'No, I said. We don't send planes like this. We keep them here for your ladies, and exhibit them for Parisians. We send much better ones to Spain.'

14 The Soviets were sending planes, men and material to help the Republican cause against Franco in the Spanish Civil War.

"There was applause and laughter. In the hall was a broad shouldered, stocky fellow — Valery Chkalov. M. M. Gromov and other pilots were also present. Valery Pavlovich turned to me, embraced me, and kissed me on the cheek.

"He comprehended not a word of French, but with the laughter, and the marshal's exit, he understood that I had answered him superbly.

'You evidently answered him well,' Chkalov said.

"I liked that.

"There was a banquet that evening, and it was necessary to wear a swallow tail coat or dinner jacket. Valery Pavlovich learned before hand how it was necessary to conduct oneself that evening. He didn't want to be the reason of any smiles. He wanted a Soviet man in foreign territory to behave and be received with the utmost dignity. Valery Pavlovich was extremely proud; not for himself, but for our country. Then, due to this passionate feeling for his country, we became fast friends.

"Valery Pavlovich came to the dinner in a dinner jacket and looked like a true Parisian. He was always a person who carried himself with dignity. He behaved with reserve, and acted with a native-born tact and strength. His achievements said it all.

"Valery Pavlovich's love for his homeland was often manifested when he was in foreign lands. He could always be counted on to be an example for the Russian people.

"I was in Moscow during May and June and was in civilian dress, since I had not enlisted in the Army. Nevertheless, Valery Pavlovich decided that I should be treated with the utmost respect.

"On May 1st, he organized a dinner and I was his and Olga Erazmovna's guest. As always, it was extremely simple and warm. Valery Pavlovich's brigade commander, Antoshin, was there. (Antoshin was commander of the 1st Red Banner Squadron, when father served with him in 1924-25. Antoshin and father continued their friendship after Antoshin was transferred to another unit — *auth*.) He was killed in WWII after reaching the rank of General-Lieutenant.

"Valery Pavlovich introduced me. It turned out that Antoshin earlier had been a guard non-commissioned officer in one of the divisions with me. We laughed at the situation: a former officer was now sitting next to a non-commissioned officer. We immediately became fast friends.

"A month later, Valery Pavlovich completed his transpolar flight.

"We knew Chkalov as a Russian hero. A hero of epic proportions—a kind of Russian folk hero; the kind you would find in the epic works of Ilya Muromets. Well, we could say that at that time the tempo was slower. But in our Soviet time, the tempo is very different. Chkalov was a true Russian example—a sharp protest against the Oblomovs among the Soviet people.[15]

"He had everything it takes to be an epic hero: the right build; the right movements; the strong will—and all this was tied to a great gift. The absence of will in a person makes him passive, spineless. Chkalov's will was the main material from which his soul was spun.

"All this was so exceptional in Chkalov, that it forced one into contemplation; forced one to emulate him—to hunt for and educate in oneself what was Chkalov-like, and to remember from where this motivation came."

As mother remembered, Alexei Alexeevich was in our home many times: "He was a charming, kind person, and a witty, happy story-teller. I met the Igantiev family after Valery Pavlovich's death. I was at their home many times along with the family of USSR People's Artist, Boris Nikolaevich Livanov."

During one such meeting, Ignatiev showed mother a photograph, which father had given him. On the back of the photograph, the following was written:

"The Earth's most valuable possession is the human being. And to such a person, one would wish to leave memories of oneself. The USSR values a person without regard to his past, but demands only honest work and a love of mankind in the present.

Please accept my warm feeling for you,

V. Chkalov

Paris. November 16, 1936"

On learning of father's death, Alexei Alexeevich and Natasha, his wife, sent a letter to father's friends, A. V. Belyakov and G. G. Baidukov. The letter was sent from a sanatorium in Sochi, at which they were resting, December 20, 1938. The letter is preserved in the Belyakov archives of the Government Central Archives of the Moscow Region.

---

15 Oblomov was the famous Russian anti-hero. A sloth-ridden man, who refused to get out of bed; created by Ivan Andreevich Goncharov, in his novel of the same name.

The letter is one of condolences, and follows:

"Dear Comrades,

"We've just read in "Pravda" the warm lines you wrote about our mutual, unforgettable friend. It seems to us no one knew him better than you, his closest hero-companions. And, therefore, there's no one who can more profoundly share our special feelings. We have lost, in dear Valery Pavlovich, such a rare friend, who from the first minute of our meeting in Paris, understood us.

"Allow us, if only in our thoughts, to embrace you warmly, and as firmly as he knew how to embrace. That's all we can say.'

"A. Ignatiev and Natasha"

FROM THE BOOK "BORIS LIVANOV"

"During the same days he (Boris Livanov – auth.) was awarded the title, People's Artiist of the RSFSR. Among the congratulations, was the following:

'Hi, Boris!

'I congratulate you, and wish you the quickest of recoveries. You're going to be bored just lying there… Hurry up and get well. The character Shvandya you were playing in "Lyubov Yarovaya" is not the same without you…

'Take care.

'Warmly, V. Chkalov'

"We first invited Chkalov on January 6, my birthday, which we usually celebrated at home. (Livanov lived in the same building with us – auth.).

"When I opened the door, there stood Chkalov, huffing and puffing in his army shirt, bare headed, looking like a Zaporozhian Cossack covered in snow. He had run up the stairs, two at a time, to the seventh floor.

"And it was always like that. Later, he came to see us almost every day.

'Valery, why don't you take the elevator?"

'I don't have the patience!'

"That evening Olga Vasilievna and Peter Petrovich Konchalovs were there, along with Kamensky, Knipper-Chekhova, Kachalov, Vsevolod Ivanov and his wife, Alexei Tolstoy, the Chagins and the Pasternaks.

"Chkalov charmed them all. His appearance was rare. It looked as if he had been cast in bronze, with the wonderful light-brown hair of a kind person. Kamensky named him 'Mikula Selyanovich.'[16]

"He told us all about his transpolar flight; about how the Americans met him; about the flowers he wished to immediately deliver to Lindbergh.

"On his return trip from America on the steamship Normandy, he was chosen 'First Passenger.' The 'First Passenger' had to select a 'First Lady.' He chose Marlene Dietrich, who was on the ship with them.

"Everything Chkalov told us was interesting. His perceptions and the relating of them seemed as easy as breathing to him.

"It seemed Chkalov could speak about anything, in any company, and on any topic; whether it be literature, theater, art, he was always 'relevant.'

"He carried my mother in his arms several times that evening, expressing in this way not only his considerable strength, but also his tenderness. He lost his mother early, and this unfulfilled feeling for her, was very strong.

"After several months, he fell ill and lost his voice. Olga Erazmovna, his wife, had to travel to Leningrad. We lived in the building opposite them, and she said: 'Evgenia Kazimirovna, let Valery Pavlovich be with you as much as possible. Take him with you when you have to go somewhere. He shouldn't be left alone. He has a need to be with people.'

"Pavel Alexandrovich Markov invited us to his wife's birthday. They lived just one bus stop from us. In the evening we had gathered together and were preparing to go out. The phone rang. It was Chkalov.

'What are you doing?'

'We're going to the Markovs.'

'I'm going with you.'

"The Markovs had many guests. Kachalov, Knipper-Chekhova were there. Chkalov was very eloquent speaking with Markov's mother. He commanded everyone's attention. There were many toasts to his health. This was one of the very last evenings we spent together with Valery Pavlovich.

"Following is a letter from Mikhail Rozenfeld, Chkalov's friend and talented journalist. He was killed in the Second World War with a bullet

16 A Russian epic peasant hero, a ploughman of the steppes. Something like our Paul Bunyan

through his chest. They say that after he was shot, he continued for some time to march with his unit, spitting blood. He finally fell—face down—everything was over.

'March 3, 1940

'Dear Boris!

'I just returned from the theater an hour ago, and although my hands are numb from applauding, I can't help myself—I had to pick up this pen…

'My heart aches that today two people were absent from the theater: Konstantin Sergeevich and Valery'…"

FROM THE MEMOIRS OF I. F. SHALIAPINA[17]

"One evening the telephone rang in my room. It was my friend Nikolai Nikolaevich Bobrov.

'Arinushka, you once asked me to introduce you to our hero pilot, Valery Pavlovich Chkalov. Well, as they say, your hour had arrived… Valery Pavlovich is inviting you to visit!'

"I knew that Nikolai was writing a book about Chkalov, but frankly speaking, I didn't believe him.

'Oh. That's enough of your jokes. You can't fool me,' I answered firmly. But Kolya (Nikolai) insisted and finally gave the phone to Valery Pavlovich.

"A rather husky, masculine voice sounded through the phone: 'Irina Fedorovna, please come. There are many friends here and everyone is waiting for you. This is Chkalov speaking.'

'Oh, stop with the nonsense, this once,' I answered rather sharply.

'Well, why don't you believe me? For proof I'm going to send a car after you, and Kolya will escort you here.'

'Go ahead, go ahead, send a car,' I laughed, and hung up the phone.

"But suddenly, I felt a terrible anxiety. What if this were true? What if I had really been talking to Chkalov? I was very nervous, and after some time, when I heard a knock on the door and in rushed a happy, excited Nikolai, I simply fell apart.

'Hurry up!Hurry up! Let's go!' he said. 'Take your guitar. Valery loves singing!'

---

17 Irina Feodorovna Shaliapina was the daughter of Feodor Ivanovich Shaliapin, widely considered to be one on the greatest performers in the history of opera.

"Now believing everything, I didn't allow myself to ask a lot of questions, and after several minutes, we were in the car and racing through the streets of Moscow.

"On the way, I peppered Bobrov with questions about Chkalov. He would only answer: 'Wait and see!'

"We rang the bell and someone quickly opened the door, and...I saw a person known to the whole world!

"A man of medium height, solid and well built, with a strong, resolute and masculine face, he immediately attracted people's attention. He wore a jacket, deerskin boots and was smoking a pipe.

"So this was Valery Chkalov! Exactly the kind of man your imagination would create: a powerful Russian epic warrior. I was staring at him, when he kindly extended me his hand. It seemed he also was examining me with care. Perhaps he was hunting for a likeness with my father. I was next introduced to Valery's charming wife, Olga Erazmovna.

"We went to the table where many people were sitting: pilots A. V. Belylakov, P. S. Golovin, A. V. Lyapidevsky and others.

"I sat next to Valery Pavlovich, and he asked me detailed questions about my father. He was a great admirer of my father.

"After dinner, we went into the next room to see the New Year's tree, and I witnessed a very touching scene: Valery Pavlovich's small daughter, Valeria, was crawling around the floor among her scattered toys. Chkalov picked her up, gave her a warm kiss, and gently placed her on the floor. He then got down on his hands and knees and began playing with her. How much kindness, spontaneity and tenderness there was in this large, rather severe looking person. It was truly an event for an artist, who could have created a marvelous picture from the scene.

"Then Valery Pavlovich took me to see his son. The boy wasn't feeling well and was lying in his bed. Though he was very young, he looked surprisingly like his father, who looked at him with pride. This was also a very touching scene.

"We again soon gathered around the table for tea, and Valery Pavlovich asked me to play the guitar and sing. I was hesitant, and shy, because I really was not a singer. It was impossible to refuse, however.

"I sang several old love songs, and toward the end my favorite: 'Leaving me, she said....' Everyone listened quietly. After I finished, there was a pause. I was frightened and decided I had sung poorly, but Valery Pavlovich turned to me and said: 'Sing that last song again. I really liked it.'

"From that evening, I renamed the song, 'Chkalov.' I sing this song rarely now, but when I do, the surprisingly marvelous figure of Chkalov appears before me."[3]

FROM THE MEMOIRS OF T. V. FEODOROVA

"...Probably, I was among the very few who spoke with Valery Chkalov on the day he died. He was killed tragically while testing a plane December 15, 1938. Valery Pavlovich called me that day, in the early morning (We lived in the same apartment building, now at 14 Chkalov Street.), and in his characteristic low, slightly muffled voice, said:

'Hi, Tanyusha! Today we have to be at a meeting at the teachers' organization. If I'm held up, then you speak to them and tell them the appeal we wrote about helping school kids wasn't just a lot of nonsense and noise, but that we're serious. We must work harder and more assertively to bring in our country's knowledgeable people—workers and scientists—to help and sponsor school children and youth.'

"I answered him:

'Valery Pavlovich, of course, I'll do as you advise. But please, you must come. You know how much they always look forward to seeing you.'

'I'll see you this evening, Tanya. I'll really try to make it....'

After my studies (I studied in the Transportation Academy), I ran home for a few minutes to leave my texts and notebook and quickly grab a bite to eat. Suddenly the phone rang. It was our friend Yegor's (Baidukov's) voice. It was troubled:

'Tanya! A terrible misfortune has occurred; I want to tell you personally—the news won't be announced until 11:30 p.m. Chkalov is dead! He was testing a plane; it didn't pull out of a dive. He was trying to save the plane until the last minute.'

"I froze. A spasm seized my throat.

"Chkalov! Valery Chkalov—our beloved people's hero—and now he's dead...

"I fulfilled his request and went to the meeting. I remember it was very cold. Tears were streaming down my face; I arrived at the House of Teachers. I stood for a while on the street. Gathering strength, I entered the hall. All around me there was lively commotion. Everyone was awaiting Chkalov.

"When I was asked to speak, I stood silently and couldn't begin. Everyone began to exchange glances: 'What's wrong with her?!' I finally began and gave the meeting the report Chkalov had requested, along with his warm greetings to them.

"And what happened? The hall exploded with applause. They didn't know, sitting there in the hall, what grief was about to engulf them.

"On a cold December day in 1938, the country accompanied Valery Chkalov on his last journey. All Moscow attended the funeral; the whole country was mourning. Standing in the honor guard, I looked for the last time at the marvelous masculine face of this Volga Russian; this courageous pilot, diplomat, scientist, kind father, and good friend.

"The pilot, Vladimir Kokkinaki, and I carried a huge portrait of Chkalov in the funeral procession from the Hall Of Columns to the Vladimir Ilich Lenin Mausoleum on red Square. Overwhelmed with grief, and among friends and family, stood a small woman—Olga Erazmovna Chkalova. She was pregnant with her third child.

"...I once later visited Olga Erazmovna Chkalova. This surprising woman was full of energy, and carrying on important social work. We conversed sitting in the garden. A tricyclist appeared on a path before us. The small, bright, blond-headed being vigorously peddled toward us; stopped by her grandmother's knees and lifted up her little flushed face. I again, after many years, saw those happy, inquisitive Chkalov eyes.

"February 2, 1974, was Valery Chkalov's 70th birthday. In his home, by tradition, gathered his friends: pilot Heroes, G. F. Baidukov and A. V. Belyakov; People's Artist of the USSR, I. S. Kozlovsky; writers and artists.

"I entered Chkalov's office and placed on the familiar desk a small miner's lamp. Georgy Filippovich Baidukov turned off the lights. And in that room, where 30 years before, we had written the appeal for youth, flashed this small underground beacon."

December 15, 1938

Front page of the newspaper "PRAVDA," December 16, 1938: - jvf

Workers of all countries, unite!
The All Union Communist Party (Bolsh.)

ПРАВДА

Organ of the Central Committee and MC ACP(B).

#345 (7670)   I   16 December 1938, Friday   I Price 10 kopeks

---

GOVERNMENT ANNOUNCEMENT

The government of the Union of SSR, with deep regret, announces the death of a great pilot of our time, Hero of the Soviet Union, comrade Valery Pavlovich CHKALOV, while testing a new aircraft, 15 December 1938.

CONDOLENCES OF THE SOVIET OF PEOPLES COMMISSARS OF THE UNION OF SSR and CC ACP(of Bolsheviks)

SPC of the Union of SSR and the CC ACP (of Bolsheviks) express to the family of Comrade Valery Pavlovich CHKALOV their condolences in connection with the death of Hero of the Soviet Union, comrade CHKALOV.

The Government of the Union of SSR, decrees:
1) A government commission to be organized for the funeral of comrade Chkalov. The commission shall include comrades Bulganin (chairman), Shcherbakov, Loktionov, Gromov, Baidukov and Belyakov.
2) Comrade Chkalov's funeral expenses will be covered by the government.
3) Comrade Chkalov will be buried in Red Square by the Kremlin wall.
4) A personal pension will be assigned to comrade Chkalov's family.

Articles printed in the above PRAVDA, December 16, 1938 - jvf

MEMORIES OF OUR FRIEND

By Heroes of the Soviet Union – G. Baidukov and A. Belyakov

On December 15, 1938, the families of Heroes of the Soviet Union, Soviet pilots, and together with them, our whole country, has suffered a grievous and irretrievable loss. Illustrious pilot, Valery Chkalov crashed while testing a new aircraft.

The name of this man is known to the whole Soviet people – from the smallest to the greatest. His name is identified in our country with exceptional bravery, love of country, and loyalty to the party of Lenin-Stalin. The name of this pilot today is known far beyond the borders of our homeland. Millions of workers in other countries saw in him a type of new person, educated by a socialist society.

It's difficult living through the loss of an outstanding pilot. It's more difficult yet to live through the loss of a comrade, whose friendship developed over the course of many years in a mutual struggle with nature's elements.

He possessed the marvelous ability to instill affection for himself in anyone who ever happened to meet or talk with this fascinating person. Openness, honesty, courage and knowledge of his profession – these are the Chkalov qualities, which made him the favorite of our people; the popular hero of our Soviet country.

How the children loved him! What happiness our school children experienced, when Valery would go to see them and speak to them about his flights! And how he loved these children. There was never an invitation to visit a school or Pioneer camp[18] that went unanswered.

A decisive, daring, fearless military pilot-warrior, Valery Chkalov was also a kind, warm, sympathetic comrade and wonderful family man. He was the kind of comrade one could have a heart-to-heart talk with – good-natured, social, responsive.

Son of a worker-boilermaker, a person of natural gifts, and coming from the people, he developed in himself the qualities of a master pilot. In his flying career, he was face-to-face with death many times, and always managed to escape what seemed to be a hopeless situation.

For more than half his life – Valery had not yet reached the age of 35 – he spent in the ranks of the Worker-Peasant Red Army, entering as a volunteer in 1919.

18 Similar to our Boy and Girl Scout camps

He flew more than 70 aircraft types in his 16-year flying career. He flew French, English, American, Italian, German, and almost all planes of Soviet construction. Master pilot Valery Chkalov tenaciously and persistently tested planes of new design, searching for defects during risky flights in order to give designers definitive evidence about the defects of their planes. In this way, the designers could improve them and provide the Worker-Peasant Red Army with an outstanding supply of aircraft.

Twice we completely entrusted ourselves to Valery Chkalov. Twice, in a tightly cohesive crew, we set out on a long, dangerous journey for the glory of our beloved homeland with Chkalov as our commander. He was not older than us in age, but we respected him as a leader comrade and commander. We trusted our commander-friend, when in the gathering darkness he landed the plane on an unfamiliar island in the Sea of Okhotsk, now carrying the name of Chkalov!

Valery was a man with a big heart, and when far from his homeland, he yearned for her. He pined for his native Moscow, for his native Vasilevo (now the village, Chkalovsk), for his wife, his son, his daughter, Lerochka (Valeria).

He was a wonderful, fiery orator. His effect on an auditorium was immense, and was explained by the fact that every listener felt the special sincerity of his words, of his speech. It's not for nothing, that many Americans, having listened to him speak in New York and other cities, spoke of him as a born orator.

Valery loved the wonderful profession of a test pilot. He possessed the most important qualities of a pilot: daring, courage, readiness to take risks, excellent knowledge of, and the ability to use the latest achievements of technology. And we all, knowing this, were certain that Chkalov would be flying for many long years; that Chkalov, when it was required, would defeat the enemy, would destroy the enemy's planes.

Valery is dead… We will bring up the young generation of pilots and navigators to be as brave and fearless as our unforgettable friend will remain in the memory of the many future generations — this Stalin protégé — Valery Pavlovich Chkalov.[19]

19 Not to praise Stalin as a source of Chkalov's achievements in the article at this time in Russian history would have meant the Gulag or death for Baidukov and Belyakov.

FOREIGN PRESS COMMENTS
ON THE DEATH OF com. CHKALOV

LONDON, December 16. (TASS). English newspapers published a report by Reuters about the tragic death of comrade Chkalov. The newspaper, "Daily Telegraph and Morning Post included a report from its Moscow correspondent, which pointed out that Chkalov "was an exceptionally courageous pilot." The newspaper reminded its readers that in 1937, com. Chkalov completed a record flight.

PARIS, December 16. (TASS). Several Paris newspapers, including "Humanity," "Maten," and others published information about the death of com. Chkalov. The newpapers recalled the heroic flight completed by com. Chkalov from Moscow to America across the North Pole.

PARIS, December 16. (TASS). "Se Suar", responding to the death of com. Chkalov, writes: "Chkalov was killed at the height of his powers. The whole world of aviation mourns him." The newspaper notes that the government of the USSR has decided to bury com. Chkalov in Red Square by the Kremlin wall.

NEW YORK, 17 December. (TASS). The Head of the US Air Force, General Arnold, in a conversation with a TASS correspondent announced that,"American military aviation deeply mourns the tragic death of Hero of the Soviet Union, Valery Chkalov."

"Chkalov," Arnold further declared, "with his achievements in the field of aviation, tied the knots of friendship between our two great nations still tighter. His death is a huge loss for the whole world of aviation."

General Arnold sent the Soviet Ambassador to the USA a letter, in which he expressed his condolences on the death of V. Chkalov.

Famous American pilot and polar explorer, Admiral Richard Bird, declared: "I express my deep condolences to the Soviet people in connection with the loss of its great pilot, Valery Chkalov. All American pilots share the grief of the Soviet people."

NEW YORK, 17 December. (TASS). Famous American pilot, Howard Hughes, having completed an around-the-world flight, sent a TASS representative the following telegram from Hollywood: "Please pass on to the people of the Soviet Union my condolences on the treagic death of Valery

Chkalov. Everyone involved with aviation in the USA, and in particular here on the Pacific Coast, everyone who had the pleasure of meeting Chkalov after his marvelous transpolar flight from the USSR to the USA, is infinitely saddened. I express my deep sympathy to his comrades."

NEW YORK, 17 December. (TASS). Famous American explorer, Stefanson, on learning of Chkalov's death, said the following:

"In the person of V. P. Chkalov, world polar aviation research lost its most important leader. Chkalov's achievements aroused amazement and personal affection for him. America shares the grief of the people of the Soviet Union concerning this loss."

CHAPTER FOUR

The Death of Test Pilot Valery Chkalov

Based on Former "Top Secret" Documents

THE 1938 VERSION

December 15, 2008 will marked the 70th year from the day of test pilot Valery Pavlovich Chkalov's tragic death.

December 15, 1938, the Soviet of Peoples Commissars (SPC) of the USSR and the Central Committee of the Soviet Communist Party (CC SCP) passed a Resolution appointing a Commission to examine the reasons for the crash of the I-180 plane and the death of Valery Pavlovich Chkalov.

"Stalin's falcon," "The leader's favorite," the people's hero had died. He died unexpectedly, like Kirov and Ordzhonikidze.[20] Stalin and his comrades-in-arms were in the honor guard by the coffin of the national hero. The urn with Chkalov's ashes was carried by government leaders led by Stalin. They carried the urns with the ashes of Kirov and Ordzhonikidze also when they died, and with similar grief. They also spoke warmly about their service to the Party and to the government from the Lenin Mausoleum. Then they firmly hid the ashes in the Kremlin recesses, together with the truth about how they died.

There was grief, and the people felt a sincere loss. Newspapers printed their praises to Chkalov in obituaries almost identical to the ones for Kirov, Ordzhonikidze, and other Communist leaders. The SPC USSR passed a Resolution about the perpetuation of the memory of V. P. Chkalov.

The Commission finished its work on December 17, 1938. The Commission's Act and all supporting documentation was immediately

---

20 Kirov and Ordzhonikidze were Communist leaders, whom it is thought that Stalin arranged to have killed in the purges.

stamped "Top Secret," and for a long time, for many decades, this material disappeared into various archives, hidden from the people.

One wonders how many people could have known, or partly guessed, the contents of these documents at the end of 1938. It turns out quite a few: the Politburo, the NKVD (KGB-jvf), Peoples' Commissars of various organizations. There were Commissions into the examination of catastrophes, Head Aircraft Designers, Directors, leading factory specialists, witnesses of the first flight, witnesses of the crash of the I-180 test plane, etc. In all, about 100 people.

It's very apparent that not one person possessed full information contained in all the documents tied to this tragic event.

Therefore, the "1938 Version" of the plane crash and the death of V. P. Chkalov that appeared without the "Top Secret" stamp, was carefully micromanaged by the government. This version was built on oral, fragmentary information and had no documented base.

1988 VERSION

(Georgy F. Baidukov relates the "1988 Version."-jvf)

After the loss of my friend and commander, in 1939 in "Roman-Gazet," I published a story with the title, "About Chkalov."[90]

It's clear that in that short book I couldn't discuss the reasons for the catastrophe, since the material about the I-180 was secret.

In 1973, the publisher, "Molodaya Gvardiya," suggested that I write a biography of V. P. Chkalov for their series of books called, "The Lives of Exceptional People (LEP)."

Having read everything written about Valery Pavlovich, I understood that without documentation concerning the I-180 aircraft, I couldn't successfully write a book for their "LEP""series.

I wrote to archives and went everywhere asking whether they had information about the I-180. But all these efforts were for nothing. Only the organs of the secret service helped. They sent me copies of the secret government commission Act on Chkalov's fatal crash written in 1938.

The Commission examined the causes of the I-180 catastrophe, and did its work on December 16-17, 1938, by order of the SPC USSR and the CC SCP(b). It consisted of Division Commander, Alekseev (Chairman), Repin, Gromov, Baidukov, Kashirin and Suprun.

In what was a surprise to me, along with the 1938 Act, I was sent an unclassified report by an expert commission written in 1955. It seemed to me so sensational, I decided to start my article with its detailed analysis. Its content follows:

"June 8, 1955

"Moscow

"The expert commission Chairman is General-Colonel M. M. Gromov. Members consist of Ter-Markaryan and Kononenko. Usachev, Belyaikin and Porai, requested that the Head Military Prosecutors Office, having become acquainted with material related to the I-180 catastrophe, appoint the commission to do its work.

"It has established the following:

"The commission is authorized to answer the following questions:

"1) What is the reason for the December 15, 1938 crash of Chkalov's I-180 experimental plane?

"2) Who is responsible for allowing the experimental I-180 aircraft to be tested.

"…The commission has established that the I-180's motor, propeller and carburetor were experimental and had never been tested before in flight. The plane lacked a regulating system for cooling the engine, without which flight would be dangerous, especially in freezing weather (-25 degrees).

"The most likely reason for the forced landing of the plane is that the motor failed due to over cooling….

"Carefully analyzing all the conditions of the I-180 plane's preparations for flight, and the conditions of the crash, the commission comes to the conclusion that the Head Designer, N. N. Polikarpov is responsible for the first test flight of the I-180 aircraft, since it was his responsibility to confirm the flight list, i. e., to authorize the first flight. The flight list is the main document confirming the full preparedness of the plane and crew for flight."

"It seems they found the responsible one, and he had to be the only one, since only he answered not only for the plane, but also for the pilot's preparedness to complete a successful first flight. But further on, the experts faulted Chkalov himself, asserting that:

"Those responsible for the flight of the I-180 are Head Designer, N. N. Polikarpov and test pilot, V. P. Chkalov.

"Polikarpov was responsible because he allowed the first flight of an experimental plane completely unprepared for flight in low temperatures: there were no air vents to regulate motor cooling.

"Chkalov was at fault, because he possessed rich experience in testing fighters in various climactic conditions, and agreed to fly without air vents. Second, he knew that to fly without air vents was dangerous and depended on his piloting skills. He intended to fly in one big circle around the airfield at such a distance that in case of engine trouble he could glide the plane in without the engine. But when the motor overcooled on his approach, he couldn't use it to reach the field and crashed into a settlement.

"M. A. Usachev, S. I. Belyaikin, and V. M. Parai couldn't prevent Chkalov and the I-180 from taking off, because Chkalov and Polikarpov possessed such commanding authority, it was impossible to consider reversing their decision."

So ended the conclusion of the expert commission, signed June 8, 1955, i. e., 17 years after the catastrophe, but which I read only 36 years after the death of V. P. Chkalov. Naturally, there was nothing left for me to do, but to compare the government Act of 1938, signed my M. M. Gromov, with the expert commission report, signed in 1955 by the same M. M. Gromov.

While comparing the 1938 and 1955 reports, I noticed that the experts didn't rely on any documents, but simply borrowed things from the 1938 report, and in the process left out important details.

The experts of Gromov's 1955 commission wrote:

"…It follows that the more probable reason for the forced landing of the plane was engine failure as a result of overcooling…"

The 1938 government commission wrote about this as follows:

"The commission considers that the reason for the forced landing was engine failure as a result of overcooling and the unreliable design of the gas feed system."

The difference in formulation is crucial, since the factory changed the controls of the engine's revolutions several times in the assembly shop.

The 1938 report said:

"The plane was allowed to fly on December 15th with uncorrected defects; the same defects which persuaded the government on December 12th to forbid the flight."

Mikhail Mikhailovich Gromov, possessing a phenomenal memory, couldn't have forgotten that fact. One has the impression that the event, which took place at the airfield with Polikarpov's experimental plane on 12/12, was left out of the experts' 1955 report consciously. They didn't want to speak of the possibility of failure of the engine controls in the fatal minutes of the I-180 flight on December 15, 1938.

The experts' 1955 report states: "…Chkalov was at fault, because he possessed rich experience in testing fighters in various climactic conditions, and agreed to fly without air vents." A pilot who refuses to fly, can't be a test pilot if he can't prove his case.

The experts stress that Chkalov "agreed to fly without air vents…"

The 1938 report also mentions this in the following formulation: "The installation of air vents was anticipated (engineer Kun's testimony), but never carried out."

The liberties taken by the 1955 expert commission in their report attracts attention, when they write: "… when the motor overcooled on his approach, he couldn't use it to reach the field and crashed into a settlement…"

The 1938 government commission said the following on this subject:

"…Judging from the conditions of the crash, the pilot continued to guide the plane until the last moment, attempting, successfully, to land outside the area covered by housing."

Chkalov was an honorable man, and until the last minute of his life he struggled to avoid crashing into housing structures in order to not to kill innocent people. But Gromov's experts asserted that the I-180 crashed into housing, and thereby belittles the test pilot, who until the last moment did everything he could to show mercy to the people below. It seems to me that if Chkalov had landed on the roof of that last barracks, it would have been a serious accident, but the pilot would have remained alive.

I was struck by the thoughtless and flippant formulations of the 1955 expert commission's report. I decided to call its chairman, M. M. Gromov, and asked:

"Mikhail Mikhailovich! In 1938, you signed the accident commission's report, which had been ordered by the SPC USSR and CC SCP(b), without any reservations. Do you remember?"

"Of course I remember," Gromov answered.

"If you remember, then tell me why your commission claimed that Chkalov knew about all the plane's defects, but wanted to fly anyway, and flew to his death of his own free will?"

"That can't be!" Gromov replied.

I didn't argue with him, since 35 years had passed from the day of Chkalov's death, and 20 years from signing of the expert commission's report. It's not surprising that an elderly person could forget certain events, and especially the details, which often play an important role.

I decided to call Ter-Markaryan, also a member of the expert commission, and a person I knew well.

"Listen, why did you sign that idiotic report in 1955 concerning the reasons for Chkalov's catastrophe on the I-180 and who was to blame for it?"

And with this person's characteristic frankness, he replied:

"Understand, Yegor Filippovich (Baidukov), Belyaikin, Usachev and Porai have children. What would they think?"

"And will the children of the dead find your strange assurances more comforting? To heap blame on the dead is very easy. This method has long been known to aviation," I answered Ter-Markaryan, and hung up the phone...

In spite of everything, the 'Story of the I-180' was found. It happened in 1973, when I went to the N. E. Zhukovsky Museum and found:

Notes on the I-180 aircraft (order 318)

Department LIS. Date:1938

Internal inventory, #b/n

Inventory Museum - #842/1 9.62

N. N. Polikarpov Fund

The discovered material on the testing of the I-180, I found in the second chapter, part IV, under the heading: 'The Last Year of Life.'

However, the secret of the great pilot's death has still not been entirely uncovered. All the material of that 1938 tragedy lies hidden, and readers ask me: "There are rumors that Chkalov himself is to blame for his death. Is that true?"

Similar questions began to be asked more frequently of this author of the book, "Chkalov." And after the publication of the 1986 memoir of M. M. Gromov, which was published after his death under the title, "My Whole Life," the questions continued.

In this interesting book, Mikhail Mikhailovich includes a sensational interpretation of the reasons for Chkalov's death, differing considerably from the formulations of the government commission's 1938 report, and even from the expert commission's 1955 report, both of which Gromov signed, along with the other members of the commissions. On pages 141 and 142 of his book, he writes the following:

"Unfortunately, not only pleasant events are printed on my calendar.

"On December15, 1938, Valery Pavlovich Chkalov was killed. This is what happened...

"Chkalov completed the first experimental flight on Polikarpov's I-180. At night on December 14th and on December 15th, serious freezing weather set in. The plane had an air-cooled engine, but no system for regulating the cooling was installed. Chkalov, however, decided he could fly one circle. Polikarpov agreed: once a pilot decides to fly...

"Chkalov took to the air and flew one large circle (far from the airfield's borders). We saw how he turned toward the airfield for landing, and began to descend. Suddenly the plane's propellers stopped. It was clear the fighter would not reach the airfield... and would land on some small homes. The plane crashed into a pile of scrap metal, the pilot was thrown from the cockpit, and he stuck his head on a metal rod lying in the small yard...

"K. E. Voroshilov appointed a commission to examine the crash. I was a member of the commission. The opinion was unanimous: the propeller stopped due to overcooling of the engine.

"Many years passed. After the war, the motor's designer and I were called to explain the reasons for Chkalov's death and to name those responsible. We again, as then, affirmed that if blame is to be placed, then one must place it on the designer, who didn't manage to install a system to regulate engine temperature, and on the test pilot..."

I suspect that Gomov wasn't able to see the final proof-read version of his book before he died, and that after he died the judgment of incompetent, unauthorized people was able to slip into the final draft under the name of it's famous author.

(M. M. Gromov is mistaken. First, he wasn't at the airfield during the first flight of the I-180 piloted by Chkalov. Second, the commission to investigate the reasons for the crash of the I-180 aircraft was appointed by an order from the SPC USSR and the CC SCP(b), not by Voroshilov.

Further, as test pilot S. A. Mikoyan, wrote, "No matter what, it's probably always possible to speak of pilots' errors." And the use of the word "fault" in this respect is far from justified. – Auth.)

In 1980, in issue 40 of "The History of Aviation and Space," a journal of the Soviet National Union of Historians of Science and Technology of the Academy of Sciences of the USSR, I read an article written by M. B. Chernobylsky, under the heading, "Questions concerning the reasons for the crash of the I-180 test aircraft":

"Many witnesses of the first flight of the I-180 aircraft at the M. V. Frunze Central Airfield say that after a normal flight, V. P. Chkalov completed a second circle at high altitude far from the airfield. They saw that as he approached for a landing, he didn't reach the airfield and crashed into a factory's scrap heap directly adjacent to the airport.

"Research into the conditions and reasons for aircraft catastrophes, show that, as a rule, they occur due to the confluence of several unfortunate and independent phenomena, the absence of any one of which might have prevented the accident.

"In this case, one of the apparent reasons for the accident is the defective engine cowling and sharp drop in temperature. It is possible that in warmer temperatures, in spite of the defective cowling, the engine might not have failed on its approach to landing… It's also important to stress that when coming in for a landing, a new phenomenon may occur—a significant rise in air resistance if the motor fails, due to the propeller's continued rotation. This fact was not published in the literature of the time and was unknown to engineers and pilots…

"Therefore, the first link in the chain of events leading to the death of V. P. Chkalov during the first fight of the experimental I-180 aircraft, is the defective cowling of the engine preventing proper regulation of its air-cooled system. The second link was a sharp drop of 20 degrees in temperature. The third and decisive link in this chain of events is the significant rise (4-5 times) in air resistance caused by 'PVP' (propeller with variable pitch) when the motor failed on its approach to landing. It was specifically this factor, which led to a sharp downward trajectory of the plane's approach and didn't allow it to reach the airfield with its failed engine.

"The crash of the I-180 aircraft happened not due to the imperfect design of the planned trajectory of the first flight or because of a mistake in piloting technique after the engine's failure. It occurred due to the unexamined, and, therefore, unexpected consequences of a failed engine with a variable pitch propeller.

"On the honorable and sad list of talented test pilots killed while researching unknown phenomena during flights on experimental aircraft, one finds the name of the great pilot, Valery Pavlovich Chkalov."

Frankly speaking, neither Gromov nor I, nor even Chernobylsky, discovered the real reasons for the catastrophe.

I will bring forth documents, which will prove, as a matter of fact, that Chkalov was murdered. They obligated him to fly on an unfinished plane, which can only be explained due to N. N. Polikarov's desire to quickly supply the Gorky Factory with a new plane to produce in place of the outdated I-16. This could be done with a report to Stalin and Molotov that a new plane had passed its factory testing program, or at least had completed a satisfactory, reliable first flight.

Following is correspondence related to the I-180 aircraft. There are 106 lists in 57 documents...

There were two important documents created on December 11th: a new list of defects and a program of testing.

In the list were 45 points, which indicated that many defects were uncovered and documented. By December 2nd they had not yet been removed.

Following are the signatures under the list: Trostyansky, Koloverzhin, Lazarev, Kurakin, Yakovlev, Nikolaev.

What conclusion can one draw on reading this list of defects? Very simple: Not having a finished engine cowling, and propeller which still needed work, not yet having an aerodynamic estimate, or an estimate of the strength of its construction, it was not only intolerable to allow that first flight, but it was dangerous even to allow a speed run with a lift of only one or two meters off the ground.

The second document: "Testing Program of the I-180." It was written on December 3rd. On December 11th, the Head Designer signed this program. On December 13th, the Factory Director confirmed it. The program follows:

"Part I. Ground testing, including 12 points. On completion of the ground testing, draw up a report releasing the plane for test flight.

"Part II. Flight testing.

    1. Test flight in a circle. 1. Hours (Minutes) – 10-15 min.

        Landing gear remains down.

After the flight, conduct a careful examination of the whole plane.

I well remember that Chief Designer, N. N. Polikarpov, was a person who could ably express himself and explain various phenomena related to the crash, but that he could not sensibly answer a rather clear question put to him on December 17, 1938, by members of the Government Commission: "Why was the landing gear lever blocked, so that the landing gear could not be raised, even in the event an extremely dangerous situation? This would have lowered head on wind resistance and increased the plane's lifting capability."

The designer must have known there were significant obstructions on the border of Central Airport, and that flying from it might demand a quick decision to lift the landing gear in order to gain altitude quickly and not tear into hangers or homes. A similar situation could arise when coming in for a landing, especially if the engine began to fail. The unfortunate Chkalov had only 500 meters to go to reach the airfield and land the plane.

Neither Polikarpov nor his deputy gave the Commission a clear explanation of the categorical prohibition to raise the landing gear on the first flight.

The day before the crash, i.e., December 14, 1938, the Head of the experimental flight station, Colonel V. Porai, and his Deputy, A. Solovev, wrote factory Director, Usahev: "In accordance with your personal directive, I report that most of the points of the plane's ground testing LIS program, by order '318,' has not been completed as of 10:00 p.m. 12/13/38.

"On completion of this program a report is to be written releasing the plane for fight testing, but since the work is not finished, the report has not been written.

"Colonel Parai, Department #4 Head
"A. Solovev, Deputy Head of Testing
"12/14/38

This means it was clear to factory Director Ushakov that the plane had not passed all its ground testing and that it was impossible to write a report allowing flight-testing for the I-180.

The double-dealing of Colonel Porai led to the signing by his subordinates on that day (14 December) of a "Report on the preparedness for the first flight of Designer N. N. Polikarpov's aircraft. Order 318." The following subordinates signed this document:

Head I-180 Testing Engineer, N. Lazarev and Flight Engineer, A. Kurakin, together with Deputy Head Designer, D. Tomashevich, Chief Engineer at OKB p/r 67, Trostryansky, chief Production Engineer, A. Koloverzhin, Factory 156 Head Technical controller, A. Yaklovlev, Head Master Controler, D. Nikolaev, Master Controller, D. Kobzev.

The report asserts that, "The defects recorded on the Defects List of 12/11/38 over the signatures of the above listed comrades, cannot serve as an impediment for the first flight. The break in the normal gas-feed system during taxiing 12/12/38 was resolved by replacing the system with a new one on instructions from Deputy Designer D. Tomashevich.

"The plane is ready for its first flight without retracting its landing gear and with restricted weight and speed in accordance with the instructions of the factory's Head Designer, com. N. N. Polikarpov.

"Enclosed: Defect List."

It's amazing how simply and brazenly Deputy Head Designer, Tomashevich, and Technical Control Center (TCC) Head, Yakovlev, rehabilitated the many extremely dangerous errors and defects — extremely dangerous for a first flight — just one day before the fatal crash of Chkalov's I-180 aircraft.

But I couldn't get Polikarpov's helpless and confused answer out of my head concerning why he wrote that very rigid command in the flight lists of 12/12, and again, three days later on 12/15/38: The command: "The first flight will be taken without retracting the landing gear and at a restricted speed, according to the instructions of Head Designer, N. N. Polikarpov."

I at last found the most fearful document relating to the I-180. It uncovered all the secrets of the restriction on speed and weight for the first flight of the I-180.

"To: Head Engineer

"Concerning unit strengthening of the wing-ribs to the spars on the I-180:

"1. Cracks in the units are unacceptable

"2. Wings manufactured by Order '318' may be allowed into flight with restricted weight.

"3. To make their replacement acceptable, the wings must be manufactured according to 318D specifications.

"4. Cracks in the 318D wings are unacceptable. In order to facilitate production of the strengthening units, I will allow the use of

D-3 with annealing before stamping, or D-2 with subsequent
tempering.

"5. I request that special attention be paid to the production of the
units, since the existing units are unsatisfactory. Also, special
attention must be paid to fitting of the units in the production
process. If absolutely necessary, I will allow the placement of
a duralumin lining under the unit of not more than 1 mm.

"Head Designer, Polikarpov, Tomashevich, Yakovitsky.

"11/23/38"

The wings of Chkalov's plane were unfit for flight!

The upper covering on the wing of the I-180 could simply tear away
on take-off, or in flight, or on an attempt to side-slip to correct calculations
on landing.

The true guilty parties for the crash are first of all the factory director,
the head designer (also the technical director of the factory), the head of
the flight station, the deputy head designer, specialists with low qualifications and other dishonest, cowardly people.

Such is the version put forth by General-Colonel G. F. Baidukov in
1988.

THE 2003 VERSION

Many publications about the tragic death of Chkalov in the mass
media over the years have contained more imaginary events than real
facts. Time has constantly and inexorably made its corrections: All witnesses have passed on, and the authors of memoirs and reminiscences
have reached an advanced age. In their works they used distorted facts
for examples and illustrations.

All authors looked at this catastrophe as an independent phenomenon,
not tied with nor affected by the social/political system of the country. The
time was 1935 – 1938. The totalitarian regime (an openly terrorist dicta-
torship) distinguished itself with its wild peculiarities. In addition, the
participants and witnesses of the crash were to some degree a consequence and result of this regime.

The first to seriously carry on quality research into the reasons for the
crash of the I-180 and the death of Chkalov was Georgy Filippovich
Baidukov. This was serious research work covering many years. As a
result we have the "1988 Version."

I had the opportunity to complete research, begun in 1997, into the reasons for the plane's crash and the death of my father using material which was partly included in my book,"Chkalov Without The 'Secret' Stamp," published in 1999.[21]

And so the most difficult and tragic part of the book is finished; the part into which I have poured a good portion of my life:"The 2003 Version."

This version has examined almost all the existing material concerning the crash of the I-180 aircraft and the death of test pilot V. P. Chkalov. It has allowed the remaining blank spots to be filled, in the history of aviation and of the government in the period of December 1 – 15, 1938.

Archival documents from 1937-1939 were found and unclassified: technical and manufacturing information about the I-180 aircraft, official orders, directions, letters, commission reports on the investigation into reasons for the December 15, 1938 crash, witness testimony, material published in the periodical press, or book publications throwing light on the various aspects of the catastrophe.

The many documents resulting in the "2003 Version" come from the following archives: The Archive of the President of the Russian Federation (APRF), the Government Archive of the Russian Federation (GARF), the Russian Government Archive of Economics (RGAE), the Russian Center for the Storage and Study of Documents of Contemporary History (RCSSDCH), the Central Archives of the Intelligence Services of the Russian Federation, the Central Government Archives of the Moscow Region (CGAMR), and small but "weighty" features from the periodical press.

All this taken together helped create a realistic picture of the catastrophe, the preparations for which lasted 13 days and culminated on December 15, 1938, at 1:06 p.m. with the tragic death of Chkalov.

And the most unpredictable conclusion, after a scrupulous analysis of all the archival documents, is that the crash of the I-180 aircraft was planned on December 12th at 12:00 noon.

The development of these events can be traced not only by the day, but also by the hour.

---

21 I had the privilege of translating that book under the title, "Chkalov: Secrets from Stalin's Archives.

November 17, 1938: Test pilot Valery Pavlovich Chkalov received permission for a leave and left for his hometown, Chkalovsk.

December 1: Chkalov was handed a telegram from the factory: "Everything is ready. Your attendance is required immediately. We are waiting."

December 2: Chkalov was already at the factory. The new fighter-plane, I-180, was presented for inspection by the Technical Control Center (TCC) of Factory #156. After a careful inspection of the plane corresponding to working drafts and technical circumstances, defects and unfinished work was noted in 139 instances.

December 5: The Head of the 1st Department NKOP, Belyaikin and People's Commissar, M. M. Kaganovich, demanded the release of the I-180 aircraft from the factory.

December 7: The I-180 aircraft was carried to the airfield on the night of December 7-8. There were 100 defects recorded in the defect list.

December 10: Factory Director Usachev, of Factory #156, ordered the plane to be prepared for its first flight. The defects were not eliminated, proper documents were issued, and the plane was not received at the flight station. There was no documentation reporting the arrival of aircraft test model I-180 from the factory. However, Flight List #1 was issued.

Due to bad weather, a taxiing exercise was carried out. Chkalov taxied the plane for 20 minutes without a parachute.

December 11: The Director ordered that the plane be prepared for its first flight.

During the testing of the motor, the shock absorber on the right landing gear slipped and settled. The plane tilted to the right. Chkalov was at the airfield. The right landing gear was repaired at the factory and toward midnight, was installed on the plane. On December 12, factory Director Usachev authorized the first flight of the I-180 aircraft. Also on December 12, the day of the suggested first flight, 48 aircraft defects were noted on the defect list. A document was prepared relative to the readiness of the plane for flight. But the required conclusions concerning the plane's preparedness for the flight were absent. Tomeshevich decided the question, when he declared that the defects would not influence the first flight.

In the evening Usachev received a phone call in his apartment from an agent of the NKVD (KGB), who informed him that the NKVD had material showing that the I-180 had many defects, which would make the first flight very dangerous! Usachev answered that the next day at noon there would be a meeting at which a final decision would be made about the first flight of the I-180 aircraft.

December 12: (Sunday).

8:00 a.m. The NKVD agent turned up at Usachev's apartment(!) and for the second time warned that they had information about the existence of many defects on the plane and that it would be necessary to cancel the plane's first flight. Usachev immediately summoned Head Designer Polikarpov, the head factory engineers, OTK Head Yakovlev, and the I-180 production control specialists.

And so the NKVD took active part in the first flight of the experimental I-180 aircraft. It's possible that factory Director Usachev had been already informed by the NKVD of the planned events for the I-180, which were to take place on December 12. The time of the first flight had already been determined for Usachev on December 11: **It was to be 12 noon, December 12th.** (This time was confirmed in December 12, 1938, letters sent to the government leadership by People's Commissar of Internal Affairs, L. Beria. – Auth.)

10:00 a.m. Usachev, Palikarpov, Tomasheviich, Taritynov, and representatives of the NKVD, Garkaev, Kholichev and Shitov, arrived at the airport.

10:00 a.m. to 10:30 a.m. Beria sends a letter to Stalin, Molotov and Voroshilov with the stamp "Top Secret," about the planned 12 noon first flight of the I-180 aircraft.

11:20 a.m. A worker at the People's Commissariat called Belyaikin and told him that the NKVD and the Secretariat of the Central Committee of the Communist Party of the Soviet Union were aware that the I-180 aircraft was to be tested in flight today, and that the plane was to be tested by Hero of the Soviet Union, Valery Pavlovich Chkalov. They said the plane had defects and the flight must be canceled.

A bit later, an NKVD representative called Belyaikin and informed him that the flight was scheduled for 12 noon, Director Usachev was not at the airport, the plane had defects and the flight must be canceled. In order to cancel the flight, Belyaikin called the 8th Department at the Central Aerohydrodynamics Institute(CAHI) but no one answered. He then immediately called Factory #1, located next to the CAHI 8th Department, and ordered the officer on duty to immediately go the flight station and personally give them his order forbidding the flight.

Therefore, factory Director Usachev, Defense Industry Commissar (DIPC) Belyaikin, and Department Heads Gorbunov and Leontev already knew of the cancellation of the I-180's first flight, with test pilot Chkalov at the controls, from the NKVD and the Secretariat of the CC CPSU.

Tomashevich, Trostyansky, Koloverzhin, Lazarev, kurakin, Yakovlev, Nikolaev and Kobzev met in Parai's office. Tomashevich, talking to no one, took the defect list and with a pencil began to make notes with accompanying remarks: "This is not a defect." "We haven't done this, nor will we." "We'll eliminate this after the first flight." A report was prepared and signed by all present that "the plane is prepared for its first flight." This phrase was put in place of one that was crossed out: "the plane in general is ready for flight."

11:00 – 12:00 noon. Usachev is absent from the airport (?!) Where was the factory director, who had been twice warned by the NKVD about cancellation of the first flight, at this crucial moment?

12:06. Belyaikin together with Gorbunov and Leontev arrive at the airport. Meeting with Polikarpov, Belyaikin gave him the instructions about canceling the flight, to which Polikarpov answered: "Okay, I hear you." At the same time, however, he said the plane was ready for the flight, and that the defects were not dangerous. Belyaikin again repeated the NKVD and Secretariat of the CC CPSU prohibition of the flight and said there could be no further discussion about it.

Usachev arrived at the airport (!).

12:10 to 12:40 p.m. A meeting took place in a separate room concerning the preparedness of the I-180 for its first flight attended by Belyaikin, Usachhev, Polikarpov, Garkaev, Kholichev,and Shitov. At the end of this meeting, Belyaikin told Usachev that the CC CPSU (as expressed by Belyaikin) had forbidden the flight of the I-180.

12:40 p.m. Chkalov arrived, greeted everyone, opened his closet, and silently began changing into his flight suit.

12:40 p.m. The following people gathered at the Central Airport:

From the Defense Industry's People's Commissariat (DIPC):
- DIPC Administration Head #1, Belyaikin.
- DIPC Department Head, Gorbunov.
- DIPC Department Head, Leontev.

From the NKVD:

- 1ST Department Head of the Main Economic Administration (MEA), Garkaev.
- Assistant Head of MEA Department #1, Kholichev
- Deputy Head of MEA Department #1, Shitov

From DIPC Factory #156:

- Director Usachev
- Technical Director, Head Designer of the I-180 aircraft, Polikarpov.
- Deputy Head Designer, Tomashevich.
- Leading I-180 Engineer, Lazarev.
- Test-Flight Station Head (TFS), Colonel Porai.
- TFS Deputy Head, Solovev
- Head Factory Military Representative, Colonel Brovko.
- Leading Subdivision Specialists.
- Chief Pilot, Test Pilot Chkalov.

At 11:00 a.m., the People's Commissar of Internal Affairs of the USSR, Lavrentia Beria, personally informed Stalin, Molotov and Voroshilov by letter of the I-180's first test flight planned for December 12.

It was Beria who called together these specialists, many of whom were sent there not to prevent the catastrophe, but to prepare, accompany and execute it.

12:50 p.m. Belyaikin arose, invited Chkalov and a NKVD representative into another room, and said that there were orders from the CC CPSU about canceling the flight, and that the flight today would be canceled. After several minutes, the whole leadership staff, including Chkalov, gathered in a Subdivision 4 room behind closed doors and continued the meeting. Porai at that time was in a Flight Unit 8 room at CAHI together with Leading Engineer, Lazarev, Koloverzhin, and other co-workers. By the hanger, technician Kurakin was warming up the plane's engine.

1:15 p.m. Happening to look out the window, Porai saw that Chkalov, with his parachute on, was getting into the plane. Usachev, Polikarpov, Tomashevich, and the NKVD representatives were standing close by. At this moment, OTK Head Yakovlev ran into the room saying that the plane was preparing for flight, that he should grab the flight registration documents and rush to the plane. As there was no time to look over the unfinished documents, he stuffed them into his pockets and ran to the plane.

Chkalov by this time was already in the plane testing the motor. Porai approached factory Director Usachev: "How dare you conduct the flight not having informed me, Head of the TFS?! You haven't filled out the documents nor signed the order for the first flight!" Usachev answered that he would sign them later(!).

Solovev, being unaware of the decision taken at the meeting, had earlier prepared flight list #2 for the first flight, stamped it, and signed in the presence of Lazarev, the I-180 Lead Engineer.

1:30 p.m. At this time Chkalov was already taxiing to the start, accompanied by technician Kurakin. Chkalov stopped the plane by the starter. The starter raised the flag, allowing the flight to begin. Chkalov gave it the gas and began his take off. At 600 to 900 feet into the take off run, the plane stopped, turned back and began to taxi to the hanger. Chkalov got out of the plane and told Lazarev that, "This is the first time a gas feed system has broken down for me on take off." Later, Chkalov told Solovev that, "If the gas feed system hadn't broken, I'd have shown how that plane could fly." These phrases by Chkalov underscore the fact that the decision was taken at the meeting to go ahead with the first flight.

Usachev and Polikarpov hurried to the plane and ordered that it not be taken to the hanger, but that the gas-feed be quickly repaired, so that a second attempt at a take off could be made. All the production workers, however, insisted that the repair would take at least three to four hours. Usachev then reluctantly agreed and ordered that the fuel be removed and the plane placed in the hanger. All measures were to be taken to repair and install the gas-feed system and to prepare the plane for its first fight in the morning.

2:10 p.m. All leadership personnel at the airport departed.

At this point a preliminary summary might be in order.

Not all of the leadership personnel present at the airport December 12th knew: that the I-180 had 48 defects; that Polikarpov had been sent a defect list by the OTK and military representatives; about the absence of almost all the normal accompanying documentation; about the absence of in-factory flight testing; about the absence of statistical examination of all the plane's basic units and systems. "The program of preliminary testing of the I-180 aircraft" was approved by Director Usachev and sent to the Air Force Research Institute only on December 13th. Much of this Chkalov did not know.

It sounds unbelievable, but it's a fact: Eight leadership personnel from various ranks of the Defense Industry and the NKVD, had been orally informed of the December 12 prohibition of the first flight of the I-180 with test pilot Chkalov at the controls by the NKVD and the Central Committee of the Communist Party of the Soviet Union—and they knew that the NKVD didn't just throw warnings around for no reason. This was at the height of Stalin's repression and purges of the aviation industry, and of the whole country, yet, in spite of this, they conducted a joint meeting behind closed doors to discuss the following question: How and in what way can we proceed with action which contradicts a government decree?

In 1938, this action could easily be interpreted as "a group conspiracy by those working for Japanese or German intelligence services." It should be noted that the NKVD played a leading role in this "group conspiracy," saying, "Enough high sounding words; it's time to get down to business."

What business? To prohibit the first flight, or to allow the first fight?

It should have been, of course, to prohibit it. The question was decided simply. Usachev commanded Porai to empty fuel from the plane and to take it to the hanger, having told all those present about the instructions by the NKVD and CC CPSU concerning prohibition of the first flight. That's all!

The flight was canceled!

But another question was being decided—how to conduct the first flight! Usachev, Belyaikin, Tamashevich, along with the silent consent of Polikarpov, insisted on carrying out the first flight, in spite of the decisions of the NKVD and the CC CPSU to cancel it. NKVD officials must ensure the execution of orders issued by their leaders; however, with such "soft enforcement," that the first flight was, as a matter of fact, allowed to take place—and not with simple silence, but with supposedly "vigorous debate."

Usachev carried out direct instructions: conduct the first flight. Otherwise, for what reason was such an august collection of responsible officials from two Peoples Commissariats told to gather at the airport on this "day of rest"? In order to hear the phrase "The plane has defects…"? They had already heard that phrase before this meeting.

The prohibition of the first test flight by the NKVD and the CC CPSU must have put such an experienced head designer on his guard—especially since he had already been arrested in 1929. But he didn't seem to be alarmed, though he hadn't signed even one technical document, report, or flight list. But this was simply prudent on his part.

It was in this situation at the meeting, when everyone agreed to conduct a taxiing exercise, and to decide after this whether to go ahead with the first flight.

What compelled them all together to make this decision?

Why did a situation, which arose on the 12th of December at a typical defense industry factory (Factory #156), in the usual course of events, while conducting a first test-flight of a new fighter plane designed by Head Designer Polikarpov, attract such "explosive" interest from the NKVD and the CC CPSU? Was it to decide extremely important questions relative to the defense capabilities of the government? Hardly. The construction of the new I-180 fighter plane didn't eliminate the gap between the aging I-16 fighter and the new German Bf-109 fighter.

There was no need for an extremely rapid development and testing of the I-180 aircraft—it was buried in the plans for 1939. Could the I-180 have become one of the world's best fighters in 1939? In explanatory notes at the end of January 1938, Polikarpov had the following to say: "The projected aircraft represents the future development of the fighter plane. Created on the basis of I-16 technology, the goal of the project is the creation of a speedy fighter plane with powerful weapons and with the capability of being quickly introduced into serial production as a replacement for the I-16 at Aviation Factory #21."

But by many tactical and technical statistics, it was already outdated by the end of 1938. For example, the "maximum speed of the I-180 aircraft was 270 mph, not the 351 mph mistakenly assigned to it by CAHI."

So what was the real reason for such "explosive" interest by the NKVD and the CC CPSU in this first test flight of the I-180 aircraft?

Let's take two steps back. Let's take a look at a little history and a little politics.

An American sociologist noted that all totalitarian regimes before the war loved aviation: Germany, Japan and Italy, for example.

At the first session of the Supreme Soviet, Stalin said: "I must admit, I love pilots. If I find out some pilot has been offended, I am deeply hurt. We must support and stand solidly behind our pilots." And so it might have seemed, even to the most informed people—if one didn't consider all the facts together, and connect all the dots.

Of course, the Stalin leadership openly used the great accomplishments of our pilots and polar explorers as its own lightning rod, attracting public opinion in the country and abroad away from the unfolding terror inside the country. Of this there can be no doubt. The coincidence of these processes was not accidental.

The style and logic of totalitarian regimes are identical, which can be seen in both the Russian and German languages. Arrests of the scientific and technological intelligentsia were part of a free labor system—and *here* there was worked out a special plan. Molotov discussed this plan partially in answering the question: "Why were such brilliant scientists like Tupolev, Stechkin, and Korolev arrested?" He answered that: "Many people talked too much... Tupolev was from that part of the intelligentsia badly needed by Soviet power. But in their hearts they opposed us, so a method was found to overcome this problem. We put the Tupolevs behind bars and ordered their secret service jailers to secure the very best conditions for them. Let them eat cake, but don't let them go. Let them work and create what this country needs—military hardware."

The logic was simple: The iintellectuals in their hearts were always opposed to Soviet power, and, therefore, could be drawn into anti-Soviet activities for which they would be destroyed. There was a solution. Better to isolate them...for their own good. In isolation, they could be supplied with all the necessary conditions for work: food, books, and even meetings with women. Combining intellectuals in a collective would create fertile soil for their work and lessen the problems of control. But most important—isolation gave the necessary cover for secrecy; very important for military purposes.

TsKB-29 NKVD was the name of the aviation experimental design bureau inside the NKVD. Organized in 1939, it was analogous to an earlier design bureau of the OGPU (TsKB-39).[22] In the TsKB-29 were located almost all the most prominent aviation designers, organizers, manufacturers, and air force weapons designers: A. N. Tupolev, V. M. Myasishchev, V. M. Petlyakov, V. L. Aleksandrov, S. M. Yeger, S. P. Korolev, A. V. Nadashkevich, A. I. Putilov, A. M. Cheremukhin, V. A. Chezhevsky, and many others (150 people in all).

The demands of Stalin and Molotov at the February-March Plenum of the CC CPSU for an "examination," or loyalty check, of the military

[22] The OGPU became the NKVD, which later became the KGB.

establishment, was perceived by the NKVD as a clear directive to massively purge the ranks of the Army, Air Force, and Navy of supposed saboteurs.

Yakov Ivanovich Alksnis, Chief of the Soviet Air Force, was a Deputy Defense Peoples Commissar for Defense Commissar Voroshilov. In October, he was selected as a candidate for Deputy to the Supreme Soviet of the USSR.

For two days, the Air Force Military Soviet discussed their accomplishments for 1937, but on November 29th Alksnis had disappeared. It was explained that the day before Voroshilov had assigned him to represent the government at a reception at the Lithuanian Embassy, but he never returned home...

They charged Alksnis with a criminal conspiracy against Voroshilov, accusing him of sending the best pilots to Spain with the goal of weakening the Soviet Air Force. In the morning of July 29, a half dead Alksnis was dragged out of his cell and shot. He was only 41 years old.

In March 1938, Chkalov was specifically invited to attend the trial of Nikolai Bukharin and Aleksei Rykov.[23] One can understand the impact this obvious farce would have had on him.

During a recess in the trial, he went up to Vyshinsky[24] and frankly announced that he didn't believe colleagues of Lenin suddenly and unexpectedly became enemies of the people.[25] Vyshinsky gave him a condescending, wry smile, and coldly, calmly answered: "You're really something, Valery Pavlovich. Is that really the point? You know, if a person offends, a statute can be found."

This conversation, of course, became known to Stalin—but, undoubtedly, in a different form and with an interpretation created by Vyshinsky. Chkalov many times intervened—with varying degrees of success—for people he knew personally, who had fallen into the hands of the NKVD.

---

23 Bukharin and Rykov were popular Russian revolutionaries Stalin had put to death after a famous show trial at the height of his purges. They, and other famous Communist revolutionaries, were tortured into publicly admitting their "guilt."

24 Andrei Y. Vyshinsky was Chief Prosecutor of the USSR and chief prosecutor for Stalin during the Purge's infamous 1936-1938 Moscow treason trials, of which the Bukharin and Rykov trials were a part.

25 "Enemies of the people" was a commonly used accusation by Stalin's prosecutors during the Purges.

It's difficult to say what fate would have had in store for him, if the December 15, 1938, crash had not cut his life short.

And what suddenly changed Stalin's mind about Chkalov? But perhaps not suddenly. And was this "falling out" to be understood and responded to by the newly formed People's Commissariat for Internal Affairs of the USSR (NKVD-jvf).

Not one action of a political nature was ever undertaken without the approval of the security organ of the CC CPSU. The Party apparatus directed the security organs always, and never for a day, nor for an hour, let slip from its unremitting control the "Chastising sword of the Party!"

It's possible to imagine that between Stalin and Chkalov there was a defining conversation sometime during the first half of 1938, which determined Stalin's relationship with Chkalov: Chkalov was a member of the Party, but not a slave of the Party; Chkalov had his own opinions, which he frankly expressed and supported strongly; the Chkalov of 1938 differed sharply from the Chkalov of 1935, and the Stalin of 1938 had also changed.

It appears that Stalin became convinced he could not make from his "Stalin's Falcon" and people's favorite an obedient executor of the wishes of this "Great Leader of All Peoples" and cast his "play-thing" aside. The trial balloons, which Stalin liked to release in his political games, were deflected and declined by Chkalov: Stalin never forgave those who refused him.

The profession of test pilot couldn't have presented them with a better opportunity to accomplish the basic task — the removal from the political and government arena of Deputy Chkalov, who had won great authority, respect, and popularity among the people of the USSR; the removal of The Great One's "favorite," whom he had quickly drawn to himself, then, no less quickly, distanced himself from.

It's generally known that the work of a factory test pilot carries with it certain requirements: At the factory, the preparation of the experimental plane for flight requires that specific safety measures be taken, especially for the first flight. Much depends, first of all, on the developed design documentation, the technical level of manufacturing, the manufacturing discipline, the equipment supplied to the flight center, and the correct cycle of standard documentation.

The Head Designer and Technical Director of the factory, Nikolai Nikolaevich Polikarpov, and the Director of DIPC Factory #156, Mikhail

Aleksandrovich Usachev were the guarantors at the factory of the safety of Valery Pavlovich Chkalov.

On November 25, 1938, Beria was appointed to the post of People's Commissar of Internal Affairs of the USSR, which he was to take over from Yezhov before December 3rd. The "Yezhovshchina" period had ended; the "Berievshchina" period had begun.[26]

At the 10th Party Congress in Georgia (June 1937), Beria announced: "Let enemies know, that anyone who attempts to raise their hand against the will of our people, against the will of the Party of Lenin-Stalin, will be mercilessly crushed and destroyed."

On August 22, 1938, Beria was appointed as First Deputy to Yezhov in the People's Commissariat of Internal Affairs of the USSR. It was clear that Stalin had selected him to replace the "Iron Commissar." On September 29, 1938, Beria headed the Main Administration of Government Security (MAGS) NKVD USSR.

On November 25, 1938, by decree, The Presidium of the Supreme Soviet of the USSR removed Yezhov from his responsibilities as People's Commissar for Internal Affairs of the USSR. On the same day, Beria was appointed to the post and continued to serve as head of MAGS.

On December 3, 1938, Stalin approved the appointment of Beria as People's Commissar of Internal Affairs of the USSR. The decree making the appointment was only published on December 8, 1938.

On December 17, 1938, Beria appointed his deputy, Merkulov, to head the MAGS. This was done after the Commission on the Catastrophe of the I-180 had done its investigation of the crash and test pilot V. P. Chkalov's death.

The first important business in which the NKVD under Beria's leadership took part was the I-180 catastrophe and the death of Chkalov. What role was assigned to the NKVD in this catastrophe, and what part did Beria play as the newly appointed People's Commissar?

Stalin's situation in 1938 seemed very favorable: a new People's Commissar for Internal Affairs; a new Head of the DIPC Central Administrative Board, Belyaikin; a new Factory Director, Usachev; a new DIPC #156 Factory; a new Head Designer, Polikarpov; a new plane not

26 "Yezhovshchina" is the name given to some of the bloodiest years of the purges under NKVD head, Yezhov. He was later himself arrested and shot, as he had arrested and shot the previous NKVD head, Yagoda. The madness of the purges fed upon itself.

having passed through any preliminary testing — but with a former "Stalin's Falcon," Chkalov, as Chief Pilot and test pilot.

For Beria the called for action was tested and simple: Determine the main executor, then prepare and "enlist" his consent. The leadership of the People's Commissariat of the Defense Industry, including the Head Designer, must understand the "importance" of the first flight, but only within the limits of specific allowed information and disinformation.

Beria created a tense, nervous, and strained environment at the factory around the preparations of the experimental I-180 aircraft by assigning extreme governmental importance to the necessity of great speed in its development, especially in the completion of the first flight. A break in the scheduled time for development would be a crime.

For the test pilot there would be special psychological treatment with the help of constant reminders of the large number of defects, constant changing of the time for the first flight, constant "discussion of problems" in the presence of the test pilot by the leadership of the factory, NKVD, and DIPC. The break in the gas-feed line is an example of the very real existence of this psychological pressure. As Chkalov said, if that break had occurred in the air, it would have caused a forced landing.

Beria had determined the main executor of the action — 29-year-old Usachev, Director of Factory #156, Party member, graduate of the Moscow Aviation Institute and former pilot.

The actions of Beria were small, but very significant and revealing in detail.

Why was action planned for December 12? Sunday was a day off. The country's leadership was resting. The offices of the NKVD and DIPC were deserted; there were no coworkers, so there could be no leaking of information. But the NKVD, i.e., Beria, was working.

Early in the morning on December 12th, Beria sent a highly placed NKVD official to Usachev's home to work out a complete and detailed plan of action. At the same time, to once again check the "readiness" of the I-180 aircraft for the first flight, Beria sent special agent Kholichev to the factory.

From 11:00 a.m. Usachev was absent from the factory: evidently to check last minute details. There could be no slip-ups. The system had to work flawlessly. Success of the plan depended on support from high places: from the authority of the Soviet Government, and from the

NKVD—Beria. They really represented "two sides of the same coin."

Having prepared very seriously and carefully for the coming operation, Beria sent letters to Stalin, Molotov and Voroshilov under the stamp "Top Secret."

The letter follows:

Top Secret

To: Comrade Stalin

In accordance with the instructions of DIPC Factory #156 Director USACHEV, the new I-180 fighter was brought to the Central Airport with 48 defects, which had been noted in the minutes of the technical control department of design engineer POLIKARPOV.

Not one registration certificate for the plane has been completed, since the head of Factory #156 Technical Control, YAKOVLEV, won't sign them until all the defects uncovered by the technical department have been eliminated.

However, under pressure from Director USACHEV, YAKOVLEV signed a registration document on the plane's wing, where he noted that he would allow the flight with restricted speed.

My source learned of this through engineer 67, GENDIN, of a subdivision of Factory #156. GENDIN, in turn, had been told this by Technical Control Head, YAKOVLEV, who was upset by the illegal demands of USACHEV.

Today, 12/12/38, at 12:00 noon, given appropriate flying weather, the aircraft, the fighter I-180, must take its first test flight.

Hero of the Soviet Union, Brigade Commander, V. P. Chkalov, will fly the plane.

In the opinion of my source, the plane's defects threaten it with disaster in the air.

To check the agent's information, special NKVD agent KHOLICHEV traveled to the factory. Assistant Director of Factory #156, SUROVTSEV, confirmed that the I-180 aircraft was sent from the factory to the airport with defects.

PEOPLE'S COMMISSAR OF INTERNAL AFFAIRS
OF THE UNION OF SSR.
(L. BERIA)

> *Com. Beria called by telephone and said that the plane's test flight did not take place today. Loginov.*

Working in the archives and examining Stalin and Voroshilov's materials, I tried, leafing through every document, to find some kind of note or phrase, uncovering the reasons for Chkalov's death. It turned out to be not a note, but the December 12th Beria letter.

Did Beria have some weighty proof in his letter to Stalin that he had formulated a plan to create a "disaster in the air?" No, Beria well understood and valued Chkalov as a brilliant test pilot, who, when he fell into a critical situation, was always able to find a way out.

Beria also knew that Chkalov's wife was pregnant, and that Chkalov would do everything in his power to save his life as the father of a third child: Beria had considered everything to the last detail.

Beria weighed all his chances for the success of the planned action; and Chkalov's chances to come out of it alive (however badly hurt). And only after all this, did Beria make the decision to "create a disaster" during the first flight, and to inform Stalin in the December 12, 1938, letter, including such nonsense as "if weather permits."

As to the "source," he was a highly placed technocrat, who understood design and construction well, and also understood that to guarantee success for the "disaster" was to equally guarantee his life. The source knew how to organize, check, and model the probability of accidents under normal flying conditions, but not in extreme situations. (Without some sort of preliminary testing of the aircraft's separate systems, their function as a whole could not be guaranteed; and, therefore, an accident could occur.)

In this way, on December 12, 1938, two official technical documents existed relative to carrying out the first test flight of the I-1890 aircraft:
- One with safety concerns—based on a report agreed to by the Head Designer and signed by the technical leadership of the factory.
- One with no safety concerns—based on a letter signed by People's Commissar of Internal Affairs, Beria, which could lead to an aircraft disaster.

The first document corresponds to the normal processes of requiring documentation for carrying out experimental flight at Factory #156. The second document contains information about carrying out the fight and was sent to Stalin under a Top Secret stamp.

The significance and importance of these documents are undeniable, but they are really aimed at only one person: test pilot Chkalov and his life.

This is the end of this version's preliminary research. The contents and analysis of the declassified archival documents show that on December 12,1938, the NKVD, i.e., Beria, planned "an aircraft accident in the air...and Hero of the Soviet Union, Brigade Commander, V. P. Chkalov, would fly the plane."

The aircraft's December 12th tragedy was averted due to an unexpected and unplanned defect—a break in the fuel line during the beginning phase of the I-180's first flight.

The events of December 12th played a special role in the life of Beria and the NKVD. In his letter to Stalin, Beria indicated the date and time of the first test flight of the I-180 aircraft with Chkalov at the controls. In other words, he was sent a "report" about the coming action and its expected consequences. But there was a breakdown, which brought an angry reaction from Stalin directed at his new People's Commissar. Consider the anger Stalin displayed at the failed transpolar flight of the Levanevsky crew, and at the delay in the trial of Zinoviev and Kamenev.[27]

It's clear the I-180 aircraft was not at all ready for its first flight.

None of the normally demanded technical documents had been prepared. Only the test pilot was ready. If the planned for catastrophe had occurred, only Chkalov could be blamed: There was no order for the first flight from factory director, Usachev; no flight list approved by the head designer. In spite of all this, test pilot Chkalov decided to fly the plane...

Therefore, representatives of the NKVD, the head designer, and the factory technical director made an oral decision, on December 12th, to allow Chkalov to make the flight.

But the main and most important written document concerning this first flight, and about which all those present at the airfield couldn't have

27 Gregory Zinoviev and Lev Kamenev were two old Bolsheviks and friends of Lenin, whom Stalin had tortured into confessing to "... forming a terrorist organization with the purpose of killing Joseph Stalin and other members of the Soviet government." They and 14 others were shot after this first of several such Moscow trials in which the defendants were absurdly accused of working with foreign governments, and of being "dangerous, hardened, cruel and ruthless" criminals.This first of what became known as the "Moscow Show Trials" took place August 19-24, 1936.

known, was the secret letter to Stalin on December 12th that at 12:00 noon, on that date, test pilot and Hero of the Soviet Union, Brigade Commander Valery Pavlovich Chkalov would indeed fly the I-180 aircraft. In this letter to Stalin, and in similar letters to Molotov and Voroshilov, Beria, through his source, confirmed the possibility of an in-flight catastrophe for the I-180.

Stalin took no measures to prohibit the flight and never answered Beria's warning letter. With his silence, Stalin gave the go-ahead to carry out this flight with its possible tragic consequences.

Only four persons, the four most powerful people in the government, knew of Beria's warning letter: Stalin, Molotov, Voroshilov, and Beria.

And these four government leaders, with full knowledge of the possible air tragedy to come, gave their permission to make this first test flight—and as a result, gave their permission to seriously risk the life of Hero of the Soviet Union, Brigade Commander, Valery Chkalov.

A small digression into Russia's criminal code might be in order:

"Socially dangerous actions (or inactions), which violate a person's rights is a crime.

"Culpability or guilt is a necessary condition for a crime to have been committed.

"Premeditation or negligence can be a form of guilt. Premeditation requires that a person foresee the incorrect nature of the action and the possibility of its negative consequences and, consciously, refuses to take action to prevent it.

"Complicity in a crime: The intentional participation of two or more persons in the commission of a crime. A crime committed with the complicity of others carries with it significantly more social danger than a crime committed alone. For example, a crime committed by an organized group is looked upon by the Criminal Code of the Russian Federation as an aggravated crime.

"A felony responsibility is also assigned to actions in preparation for a crime, for attempting to commit a crime, and for participation in a crime."

Such was the legal case for the "prohibition of the December 12th flight by the Soviet Government," according to the Accident Commission in a covering letter to Stalin and Molotov.

And what were the NKVD and Beria to do? They would wait, because there were still "many serious defects not mentioned in the defects lists."

And what did the participants and witnesses say about these events? Commentary from several of them follows:[93]

Belyaikin. Administration head of the People's Commissariat of the Defense Industry.

"Entering the flight station at CAHI, I found two NKVD representatives, Usachev, Polikarpov and the flight station head, Yakovlev. To my question, 'What's the condition of the aircraft?' they answered that the plane was ready, but that there were defects, and I was presented with a written list of defects.

"In a rather sharp exchange with Yakovlev, I pointed out it was his immediate responsibility to reveal those defects, and that he must officially write about them in order that they me removed.

"The NKVD representative demanded that they get the main point in their discussion of the I-180 plane.

"At the airfield on December 13th, I suggested to Leontiev, the head of the experimental department, that he carefully examine the mechanical condition of the plane."

Usachev. Director of Factory #156.

"At 12:00 noon on December 12th I arrived at the airport. NKVD agents and Defense Industry Administrative Head, Belyaikin were already there. They were holding a conversation in a separate room. After their conversation Belyaikin told me that the Central Committee of the Communist Party forbid the flight of the I-180. It was decided to conduct taxiing exercises first and then decide whether to make the flight or not. When the plane began taxiing to the start the fuel line broke. This defect was unexpected and wasn't noted in the defect list. The decision was made to repair the fuel line, and the flight was postponed until December 13th."

Gendin. Leading engineer of Factory #156.

"Yakovlev, Technical Control Station Head, continually talked of the plane's defects. Usachev and Tamashevich were pressing him, shouting at him. This scandalous behavior took place on December 12th in the presence of Chkalov. Chkalov was upset, and said such conversations in front of the pilot were demoralizing and have a negative psychological effect."

Brovko. The senior military representative at the factory, a Colonel.

"Anti-government action continued at the factory until the last minute, including bringing to the airport an unfinished aircraft with much left to be done and many defects and expecting it to fly. The plane was brought to the factory with these defects and with a whole series of systems not yet approved by the Flight Station. All this was done under the guise of speeding production of the aircraft, but in reality the result was an unjustified delay.

"According to a Defense Industry Commissariat report, planes make their first flights, and then, at a tortoise's pace, defects are eliminated.

"The I-180 aircraft was brought to the airfield with a huge number of defects, noted by the Test Station and by a military representative in a defect list sent to Polikarpov. Thus, on December 12th, I personally told Belyaikin of the inexcusable removal of the plane's back-up fuel pump. Before the flight, there was a serious argument, with cursing, between the Flight Station technicians, the factory director, designer Tomashevich, and in the presence of a silent Pollikarpov. This all took place before Chkalov, and it undoubtedly made him nervous, which was completely unacceptable.

"The decision by Belyaikin, Usachev, Polikarpov and Tomashevich to go ahead with the December 12th flight without completing any documentation, was criminal. Not one document or order concerning the first flight was signed and the plane, in spite of all the evidence above, was released to begin its flight. Only the breaking of the fuel line prevented it from taking place."

Porai. Test Flight Center (TFC) Head of Factory #156. A Colonel.
"On December 10th, the director was ordered to prepare the aircraft for its first flight. The defects were not eliminated, documents were not presented and the plane not accepted by the flight station. But since the weather was bad (fog the whole day), it was decided to prepare the plane for taxiing. Chkalov, without a parachute, conducted the taxiing test for 20 minutes.

"On December 11th, the factory director ordered that the plane be prepared for its first flight. During testing of the motor, and in the presence of Tomashevich, the right landing gear descended. Chkalov was at the airfield. The defects on the list had not been eliminated nor had documents been presented.

"On December 12th, a day off, the director ordered that preparations for the flight be organized. I told the director that the aircraft was not ready for flight, that documents had not been prepared, and that the Flight Station would not register the plane for flight. Usachev just waved his hand, and didn't answer me. At this time, Belyaikin was scolding Technical Control Station Head, Yakovlev."

Soloviev. Factory #156 Test Flight Center Deputy Head.

"After taxiing and a rapid run with a raised tail (the beginning phase of a plane's flight –auth.), the plane returned to the start, due to a break in a fuel line. There was a correction made in the directions of flight list #2. Made under repeated pressure from TFC Head Porai, the words 'to carry out the first flight, etc.' were changed to 'to carry out a taxiing exercise.'

"The above mentioned events (e.g., issuing the pilot his assignment without the approval of the leadership of the flight station) flowed from the system of management conducted by the highest leadership. Therefore, in this instance, we were eliminated from playing a decision-making role by the highest leadership: the Director, Belyaikin, and Polikarpov."

Ginzburg. Representative of the experimental department of Aviation Engine Factory #29.

"I was commanded to give help to the factory in the operation and maintenance of engine M-88. On examining the motor in the plane, I noticed the left fuel pump had been removed. I asked head mechanic, Leonov, who allowed the removal of the fuel pump. He answered that comrades Tomashevich and Kun, in accordance with their plan to lighten the plane's weight, had ordered its removal. I couldn't allow this violation, and wrote in the engine's logbook, 'Due to the absence of one fuel pump on the engine, I forbid the plane to fly. Factory # 29 Representative, E. A. Ginzburg.'

"Tomashevitch and Kun wanted to connect with one lever controls for fuel, afterburning, high attitude and changing speed. .I forbid it. After a series of instructions, I left on December 2nd for Zaporozhye.

"On December 5th, I again returned to Moscow. December 8th they transferred the plane to the airport. On December 9th, I called the dispatcher at CAHI'S Department 8 and asked for written permission to be present at the first test of the engine. I was denied permission. On December 10th and 11th, I called the dispatcher, who passed on to me the information that the motor worked well.

"I wasn't able to talk to the pilot or the service personnel concerning any particulars of the functioning of motor M-88. I was even more surprised, when I found out that on December 12th the first taxiing run of the I-180 around the airfield was conducted without my presence. The presence of the engine's factory representative during the first taxiing run of an experimental plane is mandatory. Without the signature of a representative of an engine's head designer, no experimental plane is allowed to fly."

Tomashevich. Deputy Head Designer, Head of Design Bureau # 1 of Factory #156.

"The organization at the factory was such that it was difficult to say who was responsible for the first flight. The Test Flight Center is an independent department, subordinate to the factory director. The aircraft was transferred from the factory to the FRS for continued factory testing with much left incomplete and a large number of defects. The aircraft was brought to the Test Flight Center prematurely. After reading the defect list of the Technical Control Center, I concluded that, 'the defects of the I-180 aircraft on December11th should not prevent the first flight.'

"I also pointed out that the question of allowing the first flight without collecting all the statistical data, was decided not by us but by higher authority. The I-180 aircraft on December 12th was ready for flight. I reported this to Belyaikin. There was a risk the landing gear would collapse during landing, because no statistical data had been collected concerning its strength. It must be admitted that the aircraft's main systems had not undergone statistical testing. Polikarpov and Usachev knew about this lack of statistical testing.

"Chkalov did not know of it.

"The motor's single fuel pump was shown in the model mock-up and in the fuel line diagram, and there were no objections by the mock-up team.

"Fuel control was redone according to the directions of Factory #33's representative. The length of the carburetor's lever and the lever in the cabin was increased. The break in the fuel line December 12th was caused by a discrepancy between a memorandum I sent to the workshop and the draft sent them by motor sector head, Kun."

Yakovlev-Ternovsky. Head of Factory #156 Technical Control Center (TCC).

"The aircraft was presented to the TCC for inspection on 12/02/38. After a careful examination of the aircraft using its drafting diagrams and technical contracts, 139 incomplete items and defects were recorded.

"Beginning December 9th, the factory director began to pressure, and even demand, that TCC technicians fill out documents in spite of the fact that several parts of the plane's systems were not completed. The control experts say they have never seen such pressure put on the technicians of the TCC by the director.

"On December 12th I was called to the Pilots' room in Department Four. Usachev was telling Belyaikin that the TCC was slowing the process leading to the plane's first flight, that it was breaking the time schedule for testing the aircraft and finding fault with every minor detail, etc. Belyaikin said that the TCC was overly concerned with trifling matters, as, for example, the absence of a second fuel pump, etc. Work in the hanger continued for almost 24 hours, and on December 12th, a series of defects and incomplete work was taken care of. Several defects were allowed to pass by the Deputy Head Designer, Tomashevich, and only after this did TCC technicians sign the document allowing the first flight.

Lazarev. Factory #156 TFC Head Engineer.

"By order of Factory Director, Usachev, I was appointed lead engineer of the I-180 aircraft for its testing program. From November 13 to December 8, I was at the factory and observed the construction of the plane and became acquainted with its mechanical parts. Work on the plane in the factory was very poorly organized and there was no coordination in the drafts. Work proceeded in two shifts and sometimes into the early morning. There was definitely a feeling of some kind of urgency in all the work. Under pressure from Director Usachev, and the head of the TFC, the aircraft was brought to the airfield without written orders of the director, and to the flight center for flight-testing without transfer documents.

"On December 12th, the planned day of the flight, 48 defects remained. A document was drawn up about the plane's readiness for flight. The required conclusions, however, concerning the plane's preparedness for flight were not included in the document. Deputy Head

Designer, Tamashevich, who announced that these defects would not influence the first flight, decided the question."

Isakov. Department Head of the Propeller-Engine Group of the Air Force Research Institute. Military Engineer of the First Rank.

"Much was not known by the mock-up team, since the designer still hadn't decided questions about covering the motor and diagrams concerning motor control. In particular, it was made clear that the system for heating air for the carburetor and the regulation of engine temperature would be taken in its entirety from the DB-3 aircraft of designer Ilyushin.

"The engine installation on the I-180 was done in a slap-dash hurried manner; only, it seems, to allow the plane to fly without eliminating defects recorded in the mock-up team's report. One could compare comrade Polikarpov's bureau with that of comrade Sukhoi's bureau, where they excel at engine installation and are examples of a serious approach to this question. The designers of the I-180 aircraft stubbornly ignored many problems, and not thinking things through, carried out a series of innovations not justified by common sense. For example, they installed their inferior heater without testing it in action."

Polikarpov. Head Designer of Factory #156, and of the I-180 aircraft.

"The organization of testing at the TFC was unsatisfactory. The equipment of the TFC was also insufficient. Therefore, testing any plane was not determinative and in accordance with regulations and methods of operation. Official registration of flights, beginning with the first flight of an experimental plane, was not accurate, and the assignment for flight was not examined. Only a general form was filled out. Serious pilot instruction, acquainting them with the plane and methods of flight, was not carried out.

"Every experimental plane has flight, design and production defects. Some of them are crucial—dangerous for flight; others, are in need of being eliminated before the first powered flights; and, finally, there are those which are not dangerous and don't affect the plane's strength or stability, and can be eliminated during the process of production. We, in our work, must achieve a situation in which the experimental plane being prepared for flight has no defects. However, we are forced to cut the time in testing experimental planes, and, therefore, allow for several defects... Such defects, which are not dangerous in a first flight, are subject to elimination after the first flight and were allowed on the I-180 aircraft. There were approximately 30 such defects."

Leonov. Factory #156 Master Mechanic of Propeller Group 5.

"When during taxiing on 12/12 the fuel line broke, I was called to work to repair it, which I finished toward morning of 12/14. The work wasn't satisfactory, however, and after the third try we were finally successful.

"On December 13th, Polikarpov and Usachev came to the plane and I again suggested making changes to the fuel control system, which, in my opinion, would have been more reliable, but the suggestion was turned down and I was ordered to set up the system as it was.

"Concerning the engine cooling system: Polikarpov said that the rear edge of the cowling could be cut in order to increase the size of the exhaust outlet. The motor would have one fuel pump, so the other would have to be removed. We put a plug in its place. This was the way the motor was when tested at the factory."

So what do the official documents show (including those published in the "1988 Version"), concerning the plane's defects identified on December 12th? They showed it carried defects, which could cause an accident or catastrophe at any stage of a first flight.

An accompanying letter to Stalin and Molotov, The December 17 Commission, which examined the reasons for the crash, noted, "all the defects remained on the plane, which caused the Soviet Government to forbid the December 12th flight. In addition, the plane carried many incomplete parts and systems, which would be extremely dangerous during flight, but which were not noted in the defect lists or documents."[94]

Examination of the official documents proves that if the flight on the I-180 had occurred on December 12th, a catastrophe would have resulted, with the probable death of the test pilot.

And what was the reaction of the top leadership of the government to Beria's warning letter that, "the aircraft's defects could result in a catastrophe"?

Stalin. It appears Stalin did not read the letter. Though there are December 12th notes of Stalin's secretary, which say, "In the morning— from com. Beria"; in the evening— "Com. Beria announced by telephone that the aircraft's test flight today would not take place. Loginov."

Voroshilov. His secretary's notes—"Today's flight has been canceled. Isaev. 12/12/38"

There was no order from the Soviet government to forbid the flight.

THE FATAL FLIGHT

And how did events continue to unfold?

December 13. The fuel line was still not repaired, since it continued to break. It was repaired several times during the day and they had to work late into the night.

NKVD representative, Shitov, reworked all the documents. Technicians were given permission to ignore normal procedures.

Aerodynamic calculations, oil and fuel system diagrams, strength calculations and the results of statistical analysis were all missing from the Test Flight Center.

Polikarpov and Usachev arrived to examine how the fuel line repairs were proceeding.

Order 318 containing the program for ground testing of the plane was received by the TFC at 8:00 p.m.

Belyaikin informed Commissar M. M. Kaganovich about what happened at the airfield on 12/12, and that the aircraft was definitely not ready, since they were still eliminating defects.

Department #1 Defense Industry Administrative Head, Leontiev, did not arrive at the airfield.

December 14. There was fog and snow; not flying weather. Usachev arrived in the morning. He railed at everyone, drove them, and ordered them to prepare the plane for flight. In answer to Porai's statement that the weather was too bad to fly in, he answered that, "Valery Pavlovich will come and he will determine whether it is possible to fly or not." Chkalov was not at the airfield.

On this day, Porai and Soloviev wrote a report to factory Director, Usachev:

"In accordance with your personal order, I report that the TFC program of ground testing for the first flight according to order 318, has not been completed, since it was received at 8:00 p. m. 12/13/38. The following points have not been completed (We will note just a few of them—auth.).

"2. A technical examination with an accounting of deviations from the draft has not been done;

"3. Measurement of the wings and other details with the goal of exposing a slowdown in production has not been done.

"10. An examination of the plane by the representative has not been done.

"11. Taxiing has been tested; flights have not.

"To fulfill this program, it is necessary to create a document releasing the plane for testing, but since this work was not completed no document was created."

In spite of this report, and regardless of the existence of defects, and the prohibition of the first flight by the NKVD and the CCCP, a document was signed on December 14th preparing the I-180 for it first flight. This was apparently done under pressure from Usachev. The document states:

"The defects shown in the defects list of December 11, 1938, over the signatures of the above mentioned comrades (Tomashevich, Kolverzhin, Trostyansky, Lazarev, Kurkin, Yakovlev, Yikolaev, Kobzev.—*Auth.*),cannot serve as obstacles for the first flight. The fuel line, which broke during taxiing 12/12, has been replace with a new one on the instruction of Deputy Head Designer, c. D. L. Tomashevich.

"The plane is ready for its first flight: The landing gear will not be raised; speed and weight will be restricted in accord with the instructions of factory Head Designer, N. N. Polikarpov."

Polikarpov didn't officially sign the document, but signed under the phrase, "I agree with the contents of this document."

This same day factory director Usachev released a factory Order releasing the plane for its first flight.

All the documents for the first flight were filled out by evening and Usachev and Kholichev both took a copy of each. The order was given to prepare the plane for flight the next day. This begs the question as to why they felt it necessary personally to take copies of all the documents.

Porai received a weather report for December 15: clear weather, but severe freezing—20 degrees below zero, Celsius.

December 15. Olga E. Chkalova:

"On December 15th, after saying good bye to me and our small daughter (He said good-bye to Igor earlier when he went to school), and agreeing that I should go the clinic for an examination (I was carrying our third child.), he again set out for the airport."

F. I. Utolin, Chkalov's chauffeur:

"It was the morning of the 15th. On the corner of Gorky and Gruzinsky Streets, Chklaov asked me to stop the car to buy cigarettes. I suggested to Chkalov that I take the car in for a maintenance check. Our car approached the railway crossing and the crossing bar was down. Valery Pavlovich got out of the car and told me: 'Take the car to the factory; I'll take the tram.'

"The Moscow weather forecast at 8:00 a.m. that day was for mostly cloudy, with stratus-cumulus clouds at about 1,500 feet. There would be a frosty mist with visibility from about one to three miles. A northeast, and at times, an east wind was forecast. The temperature would be between –27 to –23 degrees, Celsius.

Porai. "The weather was flyable; the temperature at 8:00 a.m. was –24.4 Celcius and we didn't expect it to fall further during the day. At about 10:00 a.m., Chkalov approached me in room #1 of the Fourth Department. I told him about the temperature and he answered that, 'I won't need to fly for more than five minutes,' and left for the flight room of CAHI Department Eight. The factory director arrived at the airfield between 9:00 a.m. and 10:00 a.m. and sent me an order to release the plane for its first flight with Chkalov at the controls. In accordance with this order, I instructed Head Engineer, Lazarev, to make out flight list #3, and left to check the starting layout.

"I spoke with the Central Airport's Flight Officer and asked that no other planes be allowed to take off during Chkalov's flight, and also to set out markers warning off planes which might want to land, and which might interfere with Chkalov's landing. The landing that morning would come from the Khoroshevsky Highway side and continue along a cement landing strip.

"I found Usachev and Polikarpov and told them about the weather forecast and temperature (minus 24.4 Celcius). Usachev said that it would be no problem, that the flight would only last a few minutes. After that, I signed flight list #3 and presented it to Chkalov to acquaint him with the assignment. He read it and signed that he understood the assignment. The assignment was as follows: 'The first fight will take place without retracting the landing gear and with limited speed, in accordance with instructions from Head Designer, Polikarpov. The flight will circle the Central Airport at an altitude of 2000 feet for 10 to 15 minutes. The plane will carry 441 lbs. of fuel; 55 lbs. of oil, and have a flight weight of 2.23 tons.'

"The plane was taken from the hanger at 10:30 a.m., filled with fuel. The motor was warmed up and at 12:20 p.m. was started with a healthy release of compressed air. Before it was completely warmed up, it backfired several times when fuel was rapidly increased. After it was thoroughly warmed, the motor worked smoothly, with the head cylinder reaching a temperature of 200-220 degrees Celsius. The motor was thoroughly warmed up several times during the course of 30-35 minutes.

"After Chkalov got in the plane, the mechanic, Kurakin, suggested to him that he test the engine, which he did. The assignment's directions were again repeated to Lazarev. Chkalov taxied to the start.

"The takeoff was normal with the plane properly restrained. The first turn began at approximately 160 feet with a small list. Two circles were made at an altitude of 1,800-2100 feet. During the second circle, the descent began approximately from the direction of the TIAM and the airport. The plane began the descent before the last turn and appeared to be too distant. I then lost sight of it.

"Valery Pavlovich appeared to be in a good mood before he took off. He was conversing and laughing."[95]

Lazarev. "On December 15th, at 10:30 a.m., I was ordered by Porai to take the plane from the hanger and prepare it for its first flight. The motor started well, but being cold, didn't at first react well when revolutions were suddenly increased. After being sufficiently warmed up, however, it performed this operation well. When Chkalov came to the plane, I gave him directions concerning the plane and the motor. The plane's mechanic, Kurakin, suggested to Chkalov that he test the motor, which he did just before he took off.

"In the morning, Kurakin and I once again carefully checked everything out, and I consider that everything was in good working order.

"The plane took off normally, banked to the left and began to gain altitude. Toward the end of the first circle, in my opinion, the plane was at an altitude of 1,700 to 2,000 feet. While making the second circle, the plane began to glide, made a turn, and, in my opinion, headed for a landing. It then swung around and fell from view.

"In my opinion, the plane was flying normally until the last turn."[96]

Soloviev. "On December 15th, the plane was ready for flight. In the morning, and on the director's orders, I was preparing the 'Ivanov" plane for flight as an observer. Therefore, I was absent for the release of the plane for its first flight. Lazarev, as the lead engineer, was, of course, insufficiently experienced, but this was compensated for by the experience of the head mechanic."[97]

Kozlov. "On the morning of December 15, 1938, at 9:00 a.m., I saw Porai and told him that it was −25 degrees C. and that if he decided to fly, the motor would over cool.

"As the plane began to taxi, the deputy head designer, Tomashevich, came up. I asked him what the temperature of the cylinder heads should be. He said he didn't know.

"At approximately 1:00 p.m., after the mechanic warmed up the plane, Chkalov began to test the motor. It backfired when he rapidly increased the revolutions, and then seemed to work well…

"He taxied to the start, faced the wind, and began to smoothly apply the gas. The plane made its run, and in approximately 10-15 seconds, was in the air, making one circle and half another, during which it gained an altitude of 1,700 to 2,000 feet. At about this time he was over the airport and began a smooth glide in the direction of the radio station, over which he made a left turn of 90 degrees and continued the glide at an altitude of about 350 to 450 feet. Then, making a final turn, he headed for a landing.

"At that moment, when the plane finished its last turn, there was the impression that the plane lessened the angle of its glide, and then dipped into a more severely angled glide, but this was completely normal. The I-16 aircraft, for example, often glided without its motor. After this, however, buildings blocked the plane's view and I couldn't see anything. I immediately ordered the pilot, Shiyanov, to fly the Northrop aircraft over the site of the I-180's landing to see what happened. He reported back that the I-180 was lying broken into several pieces."[98]

Polikarpov. I saw V. P. Chkalov's whole flight and judging by the plane's behavior right up until the last turn, it seemed to me completely normal. After the first circle, Chkalov began a second, apparently not noticing any dangerous indications. At the end of the second circle, beginning approximately at the radio tower, the plane began to descend reaching an altitude of about 650 feet before his last turn. We were still not aware at this point that anything was wrong. The plane then began its direct descent to a landing less than a mile from the airfield, and at little over 300 feet altitude, turned to the left and hid behind some buildings. Apparently, the cause of the crash occurred at this moment.

"From the examination of the broken plane, it's possible to conclude for certain that: the carburetor and fuel line to the fuel pump were filled with fuel; the fuel filter was not clogged, i.e., the engine's fuel system was working properly; the hand and foot controls were working all right; there was no evidence the wings and their control elements were not functioning properly; and the plane was in one piece when it hit the ground, i.e., there was no evidence any part was lost in flight.

"All evidence provides a basis to think that the cause of the catastrophe apparently lies in an interruption of engine action, or in responding to a sharp increase in fuel and engine revolution, or in some break in the fuel feed system...

"The M-88 engine must have the ability to warm up more quickly; then, in the course of such a short 10-15 minute flight, at a speed of 160-290 mph. at a low altitude of 1,640 feet, a long glide would not be necessary and the engine could easily maintain the required cylinder head temperature...

"I never received any indications concerning M-88 engine overcooling from Factory #29, from The Central Institute of Aviation Materials (CIAM), or from the engine's head designer. I also received no information from the representatives of the TFC concerning the dangers of such cold weather and the inadmissibility of flying at 1:00 p.m. on December 15, 1938. Guided by the information I've given above, I took no action to stop the factory director's order or to appeal it.

"I believe that if the pilot had paid closer attention to the engine's temperature, and periodically warmed the engine by increasing revolutions during the second circling, he would have been much closer to the airfield's border and everything might have ended favorably. The engine wouldn't have failed and in the event some problem occurred, the pilot could have made an emergency landing at the airfield.

"As I noted above, all indications are that the M-88's fuel system, although from only one fuel pump, functioned normally. It's highly unlikely that some malfunction of the fuel feed system was the reason for the crash, since neither during the testing of the engine, nor during Chkalov's flight were interruptions in the engine's work or exhaust observed."[99]

Witness Testimony to the Crash of the I-180 Aircraft.

P. V. Shirokov. Moscow Construction Autobase Brigadier.

"…A red plane appeared above the Autobase yard flying from south to north. The plane was at an altitude of not more than 45 to 50 feet. There was no sound from the motor and the propeller was turning slowly. In the beginning, the plane flew parallel to the ground, and as the plane banked to the left, to the west, its left wing dropped lower than the right. As it turned to its left, the plane began to descend still more, and at that moment it caught its left wing on electrical cables carrying a 250-volt charge. Three cables were severed, and the plane's right wing, close to the fuselage, struck a 12-13 foot electric pole. The tail section broke off sharply and the rest of the plane crashed into a pile of waste construction material."

A. S. Petrenko. Moscow Construction Autobase Shift Mechanic.

"…December 15, 1938, a plane appeared over our garage. It was flying very low. The engine was not working, but the propeller was turning and it was apparent the plane was in a glide. And right here, over us, Main Highway, Bldg. 13, the plane turned and headed toward the highway. At that moment, it struck the electric cable pole with its right wing. The plane then sharply swung to the right and struck the roof of the dryer with its left wing. After this, the plane's nose tore into a pile of planks located in the yard by the pole. The blow caused the tail section to tear off from the plane and crash into the fence… I saw that the pilot was lying face down near the fence and by the tail…"[100]

Hero of the Soviet Union, Valery P. Chkalov was received at Botkinsky Hospital at 1:35 p.m., December 15, 1938, by the surgeon on duty, Markov, and by nurse, Sviridova.

Top Secret

TO: STALIN, MOLOTOV, VOROSHILOV, KAGANOVICH

Today, December 15, 1938, at 12:58 p.m., a new plane, the I-180 speed fighter, designed by design engineer, POLIKARPOV, and piloted by Brigade Commander and Hero of the Soviet Union, com. CHKALOV, began its first test flight.

Approximately 10 minutes after it took off, the plane suffered an accident.

The crash killed Hero of the Soviet Union, com. Chkalov, who was dead on arrival at Botinsky Hospital.

The plane was destroyed. It crashed into a large pile of waste planks and wood pieces in the Moscow Construction storage area.

Our investigation before the accident revealed that as a result of the criminal actions of Factory Director #156, com. Usachev, the plane was delivered to the flight test center with defects, some or which would have inevitably caused an accident.

The I-180's test fight was assigned for 12/12 at 12:00 noon, even though the plane had 48 defects certified by the Technical Control Center of the factory. We became aware of this and informed comrades STALIN, MOLOTOV and VOROSHILOV.

At the same time, in the early morning of December 12th, I sent the Head of the NKVD Economic Administration, com. GAGKAEV, and his aid from the NKVD Economic Administration, KHOLICHEV, to Factory #156's Test Flight Center. They warned Hero of the Soviet Union, com. CHKALOV, Head Defense Industry Commissar, BELYAIKIN, and Factory #156 Director, Usachev, of the I-180 aircraft defects and of its lack of preparedness for a test flight.

Having received such information, comrades CHKALOV, BELYAIKIN and USACHEV, decided to repeat the ground-taxiing test. During the taxiing exercise, the fuel line broke. According to com. CHKALOV and the Test Flight Center Deputy Head, SOLOVIEV, of Factory #156, had the fuel line broken during flight, it would have required an emergency landing of the aircraft.

The fuel line was repaired December 14th and Factory Director, USACHEV, scheduled the test flight for December 15th at 12:00 noon.

It's necessary to note that on December 12th, when BELYAIKIN and USACHEV learned of Technical Control Center Head, YAKOVLEV's warning that the plane was unprepared for flight, BELYAIKIN and USACHEV faulted YAKOVLEV for being overly cautious and for inform-ing the NKVD about the plane's condition.

December 15th, before the plane took to the air, Factory #156 Directory, USACHEV, called Defense Industry Commissar, com. M. M. KAGANOVICH, and Informed him the I-180 aircraft, piloted by Hero of the Soviet Union, com. CHKALOV, would make a test flight. Comrade KAGANOVICH gave his approval.

The inevitable followed.

PEOPLE'S COMMISSAR OF INTERNAL AFFAIRS
OF THE UNION OF SSR.
(L. BERIA)[101]

Commissar M. M. Kaganovich sent an accompanying letter to Stalin and Molotov from Factory #156's leaders titled, "A Brief Report Concerning the Crash of the I-180 Aircraft."[102]

Secret

TO: THE SOVIET OF PEOPLES COMMISSARS
OF THE USSR, c. MOLOTOV

THE CENTRAL COMMITTEE OF THE
COMMUNIST PARTY, c. STALIN

A BRIEF REPORT
Concerning the crash of the I-180 aircraft piloted by
Hero of the Soviet Union and Chief Pilot of Factory
#156 c. V. P. CHKALOV

The I-180 aircraft is a fast, single seat, fighter plane developed from the I-16 aircraft. The experimental M-88 engine was installed in the plane.

The I-180 has a calculated top speed of 350-360 mph. Construction of the I-180 aircraft was completed at factory 156 and taken to the airport 12-7-38.

From 12-7 to 12-15, the plane was assembled, weighed, the motor ground-tested and apparent defects eliminated.

On 12-10 the plane's first taxiing exercise was conducted demonstrating satisfactory landing gear function, brakes, tailskids, and motor function. The results of the taxiing exercise were entered onto the flight list.

On 12-12, after an examination of the plane and the correction of the landing gear's right shock absorber, it was released for its second taxiing test, during which the fuel line broke. A stronger fuel line was installed; then tested on the morning of 12-14, after which a special report was issued.

The satisfactory results of both taxiing exercises and the careful and repeated check-ups, allowed us to begin preparations for the plane's first flight. A special report was issued confirming the readiness of the plane for its first flight with its landing gear in the lowered position. The following comrades signed the report:

1. Deputy Head Designer of Factory #156, c. Tomashevich
2. Production Engineer, c. Kalaverzhin
3. Chief Design Bureau Engineer, c. Trostyansky
4. Chief Operations Engineer, c. Lazarev
5. The aircraft's Chief Mechanic, c. Kurakin
6. Technical Control Center Head, Factory #156, c. Yakovlev-Ternovsky.
7. Senior Control Experts, cc. Nikolaev and Kobzev.

Head Designer, N. N. Polikarpov, approved the report. A list of defects was attached to the report which didn't affect the plane's safety during its first flight and which were to be removed afterwards. After the report was drawn up, it was issued to Factory #156 and used as a basis for Factory Director Usachev's order to release the plane for its first flight with a lowered landing gear.

It was on the basis of this order that Test Flight Center Head, Porai, issued the flight list in which the plane was to fly with lowered landing gear at a reduced speed in the area of the airfield for 10-15 minutes.

The plane underwent a careful examination on 12-15 and the engine was tested on the ground for 25 minutes before being turned over to c. Chkalov for take off (to this time, the engine had been run for a total of 6 hours and 37 minutes—4 hours and 30 minutes of which were conducted at Factory #29).

Com. Chkalov tested the engine, the control levers, the wing flaps, then taxied to the start.

The plane took off after a run of approximately 650 to 800 feet and, gaining an altitude of 350-400 feet, turned and began its first circle. The rest of the flight continued at 1,700 to 2000 feet.

Having finished its first circle over the airport, the plane began its second circle, continuing in the direction of Factory #22. It then began its approach to landing. At less than one mile from the airfield, the plane turned left and disappeared behind some buildings.

The plane was found in a wood storage area (#13 Magistralnaya Street) near Khoroshevsky Highway.

The plane, during its descent, caught and snapped cables over the storage area, and, turning, crashed into a pile of wood waste. The blow threw c. Chkalov 35-50 feet forward, together with the tail section of the fuselage, the seat and controls. The forward section of the plane was destroyed. There was no fire.

C. Chkalov was still alive and taken immediately by workers of the wood storage area to Botkinsky Hospital, where he died several minutes later.

TECHNICAL DIRECTOR AND FACTORY DIRECTOR (c. N. N. Polikarpov)	FACTORY HEAD DESIGNER (c. M. A. Usachev)
	FACTORY DEPUTY HEAD DESIGNER (c. Tomashevich)

Let's look further at what witnesses wrote of the December 15th events:

Belyaikin. "In the morning of December 15th, I went to Kashira with the Director of Factory #32, Zhezlov, and Government Administrative Head, Sokolov, retuning to Headquarters at 3:20 p.m. My secretary, Gregoriev, informed me that a disaster had occurred and that the I-180 had crashed. I immediately left for the airfield.

"On arrival at the airport, I asked Usachev who gave permission for the flight. He answered that he received permission from Mikhail Moiseevich, and that there was a document releasing the plane for flight signed by the factory director, the head designer, the head of the TCC, and chief engineer.

"I took all possible measures to prevent the release of the I-180 for flight, considering especially that it would be test flown by Valery Pavlovich Chkalov..."[103]

Ginsburg. "At 3:00 p.m. all the participants in the preparations for the flight of the I-180 and the observers gathered together. They were divided into various rooms and ordered to make written depositions. It turned out that we were in the same room as Polikarpov. When we had finished writing our accounts, all of us, 25-30 people, gathered in the reception area. They called us out one-by-one. The first was the "flight"

315

commission; the second was "political." Merkulov, appointed by Beria's deputy, headed it. Those who were sent to Merkylov after meeting with the first commission never returned. The infamous "Black Crow" limousine awaited them; right here, on the airfield.[28] My turn with the flight commission came only at 3:00 a.m., after 12 hours of tense waiting. What was I feeling? I can say only that before this day, as a young man, I had coal-black hair. After my meeting with the commission, my hair turned gray."[104]

Olga E. Chkalova. "It was about 2:00 p.m. I was home with the children, had just eaten and began to work. I was sorting through the mail and preparing answers in the name of Valery Pavlovich to the many letters he received as a Supreme Soviet Deputy.

"The phone rang often. They asked for Valery Pavlovich. The answer was the same: 'He's not here. He'll be returning late today.' Valery Pavlovich told my in the morning that he'd be going to the sculptor, I. A. Mendelevich, from the airport. Sometimes, it seemed to me without reason, people were asking me how I was. Apparently, many already knew of the tragedy... I didn't know... I continued to work. I sat. I wrote. And a life had been torn away... He was gone forever.

"The door bell rang. It was a pilot; the son of Vasily Ivanovich Chapaev.[29] (We lived in the same building.) In my conversation with him I became uneasy; it seemed he was holding something back. Apparently, he didn't have the courage to finish what he had come to tell me, and left. He left me in a terribly upset state.

"A vague suspicion began to grow, but I drove it away.

"Again the phone rang. I picked up the receiver. It was someone I knew well from the airport. She merely said, 'Hello, I'm coming to see you right away.' My anxiety grew; had something happened? And when she arrived, the terrible thought struck me. I flew to her: 'Did he crash?' She lowered her head.

"My legs seemed made of cotton; they crumbled; I fell on the divan. 'He crashed!' swirled through my mind. There were no tears. Then I lost all strength.

---

28 The "Black Crow" limousine was the Soviet "Zil" automobile used by the NKVD during the purges to pick up its victims.

29 Vasily Ivanovich Chapaev was a Russian Hero Commander during WWI and the Bolshevik Revolution, who was later turned into an immortalized, iconic, figure by the Soviets.

"That evening, four men in black leather flight coats arrived. I don't remember who they were, but seeing I wasn't sobbing and in hysterics, they in a very business like manner spoke of the funeral. I remember this now with horror, but at the time I was completely apathetic and disinterested in everything going on around me.

"People came; people went. They said something; expressed their sympathy. I was silent. What could I say? To say anything at the time that was clear or rational was beyond me. I only understood one thing: I had to find the strength to go on. There was, after all, a new life stirring in me—our child. After him, that's all there was…"[6]

Porai. " I suggest, for the following reasons, that the reason for the crash was engine failure due to:

"1. A fuel line break, since it had broken earlier. True, a new some what better fuel line was installed and a document issued that it was tested.

"2. The engine cooled, and then stopped, although it's difficult to imagine, since the flight lasted only 5-6 minutes.

"3. Fuel pump failure, since the plane's design called for two pumps, not one. Failure of the plane's controls, though this, too, is difficult to imagine happening…

"Other unfinished elements of the plane, which the technical control department allowed, it seems could not have affected the flight.[95]

Soloviev. "I consider the accident could have been caused by any one of three reasons:

"1. The overcooling of the engine and its failure when given fuel. However, I doubt that Chkalov couldn't have read his instruments (in particular, the galvanometer), and having 440 lbs. of fuel on take off, and flying very little, he could have more energetically descended and kept the engine warm.

"2. Failure of the fuel pump and interruption of fuel supply.

"3. The interruption of the fuel supply when suddenly increasing engine revolution outside the airport zone and at low altitude. By 'fuel supply,' I have in mind the whole system."[97]

Kozlov. "In my opinion, the crash occurred as a result of engine failure, and the failure was a result of overcooling or some problem with the throttle. But the fact is, that pilot Chkalov couldn't get the engine to bring the plane into the airport for a landing."[98]

Lazarev. "In my opinion, until the last turn the plane was flying normally. The last turn was caused because the engine cut out as a result of overcooling, and it turned in the hope of finding some open space in which to make an emergency landing — or something broke in the plane's control mechanism."[96]

CIAM Report of 12-16-38.

The Commission was composed of Military Engineer of the First Rank, I. M. Isakov, Central Institute of Aviation Materials Laboratory Engneer, S. A. Yevseev, and CIAM Laboratory Master, V. V. Bogomolov.

An examination of M-88 engine parts taken from the crash site was carried out at CIAM...[30] The conclusion was that, "The probable reason for engine failure in flight was the over cooling of the cylinder heads and inadequate heating of the air flowing to the carburetor."[105]

On December 17th, this CIAM Commission finished its work and sent its report to Stalin and Molotov.[106]

Top Secret

INVESTIGATIVE COMMISSION REPORT

On December 16-17,1938, the Central Committee of the Communist Party of the USSR appointed a Commission for the Investigation of the Crash of the I-180 Aircraft. It was composed of Chairman, ALEKSEEV, and members REPIN, GROMOV, BAIDUKOV, KASHIRIN and SUPRUN.

As a result of our work, we established that on 12-15, at 12:58 p.m., Hero of the Soviet Union, V. P. CHKALOV, after a normal flight and descent for a landing, was forced to land 550 to 650 yards short of the airfield, which resulted in the death of the pilot and the destruction of the aircraft.

The Commission considers that engine failure, due to overcooling and unreliable fuel system design, were the causes of the forced landing.

The engine failure occurred at a moment in the flight from which it

---

30 A lengthy and detailed technical analysis of the damage to engine parts follows, which I have chosen not to translate

was impossible to expect any favorable outcome (low altitude, absence of a landing area). Judging from crash evidence, the pilot until the last moment was guiding his plane in an attempt to land outside an inhabited area. In this, he succeeded.

The Commission further established:

1. The plane, engine, propeller and carburetor had been tested, but to this time had never been tested in flight. This obligated the flight organizers to pay particular attention to detail and give particular care in preparing the plane for flight. This was, in fact, not done.

2. There was no system on the plane for regulating engine temperature, without which flight, especially a first flight in freezing weather (-25 C.), would be extremely dangerous. Installation of controlling air vents was planned (according to design-engineer, KUN), but had not been done.

3. The plane was released for flight December 15th with a series of defects, which had caused the Soviet Government to forbid this same plane to fly on December 12th.

4. Preparations of the plane for flight, from the moment of its departure December 7, 1938, for the airfield, took place in conditions of exceptionally dangerous haste, irresponsibility, and efforts to hide individual responsibility in this area of extreme responsibility. As a result of such conditions, the pilot took the plane up not realizing its peculiarities, problems, and the conditions under which its flight preparations took place.

5. Factory #156's Party organization, carried out a whole series of actions in shamefully dangerous haste in preparing the plane for flight. The factory's Komsomol, also having responsibility for the plane's preparation, failed to motivate its people to demand from the factory's leadership the elimination of this shameful haste. The December 12th Government prohibition of the flight failed to serve as an indication to the Komsomol leadership that it should work to develop a reliable program for the preparations of the plane for flight. Having established the direct reasons and conditions leading to the catastrophe, the Commission considers the following points to be significant:

   1. Factory Director, Usachev promoted dangerous, inadmissible, and in no way justifiable haste in the preparations of the plane

for flight. For example, the I-180 was released for testing on 10-29, 11-7, 11-15, 11-25 without the proper basis for doing so. Director Usachev, directly commanding the I-180's technician, and over the heads of those in charge, created irresponsible relationships among the workers.

2. At the factory among leadership staff, for example, POLIKARPOV and his deputy TOMASHEVICH, there existed a most dangerous theory of the necessity to release planes for flight without eliminating defects "due to poor organization" (Polikarpov). Because of this it was easy to compromise decisions concerning withdrawal of unfinished planes from the airfield.

3. The method of solving serious problems by the factory designer, and in particular deputy head designer, TOMASHE-VICH, was absolutely intolerable and irresponsible. They demonstrated complete incompetence in solving many of these problems.

   For example: a. The I-180's second fuel pump was removed in the face of objections by the engine factory. b. The plane was released for flight knowing full well that the fuel feed system was inadequate. c. They decided to test fly the plane on 12-12 with 46 defects.

4. At the factory, there was no serious attention given to the placement of personnel according to their qualifications. Lead I-180 Engineer, LASAREV, didn't know the aircraft and no one informed him. He didn't give assignments and failed to check the work.

   The Head of the Test Flight Center, Colonel PORAI, was not acquainted with experimental work and the leadership failed to cover for him.

5. Experimental work was not organized and the testing of various aircraft was done in a haphazard manner "without strict determination of responsibility" (Polikarpov).

   The Commission interviewed 25 people, including Polikarpov and his deputy, the Head of The Technical Control Center, leading engineers and others, but couldn't determine the individual personally responsible for deciding the question of the plane's final preparedness for flight.

6. There was no clear leadership representative present at the factory from the DIPC (Belyaikin).

The Accident Commission appointed by com. BELYAIKIN to examine the crash of pilot MOKSHIN, stated in its report of August 5, 1938, that the test flight organization and work of Factory #156 was scandalous and warned that "it created conditions for dangerous actions, accidents and catastrophes."

Neither the factory's leadership nor c. BELYAIKIN considered the Commission's warning, or the Soviet Government's 12-12 I-180 flight prohibition, as reason to stop the criminal haste in the plane's preparations. Instead, they released it for flight with a series of major defects and in a condition not conducive to successful flight in freezing weather.

On the basis of our analysis, we have come to the unanimous conclusion that the death of c. Chkalov was the result of carelessness, disorganization, irresponsibility, and criminal negligence in the work of Factory #156.

The Commission, concluding that the PGU (Government Administration-jvf) did not pay the necessary attention to questions of the organization of leadership in experimental flight work in aviation factories, considers it desirable to obligate the Defense Commissariat and the Commissariat of Defense Industries to take the following measures:

1. Immediately examine the condition of experimental flight work in production and testing factories.
2. Reorganize test flight centers in aviation factories securing efficient order, control and leadership.
3. Work out a program for an orderly process of production and testing of experimental aircraft construction.

COMMISSION CHAIRMAN

Division Commander (Alekseev)

	(Repin)
	(Gromov)
MEMBERS:	(Baidukov)
	(Kashirin)
	(Suprun)

Top Secret

Personal
CCCP/ com. POSKREBYSHEV
Copy to: Secretary, Moscow City Council, CP/com. POPOV

On December 16th, the Party organizer of Section 67 (Polikarpov's group) informed me that in a conversation with com. Polikarpov, he told of a very alarming situation, and his fear that in connection with the latest events, he may be sent to prison because the loss was very great. He requested, that in that event, the design bureau be made secure.

Secretary of the Baumansky Regional Council of the CP, GUTIN[107]

By December 17th the Government Commission had concluded who the guilty persons were and arrested Usachev, who Beria then interrogated. They also interrogated: N. V. Lazarev, K. L. Tomashevich, Z. M. Gendin, and T. V. Volkov — the leading engineer in charge of experimental aircraft for Factory #156. All their documents were dated December 18, sent to Stalin, then filed under the heading, Death of V. P. Chkalov. It should be noted, however, that the record of Volkov's interrogation was not in this file.

The interrogations were conducted by The Commissariat of Internal Affairs: the Commissar of Government Security, Beria, and heads of various departments, mostly of the NKVD: Major G. B. Kobulov; Lieutenant G. B. Gagkaev; Lieutenant Shitov, Lieutenant Kazakevich.

During the interrogation, Beria asked Usachev:

"Who gave you the assignment to arrange this catastrophe and to kill Hero of the Soviet Union, com. Chkalov?"

Of course, the answer was, "No one."

To the question about releasing the plane for its first flight "...in spite of the prohibition to do so by the Central Committee of the Communist Party," Usachev answered that he would have released it in any event.

And to the question as to why he released the plane for flight December 15th in spite of the fact he had a warning from the NKVD that the plane should not be released for flight in such a condition, Usachev answered that he received a warning that he should carefully examine the plane, but that he did not receive instructions to not release the plane for flight on December 15, 1938.

Tomashevich said that none of the plane's basic systems had undergone statistical testing before the flight, which is called for by existing rules confirmed by the Commissariat of Defense Industries. The plane, on this basis alone, should have not been allowed to fly.

Chkalov knew none of this, and Tomashevich never noted it anywhere.

N. V. Lazarev noted that the I-180 engine had not been checked for overcooling, and had not been protected from it: there were no air vents and no skirts on the cowling. The aerodynamic statistics of the M-88 engine had not been issued, though they were supposed to exist.

Gendin noted that the M-88 engine produced by the Zaporozhky Factory quickly cooled. Either the representative of the engine factory or the appropriate representative of Factory #156 should have informed Chkalov of the engine's peculiarities — neither did. The engine was new; it differed greatly from other engines. Chkalov had never flown with them.

On the December 17, 1938, Commission Report on the Investigation of the I-180 Crash, Voroshilov wrote, "Weak." Why "Weak"? Weak because it didn't definitively assign guilt, and most importantly, it didn't assign guilt to test pilot Chkalov for his own death. That is what Defense Commissar Voroshilov wanted to see in the document.

On June 4, 1939, Voroshilov issued a signed order # 070, and stamped Top Secret, "Concerning Measures to Take to Prevent Accidents in the Units of the Soviet Air Force." In this order concerning accidents in the military units of the Soviet Air Force, it speaks in particular about factory test pilot, V. P. Chkalov:

"…Hero of the Soviet Union, and world famous for his record-breaking flights, Brigade Commander V. P. Chkalov died only because the new fighter he was testing was released for its test flight in a completely unsatisfactory condition. Brigcom Chkalov was completely informed of this situation, and more than that, having been informed of the situation by NKVD officers, Stalin personally gave instructions forbidding com. Chkalov from making flights before the complete elimination of the plane's defects.

"Nevertheless, Brigcom Chkalov on this plane filled with defects, three days later, not only took off, but began to complete his first flight on a new plane with a new engine away from the airfield. As a result, he was forced to land in an unacceptable, cluttered area. The plane was destroyed, and Brigcom Chkalov was killed."[7]

No commentary is necessary: it was a complete distortion of facts.

Stalin personally gave no instructions to Chkalov and never responded to Beria's December 12th letter. If he had, it would have been known by M. Kaganovich, Belyaikin, Usachev, Polikarpov, or, finally, by Chkalov himself.

It wasn't Chkalov who "disobeyed" the great Stalin, but factory director Usachev, who, with admirable stubbornness, persistently, and "fearlessly," and in spite of all the above prohibitions, released the plane for its first flight, saying that he would have released the plane in spite of the prohibition of the Central Committee of the Communist Party of the Soviet Union. This Usachev admitted, though he said he didn't receive instructions not to release the plane for its first flight on December 15th.

Having received the letter from Beria, why did Voroshilov not take immediate action to prohibit the flights in order to save the life of "the world famous Chkalov", but instead limited himself to the resolution in Beria's letter of December 12, 1938?

Finally, speaking of the prevention of aviation accidents in units of the Soviet Air Force, why did Voroshilov use as an example the first test flight of a factory test pilot on a new fighter being taken up for the first time? What relationship does this have to the regular programs of the Soviet Air Force?

Beria's December 15, 1938, letter to the government leadership, and to Stalin in particular, was very dry and business-like concerning the crash of the I-180 and the death of test pilot Chkalov, taking up only about 1/4 of the full text. The remaining 3/4 was a very detailed and emotional description of the December 12th events, and the unsuccessful planned "accident" of the I-180 with test pilot Chkalov at the controls.

Following is a description of events in 1939 taken from various documents covering the testing of a second copy of the I-180.

S. P. Suprun officially sent a letter to the Organizing Committee of the 18th Communist Party Congress, held March 10-21m 1939. "In honor of the 18th Congress, our Party is issuing a second copy of the I-180 aircraft in which the best pilot of our nation, Valery Chkalov, died. The first copy of this plane was to go through a program of testing: With Chkalov, the factory test pilot, and with me, the military test pilot. Now people are afraid to trust me with testing this plane on its first flight only because I am a Deputy of the Supreme Soviet of the USSR...

I ask you to issue instructions allowing me to test fly the I-180 aircraft and make its first flight. I am sure you will not refuse my request. Major Suprun, Soviet Air Force Research Institute." Suprun was given his request.

On April 19-21, 1939, Stepan Suprun completed the first taxiing and ground testing. On April 27th, Suprun took the I-180(2) up for the first time, completing two circles in 8 minutes within the airport area.

The I-180 was to have been issued in honor of the 18th Party Congress.

But why weren't "people" afraid to have Chkalov conduct that first flight? He also was a member of the Supreme Soviet and a Hero of the Soviet Union.

The I-180 aircraft on December 15th had 32 defects and was not ready for its first flight. The head designer of the I-180 did not sign a document confirming the plane's readiness for its first flight. He did not confirm the required flight list #3 for the first flight.

The I-180 aircraft was released for its first flight on December 15th with basic defects and unfinished work.

1. The plane, motor, propeller, and carburetor were experimental and had not been tested in flight.

2. The experimental M-88 engine was installed in the plane, which was significantly reconstructed by Factory #156 without the approval of the issuing engine Factory #29. The motor carried no distinguishing number, nor the name of the person in charge of its development at Factory #29. Technical documentation for in-house factory testing was missing. There were no engine aerodynamic statistics. The engine had not been flight-tested.

3. The December 12th failure of the fuel system revealed design flaws in engine control. There were constructive revisions made to fuel control, the effectiveness of which was not tested in an appropriate program, although a document to that effect was created.

4. A fuel pump was removed from the engine without the approval of issuing engine factory #29. An entry in the engine's logbook by the representative of Factory #29's head designer, forbid flights on the I-180.

5. There was no statistical testing done on the plane's basic systems, including the strength of the plane's landing gear.

6. The plane's three-bladed propeller (VISH-23) worked in two extreme positions. In the first flight, it was fixed in the take-off position.
7. Air vents were not installed.
8. The aircraft had not gone through "Part #1. Ground testing," provided for in the "Program of Preliminary Testing of the I-180 Aircraft."

It's not surprising that during its first test flight, a defect, or several defects together, or some instability, could have created an unexpected event, as occurred December 12th with the failed fuel system.

Weather conditions required serious adjustments. The temperature was a freezing –24.4 degrees C. The experimental M-88 engine had not been tested in these conditions. It was known to have a tendency to quickly overheat, and also to quickly overcool. The absence of air vents exacerbated this peculiarity, making temperature adjustment a serious engine shortcoming.

Official bench-testing of the M-88 engine in May 1939 confirmed the basic shortcomings of this motor: "There is a lack of ability to adjust from a small amount of fuel at various temperatures," i.e., "after a quick movement of the fuel control lever from using little fuel (few revolutions) to high revolutions (during rapid fuel increase), independent of engine temperature, the M-88 engine stalled." The M-88 engine was put into production in 1940.

Of course, a legitimate question arises about why Chkalov agreed to conduct the first flight of this plane with such a huge number of defects. Why did he not refuse to test it?

In the first place, Chkalov was obligated to fly because he had signed factory documents: a statement about the readiness of the plane for its first flight; a factory order concerning preparations of the plane for its first flight; a flight list. Test pilot Baidukov clearly and succinctly answered the question: "A pilot who refuses to fly cannot be test pilot. He would have to prove his case."

Second, Chkalov saw all the nervous irritability in the factory staff surrounding preparations for the first flight; he saw how stubbornly Usachev insisted upon it, and how Polikarpov acquiesced in this insistence. In this situation, he couldn't, and didn't have the right, to shrug this responsibility off onto the shoulders of another test pilot. He understood how this test could end.

Third, Chkalov didn't know of the plane's many defects, about which witnesses spoke later.

The Head Designer and Technical Director of Factory #156, Nikolai, Nikolaevich Polikarpov, carried full legal responsibility for the plane's design and for the safety of the experimental flights and the test pilot.

It should be noted that the covering letter to the Commission's report on the investigation contained 33 photographs, which I was unable to find in the President's Archives or in the FSB[31] Archives. They would help to answer many questions concerning how and why the plane crashed. By examining the scattered plane parts and the position of the pilot, it would have been possible to recreate an almost complete picture of the crash and the actions of the pilot. (This would have been possible because it was forbidden to move anything at the crash site until an NKVD representative had arrived from the nearest office.)

From all these technical details, one can come to only one conclusion—the plane should not have been allowed to make its first flight. This had been amply revealed to Beria through his "source," which he reported to the country's leadership in his December 12th letter.

The M-88 engine installed on the plane had no "distinguishing marks." What kind of an engine was it? How was it developed? Why wasn't the engine factory's representative, Ginsburg, allowed to examine the M-88 engine at Factory #156? He did not approve the plane's first flight. Why did the engine cut out? It's doubtful it was from overcooling, as Chkalov was in the air only 6-7 minutes. It's now impossible to answer any of these questions definitively.

Stalin, Molotov and Voroshilov did not forbid testing this plane. As a result of their unanimous silent decision, they denied Chkalov a chance to live. Why did Stalin behave in such a way to a person whom so many thought he loved? Perhaps, because he had outgrown his plans for him. He had become too popular and beloved by the people: he had become a person famous around the world. But perhaps it was because he had changed his views of life: he could no longer live and think like the "Great Leader" demanded.

---

31 The FSB, or Federal Security Bureau, is the post-Communist name for the organization earlier called the Cheka, OGPU, NKVD and KGB.

The daughter of the Head of Leningrad's Komsomol Organization, Alexander Kosarev, recalls that, "toward the end of 1937, Stalin called Kosarev on the carpet. He severely scolded him for not helping the NKVD to uncover enemies and traitors. Stalin told him, "So you don't want to head up this work?" A few months later Kosarev was arrested and shot. He was only 35 years old.

Early in 1938, we were discussing in our family, how Stalin had offered Chkalov government positions, including that of Commissar of Internal Affairs. Yelena Kosareva described the situation well. Stalin wanted him to "wield the executioner's ax." Father refused.

When people later spoke and wrote of this, it turned my stomach. I was ashamed that father, an infinitely honest and just person, beloved by the people, could be offered such a position. It turned out to be a kind of test: "To live, or to die." Father at that time had just turned 34.

Mother said that several months before his death, he slept with a revolver under his pillow, and his demeanor changed, which could be seen in the expression in his eyes. Photographs of the time show this plainly.

Our government had long since forgotten the individual, the creator of all happiness, prosperity and glory. The government was crushing individuals, and God forbid that anyone should fall under its millstones. And when did the government begin its work on father with these millstones?

Perhaps it was after his flights made him world famous, after he flew to America and spoke to U.S. audiences about the Soviet people, but made no mention of its leaders.

Perhaps it was when he was elected to the Supreme Soviet of the USSR as a Deputy of the Soviet of Nationalities. It was then clear just how popular and beloved he had become. Many areas of the Country had nominated him for the position.

Perhaps it was September 21, 1938, when Defense Industry Head, Belyaikin, received a letter from the commissar in charge of the Soviet exhibit to the New York world's Fair about the preparations to send Gromov's ANT-25 to the exhibit and not Chkalov's. And on December 10th, directions were received to repaint Chkalov's ANT-25, that the inscription "Stalin's Route" on the plane's side would have to be eliminated, covered over. Who gave this order?

Perhaps it had already been decided that Chkalov also would have to be eliminated, crushed.

If one looks carefully, it can be seen that all these events form a time chain, in which each link supports the next.

A short after-word to the "2003 Version" is in order:

Tomashevich was released early from prison in June 1941. The NKVD hired him immediately.

Usachev was released from prison early in August 1943.

The judgments against them were erased from their records. This was a highly unusual occurrence for the time.

On December 27, 1938, the Soviet of Peoples Commissars of the USSR passed a resolution:"Immortalizing the Memory of V. P. CHKALOV." Point #1 of the resolution set out "The Establishment of Three Annual Aviation Awards in the name of V. P. Chkalov," to be awarded by the Soviet of Peoples Commissars (Sovnarkom) of the USSR each year on December 15th.

Prize #1 – 50,000 rubles to the aviation designer who has designed the year's best aircraft.

Prize #2 – 50,000 rubles to the designer who has designed the year's best aircraft engine, or significantly improved one.

Prize #3 –50,000 rubles to the Air Force Squadron, which has achieved most in its profession during the past year.

In 1939, A. A. Mikulin developed a new engine, the AM-35. On August 20, 1940, he presented the AM-35A engine in competition for the V. P. Chkalov Prize. He considered it to be the very best engine, but did not receive the prize. Mikulin and several of his colleagues, however, did receive the title of Stalin Prize Laureate, introduced December 20, 1939, by a Resolution of the same Sovnarkom of the USSR in honor of Stalin's 60th birthday.

Thus, we can see, it is possible to answer the question Beria asked Factory Director, Usachev, in his interrogation concerning who it was that gave instructions to arrange a catastrophe and kill Hero of the Soviet Union and Deputy of the Supreme Soviet of the USSR, Brigade Commander Chkalov.

In her book, mother wrote that: "…after his famous flights, a foreign correspondent ask Valery Pavlovich what his most cherished dream was. Smiling, he said, 'I dream of having a large family. No fewer than six children.'"

This very human dream of Chkalov did not come true. He had only three children: Igor, Valeria and Olga. They, however, are raising a vigorous younger generation: four grandchildren—Yelena, Valery, Maria and Alexander; three great grandchildren—Yekaterina, Darya and Igor. And now the first great great grandchild has arrived—Ksenia.

I believe that if one of the country's leaders, at any level, had prohibited the testing of this plane, there would have been no tragedy, and father could have helped raise this younger generation and been very happy and content with his accomplishment.

Top Secret
December 17, 1938

TO: c. MOLOTOV,
SOVIET OF PEOPLES COMMISSARS OF THE USSR

TO: c. STALIN,
CENTRAL COMMITTEE OF THE COMMUNIST PARTY

The death of c. Chkalov was the result of releasing an unfinished aircraft for flight.

All the defects remained on the plane that served as the reason for prohibiting its fight by the SOVIET GOVERNMENT on December 12th. In addition, the plane had many extremely serious unfinished elements endangering flight, but not mentioned in lists, records or reports.

The decision to allow the plane to fly was given to the factory director by Commissar M.M. KAGANOVICH, who had been deceived and given incorrect information concerning the plane's readiness to fly by the factory leaders.

All this was the result of careless, disorganized, irresponsible and criminal negligence by Factory #156 personnel.

The main guilty parties to the I-180 aircraft catastrophe are:

1. The Technical Director and factory Head Designer, POLIKARPOV, who released an unfinished plane for flight.
2. The Deputy Head Designer, TOMASHEVICH, who approved the flight of a defective aircraft.
3. Director USACHEV, who irresponsibly forced an unfinished aircraft to fly.

The Commission considers it necessary to give this report on the catastrophe to the appropriate agencies in order to bring those directly and indirectly responsible to justice.

ATTACHMENTS:
1. Three copies of the Commission Report of six pages each.
2. Interrogation material, 71 pages.
3. Thirty-three photographs/three photos, 11 copies*

Chairman (Division Commander Alekseev)

	(Baidukov)
Members:	(Gromov)
	(Repin)

* (In the original cover letter, attachment #3 was crossed out—auth.)

Chkalov died tragically December 15, 1938, testing a new plane, the I-180. Stalin was purging his military at the time and Valeria Chkalova asserts, with newly declassified documents, that her father was set up to die. He may have become too popular.

Molotov and Stalin served as pall bearers with Premier Georgy Malenkov walking along side.

Georgy Baidukov is directly behind Stalin. The urn with his remains are being carried to a place of honor in the Kremlin wall.

Aircraft designer, N. N. Polikarpov. Designer of the fateful I-80.

Chkalov mourning procession to Red Square, Dec. 18, 1938.

Chkalov's remains are behind the third plaque from the left.

CHAPTER FIVE

—— ·◄◆►· ——

His Youth Stolen, Nevertheless Immortal

THE VALERY CHKALOV AIR FORCE SQUADRON IN THE GREAT PATRIOTIC WAR.[32]

In our last television interview, the famous producer, S. I. Rostotsky said: "The most important thing is that there is something to remember him by." Valery Chkalov died in 1938, having lived only 34 years, but his name has lived on through the 20th Century, and in the 21st Century he is remembered not only in our country, but beyond our borders as well. I'm not just speaking of the "near" foreign lands[33], where cities have streets, parks, aviation factories, houses of culture and educational institutions, which carry his name; e. g., in Lvov, Gomel, Minsk, Baku, Kiev.

In Prague, capital of the Czech Republic, there is a street carrying the name Chkalov. In Vancouver, USA, there is also a Chkalov street. They have also raised a monument to the crew — V. P. Chkalov, G. F. Baidukov, and A. V. Belyakov — of that first non-stop transpolar flight across the North Pole to America, which embodies a bridge between our two continents. In Seattle, in the Boeing Air Museum, stands a bust of Chkalov by sculptor V. D. Sveshnikov.

Why have people remembered this person so well and for so long? He carried something special in him that people wanted to describe, draw, sculpt, and write poems about. They imitated him; youth idolized him, especially in aviation circles. In aviation, Chkalov was known and beloved long before he became widely known for his famous non-stop flights to the Far East in 1936, and across the North Pole to America in 1937.

---

32 "The Great Patriotic War" is what we call the Second World War. On June 22, 1941, in Operation BARBAROSSA, over 3 million German soldiers and 3300 tanks attacked the Soviet Union..

33 Russians call the former Soviet Republics "Near Foreign Lands."

It wasn't only his physical appearance, which drew people to him, and which was so eloquently described by sculptor I. A. Mendelevich. He was allotted a surprising number of human qualities; such as an iron will, bravery, humility, kindness, a sense of justice, purposefulness, a love of people, an exceptional love for his homeland and its inhabitants. And people loved him, said Hero of the Soviet Union and honored test pilot, M. I. Gallai. They loved him for his humanity, for his sharply developed feeling for camaraderie, for his large and generous soul.

He had a great love for creativity; a wish to break standards, to find something new, to become one with his plane, to increase the human possibilities in controlling aircraft: "I can't overcome in myself the passionate wish to forever hunt for something new, to perfect what I do, to polish the technique of piloting."

His popularity was great. He was well known in the most distant corners of our country. People loved him sincerely. He was truly very open with everyone, and therefore his memory has been preserved in the hearts of the Russian people for many, many years.

I'd like to quote a passage from a book by Anatoly Markusha, which I like very much. Anatoly began to fly in 1938, and tells of the influence Chkalov's example had on pre-war youth:

"...On the flight field I, as almost all my comrades, thought of Chkalov, or more exactly the iconic image of Chkalov, as a fearless fighter pilot, beloved person, and a true hero of our time. And it was Chkalov who determined for me the choice of a flight school—for fighter planes, of course, the Borisoglebskaya, school from which Chkalov graduated in the first class of 47 students. And for the next 20 years I flew under the Chkalov symbol.

"My first plane was the fighter, I-5; the plane on which Chkalov created his wonders.

"Then there was the I-16, the "Ishak", or "Ishachok."

"When I finished flight school, I was sent to a combat unit and received my very own I-16, with a sky-blue seven on the tail. Opening the plane's logbook, where a record of the plane's service is recorded, on the first page I read: "The aircraft has been test flown. It is fit for service in the units of the Army Air Force. And just below it, a sweeping signature—V. Chkalov. I was overcome with happiness. Of course, in my first flight with aerobatics in my new plane, I tried to prove that, as Chkalov said,

"Whatever you are, be the very best...."As a result, I spent a week cooling my heels in the brig, and was terribly proud of it, though I couldn't admit even to myself that Chkalov also had become acquainted with a convict's bunk...

"Now I write about all this without shame. I write with the right of an heir. And also because I very clearly understand this is not about me, but about our generation. It's about the last pre-war group of fighter pilots, and most of all about him, about Chkalov, who led us all, who even after his death remained for us the most authoritative of authorities, whom we simultaneously considered our god and supreme judge.

"And more.

"After the I-16, I transferred to the 'Lavochkina,' the La-5 fighter, which was developed after Chkalov. At a front line airfield, the squadron engineer, led me to my snub-nosed, menacing aircraft, and said: "There she is. Make her behave. You only need to change four cylinders...and it'll be an animal, not a machine..."

"Looking at my new plane, I paid no attention whatever to the engineer about changing engine cylinders; I couldn't tear my eyes away from the inscription on the plane's side—"Valery Chkalov," and in smaller letters: "A gift from Gorky's farm workers."[34]

"In the skies of war, Chkalov was beside us; together with us.

"And after the war... We never quoted his words: 'Speed!. This is the dream of every pilot.' But we had the figure in our minds of which he spoke—1000 kilometers an hour! Now we've crossed that barrier for Chkalov; and together with Chkalov...

"And Chkalov stands behind me, especially when things are tough.

"Recently, I again met up with the I-16, put on permanent display in the town of Chkalovsk in the museum hanger.

"I climbed into the cockpit of Chkalov's I-16 with great emotion, took the control lever and pulled it toward me. The ailerons moved; and then I was flooded with an incomprehensible uneasiness: it didn't fly, of course, and would never fly again... The reason for my anxiety wasn't immediately clear: The plane had lost its inimitable aroma of life—the faint smell of clean fuel, the slightly bitter aroma of overheated oil, the penetratingly sharp breath of overheated enamel.

---

34 Today, the city of Gorky has been given its pre-revolutionary name of Nizhni Novgorod.

"The I-16 looks like a bullet. In it, in this amazing bullet, I can confirm by personal experience, that there exists a live, flickering soul. I didn't discover the plane's soul immediately, and she was no angel, no-o-o way! But she did repay love with love; tenderness with tenderness, and for genuine mastery, she gave the pilot life, and victory over the enemy. She gave while she could, while she was still young...

"The plane died. Only its form remained. Wonderful and eternal... But that's the way it is: life goes on. And that's as it should be.

"Thirty four years — in the prime of life. And no words can make things right; can explain; can lessen the loss."[108]

Markusha was right. During the Great Patriotic War, Chkalov was fighting shoulder to shoulder with Soviet warriors, defending our homeland.

In the partisan movement, in Byelorussia, there were two brigades and 18 detachments carrying the name V. P. Chkalov.[35]

The first partisan brigade was created in November 1942, and detachments 620 and 621 were later named for V. P. Chkalov. During 1943-1944, seven more detachments were added to the brigade.

The brigade was active in the Volozhinsky and Ivenetsky Regions of the Baronovichevsky Province; and in Dzerzhinsky, Zaslavsky and Minsk in the Province of Minsk.

The first partisan detachments were created in July and October of 1941; the second brigade in January 1943.

Five detachments totaling 1,085 partisans joined with units of the Red Army June 5, 1944.

September 28, 1941, the newspaper "Pravda" published an article: "Pilot Rozhnov's Daring Maneuver." I've mentioned him earlier. The following was written about his exploit: "A fascist fighter was on Rozhnov's tail. Rozhnov dived into a hedgerow-skimming maneuver, but he couldn't shake the Nazi plane. He suddenly remembered a trick by the young Chkalov. At the dawn of Chkalov's flying life, he flew under a Leningrad bridge. As the fascist plane began his attack, Rozhnov turned to the river. He aimed his plane at a small railroad bridge and dived between the abutments. This was daring and courageous. The amazed fascist didn't follow, but turned sharply to the side, giving Rozhnov several minutes

35 "The partisan movement" refers to the large numbers of civilians who organized behind Nazi lines to do battle with their occupiers.

and time to successfully escape the attack. The courageous pilot saved the lives of two commanders and his plane."

The fighters, I-15, I-I53, and the I-16, all given life by Chkalov, protected the skies over Russia. Amiryants wrote that "...If it hadn't been for Chkalov, it's doubtful we would have had the marvelous I-16 fighter in time to show it's ability in the Spanish Civil War against the fascists, and in the following pre-WWII events...

"If Chkalov hadn't crashed, the fate of the talented aircraft designer, Polikarpov, might have ended differently, and it's possible we would have been more prepared for our war with Germany."

Hero of the Soviet Union, Viktor Talalikhin, performed the famous "taran" in 1941 in an I-16.[36]

In the area of the village of Demidovo in Leningrad Province on August 21st of that year, Alexander Berezin, a high school teacher from the Chkalovsk Region, used the taran to take down a fascist Me-109. The pilot died, but the Me-109 never reached its target in Leningrad.

Hitler said that, "Slavs will never understand anything about air combat—these are weapons of a powerful people, a German form of battle." History, and especially the Great Patriotic War, showed that aviation was and remains a Russian form of battle. Our famous Peter Nesterov performed the first taran in 1914.[37]

The book, "The Valery Chkalov Squadron," describes how the inhabitants of Chkalovsk appealed to workers of Gorky Province on December 11, 1942, to contribute rubles for the formation of a "Valery Chkalov" fighter combat squadron.

---

36 A "taran" maneuver was an intentional ramming of an enemy plane in flight. During World War II, Soviet pilots carried out more than 580 rammings of German aircraft, most often resulting in the death of the pilots and the destruction of both planes.

37 Here is how an eyewitness described the event:
"Nesterov's plane reached the enemy plane (an Austrian Albatros-jvf) from above and rear, and rammed it like a falcon hits an awkward heron. The unwieldy Albatros after the air strike, as if being shocked, continued for a while on its course, but suddenly fell down to the side and headlong dug into the ground." Peter Nesterov failed in his risky assumptions, however, and couldn't escape death himself."

During the Second World War, the pilots who survived using the taran were mainly those who used the aircraft propeller as a sort of "circular saw".

"We appeal," they wrote, "to all the collective farm and factory workers in Gorky Province to follow our example. We're doing everything we can to help the Red Army to crush our hated enemy. We are gathering the means and building a squadron of planes to be named after our native son and patriot, Valery P. Chkalov..."[109]

The appeal of the Chkalovites struck a responsive chord in the workers of Gorky Province.

Money for building the squadron was gathered from all over the world. People gave what they could. Anna Chernova, from the Pushkin collective farm, gave 2000 rubles, saying, "...The war has been difficult for my family — my husband is at the front; I have to support three small children and my old mother. Nevertheless, I can't be indifferent to this appeal. I'm donating 72 lbs. of grain and 2000 rubles to the Red Army for the construction of an aircraft squadron. Let my modest gift strengthen our strike at the enemy."

At a meeting in the small village of Seve, 70 year old Yakov Federovich Kasatkin asked to speak: "My beloved son died bravely at the front. Here's 180 rubles. This is my life's savings. I'm giving it with the clean heart of a father who wants to avenge his son, and wants to again live a peaceful life."

From the letter of a Red Army soldier, Glebov: "I join my voice to those of my fellow workers and give 100 rubles for the creation of the 'Valery Chkalov' Squadron. Let the enemy know that to this small sum in the battle for our homeland, I am ready at any minute to add my life."

On December 18, 1942, Gorky citizens received a congratulatory telegram from the Supreme Command:

"Gorky. To the Secretary of the Communist Party of Gorky Province, com. Rodionov.

"I ask you to pass my brotherly greetings, and the gratitude of the Red Army, to the collective farmers of Gorky Province for collecting 60 million rubles in order to organize a 'Valery Chkalov' squadron of combat aircraft.

J. Stalin."[109]

The appeal of the collective farmers was well received by the industrial workers of Gorky Province: 75 million rubles was collected.

By January 1943, the first group of "Valery Chkalov" La-5 aircraft was at the front. The La-5 was one of the best fighters in the Great Patriotic War, and was created by designer, Semen Alexeevich Lavochkin.

The La-5 was outstanding for its time. It successfully countered the excellent German fighter, the Fokker Wolf 190. The Sergo Ordzhonikidze Factory #21 in Gorky, where Chkalov was a test pilot, produced this plane, and it was under the jurisdiction of Head Designer, Polikarpov. It produced many planes of his design, and is now the respected Nizhegorodsky factory, "Falcon."

The famous Soviet ace, three-time Hero of the Soviet Union, Ivan Nikitovich Kozhedub, did battle in the 240th Fighter Regiment in a La-5 "Valery Chkalov."[38]

In his book, "Faithful to the Fatherland," he wrote: "It was February 1943... They kept telling us we would soon be flying to the front. However, the planes we were training on were inferior. And this made us nervous.

"The senior regiment officer said to us finally, 'Don't worry. We'll soon get some brand new planes, straight from the factory. We'll be flying to the front to do battle with them.'

"And after several days, one frosty morning, the "Lovochkiny" appeared in the sky.

"'Are they flying to us?'

"And so they were. Much to our delight, they began to land.

"The new La-5s looked beautiful standing in a row, shining in the sun. The air was filled with the smell of their new paint. We read the inscription on the planes' sides—'In Honor of Valery Chkalov.'

"'And who are they assigned to?' asked one of the pilots, nodding toward the planes.

"'For Major Soldatenko?'

"We couldn't believe they were our planes.

"After some time, the commander called us together.

"'These planes were built with the funds of the countrymen of our great pilot, Valery Pavlovich Chkalov...'

"A plane was given to every pilot. Mine was a five-tank La-5, #75..."

Kozhedub tells an interesting story of his last battle: "Once I found a book about V. P. Chkalov in our military library. I read it with interest, and imagined how Chkalov must have trained; how he prepared for his flights, studying his plane and its systems carefully. I began to imitate Chkalov in everything, and the book about the great pilot became my favorite reference book.

38 Kozhedub shot down 62 enemy aircraft, the most by any WWII pilot.

"During the battle for Berlin, I was flying as a pair with Guard Captain Titarenko on "the hunt" in the Berlin area. We were flying over the northern part of the city. Suddenly I saw a group of "Fokker Wolf 190s" carrying bombs. The match up was uneven: two "hunters"; 40 Fokker Wolf 190s. The thought flashed through my mind, what would Chkalov do in this situation? I attacked. In my head the thoughts were swirling: 'He would take them by surprise with his daring, with Chkalov forcefulness and ability.' And in this battle I killed two enemy planes."

The First and Second Squadrons of the Baltic Air Groups Fourth Regiment received 17 of the new La-5s. On February 25, 1943, the Baltic pilots reported to Gorky citizens: "Dear friends, brothers and sisters! Full of a feeling of passionate love for your homeland and the valiant Red Army, you have given your hard earned money to build an air squadron in the name of Valery Chkalov…

"The name of this great pilot obligates us to be the same as he. Flying these planes into combat, with the words written on their sides: 'From the collective farm workers of Gorky Province,' we feel your support and it inspires us to victory. A soldiers' thank you, Gorkyites!"

This regiment produced 12 Heroes of the Soviet Union and destroyed 431 enemy aircraft, finishing the war in Kolberg, Germany.

La-5 "Valery Chkalov" planes also fought over the skies of Stalingrad in the 13th Stalingrad Regiment

The following comment by Majors Gusarev and Potanen, was one of many such, written in the guest book of the V. P. Chkalov Museum in Chkalovsk. "You were with us shoulder-to-shoulder in the days of the Great Patriotic War. Traveling along mother Volga, we have come to you, our dear friend and comrade, in order to tell you of our military service…"

Chkalov was the first hero of Gorky Province. He loved his small native village, loved the Volga, and was proud of his countrymen, about whom he often commented, "Nizhegorodskie mothers don't give birth to cowards."

The regional historian, and principal of Chkalovsk High School, V. A. Persidsky, wrote in his book, "The Valery Chkalov Squadron":

"There are people over whom time and death have no power. Such a person was Valery Chkalov. He continues to live among us, struggling with us for happiness, honor, freedom, and our independent homeland."

NOT EVERYONE CAN VISIT AN ISLAND WITH HIS NAME

The years have passed, but only one member of the crew, Georgy Filippovich Baidukov, was able to visit Chkalov and Baidukov Islands. We children of Valery Chkalov have also been able to visit Chkalov Island. It was 1986. The flight was organized the by the Central Committee of the Leningrad Komsomol League and the Ministry of Civil Aviation in honor of the 50th anniversary of the 1936 flight to the Far East by V. P. Chkalov, G. F. Baidukov, and A. V. Belyakov on the ANT-25.

The main participant in the flight was Georgy Filippovich Baidukov. Thirty four others also made the trip, including correspondents from various newspapers and magazines. (From newspapers "Pravda," "Komsomolskaya Pravda," "Sovietskaya Rossia," and from magazines "Ogonyok" and "Sovietsky Soyus," and others.) Igor, Olga and I were there, of course, along with many movie and television personnel. When we reached the Russian Far East, the regional media joined us as well.

Our trip started on July 29th. The route, of course, didn't cover the 1936 flight, but we did fly over the northern regions of our country, where weather conditions were favorable. We flew over the Rybinsky Water Reservoir, Vorkuta, the small village of Mirny, and over the endless Siberian Taiga.

Already on the plane, in spite of the late night hour, correspondents began to work with Baidukov. Taping his authoritative answers to questions and filming him. The history of our country came alive before us: the first heroic five-year plans, the achievements of Soviet people, of our fathers. He somehow especially clearly defined the meaning of the 1936 flight for the formation of aviation in the young Soviet nation. Georgy Filippovich was an interesting storyteller, and to listen to him was pure pleasure.

I didn't sleep that whole night. And even when the filming stopped, they continued to ask him fascinating questions. I eagerly listened to the answers, trying to remember them all. I was interested, of course, in the details of the flight's preparations, in the difficulties during the fight, the landing, father's behavior in difficult situations, and descriptions of his ability. Who, besides a witness and direct participant in the event, could answer these questions today?

The eight hours to Khabarovsk went by almost unnoticed. And from the taxiing plane we could see Young Pioneers with flowers and groups of people who had come to greet us — in a pouring rain.

Georgy Filippovich was the first to exit the plane. There were greetings, congratulations, handshakes, smiles, and masses of roses, which were presented to each of us. Georgy Filippovich and Igor gallantly gave their bouquets to Olga and me.

We held a meeting inside due to the poor weather, and after a short rest, we continued the flight. We transferred from the Il-62 to two AN-24s. They divided the press corps into two groups.

In an hour and a half we were met at Nikolaevsk-on-Amur. Flowers were again presented to us, but this time they were field flowers: daisies, carnations, and bread and salt, which we tasted with pleasure.[39]

We placed our flowers on a monument in honor of the flight, which had been erected on the square in front of the airport building.

And starting from that moment, it seemed that doors from the past were opening — I was touched, tears rose in my eyes. We were walking on the same land our father had trod many years ago!

The road to the city passed a "Chkalov" bus stop, by an old airport, which ran along the Amur River. There was a light fog and the opposite shore was barely visible.

I won't describe in detail, this lower Amur River land, but only note that the city had prepared well for the celebration.

The City Communist Party had prepared a broad program, including meetings with young Pioneers in Pioneer Clubs, with aviators — the winners in 50th Year Anniversary Chkalov Flight contests. In the meeting with the aviators, Baidukov awarded prizes to the winners and very interestingly answered questions. The program also included meetings between youth and the city's "Honored Citizens," official gatherings, city tours, exhibitions, and much more. It should be noted that Georgy Filippovich was Nikolaev-on-Amur's "Honored Citizen #1."

In spite of the limited time, we were able to meet with many interesting people and activists interested in their work and their city. I'd like

---

39 Greeting guests with freshly baked bread and salt is an old Russian tradition. Each guest tears a piece of bread from the large loaf and dips it in the salt.

particularly to mention V. M. Yuzefov, director of the regional museum, and his colleagues, who record the details of the region's history.

A word must be said about the richness of the area: the yet uncounted unique and beautiful stones, and the many experts and collectors who studied them. The region still holds much of value underground, and one can only envy the marvelous museums, which display a small portion of this wealth.

Trying to examine the source of the patriotic feelings of these lower Amur River inhabitants necessarily turns one to the history of the city. It's just impossible not to love a city with such a history! Our famous pioneer and explorer of the Far East, Admiral Gennady Ivanovich Nevelskoy, founded the city in 1850 at the mouth of the Amur River, joining this land to Russia without firing a single shot—"Under the trilling of a boatswain's whistle."

Nevelsky was first to prove that Sakhalin was an island, that the Amur didn't disappear into the sand, and that it was navigable. He discovered the bay and named it Bay of Happiness. And it was there that our culminating activities took place for the celebration of the 50th Anniversary of the 1936 Chkalov flight. A monument was raised on the place of the ANT-25's landing.

The First Secretary of the Regional Communist Party, A. K. Cherny, Chairman of the Regional Executive Committee, N. N. Danilyuk, Commander of the Far Eastern Military, D. T. Yazov, Head of the Red Banner Military Border Patrol, V. D. Butenko, took part in the celebrations.

The program envisioned two variants for August 2nd: If the weather was good, we would fly by helicopters to Chkalov Island; if it was bad, we would be taken on board a steamship, where formal ceremonies would take place.

The weather that day turned out to be beautiful! Blue sky, warm sun, cool sea breeze. Nevertheless, from early morning, boats were traveling to Chkalov Island, many carrying those wishing to take part in the celebration. Many came to the island independently on their own small crafts.

At 1:00 p.m. we flew in a helicopter of the regional military command to the island. We were nervous, of course, and looked constantly out the helicopter's windows. The pilots purposely flew along the Amur in order to show us the surprising beauty of its mouth.

And suddenly, the Bay of Happiness appeared — and the sharp cliffs of Belyakov Island. The tiny homes on Baidukov Island came into view. And, at last, Chkalov Island! I was so choked up I saw nothing; I understood nothing. We landed!

The helicopter's door opened. So many people! Correspondents immediately surrounded Georgy Filippovich. An avalanche of questions: "How does it feel to return?" "How has the island changed?"

We stood in the back, choking back tears, and happy that dark glasses covered them. Volodya Mikhalenko approached with a microphone; we hadn't the strength to speak.

We went with everyone else to the monument. Party Secretary, A. K. Cherny, opened the program. He noted the huge significance this historical flight had for the country, for the Russian Far East, where aviation at the present time is the main form of transportation, and is now an active participant in the economic development of the region. Baidukov told of the final hours of the flight, of zero visibility, of the virtuosity of the commander in landing the plane on the island.

Next, the shroud was removed from the monument. A bas-relief of the three heroes stood out sharply. A portrait likeness of father was apparent, or more exactly, the elements of his character: the masculinity, the concentration in flight, and the strong lines of his mouth. The monument stretched 20 feet into the air, and on the top was the legendary ANT-25.

We carried our flowers to the foot of the monument. Baidukov and Cherny placed their basket of flowers first; Igor and Yazov second; Olga and I third. The inscription under the bas-relief, read:

"The ANT-25 landed on this spot on July 22, 1936, after completing a non-stop flight from Moscow to Petropavlovsk-Kamchatsky to Udd Island (now Chkalov Island). For the successful completion of this assignment, crew commander, V. P. Chkalov, co-pilot G. F. Baidukov, and navigator A. V. Belyakov were awarded the titles of Hero of the Soviet Union."

After the monument dedication, our first wish was to get to know the island! It would have been nice, if no one had been there, if I had been alone, to lie on this rocky beach and sob my heart out. But this moment passed, and we rushed to see the first memorial, which was put up in 1936 by sailors. It was a simple metal tube with a red-winged plane and inscription at the top.

We didn't have time to go to the shore washed by the Okhotsk Sea. People asked us to pose with them for photographs, to sign autograph booklets. We hurried to the other side of the island, to a lake. Along the way we collected interesting stones, picked flowers, grasses, and rose hips. All this was to remember this island carrying our father's name.

We stopped and looked around. The vegetation on the island was low growing and sparse, and therefore gave the impression of expansiveness and freedom. From the sea, in which the island is a mere speck, blew a fresh breeze. On the other side of the island, was the Bay of Happiness, which, after almost 100 years, for the second time justified its name for the three Soviet air explorers.

There was no time for further exploration. We were called for dinner: fish soup from sturgeon. In spite of the fact there was twice as many people on the island as had been planned for, there was enough fish soup for everyone.

After dinner, we said good-bye to the island. We left carrying with us a feeling of extraordinary love for this island, which a mere three hours ago was unknown to us; only a geographical spot on a map. We carried with us a huge desire to come again; next time with the whole family, so our children and grandchildren could see this land...

We returned by a shorter route over the Taiga. Again, we saw the island swimming in the sea below us. We looked out the helicopter's window trying to understand our emotions; saying good-bye to this small piece of land, which had become so dear. From this altitude, it seemed still more beautiful. Stretching along the main land, as if trying to protect it from the cold Sea of Okhotsk. We could see many lakes. The shore on the Bay of Happiness was cut with many small bays and inlets, which appeared so cozy from our altitude.

In only 15 minutes, our helicopter landed in Nikolaevsk-on-Amur. Slowly, as if in a dream, we exit the plane. Saying our good-byes, our souls are spilling over with the many marvelous impressions and memories.

The following day we say good-bye to our hospitable hosts and fly to Khabarovsk. The two days in Khabarovsk passed quickly. Igor, Olya and I were asked to speak many times, since Georgy Filippovich had to immediately fly to Moscow. We visited flight re-training schools, an aviation museum, and the regional museum. We visited the spot in the city park, where father spoke to a gathering on August 2, 1936. One can sum up Khabarovsk quickly: it is a beautiful, modern city; clean and green.

And so our trip ended. On August 5th, we returned to Moscow.

AMERICA'S CHKALOV COMMITTEE PROMOTES SECOND TRIP TO CHKALOV ISLAND

I was able to visit Chkalov Island one more time, in 2001, for the 65th anniversary of the flight. Our country didn't celebrate the event. It was a period of government and economic reorganization. We paid tribute to everything American, including its ideology, forgetting about our wonderful history—about the people who brought fame and respect to our country.

And if it hadn't been for the persistent wishes of members of America's Chkalov Committee, Jess Frost and Carl Dugger, to visit the island where the legendary crew landed, our family probably would have done nothing.

I won't go into how all this was organized, only to say that the aviation factory at Komsomolsk-on-Amur, KNAPPO, and Government Duma Represenative, Vyacheslav Ivanovich Shport, from the Kabarovsk Region, gave us tremendous help and support.

Unfortunately, neither Igor nor Olga could participate in this trip. And no one could come from the Baidukov and Belyakov families.

There were only seven of us in this small delegation: the two Americans—Jess Frost and Carl Dugger; V. I Shport; a top correspondent from the magazine, "Russian Federation," Yulia B. Zakhvatova; television producer, Yury P. Salnikov, and cameraman, A. Polyakov and I.

We flew on a KNAPPO airliner to Komsomolsk-on-Amur, then on a factory helicopter to Nikolaevsk-on-Amur. They received us marvelously in all the cities. Of course, there were meetings with the mayors of these cities as well as with the citizens. It seems the farther one gets from the center of our country, the more kind and hospitable the people become. They remember and respect our history.

I received great satisfaction meeting with the people of the lower Amur River region. After our presentations, and a showing of the film "Valery Chkalov," people came up to us, remembering our trip 15 years earlier, asking questions and asking us to pose for pictures with them. A middle-aged woman came up to me and said it was she, who had cooked fish soup from Sturgeon at that time. She was a young girl then, and had been sailing with her father on a lumber hauling ship. I again saw the love and loyalty these people have for their city.

The mayor of Nikolaevsk, V. S. Voitsekhovsky, impressed me greatly. To my question as to how they were doing economically, he answered laconically, "We're enriching ourselves." I was struck by this answer, since usually they speak of the difficulties, the absence of materials, etc. I sincerely wish the best to this wonderful city, its people and its leadership.

The following day we flew to the island. We flew in two helicopters, one belonging to the city. The weather was foggy so we were forced to land on Baidukov Island instead. But this was great for me, since we didn't get to visit Baidukov Island on my first visit. Everything on the island was in bloom: the wonderful rose hips, yellow lilies, and other exotic flowers. The island is large and beautiful, but there is no fishing industry and the small peasant huts are falling down. If there are visitors to the island, they are likely to be poachers. I gathered attractive rocks and grasses for the Baidukov family.

When the fog lifted and the clouds disappeared, we left for Chkalov Island. It had changed little in 15 years. It seemed to me there were fewer bushes and shrubs. The monument had aged. Repairs needed to be made, since vandals had damaged it.

I didn't expect to be so emotional, visiting the island a second time. After walking around a bit and calming down, I went to the monument, where guests from the helicopters and local fishermen had gathered. A spontaneous, improvised meeting took place in which Jess Frost spoke to the group in Russian. He said in part, "My dream to visit the place on Udd Island where the Chkalov crew landed has been fulfilled!" Jess is the first, and probably the only American, who has visited all three places where the famous Soviet crews landed — Chkalov Island, and San Jacinto, where the Gromov crew landed.[40] And, in his home in Vancouver, he participated in the building of the Chkalov Monument, dedicated in 1975.

---

40 Mikhail M. Gromov landed in San Jacinto, CA, July 14, 1937, 24 days after Chkalov landed in Vancouver. With advice from the Chkalov crew that they carry three times as much oxygen and anti-icing liquid, and fewer other supplies, he and crew members Yumashev and Danilin, set a world record of 6,308 non-stop miles in the ANT-25(1).

We were surprised to find that on Chkalov Island we were located 3,780 miles from Moscow, and only 4,010 from America. The Americans found this ironic.

After the meeting, we wandered around the island. There was not the organization you find when VIP individuals are present; no one asked us to hurry, and we did pretty much as we pleased. The weather improved and the sun came out. We boarded the helicopters and flew to the other end of the island where fishermen were working. They catch white whales (белуха), train them, and sell them to large aquariums and "Sea Worlds" worldwide.

They say that if you pet or stroke a white whale, you will be happy, so of course, I did so. I don't know if I'm any happier, but I do know I have a tremendous reservoir of pleasant memories and good will toward this island, which has become so dear to me, and toward the people who catch and "educate" these white whales.

The Russian people are proud of their hospitality. And here on this small island, so open and vulnerable to the sea's winds, where fishermen work only in the summer, and where in the Spring and Fall migrating birds completely cover its surface, tables laden with food suddenly appeared as if by magic![41] The dinner consisted mainly of various, delicious fish dishes.

The wonderful Marchenko family is one of families in this small fishermen's colony. The father is 65, having worked on Chkalov Island for 29 years, and later on Baidukov Island. His daughter, Albina, was born on Baidukov Island in 1959 [42] and has two daughters and a son. The family has worked here many years catching white whales. The youngest daughter was brought here as a 1 1/2 year old child in 1991, when her parents began working in this small fishing colony.

In all the commotion, Yury Salnikov took an interview from Albina: "Are you an optimist?" he asked.

"We have to be optimists," she answered with particular dignity, straightening her hair, and a bit nervous. Albina is a simple, but very beautiful woman, tanned and healthy from the open island's sun and sea winds.

41 Carl and I can testify to this, and have never been able to understand how, from these small, run-down fishermen's huts, such an elaborate, delicious meal could have been prepared.
42 It must have been an interesting birth—there are no hospitals or medical help on either island.

"How's your life here?"

"It's okay. We work, bring up our children, and hope for a better life."

"Is there a chance of that?"

"If there was no chance of that, the country would fall apart completely."

"They say it's falling apart now."

"As long as there are good people in the country who can organize and lift the country up, everything will be all right."

It was a pity to leave this island, which I had come to so love on my first visit. This time also, of course, I collected interesting rocks, grasses and moss. The island presented me with a gift to remember it and my father—I found a small white stone in the shape of a heart. The sea brings these stones to this surprising island. And the wonderful Albina, who was born on Baidukov Island, presented me with a beautiful, warm, amber colored stone to remember them by. I took some of the island's plants to our dacha at Serebryany Bor in Moscow and planted them in our garden. They have grown, and today are blooming with beautiful, small lilac blossoms, reminding us of this dear, distant island.

Sitting in the helicopter on the way back, and not being able to converse due to the noise, I gave myself to my thoughts, one of which was particularly persistent. How nice it would be if the Baidukov and Belyakov families could visit the island—grandchildren, great grandchildren and great great grandchildren. How nice it would be to see them gratefully place flowers at the foot of the monument to their heroic ancestors.

A Young Man Gone, But Immortal

Years have passed, but the memory of Chkalov continues to live in the hearts of the people. A new, young generation of pilots has grown up, and is being pulled toward the vast, unexplored expanses of the universe. A new field of science and technology has sprung up: astronautics—and a new specialist—the cosmonaut.

Our first cosmonaut, Yury Gagarin, completed the first orbit of the globe on March 12, 1961, fulfilling a Chkalov dream. Speaking at a celebration in Star City near Moscow dedicated to what would have been Chkalov's 60th birthday, Gagarin said, "We pilot-cosmonauts owe a lot to Valery Pavlovich. Although we didn't know him personally, we considered it our duty to be Chkalovites…"

On June 22, 1962, having visited the V. P. Chkalov Museum in Chkalovsk, pilot-cosmonaut, and at that time Major Gherman Titov, wrote in the guest book:

"I have long dreamed of visiting the home of the great pilot, and today I climbed the steep Volga shore to this historic spot tied with his life. With help from his great achievements, the Soviet people have laid the first highways to space. Through his work and selfless labor, he created a foundation for us, for our generation, and gave us the possibility to fly into space.

"Therefore, with love and gratitude, we preserve the memory of this wonderful person; this outstanding pilot, Valery . P. Chkalov."[43]

Cosmonaut #13, twice Hero of the Soviet Union, aviation General-Lieutenant, Vladimir Shatalov, was born in 1927. When Chkalov died, he was 11 years old. Chkalov was Vladimir's idol. He cut out and saved his portraits as his most valuable possession. On hearing of Chkalov's death, he burst into tears. He then found a piece of paper and wrote in his child's hand: "The great pilot of our time, Valery Pavlovich Chkalov, died today. He then carefully folded it and placed into a glass ampul, which he soldered close. When his family escaped from the besieged Leningrad during WWII, it was lost...

Pilot-Cosmonaut and Hero of the Soviet Union, Valery Bykovsky, wrote in the newspaper, "Gorky Pravda": "I was fortunate to visit the home of Valery Pavlovich Chkalov. It's really not necessary to say how especially dear his name is to us cosmonauts. Our profession and the fate in aviation for many of us was determined by the influence of the vital achievements of your famous son. In Chkalov we see the symbol of exceptional courage, a creative approach to his profession, and an undying love for his homeland.

"...In the hanger, I saw the plane about which all pilots know—the famous Chkalov red-winged ANT-25. As I examined this plane, I came to realize clearly that in addition to the impressive expertise of the crew, they had to possess a huge amount of courage, and, if you wish, daring...

---

43 As the photo on page 8 explains, the Valery P. Chkalov Cultural Exchange Committee hosted Titov in Vancouver in 2000 at the 63RD anniversary of the transpolar flight. He was the second person in space and the first to stay up a whole day, completing 24 orbits. He spoke very eloquently to the Vancouver City Council of the need for our peoples to work together to preserve this small, vulnerable planet.

As for us pilot-cosmonauts, we strive to continue the glorious tradition begun by Chkalov during the birth of our country's aviation."

Test pilot and Hero of the Soviet Union, Georgy Mosolov, remembers: "I received my ticket into the sky at an air club named 'Valery Pavlovich Chkalov.' They didn't have to lecture us about how learning to fly at an air club bearing the name the famous pilot placed obligations on us. Each of us understood it well. There were many discussions about how Chkalov would have fought various battles... The image of Valery Pavlovich was before us all during the severe conditions of the war... For many of us, Chkalov was the most important example of service to the homeland.

"...From my very youngest years, I have carefully kept as a valued memento, a portrait of the pilot in his flight helmet and goggles, taken from the magazine, 'Building the USSR.' On my desk today, under the glass, is a photograph of Valery Pavlovich Chkalov."

In 1977, in an aviation town outside Moscow, a memorial was dedicated to the 40th anniversary of the two flights across the North Pole to America by Chkalov, Baidukov and Belyakov, and Gromov, Yumashev and Danilin. In 1997, a marker was put up at the Chkalov Airport in honor of the 60th anniversary of the flight.

In 1967, the Air Force Scientific Institute was given the name Valery Pavlovich Chkalov. A short history of the institute follows: In September 1920, by order of the Revolutionary Military Soviet, the country's first experimental institute was created to research and test military aviation technology. It was based at the Central Moscow Airport on Khodinsky Field.

After several reorganizations, in October 1927, the experimental institute was re-formed into the Scientific-Testing Institute of the Red Army. It was at this institute that Chkalov, Badukov, Kokkinaki, Suprun, and many other outstanding pilots worked in the 1930s.

On July 1, 1944, this institute was awarded the Order of the Red Banner.

In 1960, the institute was moved to the city of Akhtubinsk in the Province of Astarakhansk. All testing of military aviation systems took place there. The aviation authorities then decided to combine all scientific-testing institutes into one government organization: the GK Air Force Research Institute. In 1970, it was awarded the Order of Lenin. In 1990, this institute was given its contemporary name: The Chkalov Government Test Flight Center.

All military planes serving in the Russian Air Force, and all military planes exported to foreign countries today are tested and approved there.

VANCOUVER IMMORTALIZES CHKALOV

As I've already written, in 1975, the Americans in Vancouver, where Chkalov crew's red-winged ANT-25 landed in 1937, decided to immortalize the memory of the flight for their city. They consider the transpolar flight to be an important part of the history of this small city in Northwest America. In 1937, immediately after the flight, Vancouverites wanted to erect a monument to the crew.[44]

In 1974, a committee was formed to collect donations for a monument to honor the historic flight. The committee was headed by a well-known public figure, Mr. Norman Small. The Americans worked with enthusiasm. Money was collected by "passing the hat around the circle," as we say. People gave what they could. The monument had to be built in people's spare time, on their days off. Something like our Leningrad "Subbotnik" days.[45]

The monument was completed by June 1975. It symbolized a bridge between two continents, under which was a map of the polar region with the North Pole marked directly under the center of the bridge. Our country contributed also, sending two bronze plates. The contour of the ANT-25 flying over the North Pole was cut into one; the other contained excerpts from newspapers in both Russian and English with the names of the Chkalov crew also included.

Chkalov crew members Georgy Baidukov and Alexander Belyakov, 67 and 77 years old respectively, were invited to the monument's dedication.

They also decided to invite the crew commander's son, igor Valerievich Chkalov, and a doctor, Anatoly Ivakhnenko, for Belyakov, who wasn't feeling well, as well as Irina Fedorova Bostorina, a niece of Valery Chkalov.

---

44 Due to complications in U.S.-Soviet relations and the exigencies of the coming World War, the project was forgotten.

45 "Subbotnik" translates roughly into a "Saturday" worker. People were to contribute their time "voluntarily" for socially useful work on their days off.

As Baidukov remembers: "Our American friends suggested we fly on an American Boeing 707 airliner, which flew to New York or Washington, D. C. with stops in Paris or London.

"I shuddered at the suggestion. How could we fly across the Atlantic Ocean to the American city, Vancouver? It was raising a monument to Soviet pilots, who had shown the world 38 years ago that the shortest route between Moscow and the Northwest United States was across the Arctic Ocean and the North Pole.

"No, we just couldn't fly across the Atlantic. Neither the Soviet nor the American people would understand this.

"The Americans understood our objections and kindly suggested we fly across the North Pole in their gigantic Boeing 747, with an excellently prepared crew.

"This was pleasant to hear. The suggestion was interesting and seductive. But we had other thoughts. Wouldn't it be better for us, for Soviet aviation, to show the world we were flying the 38-year-old route using our own technology?

Members of the Chkalov Memorial Transpolar Flight Committee pose in front of the monument with Soviet cosmonauts Alexei Leonov, Valeri Kubasov and Boris Yegorov in 1975. From left to right: Fred Neth, Chuck Cunningham, Ken Puttkamer, Dick Bowne, Norman Small, Alexei Leonov, Boris Yegorov, Pete Belov, Jess Frost, Dick Osborne, Valeri Kubasov and Alan Cole.

"Everyone liked this idea. The old stubborn pilots of the Chkalov crew insisted, and the Ministry of Civil Aviation decided to fly to the celebration in America along the 1937 route in the new IL-62M airliner.

"And so, once again across the Arctic Ocean; across the North Pole!"

There were only 25 days to departure when misfortune struck—Alexander Vasilievch was taken by ambulance to the hospital. Following an old tradition, our friend decided to cut the grass at his dacha with a scythe. It proved to be too much for him. He suffered a serious heart attack and was now lying in the hospital.

The doctors objected to him taking the trip, even if one went with him. And the "guilty one" himself, our old hero warrior, was set on going, set on fulfilling his duty. Not even a specially organized medical commission could talk him out of this flight to the U. S.

In order to be sure things would work out as planned, we asked Aeroflot to conduct a training flight. Our doctor was pleased with the installed equipment designed to care for us, for us "old people," in case of problems.

At Sheremeteva Airport, in the morning of June 18, 1975, the IL-62M "USSR 86614" was preparing for departure. Besides our delegation, there was a doctor, interpreters, and press representatives from film, television and radio. Overseeing the flight was Hero of Soviet Labor and Distinguished USSR pilot, A. Vitkovsky. Y. Zelenkov commanded the crew with co-pilot I. Ryazanov. V. Ryzhov and V. Stepanenko were navigators, with V. Kirilov the flight engineer, and I. Klochko the radio operator. Three American pilots, Yaroslav Kostol, navigator Jay Berke, and radioman Dokol Kirba rounded out the crew. Their assignment was to help the crew in the event of difficulties in the air over Canadian and American airspace. This help was welcome.

At 9:45 a.m., Alexander Vitkovsky took the plane into the air and set a course to the North Pole. Before he took the plane up, Vitkovsky told the press: "In 1937, the flight of the ANT-25 was a genuine world-wide historical achievement; today's flight is just an ordinary transcontinental trip."

After 4 hours and 26 minutes, the IL-62M was already over the North Pole, where it turned to the right toward the Alaskan Meridian, which we crossed and headed to the Pacific Ocean. We then followed the Canadian coast to Seattle, where we made our first American landing. A flight over the North Pole had indeed become ordinary for Aeroflot flights!

Vitkovsky later said, "Like an old pilot, I understood that today's flight became possible thanks to the flights completed 38 years ago by those first transpolar adventurers."

After 11 hours, they landed in Seattle. Eleven hours! Not just six times faster than they flew in 1937, but also four hours faster than the usual Aeroflot flight to Seattle. But that was not surprising. This second flight along the Chkalov route was beautifully executed.

And so, as they had at that earlier time, the Americans met our famous old veterans with enthusiasm. There were touching moments, when Americans returned souvenirs to Baidukov and Belyakov given to them after their flight in 1937. The souvenirs were surprisingly simple items: biscuits, canned goods, cigarettes, post cards, screwdrivers, and other small instruments. The pilots had no room, of course, to carry true souvenirs with them. They gave away everything they had and 38 years later returned home with a basket of biscuits, and other items, which now lie in a place of honor in the museum in Chkalovsk.

In America they visited Vancouver, Portland, San Francisco, and Washington D. C. In the capital, Baidukov, Belyakov and Igor were received in the White House by President Gerald Ford, who said that: "We consider what these people did in 1937 to be one of the major accomplishments of the century."

At the dedication of the memorial to the flight in Vancouver, which took place on June 20th, one of the American speakers said: "We're obligated to make a world in which American and Soviet peoples become friends and work together; not only for our generation, but for our children, grandchildren and great grandchildren. We must all strive to make this happen…"

On the outskirts of Vancouver that day a street was opened and named Chkalov. Today, you couldn't recognize it—all around are large buildings and stores; the fields with daisies are no longer to be found.

Dedication of Chkalov Drive. Igor Chkalov has just unveiled the sign. It was difficult to convince him and others that this location would soon become one of Vancouver's busiest locations.

It has become a tradition for committee members to lay a wreath at the Kremlin Wall where Valery Chkalov's ashes are buried. From left to right in 1984, front row: Valery Chkalov, Jr., Dick Osbourne. Back row: Jess Frost, Ina Chkalov, Igor Chkalov, Alan Cole, Dick Bowne.

Chyanna Dyer (center), a Vancouver fourth-grader (singing "Let There Always be Sunshine," in Russian, presents a bouquet to Russian delegation head, Vadim Zdanovich, in November 1986 at one of the many tributes paid at the monument to the courageous Chkalov crew.

The Chkalov Cultural Exchange Committee, after meeting with the Chkalovsk City Council, February, 2004, on Valery Chkalov's 100th birthday.
From left to right: Bruce Romanish, Sue Tellock, Doug Lasher, Jess Frost, Dick Bowne, Rodi Lasher, Buck Heidrick, Dave Dumas, Marsha Fromhold, Carl Dugger.

Russia Immortalizes Chkalov

Well, and what of our country, that so loved Chkalov? What has it done to immortalize his memory? A great deal, of course.

In addition to what I've already mentioned—streets, cites, villages, educational institutions and Chkalov Island—there is a series of geographical points named in honor of Valery P. Chkalov: two mountains in the Antarctic, and Cape Chkalov on Franz Joseph Land in the Barents Sea. There is a mineral named Chkalovite, and a small planet "Chkalov," as well as a "Chkalov" steamship, which sails out of Yenisei Bay in the Kara Sea. All this was done on the initiative of researchers, scientists and pioneers.

Three metro stations carry his name—in Moscow, St. Petersburg, and Tashkent. The steamship "Valery Chkalov" plies the waters of the Volga River.

For his 100th birthday, in 2004, they were planning to put up a monument in Moscow. True, during the period of reconstruction in the '90s, they changed "Chkalov Street" near the Kursk Railway Station back to Zemlyanoy Val.[46]

In 2002 Yevgorevsk College of Civil Aviation was named after Chkalov, and in 2003 Moscow School #397 received the Chkalov name.

A photograph found its way on board the International Space Station during Basic Expedition #5. Cosmonaut and Hero of Russia, Valery Korzun, said the photo was taken there by the supply ship "Progress," which docked with the station June 29, 2002: "The photograph was located in the service module on the panel by my bed. The panel contained other subjects reflecting the theme of aviation.

"Usually, cosmonauts setting off on a space mission will take photos of the family, relatives and friends, or those who have left an indelible impression in their lives. Valery Chkalov—the legendary pilot—was, and remains, an idol for all pilots and cosmonauts.

"My parents named me Valery in honor of Chkalov. I have devoted all my life to aviation and aeronautics, and Valery Chkalov has always been my model as a professional and as a person.

"Before my flight to the International Space Station, Victor Taran, an

---

46 After the fall of Communism and the dissolution of the USSR in December 1991, many Soviet names were changed back to their original pre-revolutionary names.

aeronautics specialist and collector of aviation and space subjects, gave me a unique photograph of the young Valery Chkalov with his instructor and fellow pilots taken at the Borisoglebsk Aviation School. I decided to take this photo to the Space Station.

"This photo of Valery Chkalov was with me on board the International Space Station for six months, and is proof that Valery Chkalov was the 4th member of Basic Expedition #5.

"On December 2nd, I carried him with me on board the shuttle "Endeavor", which landed at Cape Canaveral on December 7th.

"February 2, 2004, will be Valery P. Chkalov's 100th birthday and the memory of this legendary pilot and marvelous person is alive today and will live forever in the hearts of pilots and cosmonauts."

Statue of Valery Chkalov in Nizhni Novgovod, the capital of his home province.

"Chkalov Steps" leading from the Vola to the Nizhni Novgovod statue of their native son.

Epilogue

The Serb writer, Milord Pavich, very eloquently noted that, "every book has a melody, has its own sound. All that's needed is an ear."

I would like our young generation to listen to the sound — the melody of love for a homeland, the melody of pride in Russia!

Gennady Ashotovich Ameryants said:

"Who knows how much we have lost with the death of only one person — but — Chkalov?

"And how important it is for the country to produce his heir — a citizen, hero, and skilled master...

"Heroism and selfless devotion — these are eternal qualities, like gratitude and beauty in mankind; as ineradicable, probably, as wildness and baseness.

"True heroes are truly rare. But it is they, with their powerful example, who have the ability to lift, to save, to elevate the individual, the nation, and humanity as a whole. Neither government nor wealth has the power to do this."

My father, Valery Pavlovich Chkalov, very simply and perfectly defined his place in aviation and in life with the following:

"There, where it is difficult and unknown; there I find my place.

"There, where we speak of the happiness of my people; there I search for my life's calling.

"All the rest — honor and danger — don't concern me.

"Only in struggle do I feel life. Without it, I lose the feeling of its greatness."

(V. Chkalov)

APPENDIX

THE WHITE HOUSE

WASHINGTON

July 23, 1975

Dear General Belyakov:

It was a special pleasure to welcome you, General Georgi Baidukov, and Colonel Igor Chkalov to the White House, and I want to thank you for the handsome punch set you presented as a memento of our meeting.

I was pleased to join in the commemoration of the historic transpolar flight you, General Baidukov and Valeri Chkalov, the father of Colonel Chkalov, made from Moscow to Vancouver in 1937. The replica of the ANT-25 single-engine monoplane you flew and the copy of your logbook will serve as lasting reminders of this pioneering feat.

Your recent visit to the United States gave the American people an opportunity to reaffirm their desire to work together with other peoples to promote peace and progress for all mankind.

Sincerely,

Gerald R. Ford

Lt. Gen. Aleksandr V. Belyakov
Moscow

THE WHITE HOUSE

WASHINGTON

September 30, 1985

Dear Friends:

Senator Daniel Evans saw that I received the
copy of Beautiful Vancouver U.S.A. which Alan
Cole and Mayor Bryce Seidl inscribed for me.
I am pleased to be remembered with this handsome volume of photographs, and your special
thoughtfulness in calling my attention to the
section on the Chkalov Monument, prior to the
forthcoming summit in Geneva, is indeed appreciated. Please know that I'm deeply grateful
for your prayers and goodwill as we seek the
peace which all freedom-loving peoples desire.

With my best wishes,

Sincerely,

Ronald Reagan

Members of the
  Chkalov Transpolar Flight Committee
c/o The Honorable Daniel J. Evans
United States Senate
Washington, D.C. 20510

SIGNIFICANT DATES IN THE LIFE AND WORK OF VALERY PAVLOVICH CHKALOV

1904, February 2 – Born in the village of Vasileva Slaboda in Nizhegorodskaya Province.

Father – Pavel Grigorevich Chkalov, a peasant in rural Vysokovo, Balakhninsky District, Nizhegorodskaya Province.

Mother –Arina Ivanovna Chkalova (Kozhirnova), peasant from the same rural area.

1911-1915 – Village school in Vasileva Slaboda.

1915-1918 – Technical school in Cherpovets.

1918-1919 – Work as a blacksmith hammerer in a ship repair boatyard in Vasileva. Fireman on a Volga River dredger. Fireman on the "Bayan" steamship.

1919-1921 – Metal worker at the Red Army's 4th Aviation Park for aircraft repair and assembly. Volunteer.

1921-1923 – Yegorevskaya Military-Theoretical Pilots' School.

1923 – Borisoglebskaya Military Pilots' School.

1923-1924 – Moscow Military Aviation School for Advanced Piloting. Serpukhovskaya Advanced Aviation School for firing, bombing and air combat.

1924-1927 – Fighter pilot in the Leningrad 1st Red Banner Aviation Fighter Squadron.

1927, February 27– Married Olga Erazmovna Chkalova (Orekhova), a school teacher in the Vasileostrovsky Region of Leningrad.

1927-1928 – Unit Commander in the Bryansk Aviation Brigade squadron.

1927 – Participated in an air parade over Moscow in honor of the 10 anniversary of the October Revolution.[47] Received an official notice of appreciation from the People's Commissar of Defense for outstanding mastery of flight.

1928, January 1 – A son, Igor, was born.

---

[47] Russia was still using the Julian calendar, which was 13 days behind the Gregorian calendar at the time of the Communist Revolution on November 7, 1917.

1928-1930 – Aviation instructor for a Leningrad aviation club, Society of Friends of the Air Force.

1930-1933 – Test pilot, Red Army Air Force Science and Testing Institute.

1933-1938 – Test pilot at the aviation industry's factory for testing and experimental construction.

1935, May 5 – Awarded the Order of Lenin

1935, May 10 – A daughter, Valeria, was born.

1936, July 20-22 – Completed non-stop flight: Moscow — Petropavlosk-Kamchatka — Udd Island.

1936, July 24 – Awarded the second Order of Lenin and the official title of Hero of the Soviet Union.

1936, November – Chosen to be a member of the Administration Soviet of USSR Civil Aviation.

1936, November – Participated with Baidukov and Belyakov in the Paris World Aviation Exhibit.

1937, June 18-20 – Completed non-stop, transpolar flight: Moscow — North Pole — Untied States of America. Awarded the Order of the Red Banner.

1937, December 12 – elected Deputy to the Supreme Soviet of the USSR.

1938, March – Chosen to be a member of the Aviation Soviet of the Defense Committee

1938, December 15 – Met a tragic death while testing the I-180 fighter plane.

1938, December 18 – Buried in Red Square by the Kremlin wall.

1939, July 21 – A daughter, Olga, was born.

REFERENCE LIST

RUSSIAN ARCHIVAL ACRONYM DEFINITION

АПРФ – Archives of the President of the Russian Federation
ГАРФ – Government Archives of the Russian Federation
РГАЭ – Russian Government Archives of Economics
РЦХИДНИ – Russian Center for the Preservation and Study of
    Current History
РГАНТД – Russian Government Archives Scientific and Technical
    Documents
ЦГАМО – Central Government Archives of the Moscow Region
ЦФСБРФ – Foreign Policy Archives of the Russian Federation

1. M. Charnley. *Wright Brothers*. Detizdat. ЦК ВЛКСМ
   (Leningrad Komsomol Central Committee) 1938.
2. V. A. Persidsky. *Vasileva Sloboda*. Chkalovsk. Regional Notes,
   N-Novgorod. 1998.
3. V. P. Chkalov family archives.
4. *Our Chkalov. A Collection of Memories.* O. E. Chkalova.
   "Molodaya Gvardia". 1969.
5. N. F. Popov. *First Flights.* "Pravda", December 18, 1938.
6. O. E. Chkalova. *Valery Pavlovich Chkalov.* Volga-Vyatkoe Book
   Publisher. Gorky. 1978.
7. N. Dobriukha. *"Valery Chkalov. A History of Flight and Death."*
   "Komsomolskaya Pravda", December 14, 1994.
   N. Dobriukha. *Aviation Revolutionary.* "Nizhegorodskaya
   Pravda." September 22, 2001.
8. *Our Chkalov. A Collection of Memories.* O. E. Chkalova.
   "Molodaya Gvardia". 1963.
9. Valery Chkalov. *Pages of Memories.* Volga-Vyatkoe Book
   Publisher. Gorky. 1972.
10. G. Baidukov. *Flight Commander.* Pub. House "Zvonnitsa." 2002.
11. "Historical Archive" #3, 1957, pp. 233-234. "A New Document
    of V. P. Chkalov."

12. A. Serov. *The Country's Best Pilot*: "Pravda," December 18, 1938.

13. S. Suprun. *The Chkalov Style.* "Pravda,"December 18, 1938.

14. M. Gallai. *The Third Dimension.* "Molodaya Gvardia." 1979.

16. G. Bocharov. *A Meeting With Mary Hemingway.* "Komsomolskaya Pravda,"February 1, 1978.

17. I. Spirin. *Into the Blue Sky.* "Soviet Russia." 1960

18. V. P. Lukin. *'Nizhni Novgorod."* #3, 2001

19. G. Maksimovich.*The I-180: The Secret of Chkalov's Death.* Publishing House ""Vokrug Sveta." 1995.

20. G. Baidukov. *Chkalov.* "Molodaya Gvardia," 1977

21. P. M. Stefanovsky. *Three Hundred Strangers.* Pub. 2. Military Pub., 1975.

22. ЦГАМО, f. 4610, op. 1, d. 15, p. 9-14

23. РГАНТД branch. f. P-217, op. 3-1, d. 28, l. 1-4

24. РЦХИДНИ, f. 17, op. 165, k. 55, l. 116-130.

25. РГАЭ, f. 7515, op. 1, d. 81, p. 256-260/

26. G. A. Amiryants. *Fighter Pilot.* Mashinostroeneia. 1997.

27. АПРФ, f. 3, op. 50, d. 687, p. 3

28. РГАЭ, f. 9570, op. 5, d. 85, p. 2,3.

29. АПРФ, f. 3, op. 50, d. 687, p. 8, 9.

30. АПРФ, f. 3, op. 50, d. 687, p.24-25

31. АПРФ, f. 3, op. 50, d. 687, p. 26-27/

32. РЦХИДНИ, f. 17, op. 3, d. 19, Protocol #32, p. 256, p. 52.

33. РГАЭ, f. 9570, op. 5, d. 68, p. 102-103.

34. АПРФ, f. 3, op. 50, d. 687, p 33-36.

35. РЦХИДНИ, f. 17, op. 162, d. 19, Protocol #37, p. 32, p. 73, 74.

36. РГАЭ, f. 7515, op. 1, d. 16, p. 158.

37. *Along Stain's Route.* Pub. Central Committee of the Communist Party. 1937

38. V. P. Chkalov, G. F. Baidukov, A. V. Belyakov. *Two Flights.* Military pub. 1938.

39. АПРФ, f. 3, op. 50, d. 685, p. 8-9.

40. АПРФ, f. 3, op. 50, d. 685, p. 7.

41. РГАЭ, f. 7515, op. 1, d. 14, p. 275-276.

42. "Historical Archive," #4, p. 29, 1995.

43. АПРФ, f. 3, op. 50, d. 687, p. 10-11.

44. АПРФ, f. 3, op. 50, d. 685, p. 17.

45. АПРФ, f. 3, op. 50, d. 685, p.24-26.

46. ГАРФ, f. 3316, op. 12, d. 796, l. 6.

47. РЦХИДНИ , f. 17, op. 3, d. 980, l. 50.

48. РЦХИДНИ , f. 558, op 1, d. 3197, l. 3.

49. РГАЭ, f. 8328, op. 1,d. 834, p. 71-74.

50. РЦХИДНИ , f. 17, op. 3, d. 981, Protocol #43, p. 144, p. 29.

51. АПРФ, f. 3, op. 50, d. 687, p. 55.

52. РЦХИДНИ , f. 17, op. 3, d. 981, Protocol #43, p. 144, p. 29.

53. РЦХИДНИ , f. 17, op. 162, d. 20, Protocol #43, p. 416, p. 95.

54. РГАЭ, f. 7515, op. 1, d. 6, p. 5.

55. РЦХИДНИ , f. 17, op. 162, Protocol #45, p. 349, p. 179, 180.

56. РГАЭ, f. 7515, op. 1, d. 7, p. 26.

57. РГАЭ, f. 7515, op. 1, d. 7, p. 25.

58. РГАЭ, f. 7515, op. 1, d. 7, p. 24.

59. РГАЭ, f. 8328, op. 1, d. 688, p. 49.

60. АПРФ, f. 3, op. 50, d. 688, p. 43-45.

61. АПРФ, f. 3, op. 50, d. 688, p. 42.

62. АПРФ, f. 3, op. 50, d. 688, p. 2, 3.

63. АПРФ, f. 3, op. 50, d. 687, p. 64.

64. АПРФ, f. 3, op. 50, d. 688, p. 49.

65. "Historical Archive," #44, p. 53, 1995

66. Y. Kaminsky. *The Doomed Flight: Disappearing Fame.* Puzzles and Secrets of the 20th Century. "Smena", #1, 1992.

67. РЦХИДНИ , f. 17, op. 162, d. 21, Protocol #49, p. 313, p. 46.

68. РГАЭ, f. 7515, op. 1, d. 71, p. 187-192.

69. РЦХИДНИ , f. 17, op. 162, Protocol #45, p. 481, p. 53-55.

70. ГАРФ, f. R-9552, op. 8, d. 46, p. 1-25.

71. G. Baidukov. *Chkalov.* ZHEL, "Molodaya Gvardia," 1977

72. РЦХИДНИ , f. 17, op. 162, d, 21, Protocol #49, p. 512, p. 58

73. ГАРФ, f. R-9552, op. 8, d. 27, pp. 2, 4, 9, 7.

74. РГАЭ, f. 7515, op. 1, d. 72, p. 42.

75. Valery Chkalov. *Our Transpolar Flight.* OGIZ. Gov. Pub. Pol. Literature. 1938.

76. E. A. Olkhina. *Vihljamur Stefansson.* Pub. "Nauka", 1979.

77. Foreign Policy Archives of the Russian Federation. f. 192, op. 4, port. 31, folder 28, l. 113.
78. Foreign Policy Archives of the Russian Federation. f.129, op. 21, port. 10, folder 23, l. 85.
79. G. Reznichenko. *A Life Given to the Sky.* Pub. Political Literature, 1983.
80. Air Force General Colonel, V. V. Kovalenok. *Moscow – North Pole – USA.* Zhukov Air Force Academy newspaper, "Vpered I Vishe." June 20, 1997
81. АПРФ, f. 3, op. 50, d. 687, p. 111-113.
82. РГАЭ, f. 7515, op. 1, d. 7, p. 170-171.
83. АПРФ, f. 3, op. 50, d. 687, p. 102-104.
84. ГАРФ, f. 5673, op. 1, d. 110, p. 393.
85. V. P. Chkalov Museum. Chkalovsk. N-Novgorodskaya Province.
86. L. Kudrevatykh. *With Valery Chkalov.* Pub. "Pravda", 1958.
87. T. Fedorova. *Over Moscow.* "Sovietskaya Rossia." 1978.
88. B. M. Filippov. *Notes "Domovogo."* Pub. "Sovietskaya Rossia". 1978.
89. Boris Livanov. *Composition in Life and Creativity. Articles. Letters. Memoirs of E. K. Livanov.* All Russian Theater Society. 1983.
90. G. F. Baikukov. *If We Speak the Truth.* "Air Transport", December 10, 13, 15, and 17, 1988.
91. V. V. Chkalova *Chkalov Bez Grifa "Secretno" (Chkalov: Secrets from Stalin's Archives).* 1999.
92. АПРФ, f. 3, op. 50, d. 658, p. 1-2.
93. АПРФ, f. 3, op. 50, d. 658.
94. АПРФ, f. 3, op. 50, d. 658, p. 17.
95. АПРФ, f. 3, op. 50, d. 658, pp. 42-45.
96. АПРФ, f. 3, op. 50, d. 658, pp. 47-50.
97. АПРФ, f. 3, op. 50, d. 658, p. 64.
98. АПРФ, f. 3, op. 50, d. 658, pp. 83-84.
99. АПРФ, f. 3, op. 50, d. 658, pp. 33-37.
100. Archive Reference Central Archive, #10/a-2739 from 18-08-99.
101. ЦА ФСБ РФ, f-3987, t. 5, l. 161-166.

102. АПРФ, f. 3, op. 50, d. 658, pp. 4-6.

103. АПРФ, f. 3, op. 50, d. 658, pp. 38-40.

104. E. Ginzburg. *The Last Flight of Valery Chkalov.* "Air Transport", #32, August 1988.

105. АПРФ, f. 3, op. 50, d. 658, pp. 57-58.

106. АПРФ, f. 3, op. 50, d. 658, pp. 18-23.

107. АПРФ, f. 3, op. 50, d. 658, p. 96.

108. Anatoly Markusha. *Immortal Leader.* "Molodaya Gvardia." 1974.

109. V. A. Persidsky. *Air Squadron "Valery Chkalov."* Nizhni Novgorod, 1992.